Cambridge Studies in Modern Political E

Editors
SUZANNE BERGER, ALBERT HIRSCHMAN, AND CHARLES MAIER

Changing boundaries of the political:
essays on the evolving balance
between the state and society,
public and private in Europe

Sponsored by the American Council of Learned Societies
and the Joint Committee on Western Europe
of the Social Science Research Council

Changing boundaries of the political

Essays on the evolving balance
between the state and society,
public and private in Europe

Edited by
CHARLES S. MAIER
Harvard University

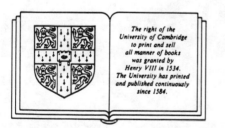

The right of the
University of Cambridge
to print and sell
all manner of books
was granted by
Henry VIII in 1534.
The University has printed
and published continuously
since 1584.

CAMBRIDGE UNIVERSITY PRESS
Cambridge
New York   New Rochelle   Melbourne   Sydney

Published by the Press Syndicate of the University of Cambridge
The Pitt Building, Trumpington Street, Cambridge CB2 1RP
32 East 57th Street, New York, NY 10022, USA
10 Stamford Road, Oakleigh, Melbourne 3166, Australia

© Cambridge University Press 1987

First published 1987

Printed in the United States of America

Library of Congress Cataloging-in-Publication Data
Changing boundaries of the political.
(Cambridge studies in modern political economies)
Papers prepared for a series of meetings of the
Joint Committee on Western Europe.
Includes bibliographies and index.
1. Europe – Politics and government – 1945–
2. Europe – Economic policy.   3. Europe – Social policy.
4. Privatization – Europe.   I. Maier, Charles S.
II. Joint Committee on Western Europe.   III. Series.
JN94.A2C42   1987   940.55   86-33406

British Library Cataloguing in Publication Data
Changing boundaries of the political: essays
on the evolving balance between the state
and society, public and private in Europe.
– (Cambridge studies in modern political
economies).
1. Europe – Politics and government – 1945–
I. Maier, Charles
320.94   JN12

ISBN 0 521 34366 6 hard covers
ISBN 0 521 34847 1 paperback

Contents

v

vi   *Contents*

Contributors

LAURA BALBO
> Department of Sociology, University of Milan, Italy, and Member of the Chamber of Deputies of the Italian Parliament

SUZANNE BERGER
> Department of Political Science, Massachusetts Institute of Technology, Cambridge, Massachusetts, U.S.A.

GERALD D. FELDMAN
> Department of History, University of California at Berkeley, Berkeley, California, U.S.A.

JOHN H. GOLDTHORPE
> Department of Sociology, Nuffield College, Oxford University, Oxford, England

ELLEN IMMERGUT
> Department of Political Science, Massachusetts Institute of Technology, Cambridge, Massachusetts, U.S.A.

MILES KAHLER
> Graduate School of International Relations and Pacific Studies, University of California at San Diego, La Jolla, California, U.S.A.

CHARLES S. MAIER
> Department of History and Center for European Studies, Harvard University, Cambridge, Massachusetts, U.S.A.

CLAUS OFFE
> Department of Sociology, University of Bielefeld, Bielefeld, Federal Republic of Germany

MASSIMO PACI
> Department of Sociology, University of Ancona, Ancona, Italy

JAN PEN
> Department of Economics, University of Groningen, Groningen, the Netherlands

vii

ALESSANDRO PIZZORNO
*Department of Sociology, Harvard University, Cambridge,
Massachusetts, U.S.A. and European University Institute, San
Domenico di Fiesole (Florence), Italy*
PAUL STARR
*Department of Sociology, Princeton University, Princeton, New
Jersey, U.S.A.*

Acknowledgments

The chapters constituting this book formed the basis of discussion at a series of meetings of the Joint Committee on Western Europe of the Social Science Research Council and the American Council of Learned Societies. We are grateful to the authorities of the Center for Interdisciplinary Research at the University of Bielefeld, West Germany; the European University Institute, San Domenico di Fiesole (Florence), Italy; Nuffield College, Oxford, England; and the University of Granada, Spain, for providing congenial meeting sites and intellectual hospitality. We acknowledge with gratitude the Ford Foundation for supporting the costs of these conferences and related travel. Francis X. Sutton, who was then our interlocutor at the Foundation, was especially receptive to the Joint Committee's premise that understanding Europe required serious reflection on history and more than a simple review of the current common problems of industrial society. Susan Brown, Claire Fuller, and Meri Whitaker provided invaluable editorial assistance in the preparation of this manuscript; and Robert A. Gates, former staff associate, and Nikiforos Diamondouros, current staff associate of the Social Science Research Council, offered continuing help and encouragement.

An earlier version of Chapter 2 (Offe) appeared in *Social Research*, vol. 52, no. 4 (winter 1985); of Chapter 4 (Maier) in *Urbi* (Paris, 1987); of Chapter 5 (Paci), in *Stato e Mercato*, no. 6 (December 1982); and of Chapter 11 (Goldthorpe), in *Stato e Mercato*, no. 7 (April 1983).

CSM

Introduction

CHARLES S. MAIER

The chapters in this volume are the results of the second research cycle of the Joint Committee on Western Europe of the Social Science Research Council and the American Council of Learned Societies. A first volume of papers, published in 1981 as *Organizing Interests in Western Europe*, examined the changing structures of representation and interest intermediation. Collectively, as Suzanne Berger explained in her introduction, those essays argued for a model of the relationship between state and civil society that significantly departed from the paradigms of American social science in the 1950s and 1960s. Whereas this earlier work described a system of decentralized competitive pluralism, the contributions to *Organizing Interests* suggested that policy emerged from a more restrictive collaboration of state agencies and large producer interests. The authors explored the growth, the patterns, and – just as significant – the limits of what is often termed "corporatism".[1]

The contributions to this second volume take up a theme that is an outgrowth of our earlier work. Beyond the issue of the representation of interests and opinions lies that of the claims of politics in general. When the then members of the Joint Committee on Western Europe framed this inquiry, they were acutely aware that the agendas of political discussion in Western Europe and other industrial countries had become crowded with issues that had not been subjects of controversy for many years. These intrusive issues included questions of family and sexual relationships, of environmental degradation, fundamental dilemmas of national security and sovereignty, and the heightened perception of economic vulnerability. Of course, all these areas had been periodically subject to political discussion and settlement. Now, however, they all had to be reexamined, debated, and renegotiated.

This renewed politicization of important social issues brought not

1

only a new agenda but also new institutional mechanisms. The existing framework of parties and interest groups often seemed unresponsive to the newly perceived problems; claimants turned instead to new movements or networks. A change in the substance of politics interacted with a change in the instruments of politics.

The concept of the changing boundaries of the political has proven to be an enticing but elusive one. In the first instance, the notion of changing boundaries of the political has meant, as stated above, a new political agenda. It would be misleading to identify this with a simple growth in state power. Explicit debate over issues earlier left to the family, the church, or the market need not imply that society has tightened its fabric of constraint or established more binding legislation in areas once deemed private. The locus of constraint certainly shifts, but one cannot claim in advance that the aggregate resort to constraint in social life is either greater or less. Emancipation has been as much an objective of politics in the modern era as order has been.

Some of the most striking political interventions have been either to reduce *private* power, or to roll back accumulated *public* authority on behalf of rights of privacy or property. Abolishing serfdom or slavery is a classic example of the first intervention. Striking down prohibition or blue laws or anti-abortion statutes, easing divorce, selling state oil properties, or reducing taxes furnish examples of the latter. (Public authority can also be used to "create" new property rights, for instance, by enlarging copyright or patent protection, or allocating television channels.)

To survey the changing boundaries of the political thus requires asking first whether political changes tend to expand authority (conscription or manpower controls in wartime represent a clear example), or to diminish authority, private or public, or merely to displace it from one set of institutions to another. Care of the elderly is transferred to the state, or police security functions are taken over by private agencies. Then the task becomes one of tracing the shifting of power – or of the instrumentalities used to satisfy public needs. Massimo Paci's chapter, for example, seeks to trace how Western nations have first centralized and then decentralized anew the provision of social welfare assistance, shifting it from families and religious providers to the state and then increasingly delegating it back again. Miles Kahler's chapter raises similar questions about the macroeconomic and security functions of the modern state: Which aspects of economic regulation have been delegated "upward" to the European Economic Community? Which aspects devolved "downward" to corporatist producers? To what extent do continuing defense and security needs set limits to the attrition of national sovereignty?

Europe, of course, does not provide the only arena in which to study the changing boundaries of the political. Equivalent trends have emerged in almost all world societies of any magnitude and historical tradition. But as so often is the case, European political developments since the late 1960s have shaped our awareness and ideas. The students' and workers' protests in France and Italy; the rethinking of national identity and security issues, whether through *Ostpolitik* or the arms race; the explosion of women's and family issues in the 1970s; the questioning of the welfare state in the wake of persistent stagflation; the apparent revival of religious loyalties and their public impact, have all forced a rethinking of earlier models. A continent that many observers easily pigeonholed as a routine specimen of "advanced industrial society" has again proved its complexity, its surprises, and its incorporation of significant historical developments.

What is the political?

In discussing the chapters in this volume, defining the political was a recurring dilemma. Politics was sometimes used to describe the site of argumentation or action: A political issue in this sense was one debated in legislatures or state bureaucracies. Second, politics sometimes seemed to refer to just the level of controversy an issue created: A dispute was sometimes claimed to be political when it made the news. (In fact, what was usually occurring was that the process of making an issue political made it newsworthy and controversial.) Relatedly, political might mean public: An issue was political when it concerned or was discussed by men and women associated only by citizenship or by affiliations more encompassing than the family, church, club, or business.

Reflection suggested, however, that public and political might be overlapping, but not congruent, categories, even if ordinary language tends to oppose "political" and "private" almost as completely as "public" and "private." Some allocations of space, such as parks, marketplaces, and theaters, establish a *public* domain, as do some codes of dress, such as women's veils in Islamic society or gloves for the nineteenth-century European bourgeoisie. They can also send more specific *political* messages: The gardens of Versailles and the foyer of the Opera are statements about power, as is the reappearance of the veil or the wearing of cockades or sashes in a revolution. Changes in the public sphere, furthermore, evolve along with changes in politics: The nineteenth-century public sphere involving a flourishing local press, face-to-face electoral meetings, or even the candidates' parade has yielded to the less participatory and more plebiscitary interactions of television and spectator politics.[2] Nonetheless, the public and the political need to be kept conceptually distinct even when they interact.

At its minimum, "political" seems to refer to issues that become enforceable subject to some sort of imperative decision-making, potentially coercive, by the state or by some other recognized (or insurgent) jurisdiction.[3] In this respect the political differs from an ideal-typical economic sphere (as liberals conceive it), where actors voluntarily trade what they construe as equivalents of value. The political also differs from the impulses to action within families or other primary associations, which may generate loyalties at least partially free of constraint as we ordinarily use that term.

But if the capacity for enforcement is necessary for the idea of the political, it is not sufficient. Constraint alone can hardly define the political; it serves as an instrument of cohesion in businesses, schools, and families – each of which can have its politics but does not usually constitute what we understand as the political realm. Some normative aspect inheres in the political: For Aristotle, man's nature was completed only in the polis; only gods or brutes could be complete beings in isolation.[4] Even for legal positivists the concept that valid law had to express a recognized norm, or obligation binding the community, remained as crucial as the capacity for enforcement.[5] The political realm stakes a claim to a universal jurisdiction by virtue of superior normative legitimacy, not by power alone.

Representation, force, and love: the changing quality of the political

The shifting of issues into or out of the political realm is one sort of transition, but not the only one. The redrawing of the boundaries has been accompanied by a changing intensity of what takes place within the perimeter of the political. One might tentatively talk of hard politics and soft politics. During the 1950s and early 1960s social scientists tended to predict that under conditions of long-term economic growth, political issues would be transformed into administrative and noncontroversial routines: Politics would dissolve into social engineering. Recent years, however, have suggested some revival of belief in the autonomy and harshness of politics – a renewed sense that constraint and not technology must be its final recourse. Even if the traditional state has grown less clearly bounded a unit – delegating authority to both supranational bodies and organized interest representatives within – a search for political "decisionism" seems to be resurgent. It is no coincidence that left-wing circles have been intrigued by Carl Schmitt, with his invocation of the friend–foe division as the *ultima ratio* of politics.[6]

This perception of the political as a final appeal to transforming power has informed several of the chapters in this volume. It underlies Pizzorno's notion of the "Gregorian moment" and what in discussion was treated as the "Hobbesian moment," in which the modern state emerged to organize, limit, and enforce the world of moral alternatives. The theme of politics as an elaboration of "when push comes to shove" is a recurrent if wintry one. While neo-Marxist theorists grudgingly admire Schmitt, Schmitt wrote on Hobbes's *Leviathan*, and Hobbes in turn had translated Thucydides, who in one of his most memorable passages had written, "The strong do what they can and the weak suffer as they must."[7] Hard politics is back, at least as a theoretical possibility.

This pessimism has not been the dominant mode in Anglo-American thinking about politics. In an early essay, which could not be included here, Alan Silver argued that one of the major British and American ways of thinking about the political – the tradition based upon a Scottish Enlightenment belief in natural sympathy and sociability – was at fundamental variance with the Hobbesian mode. Instead, its adherents envisaged the political order as based upon the affective bonds that united small primary groups, an optimistic conviction that ran from Thomas Jefferson to the sociologists of the "Chicago School" in the early twentieth century.[8] Thus one might envisage three qualities of the political. The tradition from Hutcheson to Silver's social scientists saw politics as friendliness; the generation of social scientists after World War II conceived of politics as functionalism; the question now arises whether once again politics must be understood as force.

The difficulty with politics as force, however, is that it tends to become an end in its own right. Ostensibly, Schmitt may have sought only to reduce politics to its lowest common denominator, as an internal analogue of war or as a higher form of tribalism, to separate friends and foes, to protect "us" from "them." But realpolitik is seductive, not merely descriptive. Force is all the more addictive when it appears as a resource for transforming society, whether on the part of an exalted Saint-Just or of Joseph Conrad's "frail, insignificant, shabby, miserable – and terrible" professor, whose political fantasies are constructed around the fact that "The world is mediocre, limp, without force. And madness and despair are a force. . . . Madness and despair. Give me that for a lever and I'll move the world."[9] It is probably a defect that this collection includes no chapter on terrorism. Offe specifically excludes terrorism because its means are not regarded as legitimate, even if its ends be political. But it might have been more appropriate not to exclude it. If we view terrorism as more than mere derangement, it implies a commitment to transformation of the political order albeit one that overrides ordinary ethics and human sympathies. And even if those of us who enjoy the privilege of not living in Belfast, Beirut, or Bilbao would dismiss outright terrorism as merely pathological, less violent, but still intense levels of political engagement must be made comprehensible. The claims of the political involve the fervor of commitment as well as the scope of the agenda.

In this collection the claims of the political remain a crucial problem for Pizzorno, Berger, and Offe. Pizzorno seeks to isolate the characteristics of "absolute politics," which is the endeavor authoritatively to orient the long-term ends of society. The most emblematic episode in the defining of this goal he finds in the struggle of the Gregorian papacy. The Investiture Conflict exemplifies the claims and the ideological or spiritual resources of the thrust for absolute politics – a drive that would later be taken on by the territorial state. For Berger the issue of the claims of politics is exemplified by the infusion of Catholic religious "integralism" into political activity; while for Offe it lurks behind the emergence of recent West German movements such as the "Greens," antinuclear activists, and others who aspire to more existentially defined goals than those sought by traditional party politics. In each case politics has claimed a new scope and greater militance as it aspires to recast society or at least to claim a domain that is uncontested by other principles of authority. Certainly a new or renewed militance has transformed the quality of the political since the early 1960s.

The militant cannot renounce force as a political resource. But militance involves more than merely restoring the hard politics of Machiavelli or Hobbes or Schmitt. It exalts politics as a vision of transformation. If we seek a description of politics adequate to comprehend Offe's new movements or Berger's integralists, Rousseau is a more helpful source. For Rousseau believed that Hobbes's reading of the state of nature was incomplete. If men were ferocious in the state of nature, it was because "they believed themselves each other's enemies," not because they were hostile by nature. Reciprocal fear was the source of cruelty; political development meant moral education, that is, an education in pity by the exercise of empathy: a progress that perhaps recapitulated Rousseau's own psychological effort to overcome his awareness of early parental loss. Crucial to this moral and political recuperation was the development of representation – whether representation by means of written languages or through political institutions.[10] At the same time, representation meant indirect communication and the sacrifice of direct participation. It compensated for estrangement but testified to its persistence. "Praise of 'the assembled people' at the festival or at the political forum is always a critique of representation."[11]

For Rousseau, the problem of the political – "Man is born free but everywhere he is in chains" – resulted from the estrangement inflicted by society, even though society itself was a response to human needs for love. Political action must endeavor to make society less problematic for "authentic" existence – not only through specific reforms sought, but by virtue of the very method of conducting politics. In this respect the boundaries of the political had to expand for Rousseau and his heirs, and the quality of politics had to change simultaneously. For the true militant no aspect of an inauthentic society can be allowed to stand immune from politics. Nothing is nonpolitical; in which case, however, politics is permitted any recourse and easily degenerates into *épuration* and purge. As Montesquieu implied, if politics seeks to legislate love, it will end with violence. "I am putting the sword into your hands," even his rational Persian prince is driven to command. "I am entrusting to you the dearest thing I now have in the world, my vengeance. When you start on your new duties, leave pity and tenderness behind. . . . Make my seraglio what it was when I left it; but begin by expiation; exterminate the criminals, and strike dread into those who contemplated becoming so."[12] Vengeance crowds out sympathy, and militance tends to become a political goal in its own right, not just a means to achieve a program. Here is an aspect of contemporary politics that few observers would have still believed compelling a quarter-century ago.

What is politics for?

The minimal criteria for the political cannot include any particular purpose defined in advance. As Max Weber wrote, "It is not possible to define a political association, not even the State, by giving the purposes of its transactions. From provision of food to the protection of art there has been no purpose that states have not occasionally followed, none, from guarantees of personal security to establishing law."[13]

The purpose of politics presents a more complicated problem than the purpose of power, which is often construed, like sex, as providing an elementary gratification in its own right. Historians and commentators have divided over the objective of political activity. Does it have an instrumental purpose, and if so, which? Or is it carried on for its

own sake, as an expression of community or a sort of game? Moses
Finley has made the distinction between historians who have described ancient politics as "a way of life" and his own view that "the
devices and spectacles were part of a process leading to the achievement of social goals. Politics, in other words, were not just open-
ended procedures; they were about issues."[14] For Finley, as for many
others, the issues behind ancient politics were ultimately those of
class and social stratification: Politics served hierarchy. If a hierarchical
social order provided enough general benefits to retain the loyalty of
its plebeians, at least until the late Roman Empire, it still gave more
to those at the top.[15] The alternative vision sees the political structure
as a world of values, genuinely circumscribing a whole community,
in which inequality is incidental and hardly the "purpose" of ritual,
assembly, oratory, and civic architecture. Power is part of such a
political order, but not its purpose. Clifford Geertz has recently
claimed that the precolonial state in Bali was designed to institute a
symbolic order of ritual:

Power, defined as the capacity to make decisions by which others are bound,
with coercion its expression, violence its foundation, and domination its aim,
is the rock to which . . . most of modern political theory clings. . . . Bali comprised such an alternative conception of what politics is about and what power
comes to. A structure of action, now bloody, now ceremonious, the negara
was also, and as such, a structure of thought. . . . The dramas of the theatre
state, mimetic of themselves, were, in the end, neither illusions nor lies,
neither sleight of hand nor make-believe. They were what there was.[16]

Of course politics must have some purpose. It is about rule, and
rulers must provide security and render justice. That is, they must
protect the community's historical continuity against enemies abroad
and sometimes at home, and (assuming they wish to enjoy legitimacy
and not merely impose force) they must distribute goods and honors
according to criteria deemed as equitable. Even a "theatre state" must
provide these minimal services or else it perishes, as did the Balinese
monarchy before Dutch rifles. Sometimes, as in the 1930s, the minimal
tasks seem fraught with almost insuperable difficulty. In other eras
they seem unproblematic and accomplished by mere administrative
procedures. Both major tasks of politics seemed resolvable by automatic rules in the 1950s and 1960s. The security problem was referred
to the North Atlantic Alliance. Two decades of economic growth made
the challenges of economic distribution less urgent, which in turn
lowered the threat of revolutionary challenges to welfarist capitalism.
The centrist tendencies in the European parliamentary systems (the
supposed "Americanization" of politics, the growth of catch-all par-

ties, "the waning of opposition")[17] facilitated the establishment of a consensus on security and distribution.

What the last two decades have suggested, however, is that these primordial tasks are not sufficient. Claus Offe's discussion presupposes that a new task for politics emerged after the 1960s. Politics was called upon by newly mobilized sectors, often youth or women, to guarantee the quality of life: to protect the environment against despoliation, to create a milieu for authenticity and participation. This new agenda could not be advanced by traditional parties but required more spontaneous movements less grounded in preexisting interests. As Suzanne Berger also stresses, the quality of association and commitment provided by the movements were themselves part of the objective. Fraternity, the most elusive goal of the revolutionary tripod, was restored to politics as goal and as method. Offe's critics have asked whether the movements he traced would make an enduring and significant contribution: Did not their existential issues represent merely the luxury concerns of a wealthy elite? Movements have arisen periodically, especially in German history, but sooner or later disintegrated, or were coopted, or bureaucratized. Yet the merit of Offe's chapter is not to establish that movement politics, the "new paradigm" as he calls it, will carry the day, or revert to marginality. It is rather to demonstrate that issues built on goals of self-actualization and highly diffuse concerns for the quality of life now shape the political agenda and challenge traditional organizations and even perceived social divisions.

Suzanne Berger's case study of the disintegration of the Catholic subculture raises an analogous problem. Berger suggests that the dissolving of a cohesive network of church-affiliated social organizations in France (and presumably wherever they were important) has had a profound effect in generating political and labor activism. Nonetheless, she rejects the simple model of political displacement that views the religious energies of Catholic militants as merely sluiced into a surrogate faith. Indeed, the Catholic activists bring a continuing "integralist" approach to their new loyalties. Not only do they seek particular programmatic objectives, they also want to transform the conduct of politics, insisting that their organizations reject compromise and halfway involvement. The movement must serve as beacon for the wider society, and the intensity of political mobilization is as important as any specific result. The vision is a recurrent one, as Blake's lines let us recall:

> I will not cease from Mental Fight,
> Nor shall my Sword sleep in my hand

Till we have built Jerusalem
In England's green and pleasant land.

Re-forming the political

Berger and Offe's essays raise the question as to why the demands
for a melting down and remolding of political life have become more
urgent since the 1960s. Offe suggests that political parties have become so highly aggregated in their appeal that they sacrificed their
older, emotionally rewarding ties with primary class or religious
groups. As their appeal waned on the "input" side it was undercut
even further as their political "output" likewise became more diffuse.
In effect a colorful politics of parishes and patronage became bureaucratic and administrative. Parties and interests appeared in the gray
on gray of Hegel's philosopher.

Pizzorno's chapter suggests, however, that it is also revealing to
address the issue in a long-term perspective and to ask about the
tendential thrust toward "absolute politics." Major historical forms
of regimes embody successive aspirations for politics. The Greek polis
did not differentiate the political domain from a fabric of social and
religious functions. The late Roman Empire, while compelling political
obedience, allowed Christian-Stoic claims on one's interior loyalties.
The feudal principality allowed religious structures a competing degree of sovereignty. For Pizzorno, the major point of departure for
modern politics was apparent as early as the church's effort to claim
wardship of Christian society's long-term goals. In effect, to organize
a structure that safeguarded its subjects' eternal interests (salvation),
the eleventh-century church also adumbrated the later vocation of
the state.[18]

Only a universal church could have claimed such a mission, which,
of course, was never uncontested. Five hundred years later, after
irretrievable schism and a century of religiously motivated civil wars,
spokesmen for "the political" recognized that secular rulers must be
granted the authority to subordinate religious claims and save territorial communities from the bloodshed unleashed in the name of
contending faiths. The counterpart to the Gregorian moment might
thus be described as the Bodinian or Hobbesian moment, asserting
the fairly absolute claims of state sovereignty and, aside from certain limiting conditions, denying the legitimacy of resistance in a
settled commonwealth.[19] The theorists of the state in the century
after the wars of religion called for the aggrandizement of the political and shaped the concept of an overriding sovereignty. Nonetheless, this search to define the state could also initiate a process to

restrict the scope of government. Liberal spokesmen and later the enlightened monarchies certainly wanted government to keep a monopoly of regulatory power over how subjects acted. What subjects believed, however, could be restored to a nonpolitical sphere. By the eighteenth century Smith and others in Britain could call for a similar divestiture of the economic sphere. Bounding the sphere of the political might actually strengthen the state and sanction the richer development of what is often termed "civil society." Two centuries later, however, we may have come to the end of that trajectory.

Today it is less the state itself than civil society and its discontents which prompt efforts to change the boundaries of the political. The idea of civil society is that of a highly developed web of organizations that are outside the state (even if they are often actually created by the state). As Hegel defined the concept, civil society "is the difference intervening between family and state, even if its formation follows that of the state, because as a difference it presupposes the state which it must have as independent object for its own existence. The creation of civil society, moreover, belongs to the modern world."[20] Civil society includes the exchange of individual labor, a legal system, police, and corporate organization. For the realm of ideas and communication, Jürgen Habermas's "public sphere" serves as a parallel concept, including the organization of civic or bourgeois opinion as represented by associations and the media. Civil society and the public sphere are both topographical concepts. They suggest collective networks and intermediate bodies beyond the individual or the family, but "below" the state.

Certainly much of liberal thinking from the eighteenth century on was based upon the theoretical distinction between the state and civil society. For many thinkers the relationship was unproblematic. The world of associational interests civilized man and made governance easier.[21] Or else the belief in an underlying sympathy could allow some thinkers virtually to forget about the problem of interests. Citizens could virtually vault over civil society and proceed from face-to-face unorganized relationships to political trust. Elective affinities became electoral affinities. But the problem for many of the new political actors seems to be that civil society has become too engrossing. The distinction between the state and civil society seems to have largely collapsed.

Certainly for the protagonists of Berger's and Offe's chapters civil society has effectively ensnared and suffocated politics. Catholic militants or antinuclear demonstrators want to reduce the claims of mediating structures, link up individuals or small groups directly to politics, and create through politics the integrity that the heirs of Scottish philosophy felt was provided by human nature. To a degree these actors sense a failing of political "outputs"; they want different decisions. But the greater failing may be that of "inputs": The former mediating institutions, conventional parties and organized interests, no longer command loyalty. Changing the boundaries of the political thus entails changing the nature of associational life in general. Indeed, the legacy of the political changes instituted in Europe since the 1960s may consist primarily of the new fabric of movements, networks, local party activity, lay religious bodies, school councils, and the like more than regime transformations. In short, a legacy of caucuses that, as Offe points out, seek to occupy or create the sphere of the political within civil society.

The confrontation of politics with society

It is no accident that two studies germane to the themes taken up here appeared in France at the very moment intellectuals revealed acute disillusion with the Socialist government elected in 1981 and with Marxist projects in general. Both works took as their historical starting points the aftermaths of ideological conflict and civil upheaval. Pierre Rosanvallon urged a reevaluation of stodgy, despised Guizot. No longer the bourgeois conservative, but the exponent of a political sociology needed to reconcile liberty and democracy in the wake of the Revolution, Rosanvallon's Guizot sought to heal France's political lacerations and to "constitute government by the action of society and society by the action of government." This was not merely a rearguard defense against 1789, but a modern search for institutional solutions, for citizens with real "capacities" and expertise. The key was "social power" not limited government: "the reconstitution of the social bond without recourse to the idea of contract and without return to an organic vision of orders."[22] Rosanvallon asked that the French rethink Guizot's questions, if not endorse his answers.

Jacques Donzelot's starting point was the revolution of 1848 and the subsequent effort to create the "social" realm. The social was different from society: Society might remain a murky entity, subject to collective passions, hard to reform (like Le Bon's crowd), but the social was a network of solidaristic ligaments encouraged by the state. It would comprise insurance *caisses*, professional associations, social legislation, republican festivals, even as it dissolved archaic concepts of individualism and democratic will. For Donzelot, Durkheim and Duguit played the role that Guizot served for Rosanvallon – but he felt uneasier about their success. The triumph of the welfare state in the twentieth century based on their principles represented a surfeit of the social. By the 1960s it would provoke two reactions: *"changer la vie,"* the Left's demand to revalidate the claims of individual historicity that erupted in 1968; and "changer la société," the Club Jean Moulin's Tocquevillian concern about the encroachments of welfare statism that blocked initiative and reform. Donzelot distanced himself from both these positions to emerge with his own paradoxical critique of the welfare state. "Conceived *in the name of the social,* the welfare state developed *at the cost of the effective life of society."*[23] Donzelot apparently wanted more politics; Rosanvallon more of the social. Both lamented the fissure between the two.

These reflections introduce the problems raised by the chapters in Part II of this book. They are concerned less with defining a political order than with the limits of politics in its relation to society. Somewhat in the spirit of Donzelot, Massimo Paci asks that the critique of the welfare state not be rejected out of hand. Paci follows the interplay among three sources of welfare and public assistance: the family and other traditional primary groups, such as the church; the market with its development of commercial insurance and medical and pharmaceutical services; and state-financed social insurance or health administration. Neither of the first two strands ever disappeared, and each, in fact, contributed particular strengths. What is striking today is the revival of the voluntary nonprofit sector of public assistance, as the welfare state comes under attack for both its costs and its bureaucratic deformities. The proliferation of self-help groups also restores to group initiatives a new vitality in the human services. Paci's chapter seeks to trace the phases of these welfare sectors and to explain under what conditions the role of state welfare became predominant and then apparently faltered.

Laura Balbo's chapter applies a similar schema to the particular interventions around family and women's policy. She, too, characterizes the present situation as a post–welfare state era in which the complexity and fragmentation of family relations renders the universalist approaches of the classic welfare state less serviceable.[24] Balbo also stresses the role that women played in each phase of family policy. Women were not merely the passive objects of legislation, but brought nurturing and family managerial capacities upon which each stage of welfare policy – and, ultimately, definitions of citizenship – had to rest.

Paul Starr and Ellen Immergut's survey of the state's role in health care also tells a similar story of recent rollbacks in the state's commitment in the health sphere. Besides supplying an admirable survey of medical care provisions, this chapter asks us to think not merely about the relationship of the political and the private, but about the overlapping distinction between what is political and what is "technical." The modern bureaucratic state, Starr and Immergut argue, has to recognize a sphere of technical issues, resolvable allegedly according to an impartial scientific expertise. Access to specialized care in Britain might be a political issue but can usually be handled as a technical medical decision. But this reservoir of decision making can become politicized in its own right; it certainly allows countervailing power to develop in the case of physicians. And, of course, the appropriate place to draw the boundary will remain a highly charged question in a pluralist society.

In all of these chapters, the authors take note of the tendency to roll back state intervention or political initiative. Of course, some of that impulse derives from the costs of public welfare. The economic constraints are discussed explicitly in the final chapters by Pen and Goldthorpe. But the trend away from public intervention in the human services is not motivated by considerations of cost alone. Balbo and Paci and Starr suggest that political intervention was the appropriate instrument when claims of universal citizenship had to be established, but unwieldy in meeting the more "customized" welfare or medical needs of contemporary society. Along with the market, say, for machine tools, travel, financial services, and most commodities, so too the market for social services has become far more differentiated than previously. Just as family medical care has yielded to group practice with specialization, so pension plans require differentiation, while a proliferation of therapists and self-help groups respond to differential emotional needs. State intervention retreats, not merely because of a conservative assault on its funding, but also because needs are highly specific.

The challenge to the political is also a result of the complexity of technical issues, as Starr and Immergut emphasize, and as is also demonstrated in Feldman's case study of science policy in an earlier era. The relationship of the political to the technical is a problematic one. State intervention into economic and social life has usually been justified as a way to make life less arbitrary, to reduce the role of "chance" or "fate" in people's access to medical care or education or basic subsistence. Some interveners believed, in fact, that the political process itself would become more scientific, rational, and administrative and less a contest of wills or interests. Technological solutions supposedly allowed costless enhancement of outputs by virtue of innovation. Administration would provide a sort of government technology: a cybernetic system that would eliminate political disputes.

The governance of men, to repeat an old claim, would be replaced by the administration of things. It was forgotten that the essence of politics lay in the clash of wills, not the discovery of knowledge.

Logically one would expect that the recourse to politics and the belief in technology would vary inversely. As one system evoked distrust, political consumers would turn to the other. Nonetheless, the 1970s brought a rising resistance to both technology and politics. This was in sharp contrast to the confidence of the two previous decades, which saw technologies as more promising (whether medicine, energy, or economics) and politics as less necessary. The result, however, has not been a coherent reaction. On the one hand, the distrust of politics leads people to search for technocratic social policies that apparently transcend conflict, promise growth, and in general have a self-evident validity. On the other hand, there is a growing disillusion with scientific and technological approaches to community problems. The techniques arouse skepticism even while the expense makes political review more urgent. One clear sign of the changing boundaries of the political is that issues formerly accepted as susceptible of technical resolution no longer seem cut-and-dried. Paci and Starr and Immergut show that we have witnessed a cycle in health care. The state was originally invoked to separate the diseased from the healthy (first through quarantine then by eugenics) and prevent epidemic, then called upon to generalize medical benefits for individuals and, finally, was mandated to recapture political control of health from partially discredited experts. Revealingly enough, each stage of the solution produced a new problem. The crisis of costs arose out of the expansion of benefits, for doctors and researchers were granted almost unsupervised budgets as a price for their acquiescence in an enlarged state role.

This is one aspect of the problem Starr and Immergut describe; another emerges from the Feldman chapter. There is traditional tension between the scientific expert, protected by systems of peer review and independent establishment of research priorities, and democratic control. Feldman reminds us that the claim for scientific independence is sometimes asserted against the Left, sometimes against a know-nothing Right. His contribution raises the question as to the circumstances that politicize the conduct of science. Conflict over scarce resources is one catalyst, today as in the 1920s. Ideological implications of science also politicize: Whether in the case of eugenics, debates over genetic determination of different human traits, or the feasibility of the Strategic Defense Initiative, much science has its own built-in political agenda, thus making its support a question of will and power. Feldman also prompts a comparative analysis of how industrial societies fund basic research that can offer only long-term profits. The German state, he reminds us, has conceived of scholarship as a public resource since the eighteenth century and has endowed it directly. The United States, in contrast, has until recently relied more on structuring a favorable market for research results by confirming property rights for innovation. American policymakers bestowed land on railroad builders and frequency bands on radio and television broadcasters, and most recently the Supreme Court has decided that patent protection can be extended to new forms of life.

If for the moment there is a faltering of confidence in both the technical and the political, what sources of regulation can replace them? For some activities the organized routines of the family and voluntary groups have reemerged as the appropriate structures; for others, the market. But the search for cybernetic or self-regulating systems to replace political action is more widespread than in the market arena alone. Many of the social science paradigms that seem ascendant today can be understood in terms of an effort at political devolution or a quest for software utopianism. They incorporate an effort to cast off the burden of political conflict and clashing preferences in favor of culturally or even biologically programmed social programs. Sociobiology suggests one model; rational expectations, another; there is a restoration of jurisprudential caution in the law after a generation of sweeping social decisions. All of this bespeaks a search for less political and more self-regulating social programming.

Insofar as there is a search to reconstruct homeostatic institutions that need not rely on political decisions, current developments can be judged in longer-term perspective. The current yearning to retreat from politics fits in with epochal oscillations. The Enlightenment strand of thought that culminated in a Holbach or Bentham believed that politics could shape society. The conservative Romantics rejected this notion but assigned a virtual self-policing power to society and church in their own right. Only early-twentieth-century political thinkers rediscovered the political construction of society, whether through Leninist or Weberian scenarios. If civil society could constitute the political, then the political could recast society. My own chapter in this collection seeks to argue that some of our most basic conceptual categories, those involving the demarcation of time, are influenced by struggles for collective power. It is only logical that an activist state or contending social groups should try to mold two of the scarcest social resources, space and time. Corresponding to the differing phases of political organization – premodern, liberal, and different postliberal approaches – are corresponding stages of spatial and temporal ordering.

The present moment, in summary, seems rich in contradictory possibilities. On the one hand, there is a rediscovery of the political, a renewed insistence upon collective will and power. The belief in "decisionism" emerges after the disappointment with welfare state functionalism and disillusion with the belief that bureaucratic settlements or technological fixes can replace politics. But as politics in turn falls short of its promises, what seems to emerge is not a renewed civil service functionalism, but a yearning for intermediate institutions (family and religion), or programmed routines and social science protocols that would make politics unnecessary. Sometimes, to be sure, these intermediate institutions spearhead a new political assault: Religious integralists, whether defenders of Catholic schools in France or assailants of secular humanism in the United States, call upon religion not as a nonpolitical recourse but as a highly politicized one with which to browbeat their opponents. Nonetheless, they benefit from a wider movement that does seem to long for relief from politics and wishes to shrink the jurisdiction of the political. Albert Hirschman has suggested that people naturally oscillate between throwing their efforts into public causes and private satisfactions, switching from the one arena to the other as they become successively disillusioned with the meager results of the one that has occupied their lives.[25] A similar logic of satiation and disillusion may govern collective choice among institutional approaches to regulating collective life, such that political and infrapolitical institutions exert successive appeals. But it would be naive to believe that the old infrapolitical institutions – markets, families, churches – can be reconstructed in the same pattern they had before they were melted down in the 1960s and 1970s. Changing the boundaries of the political in the previous generation required dissolving old classes and interests and establishing new clientelistic, ethnic, and gender affiliations, which were often then given official protection by newly created political linkages: regional governments, corporatist consultative bodies, PTAs, church councils, and the like.[26] Coherent public policy programs may appear stymied. But that does not mean that bourgeois families, hierarchic universities, an orderly clergy, a functioning market, and benevolent physicians are still in the wings, like unaging actors, ready to be called back onstage. Politics was itself appealed to, in the late 1960s as in earlier eras, because of the transformations of civil society already under way. As we return to the regulatory mechanisms of civil society we will doubtless find them further changed.

The same holds true not only for civil society but for the major institutional framework in which we live, the nation-state. As Miles Kahler suggests, the hope of supranational integration, the confidence that a transnational functionalism would dissolve its boundaries, that in effect the Common Market or the advance of satellite telephone and television communication would dissolve political borders, was excessive. Nonetheless, we cannot simply unfurl the old flags. Interdependence may not be integration, but it does represent an economic diffusion of sovereignty that has few precedents.

The changing boundaries of political economy

The stresses and strains cited in previous sections emerge clearly in the sphere of political economy: what John Goldthorpe terms in his essay the Keynesian impasse. The economic symptoms are well-known: the advent of a decade of "stagflation" and the decline of the sustained growth from the late 1940s to the mid 1970s that more than doubled real income in Western Europe. Nonetheless, Goldthorpe argues, the Western economies seemed hardly able to do without some Keynesian demand stimulation as the cost of avoiding intense class conflict. And even after the recession of the early 1980s, structural unemployment in Western Europe, persistent budget deficits in the United States, and massive Third World international debts suggest continued vulnerability.

The faltering of economic growth in the 1970s obviously had to exert a profound impact upon political life and itself reflected political change.[27] The fault line between the market and the state where the stresses of economic stagnation are most likely to cause political tremors lies in the area of fiscal politics. The level and shape of government budgets reveal both an earlier confidence that the state could intervene to reshape society, and the contemporary reluctance in Western states to extract the resources needed to meet these ambitions. Jan Pen's contribution points up that a major part of the government's claim on GNP is really just as a transfer agency, not a final consumer. The budget summarizes a redistribution of resources that goes forward even more extensively in bad times (as intended to do) than in flush times. Pen writes "The danger exists that the welfare state breaks down at the moment that it is most urgently needed." In part this may happen because the welfare state was confirmed (if not originated) at the beginning of the era of postwar growth in which societies were best prepared to get along without it.

If public expenditure represents primarily a transfer of resources from some groups to others, how does the public sector place a real burden on the private economy? One such burden might be misdirection of resources so that government employment and authorizations pull people out of "productive" occupations and make them paper pushers.[28] Another impediment might lie in the fact that taxes preclude profits. Pen argues that in a capitalist economy, profits must be redressed and wages restrained. Labor can enjoy either the gains of higher public spending or higher real wages drawn from a thriving private sector – but not both. Without some political bargain, Pen argues, however, the public sector share of national income is likely to increase further – or else the cost of decreasing it (one might read the evidence since 1981, when this chapter was drafted) is likely to be very high.

Pen's chapter might be termed classically Keynesian. It focuses on the central motor of investment in a growth economy; it dismisses the negative role of government spending in its own right, concentrating instead on the issue of how it is to be financed; it stresses real and not monetary quantities, and allows for demand reflation as a source of growth. On the other hand, Pen is discussing a decade when Keynes's long-term predictions began to seem shortsighted. The thrust of the *General Theory* was to argue against a century of teaching that "parsimony," or saving, was the key to national wealth. Instead, the major problem was deficiency of demand, and Keynes envisaged an era in which savings would become less necessary and the scarcity value of capital would disappear. Implicitly, Keynes seemed to assume that capital accumulation was a real need only for the era of heroic industrialization. Pen's figures suggest that we have almost reduced savings to the figures that might be appropriate were Keynes's vision of unexerting abundance correct; Europeans and Americans save far less than they did a generation ago and certainly less than the Japanese. Nevertheless, there is no reason to believe that a post-smokestack economy requires less capital than one still stuck in the age of hardware.

Pen examines the economic vulnerability of a capitalist economy in a period of low growth and high redistributive aspirations. John Goldthorpe focuses on the political dimensions of economic constraints. Pen envisions the application of incomes policies within a consensus on private accumulation. Goldthorpe suggests that the whole legitimating structure for private accumulation may be irreversibly eroded. For Goldthorpe, the decades of postwar growth provided a social democratic bonus. They allowed the postponement of hard political choices about redistribution by generating a continuing dividend that could be allocated easily, and adjourned questions of economic power and legitimacy. With the end of such robust growth, the era of sunshine social democracy has ended. Capitalism itself has no inherent legitimating claims but has rested upon earlier habits of deference that were bound to be subject to attrition as democracy was increasingly rooted and all classes won full civic participation.[29] The alternatives for Goldthorpe thus seem unpromising: A consistent return to the new laissez-faire will lack political legitimacy and may provoke sharp conflict. But the political coalition that would purposefully stride ahead to greater democratization of the economy is too weak to prevail.

As Pen's and Goldthorpe's contributions suggest, one major reason behind the clamor of the late 1970s and the 1980s to retrench the boundaries of political intervention has been that the great political economy settlement of the postwar era no longer seems binding. As Goldthorpe notes, this social *Ausgleich* rested on organized labor's general acceptance of the continuing role of private investment and control of capital. On the other side, employers ceded a "Keynesian" commitment to high employment and extensive social welfare. To be sure, this was a Keynesianism that could remain untested in large measure and whose victory in the United States, West Germany, and Italy was fragmentary and contested. Still, the major lines of compromise held up throughout the era of high growth. With the economic slowdown of the 1970s, this postwar settlement seemed far more fragile. During the disturbingly high and continuous inflation of the 1970s it appeared that any renegotiation of the settlement must favor labor with a stronger voice in investment decisions or over national economic policy. In fact, organized labor has been so weakened by recession and changing patterns of employment, which have beleaguered its traditional industrial citadels, that renegotiation has often meant retreat. That is, new conservative coalitions have managed to find support for strategies of exclusion; greater democratization of the economy has hardly been necessary. Although it is hardly likely that such a political victory for a reinvigorated market capitalism can remain permanent – bad times will discredit it, good times will reinvigorate a social democratic opposition – it is also unlikely that the structures of working-class representation will be simply restored.

Some implications

The chapters of this volume describe contradictory phenomena: More issues have become political as the line between private and public matters has been renegotiated. Simultaneously a new caution has inhibited political efforts to regulate civil society, and is reflected in perceptions of a so-called crisis of the welfare state, calls for tax relief, or disillusionment with "bureaucracy". Social scientists have no sooner managed to analyze a generation of corporatist delegation of regulatory functions to private interests than they have had to note that authoritative political choices among conflicting values cannot simply fade away. Why do we claim such trends? One criterion of a historical transition is a widely perceived sense of accelerating change. Another criterion is the simultaneity of change – the loosening and reknitting of many political and social relationships at once, whether those constituting the nation-state or trade unions and businesses, or families, church, and cultural apparatus. But why now? One inherent difficulty in analyzing systemic changes is that the more one searches for totality or complex interaction, the less one can plausibly find an agent outside the system or a clear starting point within. By seeking endogenous causes, the social observer is thrown back upon dialectic and the self-transforming capacity of society.

Perhaps it would be more fruitful to explain not why the political domain is in such flux, but why the changes did not develop more gradually and less concertedly, why they could be postponed for so long. There are not many periods in modern history that appear as plateaus of equilibrium equivalent to the quarter century or so from the late 1940s: perhaps the decades in Western Europe after Utrecht, from about 1715 to 1740, or the high-Victorian equilibrium of the 1850s and 1860s. To explain this recent stability one might adduce the demands of reconstruction after World War II, the eclipse of an authoritarian Right, the ideological inhibitions on the Left engendered by the cold war, the prestige of American models of technological expansion and social science behavioralism, the robustness of economic growth, and so forth. At the same time, however, the very prosperity of the 1950s and 1960s may ultimately have worked as a solvent upon the structures of civil society even as it made the immediate task of government seem easier.

In certain epochs politics becomes hammer and anvil for civil society. In revolutionary periods politics tackles the organization of the economy, the definition of property and value, the measurement of time and space, the equilibrium of the family, and the reconstruction of language. To maintain a sphere for private life in such epochs one must have either the resources to be an epicurean or the fortitude to be a stoic. At other times, politics appears a depleted resource, no longer able to convince and at best able to compel. This is the situation Donzelot laments when he charges that the social has swallowed up the categories of the political: citizenship, sovereignty, parties, public opinion, and the other once clear-cut entities of nineteenth-century liberals.[30] If this is so, the problem is not overloaded democracy but insufficient civicness. In such circumstances we end up despairing or indifferent about political solutions for apparently intractable problems (public education in the United States, peace in Northern Ireland, the efficiency of the state in Italy). But faith in political solutions does not decline alone. As it ebbs, skepticism also grows about the possibilities for "technologies" or outside experts or independent bureaucracy. Not all efforts to reclaim the private from the political yield successful outcomes. We may want the market but end up with the Mafia. Likewise we get the informal economy of once public institutions: private police forces, glittering hotels in wasted cities, enclaves of gentrification in urban ghettos. Renouncing the possibility of using politics to shape civil society, we nonetheless inherit politics as force to contain the conflicts we can no longer resolve. Some of the chapters in this volume suggest the disillusion that might well have emerged from the ambitious agendas of the welfare state. Nonetheless, to retreat from the political can never eliminate politics as constraint and would leave us all less citizens than survivors.

Notes

1 To a degree, the critique implicit in *Organizing Interests* paralleled that made by Otto Kirchheimer under the impact of fascism about the earlier generation of pluralists: "In the pluralists' zealous endeavors to destroy the image of the centralized state and to install the free reign of the voluntary groups on its ruins with a kind of vast 'super clearing-house' as a coordinating agency, social reality of group life in industrial society was invariably romanticized." See "In Quest of Sovereignty," in *Politics, Law, and Social Change*, Frederic S. Burin and Kurt L. Shell, eds. (New York: Columbia University Press, 1969), p. 162.

2 For a now classic study of the bourgeois "public sphere" and its political implications, see Jürgen Habermas, *Strukturwandel der Öffentlichkeit* (Neuwied and Berlin: Luchterhand, 1962); and, for the decline of the public sphere, Richard Sennett, *The Decline of Public Man* (New York: Random House, 1978).

3 This list of diverse meanings for the "political" was proposed in discussion by Philippe Schmitter. By focusing on the state as the source of potential coercion, one need not exclude from the purview of politics those institutions that function with the encouragement of public power (such as corporations or schools) and that often generate their own politics. For that interrelationship, see most recently Michael Burawoy, *The Politics of Production* (London: Verso, 1985), esp. p. 11.

4 *The Politics of Aristotle*, Ernst Barker, ed. (New York: Oxford University Press, 1958), p. 5 (1253a.9).

5 See Hans Kelsen's discussion of norms (the "ought"), as a criterion for positive law, and not merely a characteristic of a less realizable justice or natural law, in *General Theory of Law and State*, Anders Wedberg, trans. (Cambridge, Mass.: Harvard University Press, 1945), pp. 35–37, 45–49.

6 See Carl Schmitt, *The Concept of the Political*, George Schwab, ed. and trans. (New Brunswick, N.J.: Rutgers University Press, 1976). For the social democratic interest in "decisionism," see Alfons Söllner, *Neumann zur Einführung* (Hannover: SOAK, 1982), pp. 70–73. Although Otto Kirchheimer, who had been Schmitt's student, could criticize his professor – cf. "Bemerkungen zu Carl Schmitts 'Legalität und Legitimität,'" in *Von der Weimarer Republik zum Faschismus* (Frankfurt am Main: Suhrkamp, 1976), pp. 113–

51 – he also shared Schmitt's idea that the liberal order embodied an unresolved compromise over who exercised decisive authority. See "Bedeutungswandel des Parlamentarismus," in *Von der Weimar Republik zum Faschismus*, pp. 58–63, and most notably "Weimar – and What Then?" reprinted in Burin and Shell, eds., *Politics, Law, and Social Change*, esp. pp. 71–74.

7 Thucydides, *The Peloponnesian Wars*, Book V par. 90.

8 Allen Silver, "Small Worlds" (draft essay). For a recent effort to restore Francis Hutcheson's key role in influencing the Jeffersonian idea of the pursuit of happiness, see Garry Wills, *Inventing America: Jefferson's Declaration of Independence* (New York: Random House, Vintage, 1979), pp. 149–64, 240–55.

9 Joseph Conrad, *The Secret Agent* (New York: Doubleday, Anchor, 1953), pp. 251–53.

10 This is Jacques Derrida's reading of Rousseau's "Essay on the Origin of Languages," in *Of Grammatology*, Gayatri Chakravorty Spivak, trans. (Baltimore: Johns Hopkins University Press, 1976), pp. 187–88, and 216–19. Cf. Judith Shklar's discussion of how Rousseau searched for the teacher/legislator/parent in "Rousseau's Images of Authority," *The American Political Science Review* 58 (1964), reprinted in Maurice Cranston and Richard S. Peters, eds., *Hobbes and Rousseau* (New York: Doubleday, Anchor, 1972), pp. 333–65. As for Hobbes, the nasty and brutish quality of the state of nature seems to derive from the structural insecurity it must breed even among modest men (the prisoner's dilemma evoked in *Leviathan*, Part 1, chap. 13) and/or the psychological need for honor and eminence (Part 2, chap. 17).

11 Derrida, *Of Grammatology*, p. 296.

12 Montesquieu, *Persian Letters*, C. J. Betts, trans. (Harmondsworth: Penguin, 1973), letter 153, p. 274.

13 *Wirtschaft und Gesellschaft*, chap. 1, para. 17, no. 2. The alternative to Weber's position is to make the purpose of the state so general that it can comprehend almost every case. Cf. Georg Jellinek's discussion of the state as a legal association that seeks by planned and centralizing activity to advance a people's interests in terms of individual, national, and human solidarity: *Allgemeine Staatslehre*, 3rd ed. (Berlin: Springer, 1929), pp. 263–65.

14 M. I. Finley, *Politics in the Ancient World* (Cambridge: Cambridge University Press, 1983), pp. 96–97; the opposed view he cites is that of Christian Meier, *Die Entstehung des politischen unter den Griechen* (Frankfurt am Main: Suhrkamp, 1980), p. 258: "Politics was so intensely a way of life and being that it could not serve as a means to ends arising from interests out of other sectors of life." Citizenship and politics were absolute, but limited in scope and could not call into question social inequality (pp. 268–71).

15 Finley, *Ancient Politics*, pp. 97–121.

16 Clifford Geertz, *Negara: The Theatre State in Nineteenth-Century Bali* (Princeton, N.J.: Princeton University Press, 1980), pp. 134–36.

17 See Otto Kirchheimer, "The Waning of Opposition in Parliamentary Regimes" [1957], reprinted in Burin and Shell, eds., *Politics, Law, and Social Change*, pp. 292–318; and "Germany: The Decline of Opposition," in Robert A. Dahl, ed., *Political Oppositions in Western Europe* (New Haven, Conn.: Yale University Press, 1966), pp. 237–59.

18 This is also Harold J. Berman's underlying argument. See *Law and Revolution: The Formation of the Western Legal Tradition* (Cambridge, Mass.: Harvard University Press, 1983), pp. 113–19. Berman asserts, pp. 31–41, that the concept of an autonomous legal tradition, as the search for universal standards of procedural and substantive equity beyond the ruler or mass pressures or even social convenience, is in crisis today; the tone is reminiscent of Albert V. Dicey's concern in *Lectures upon the Relation Between Law and Public Opinion in England During the Nineteenth Century* (London: Macmillan, 1905).

19 I rely on Quentin Skinner, *The Foundations of Modern Political Thought*, vol. 2: *The Age of Reformation* (Cambridge: Cambridge University Press, 1978), pp. 284–301, 349–58.

20 G. W. F. Hegel, *Grundlinien der Philosophie des Rechts*, supplement to paragraph 182 (Frankfurt am Main: Suhrkamp, 1970), p. 339.

21 See Albert O. Hirschman, *The Passions and the Interests* (Princeton, N.J.: Princeton University Press, 1977).

22 Pierre Rosanvallon, *Le moment Guizot* (Paris: Gallimard, 1985), citations from pp. 42, 45. Cf. pp. 35–63, 98–104.

23 Jacques Donzelot, *L'invention du social: Essai sur le declin des passions politiques* (Paris: Fayard, 1984), p. 224. Donzelot's third way would be to reconstitute the political within society by encouraging frank negotiations among interests: a continuing negotiation that allowed for political will and representation without archaic '68ism or a corporate euthanasia of politics from on high.

24 For a similar argument that no unified model of the family now exists to permit a coherent family welfare policy, see Antoine Prost, "La politique de famille, 1938–1981," *Le Mouvement Social*, no. 129 (October–December 1984): 7–28.

25 Albert Hirschman, *Shifting Involvements: Private Interests and Public Action* (Princeton, N.J.: Princeton University Press, 1982).

26 For this argument in relation to women, students, and youth, see Yasmine Ergas, "Allargamento della cittadinanza e governo del conflitto: le politiche sociali negli anni settanta in Italia," *Stato e Mercato* 6 (December 1982):428–64, and now in Ergas, *Nelle maglie della politica* (Milan: Franco Angeli, 1986), pp. 82–110, esp. pp. 101–105.

27 For a summary of the forces behind this economic transition, see Charles S. Maier, "Inflation and Stagnation as Politics and History," in Charles S. Maier and Leon N. Lindberg, eds., *The Politics of Inflation and Economic Stagnation* (Washington, D.C.: The Brookings Institution, 1985), pp. 3–24.

28 This analysis, argued most forcefully by Robert Bacon and Walter Eltis, *Britain's Economic Problem: Too Few Producers* (London: Macmillan, 1978), has fewer adherents than when it was made five years ago. After all, the Thatcher government reduced the public sector claims, but without private enterprise rushing in to employ more workers.

29 For the depleting moral legacy of capitalism, see John Goldthorpe, "The Current Inflation: Towards a Sociological Account," in Fred Hirsch and John Goldthorpe, eds., *The Political Economy of Inflation* (London: Martin Robertson, 1978), pp. 186–214; and Fred Hirsch, *Social Limits of Growth* (Cambridge, Mass.: Harvard University Press, 1977).

30 Donzelot, *L'invention du social*, pp. 10–12.

Part I
Re-forming the political

1

Politics unbound

ALESSANDRO PIZZORNO

"Am I both priest and clerk? Well then, amen."
Shakespeare, *The Tragedy of King Richard II*, IV.1.173

Absolute politics and the reflexive power of politics

Behind the idea of politics having boundaries, and of these dilating
and contracting, it is not hard to discover, in both individual and
collective representations, the image of a state of affairs – and the
hope for or terror of it – where no boundaries at all are set around
the practice of political commitment and the exercise of political will.
Everything social would then be placed *sub specie politicae*, interpreted
through politics and seen as transformable by politics. I will call "absolute politics" the state of affairs reflected in that image. It will be
the object of this inquiry. This will therefore deal with the circumstances under which politics can be seen as the type of activity entitled
to dictate the rules of conduct for all relevant social activities, while
these, in turn, are being evaluated essentially for the political consequences they may bear. Under such circumstances political action
can be seen as the only type of action capable of transforming society
and therefore the only one through which the life of humanity, or of
a nation, can be improved to approximate a given ideal. Political
vocation as well as participation in politics are predicated as the highest of possible individual choices. They dictate to a person aims which
will prevail over those dictated by his or her own self-interest.

Absolute politics will be taken, therefore, not so much, or not only,
as representing a certain mode of organizing a political system but
rather as a mode of conceiving of and possibly also handling the
instruments meant to bring about a desired form of society.

The logical premises which justify this absolute mode of relating
to politics can be stated in the following terms: If only good society

can breed good human beings, then political action which brings about good society should constitute the supreme moral activity. To the extent that every human activity – be it educational, professional, artistic, or recreational – can be judged morally, it should first be judged politically. Politics is what projects human activity toward its future. What counts in it is not the well-being of present human beings but rather the achievable happiness of a humanity to come. Moral obligations are not toward the living but toward that future humanity, with the possible exception of those contemporaries who are committed to the task of bringing about that end state.

Thus described, absolute politics may appear to be an extreme, almost pathological mode of conceiving politics, one in which total commitment and devotion to a cause practically abolish the immediate, day-to-day circumstances of political life. But the idea of absolute politics does not stand apart; one cannot sever it easily from the more normal occurrences and attributes of modern political life. One needs only to remember that the state is the institution that can legitimately require from its members the sacrifice of their lives.

Moreover, in the modern state, politics sets the boundaries between itself and the other activities. To define what is within or what is without the scope of politics, one needs laws, or abolition of laws, hence political decisions, political activity, and discourse. This we may call the "reflexive power" of politics. In it are the roots of the absolute conception of politics. If politics decides about its own boundaries, there will be times when these will overexpand, and be set, so to speak, nowhere.

Absolute politics, therefore, cannot just be explained away as if it were some temporary, or cyclical, pathology of ideological deviance. Some more permanent mechanism of our institutions is at work. We must look into it more closely.

Politics and religion hydraulically modeled

Consider Talmon's view of absolute politics as "the assumption of a sole and exclusive truth in politics. It may be called political Messianism in the sense that it postulates a preordained, harmonious and perfect scheme of things, to which men are irresistibly driven, and at which they are bound to arrive. It recognizes ultimately only one plan of existence, the political. It widens the scope of politics to embrace the whole of human existence."[1] This comes close to what we mean. But then the author makes clear that what he intends to describe is "a state of mind, a way of feeling, a disposition, a pattern of mental, emotional and behavioristic elements, best compared with the sets of attitudes engendered by a religion."[2] It is the state of mind originated in the works of *philosophes* and ideologues such as Helvetius, Holbach, Rousseau, Morelly, Mably, and the Jacobins. Against it, Talmon places the "state of mind" of the liberal-democratic school. The inquiry does not go beyond the reconstruction of such states of mind. The conditions for the occurrence of one rather than the other "school" are not explained, and no relation is shown between one or the other style of politics and the phenomenon of the reflexive power of politics.

Talmon was preoccupied with the logical reconstruction of absolute politics more than with the explanation of its occurrence. Nonetheless he hints at a sort of causal factor when he states that with the "decline of religious authority . . . and the rejection of the Church and of transcendental justice, the State remained the sole source and sanction of morality."[3] He locates that process in the eighteenth century. But has the state everywhere after the eighteenth century become "the sole source and sanction of morality," or only in certain countries and for certain moments? If the first is the case, totalitarian democracy should be found everywhere. If the second, how are the variations to be explained?

Talmon's position is not an isolated one; rather, it represents a version of the almost century-old and widely diffused idea that certain forms of politics are just secularized expressions of religious attitudes and feelings. Recently this idea has been given new currency with the theory of the so-called secular religions. This is the name given to those doctrines that appear to have replaced bygone faith, placing in this life, in a remote future, the salvation of humanity in the form of a social order yet to be created. The secular religions induce in their followers the same traits considered by Talmon: total devotion to a cause, absolute belief in the truth of that cause, intolerance, fanaticism against other causes, moral judgments dependent on political belief, and possession of a global view of the world, including a view of a future society to be realized through political action.

This theory becomes systematic with Julien Freund[4] and finds a lengthy and richly documented treatment with J. P. Sironneau. It can be summarized by this general statement: "Le sacré ne disparaît pas, mais se réinvestit dans d'autres spheres de l'activité humaine, en particulier dans la sphère politique."[5] The theory is built on what we may call a "hydraulic" model: The flow of the sacred runs through the duct of religious institutions, and when those are, for some reason, obstructed, part or the whole of that flow will find its way through another duct, specifically through the political one.

For these types of models to be workable, though, stringent requirements should be respected. In particular, the nature of the flow should be specified, so that one could observe it separately from the ducts in which it flows. Also, the nature of the ducts should be specified, so that one could distinguish them independently from the content they convey. Finally, the material that obstructs this or that duct should be specified in terms of categories generated by the same theory that defines ducts and flows. These requirements are not satisfied by the versions of this theory so far advanced. Either the "sacred flow" is always the same – and in this case there is no way of distinguishing religious from political institutions and movements – or it changes, and in this case nothing is learned about political phenomena by calling them "religious."

The hydraulic theories of "political religions" are popular because they operate as "umbrella theories" for two deep-seated ideological positions. One is the secular view of politics, based on the idea that absolute politics is a form of pathology because it mixes religion with politics. Let the absolute be expunged from politics and politics will be sound again. Another is the conservative view of limited politics, based on the idea that shared values are badly needed in society, but that they are *not* the business of politics. Hence absolute politics is not politics, it is just a distorted, perverse mode of religion.

Both views are too simple. But they make a good point by calling attention to the relations between politics and religion. It is the point that also Hegel made, in a famous paragraph (270) of *The Philosophy of Right*, when he saw the origin of the state "as a self-consciously rational and ethical organization" as lying in the dissolution of the religious unity of the West. Similarly Marx, in "The Jewish Question," saw the state as taking up the traditional function of the church, the function of creating an *illusorische Gemeinschaft*. Society is divided into classes and conflicting interests. Some all-embracing institution is needed to give the illusion that society can be united. When the church, itself ridden and divided, became unable to do so, the state emerged in its place. But there is no real theory here, just suggestions. One would like to understand better what mechanisms bring about the "functionally equivalent" institution when it is needed. And what are the "normal" functions of the political institutions when the church seems to be in charge of the unifying function, and, vice versa, of the religious institutions when the unitary function is to be found in the state?

When did the age of the "political" appear?

One way of dealing with these questions is by considering that "politics" as a distinct category has only a recent historical origin. Whenever that origin may be placed, it is only after that moment that one is entitled to speak of politics as a separate activity. Before, religion and politics must be considered undifferentiated, without any way of saying what is political and what is religious in a certain function or in a certain activity.

"Contextualist" historians make this point very forcefully:

The absence of the "political" in the Western vocabulary before the thirteenth century indicates that the idea behind it was not yet or only dimly grasped: and the success of the papacy in the West and the lack of success on the part of Western kings and emperors against the pope was in fact due to the absence of the political norm as a separate and distinct category of thought and action. To say that the "political" was merely another name for the "temporal" or "royal" and the like would be a facile way out of facing difficulties . . . The emergence of the "political" and consequently of the "citizen" – as distinct from the Christian – was to herald the end of the medieval Western period.[6]

Similarly, Q. Skinner, in concluding his *Foundations of Modern Political Thought* (1978), writes that "the most important preconditions for the acquisition of the modern concept of the State" are, first, the formation of a discipline of political science as a separate branch of moral philosophy. Second, that the territorial state be conceived as autonomous from any external and superior power in particular from the empire. Third, that the authority of the state be construed as not recognizing rival jurisdictions in its territory – in particular the jurisdiction of the church. "Finally, the acceptance of the modern idea of the State presupposes that political society is held to exist solely for political purposes."[7]

All points are well made. What one should not, however, derive from them is an idea of "modern" politics as an activity in which "godly ends" are simply expunged and nothing of that nature put again at their place. Consider the case of the French Politiques of the late sixteenth century Michel de l'Hôpital, Bodin, and their friends, whom Skinner shows to be the first ones clearly to spell out in practice that the state should not set godly ends to its activity. Against them, the religious extremists used "godly" names in the declaration of their goals. In what did the difference consist? Both had long-term ends in mind. But they differed about the collectivity that should tend toward those ends. For the ones, it was the territorial collectivity of the state. For the others, it was a collectivity of believers who joined together because of their belief. In other words, godly, or otherwise "spiritual," or "ultimate," ends can always be found, in varying degrees, in the pursuance of those activities to which it is today usual to assign the generic name of politics: They aim at bindingly committing the future of a certain collectivity. What makes the difference is the nature of the new ties, not the presence or absence, or degree, of religiosity in the intentions of the actors. What some call "modernization of politics" is this sort of change: a process not of secularization of values – or not as a prime motor – but of territorialization of binding ties, with all the consequences. (Skinner is therefore right in premising his analysis on the appearance of the concept of the state, and not of politics.)

On the other side, attributing a political rather than religious nature to certain activities in traditional societies is also misleading. Consider the distinction forcefully analyzed by Gerd Tellenbach in his classic work on church and state at the time of the Investiture Contest between the Cluniac movement and the Gregorian reformers who emerged out of it and gave rise to the ecclesiastical revolution of the eleventh and twelfth centuries. The former are described as having in mind the moral reform of monastic life, as being otherworldly oriented, not inclined to fight with the emperors but, on the contrary, ready to cooperate with them. The latter are described as aiming at the general reform of the whole Western church, as hostile to the empire they hoped to subordinate, and carrying out a program which amounted to a political revolution. Hence, one is told, Cluny's aims were not political but merely religious, whereas Hildebrand's aims were typically political.[8]

The characterization seems plausible. We have no difficulty today in calling "nonpolitical" a program of establishing new rules of asceticism, moral behavior, regularity of life and work in a monastic or ecclesiastical organization. Whereas what could be more "political" than a strategy of increasing the authority of the Church of Rome over the empire? But the actors of that story, aside from not using that word, did not see a difference of quality between the two types of action; only, if at all, divergences of method. Both movements aimed at purifying and enhancing the clerical vocation and status in Christendom. Both acted according to a commonly accepted interpretation of Christian doctrine. That we see it differently today and that we can consider the Gregorian reform as the first of the great *political* revolutions of the West[9] is *our* problem. It is that by *then* and *now* at least the consequences of *then* have intervened – and among these, as for our case, the building up of the premises for absolute politics.

A second example may be taken from a more recent but already classic work on the same historical period, the work on the three orders of feudalism by Georges Duby. Analyzing the "Estoire des ducs de Normandie," written toward the end of the twelfth century by Benoît de Sainte-Maure, Duby notices that political discourse begins to appear here devoid of references to redemption and to how the distribution of dignities of the heavenly city is reflected in the worldly city; features which characterize "political" discourse in the previous centuries: "This is the fundamental, the tragic change – this fall, this plunge from the dizzying heights of theology, to which the bishops of the year 1000 had been raised by the imaginings of the pseudo-Dionysus, toward the abysmal depths of that petty, trivial thing that we call politics."[10]

Again, Duby sees modern politics – what "we call politics" – emerging from the fall, or weakening, of some religious (theological) discourse. But this he detects in a text of the twelfth century. It seems that each time that religious discourse fades away, politics as we conceive it – better, as we ought to conceive it, as this "petty, trivial thing" – emerges. There will be moments in which some religious discourse will be reintroduced, but in those cases people, instead of doing politics, will be doing religion in disguise. Things cannot be so simple.

Let me divide issues here. One is the issue of the birth of politics, *modernly conceived*. The second issue is our original one: When were the premises for absolute politics built into the Western institutions? This I will now pursue, but some detours are required.

I began by quoting a type of theory which maintains that the premises of the phenomenon of absolute politics should be traced back to the process of differentiation of politics from religion. The historical examples I then referred to exposed the difficulty of determining the origin and nature of such a process. Indeed, the very concept of a differentiation of functions is an ambiguous one. The idea is that two types of functions that are now performed by two different individuals or structures were previously undividedly performed by only one individual or structure. In evolutionary structural-functionalism this represents the central idea for a general theory of social change. But what is in general left unexplored or not made explicit is how this differentiation comes about and why the two deriving branches are what we think we see in divided institutions now (politics and religion) and not other conceivable ones. From the experience of the modern institutional division we are simply asked to infer the constancy in all societies of separate analytical functions. The emergence of separate structures (church and state, for instance) are then explained as a process of emancipation of the one from the other. This is not very illuminating.

The historiographical analyses I quoted above may suggest an alternative reconstruction of the process of social change. It would aim at describing the shifting nature of the ties and of the boundaries that identify that collectivity to which ultimate ends are assigned – and which therefore determines the ultimate identity of individuals. Phases of absolute politics would then be seen as playing a crucial role in this type of passage.

The Gregorian moment, or the spiritual drive to power

This view of the processes of social change, and of the role of episodes of absolute politics in them, has led me to choose the "Gregorian moment" as the most emblematic episode in Western history. It lies at the roots of the transfer, as it were, of the collective responsibility for ultimate ends from a collectivity having the boundaries of Christianity, and including all believers tied by this particular bond of faith, to separate collectivities defined by the territorial boundaries of one state and including all the individuals identified by their living within those boundaries.

The process takes its move from the struggle between the two dominant structures of the old society. It is the struggle between the church and the empire, or, according to an alternative contemporary terminology, between "power spiritual" and "power temporal." It could appear, but it is obviously not, the struggle between two "functions," the religious and the political, and therefore a process of functional differentiation. It is, instead, a fight between groups of individuals, partly identified by their position and their functions, but tied together by their idea of the nature of the collectivity that should be responsible for the ultimate ends of the human (Christian) beings, and therefore by their idea of what their common long-term – indeed "eternal" – interests were.

That the two parties were identified by the terms "power spiritual" and "power temporal" can be revealing, but only if one first solves a hermeneutical puzzle. How can these two terms "spiritual" and "temporal" make sense for us? They do not belong to our vocabulary – or, at least, not to one universally agreed upon today, even if somebody could pretend that the terms mean something for him singularly. How can we account for a conflict between an agent "spiritual" and an agent "temporal"? How can we gauge that the "spiritual" as such won or lost? Indeed, for the very participant, what could the sense of such a conflict have been? What were the weapons used by each side that the other might have feared? What the resources that each side displayed and the other might have wished to possess? Analogous problems do not emerge when one thinks of two territorial states, or two armies, or two political parties, or two corporations, or even two social classes fighting each other. In these cases it seems easy to tell who wins and who loses since it is possible to establish what the antagonistic interests of the two parties were, or were imagined to be, before and after the events. In a conflict between some agent spiritual and some agent temporal the "interests" of the parties cannot be defined (at most the interests of individuals caught in specific situations). The stake can only consist in a new form of society, and in that end-state no agent as defined by the previous form would be recognized with the same identity. When conditions like these occur one is dealing with a case of absolute politics.

And, indeed, in the Gregorian project the drive toward absoluteness was openly put. It was a project aimed at securing autonomy and superiority for the class which was in charge of spiritual resources, and was seen as the only one capable of leading society toward a desirable long-term end. The very definition of this end, as well as the provision of the resources needed to pursue it, and the instructions on how to use these resources, came from that class. Such a monopoly of "spiritual resources" grounded the demand for the advent of an order in which that class would be autonomous and, in some form, superior (what this really meant will be spelled out below).

How could these resources lead to such pretense? What form did they take, how did they operate? To find an answer one must look at four fundamental modes of control for which the agents of spirituality, the ecclesiastical class, were practically alone in charge. These controls are of knowledge, of normative procedures, of the states of devotion, and of the definition of the enemies. They must be analyzed one by one.

The control of knowledge

The control of knowledge represents the most typical and, generally, the most powerful of "spiritual" resources, especially insofar as it rests on the basis of an all-encompassing vision of the long-term, ultimate ends of society and the individual. Ultimate (i.e., long-term) ends are to be defined as implying uncertainty, while proximate (i.e., short-term) ends imply practical certainty. In other words, decisions in view of long-term ends provoke consequences that are unknown, uncertain, unpredictable. This uncertainty can be overcome by some form of transcendental knowledge.

Let these definitions stand, for the moment, as they are. The smallest development of the attempt to justify them would take us too far.[11] Let it be added that the activity of providing knowledge about ultimate ends introduces into the horizon of individual and social choices a needed degree of certainty. The capacity to provide that type of knowledge constitutes a powerful resource in the hands of

some groups of specialists. In our case, it was in the hands of the
ecclesiastical apparatus. They controlled the supply of that knowledge
monopolistically, as it were. And this was, as usual in traditional
societies, an important source of power. But there was more. The
knowledge needed for transcendental certainty was also tied to another form of knowledge that was "transcendent," so to speak, in a
spatiotemporal sense and was therefore an essential component of
the collective identity. Indeed, the use of Latin as the language capable
of transcending the local-boundedness of unwritten vernaculars, as
well as the specific cultivation of writing and record keeping, allowed
the ecclesiastical class to mediate any type of extralocal, and therefore
all "political," communication and discourse as well as any communication through time, either from the past (the cultural tradition)
or to the future (the language of salvation, of ultimate ends). The
identification of the Christian community through time, and within
its boundaries in space, was therefore assured through this control
of "transcendent" knowledge, which bore to ordinary, daily, unorganized knowledge the same relation that the "general" bears to the
"particular": It gives meaning to it. That is, it makes communication
possible, generalizable, durable. Most of all, it makes the past and
the future meaningful within the whole.

Moreover, the arcane nature of the church's knowledge – knowledge that the untrained could not understand, that lies behind
appearances[12] – can also be seen as an expression of ecclesiastical
superiority grounded on the control of future events; it implied the
skill to foresee consequences left hidden to the layperson.

Awareness of all these facts provided the partisans of the superiority
of the spiritual power with their central argument: As knowledge of
the "general" is superior to knowledge of the "particular," since one
cannot grasp the latter without having first understood the former,
so spiritual power is superior to the temporal one. It follows that a
ruler cannot take day-to-day decisions successfully if he is not enlightened by knowledge of the general ends of society. And this only
the spiritual (ecclesiastical) class possesses.

Throughout this Gregorian moment one sees a class in control of
knowledge move to assert its general authority on society. Organized
knowledge is mobilized in its function of defining ultimate ends and
of giving general meaning to the symbols of communication. These
are the conditions that enable a society to live beyond the momentary
and beyond the local.

The control of rules

Knowledge of ultimate ends might be considered, as it were,
a once-and-for-all operation. It is of the nature of the general and

hence of the relatively unchanging. Its continuous presence in a society is assured by rituals that reiterate the same content, the same message. But at the lower level of everyday life, of short-term goals, of particular and possibly divergent and conflicting orientations of action, more specific rules are needed. Before the dissociation of the spiritual, the ecclesiastical class had the power to emit these rules and to adjudicate when violations or conflicts arose. It thus controlled the collective and the interpersonal, the ultimate and the proximate.[13]

Traditionally these two components of the spiritual domain, definition of identity and normative regulation, were not clearly distinguishable. Sin, for instance, tended to be seen as an all-or-nothing case. One was a Christian and hence destined to salvation, or otherwise one was excommunicated and expelled by the Christian community. And crime tended to coincide with sin.[14] When the spiritual-temporal levels began to separate, the ecclesiastical class organized itself to explicitly renew its control of the regulation of proximate ends. This endeavor is manifested in the reorganization of the canon law as well as in the distinction between the two types of power, different but both pertaining to the spiritual realm. In the ecclesiastical terminology one came to be called power *ordinationis* (related to sacraments, to liturgy and ritual), the other power *jurisdictionis* (related to the church as a legal corporate organization). Both eternal knowledge and daily regulations should then stay in the hands of the spiritual apparatus.

The control of devotion

A third important spiritual resource is the capacity to control what can induce devotion. Devotion is that attitude of mind, or that project of life, thanks to which individuals determine to "devote" their activity, time, and riches to a collective cause that transcends their self-interest. The very definition of what "self-interest" in certain circumstances may be, or is perceived to be, is obviously involved in the definition of a particular form of devotion. To shut oneself in a monastery, to bequeath all one's riches to the church, to die for a cause, religious or political, may perfectly be included in the category of self-interested actions if the "self" in question includes also the soul of the person after death. In this sense, control of devotion is strictly linked with the first of the resources we have here listed, the capacity to define personal identity through the definition of ultimate ends. While this capacity, grounded on eschatological knowledge, leads to assigning a certain collective identity to a society (to defining it, for instance, as the "Christian society," that is, a society different from all others because of the nature of the ultimate ends it sets for all its members, irrespective of their differences in language, blood ties, territorial or political allegiances), the management of devotion can establish particular standards in the intensity of the identification of an individual with the collective ends. States of devotion can be achieved to an exceptionally intense degree throughout their life by exceptional persons, or in decisive exceptional moments by normal persons.

The exceptional *persons* are those whom Weber called the religious "virtuosi." The exceptional *moments* are mainly to be found in a practice that developed when the church's monopoly over devotion was threatened.It can be illustrated by the example of a wealthy man on his deathbed, who must decide where (to whom) his wealth will go. It is obviously a crucial moment for a definition of his identity, of what he (his soul) has been (in the succession of the unlimited calculations that have brought him to accumulating that wealth), and of what his soul (he) will become. If he is a "devoted" man, that is, if the church has convinced him that the identity of his soul can be only defined within the collective identity of the triumphant church, or, in other words, that "his" ultimate ends coincide with the ultimate ends of the Christian society, then he will bequeath his wealth, or part of it, to the church.[15] Most of the wealth and therefore of the temporal power of the church, came, for centuries, from this "politics of devotion," as well as from that other type of "politics of devotion" which brought men and women to spend their whole life of industrious and zealous commitment to nonselfish ends in monasteries where, in times of disorder and waste, wealth was orderly and continuously created, accumulated, transmitted.[16]

The very essence of the church as the warden and promoter of the collective identity of Christianity lies in its control of the techniques of devotion. When it loses, at least partially, this control, and the devotion – that is, the allegiance – of a population is captured by other collective identities (the state, or the heretic movements), also its power will decrease. And when the state, or a political movement, is able to control devotion in an absolute way, then absolute politics in the stricter sense will set in.

The definition of the enemies

Fourth, and finally, spiritual power includes the operation of defining the enemies. An institution entitled to decide who my enemies should be – enemies that I will have, at times, the right to kill, enemies of life and death – has a deeply penetrating power. In the contemporary world there is no doubt that only the state has such a power, such an authority. We can even date the birth of the modern state at the moment it conquered and held alone this authority. But until Christian society existed as a larger and more comprehensive unit than the particular peoples, nations, and communities that composed it, "legitimate" enemies were only the infidels and, at times, the heretics, that is, those who refused to share the same definition of ultimate ends. Wars among Christians were waged and people killed, but that was not legitimate: A soldier who killed enemies in battles that were not against infidels had to make penance.[17] One can say that as the church was in charge of the definition of ultimate ends, so it was in charge of the definition of ultimate boundaries. And boundaries were not territorial but spiritual. As soon as the infidels, or the pagans, wherever they lived, were converted, collectively or individually, they integrated the Christian society. This has been the fundamental, long-term function of the church in the formation of Western civilization: offering a set of symbols of a common identity, which made it possible to establish who belonged and who was excluded, irrespective of cultural origins, and to test the bids for belonging.

Boundaries were also defined, by processes of individual or group exclusion, toward the heretics and the excommunicated. These were, so to speak, the "internal enemies." And here the control of the definition of boundaries rejoins the control of adjudication and punishment, since the essence of punishment for a long time consisted in forms of exclusion from the collective body (death being obviously one of these, excommunication another, shame a lighter and temporary one, etc.)

These four components of what has traditionally been called "spiritual power" seem to operate partly in times of *routine* (as the controls of knowledge and of the formation of rules) and partly in *exceptional moments* or for exceptional persons (as the controls over the inducement of devotion and over the definition of the enemies). On another dimension, the controls both over norms and over the definition of the enemies seem addressed to the *maintenance of the boundaries* of the collectivity: of the internal, or cultural, boundaries, against the disruption brought about by deviant behavior; of the external boundaries, against invaders. Whereas knowledge and devotion are the basis for the *overcoming of boundaries*; they create room for some form of unbound commitment.

The ritual power of the weak

The types of control so far described have one aspect in common: They assume the collectivity to be a unified entity. They seem to deny the presence of differences and divisions. But consider now, in a ceremony legitimating the authority of some powerful warrior, the strange presence of the ecclesiastic. In his capacity, he is a person removed from worldly power, excluded from the use of force, and yet he seems an indispensable figure when power has to be recognized and accepted by the collectivity. This would be a difficult fact to explain, were it not so common in societies throughout history. The need for the presence of the powerless components of a collectivity in the very moment in which power receives recognition and becomes "authority" has been called, in a formula, "the ritual power of the weak." It may take the form of status reversal (the underling comes up uppermost); of the ritual humiliation of the powerful (as in the formula *servus servorum dei* in the consecration of the pope); of pledges to serve the weak (as in the vigil of the medieval knight); or of similar techniques of chastening of the powerful. In tribal societies, the presence of the weak is often direct, and is circumscribed to what Van Gennep named "the liminal phases" of society, that is, to rites of passage proper. But with increasing complexity in the social division of labor "what was in tribal society principally a set of transitional qualities 'betwixt and between' defined states of culture and society has become itself an institutionalized state."[18] This state is embodied in the ecclesiastical profession.

This strange power accorded to the powerless classes of society, or to its representatives, in the ritual processes during which power becomes recognized may receive two interpretations. One is the "structural interpretation," Machiavellian in its nature. The ritual power of the weak is seen as slightly more than a mystification. More exactly, it is seen as a cunning technique of social control making it easier for the powerful to govern society. The very temporary phases in which the powerful are humiliated, the statuses reversed, the powerless given experience of authority, are simply outlets, illusory states from which the subordinate classes return more acquiescent and submissive to daily productive life. When a whole apparatus is created to represent the powerless, their representatives join the real powerful in the sharing of the benefits of power. Thus the illusion is perfected.

The alternative interpretation we may call "communitarian." At the basis of the ritual power of the weak is the need for the community to periodically reassess its unity. The presence of the powerless in the process of the formation of power is the guaranty of the collective identity. In that process, the weak and the strong classes join together in some sort of mystical union. This is not just a momentary, or illusory, union. The powerless classes have something of relevance to give to the powerful, aside from the guaranty of unity. Being powerless and unsuccessful, they live in a special tension toward the future, where some sort of redemption may take place, which would put an end to their misery and subjection. The classes which already have power and success now, have less reason to know any tension toward the future. But the collectivity as a whole may require this tension, thus needing the special contribution of the lower classes, or their representatives.[19]

The two interpretations do not necessarily contradict each other. The one or the other will be closer to the facts according to the degree of danger or tranquility confronting the collectivity. When the collectivity is *not* in danger, the ritual power of the weak will not influence the daily social hierarchies. When the collectivity *is* in danger, the normally powerful have as much to lose as the normally powerless. The solidarity generated in rites will tend to be true also for a daily instrumental sphere. Ritual states will then naturally develop into collective action. As a consequence the relative social position of the ritual class – which is in charge of rites and sacrifices, and also represents the weakest part of society – will be enhanced. Their vision and style and procedures will inspire more than usually the governance of society. This will be also a moment in which a tension toward the future is needed to overcome the state of uncertainty. In other words, the duration of the collective identity in time is seen as the real common interest for both parts of society.

Transcendental and absolute politics are of that nature. Renewal or tightening of collective identity, tension toward the future, toward a radical change of the situation, are among its essential ingredients.

Teaching versus command

To define the ultimate ends of social activities, to determine who the enemies of society must be; to prescribe the rules of daily life and to induce states of devotion in special individuals or in special circumstances; to receive ritual power through the representation of the weak – all that seems power enough, seems all that there can be in terms of social resources of power. With one exception, indeed a fundamental one; the skill in the use of force. The capacity of employing force was to be considered the real alternative to power spiritual. Indeed, the ecclesiastical reform movement had its origin mostly in the movement for God's truce.[20] And when they conquered the papacy, the reformers hoped to find in the preaching of the Crusades a mode of restating the right to assign spiritual goals to the use of arms.

This notion of the use of force as something distinct and specific still haunts us today when, for instance, in Weberian terms, we conceive of the state as the institution having the monopoly of the (legitimate) use of force; or when we draw a radical distinction between consensus and coercion in the relation between rulers and ruled. And if one merely has in mind relations between individuals, surely there are reasons for making some distinction between the individual who, with use of muscles or threat of weapons, coerces another to do something, and the individual who induces the other to do the same thing with the use of resources, which, whatever they might concretely be, may be called "spiritual." Of this second person we will say that he *intrinsically* controls the other's will. But if one considers the use of force in political and military terms, when collectively organized action is implied, then this distinction is much less neat. Weber himself remarked how military organizations and military action are made possible by types of social relations very close to forms of religious devotion. And one must be aware at least of the unavoidable circumstance that in commanding the use of force, force cannot be used. Something else must be at work.

The fact is that two quite different dimensions are hidden behind this age-honored dichotomy of the forms of control. On the first dimension, the dichotomy refers to a differentiation in the timing and scope of the effects of control. Spiritual is that control that *takes time* to bear effects. Consider its most typical form, *teaching* (the function of teaching distinguishes all priestly classes in traditional religions), and contrast it to *command*, the most typical relation of control premised to the use of force. Teaching operates in the long term and in a generality of situations. Command has immediate effects. Even if its execution is delayed, the content of what has to be done is specifically defined by the command itself (notice that according to the scholastic formula, to the temporal sword belonged the *usus immediatus*). Moreover, the jurisdiction inherent in the two forms of control has different types of boundaries. Teaching, implying conversion and proselytism or, in some form, modification of identities, has no predetermined boundaries limiting its message and moves without fixed horizon; its audience cannot be jurisdictionally defined. Command, on the other hand, has specific content and predetermined boundaries. Who must obey is established in advance. Outside its jurisdiction lie only enemies (external or internal, infidels, criminals, heretics, etc.), who then are the objects of the use of force.

If on the first dimension the distinction is based on the *modes* of influence between persons and groups, on the second dimension the distinction refers to the *reasons* for obeying a command. Here the essential alternative is between obeying a command because it emanates from a certain office or, instead, because it is expressed by a certain person, to whom the complaint is personally linked by certain special ties (in general, of consanguinity). The first principle had emerged in the cosmopolitan community of the Roman Empire and had been adopted by the ecclesiastical organization of a religion which proclaimed to be "catholic," that is, worldwide and aiming at assembling men of every kind. The second was constitutive of the German nations which were occupying the empire, and is present in so long-lasting political criteria of identity as "dynasty," "kinsfolk," "people," "race," and the like. When the German nations settled on large territories, the principle of consanguinity could not maintain its former centrality. Relations of dominion were grounded mainly on bonds of personal loyalty. Against the primacy of personal loyalty, when it had autonomy enough to stand for something, the church clearly stood for universality, impersonality, as well as supraterritoriality. Authority, for the church, had to be "an effluence of office."[21]

The distinction between the reasons for obeying based on office or based on persons has long remained central in the formation of political identities in the West. It does not correspond – it should be clear by now – to the spiritual/temporal distinction. Both principles belong to things spiritual. A reason for obeying based on the conception of a durable community of blood, derived from common (divine) ancestors, is as spiritual as a reason for obeying based on membership in a salvific community of souls, only of a fundamentally different spirituality. They were therefore doomed to clash.

It is, throughout history, a well-known type of clash. Traditionally it was solved by circumscribing the individualistic tensions toward salvation within the circles of the "world renouncers." In the West a different course unfolded. The potentially centralized supraethnic, and supraterritorial organization of the functionaries of salvation found in two principles – that salvation should be individual and that norms should be applied universally – a potent weapon to expand spiritual control beyond all boundaries. The door was open for the world renouncers to become world transformers. Neither the fathers of Cluny, nor the Gregorian reformers, nor even the great lawyer-popes of the thirteenth century had such a passage clearly in mind. But that original connection between world renunciation and world transformation did not remain a historical oddity. It was to become a recurring theme of the absolute style of politics and is still to be observed in the structure of personality of some protagonists of the style in our time.

Conditions for a politics of transcendence

In the three preceding sections I have tried to establish that a particular historical dissociation of the spiritual from the temporal powers is at

the origins of the Western style of politics and its "absolute" manifestations. I have consequently tried to define the nature of these two
powers. The understanding of the meaning of this distinction is generally taken for granted. Even people who do not believe in some
spiritual reality, or who give of it some philosophical and not religious
description, accept the idea that a "spiritual" apparatus may have
power, without asking what type of power this is. At most, reference
is made to the meaning that the religious phenomena have for us
today. This compounds the confusion because as politics is not what
it was, so also religion is not. When they confront similar phenomena,
anthropologists are more cautious. The cultural distance between
them and their objects being wider, their reconstruction is bound to
be more theoretical. They have no nominal analogies to rely upon or
traditional canons to trust. They therefore are led to justify their categories more systematically. Analogously, I tried to make sense of
what was called "power spiritual" by seeing it as a compound of four
types of power, or control: control of the organization of knowledge,
of the production of norms, of the inducement of devotion, and of
the definition of the enemies of society. These are forms of activities
and attitudes that exist in the most different societies, independently
from any belief in some extraworldly reality. Moreover, they are not
part, or are only part very indirectly, of what we consider to be
religious phenomena today. The same can be said of the ritual power
of the weak, whose representation, in our example, was another
function of the ecclesiastical apparatus.

The dichotomy "spiritual/temporal" is therefore released from its
commonsense reference to the dichotomy "religious/political." More
analytically, the essential reference becomes "ultimate" (or long-term)
as against "proximate" ends. For the term "temporal," this reference
is included in the linguistic root "temporary." As for the term "spiritual," the reference to the dimension of time, of duration (if eternal,
or just long-term, is a question of measure) renders the only meaning
acceptable to nonbelievers. The consequence of this analysis for our
inquiry is to look at Western politics as composed, in various ways,
of these two modes of power.

Two general visions of what the governance of society should be
about also correspond to this dichotomy of the two modes of power.
In one vision, a dominant group, cohesive because of personal ties
and loyalties, possessing the means for the use of force, is seen as
demanding obedience from the rest of the population. In the other
vision, a group of "teachers," ostensibly weak as for the use of force,
but inspired by a common conception of the long-term ends of society
and possessing the means of an intrinsic control of individual wills,

is seen leading the collectivity toward a transformation of the conditions of social life. These two modes of power, and the corresponding visions of politics, do usually coexist and complement each other. When they separate, and the second tends to dominate, we have absolute politics. We need now to ask under what circumstances this is likely to occur.

The temporal mode of power is based on personal loyalties and on the efficacy and immediacy of the transmission of commands. When circumstances are such that personal ties lose stringency and command backed by force is precluded, made inefficacious, or otherwise hampered, the action of the collectivity must be spurred through spiritual means. Teaching, or other forms of intellectual discourse, rituals, techniques of devotion, representations of impending threats to a common identity, become then prominent. Such circumstances can be brought about, for instance, by processes of rapid social and geographical mobility. Then traditional communities break down and customs are weakened or invalidated. Generally, one might say that any process of individualization undermines the contribution of personal hierarchical ties to social order. The breakdown of central authorities, territorial fragmentation, and, in general, the dismemberment of the agents of force as well as breaches in their chain of command, on the other hand, have thwarted the possessors of force in their attempts to reinstate subordination. The jurisdiction of command contracts. The jurisdiction of spiritual authority expands and is assumed to provide the criterion for identifying what is to be done, on what grounds, and with or against whom.

If the weakening of personal or other form of *immediate* social ties is a necessary condition for the possibility of the spiritual apparatus to take command, other circumstances must intervene for a real politics of transcendence to develop. The historical example we may refer to is the difference between Eastern and Western Christianity.[22] Analyzing these differences in an ideal-typical way, one finds on the one (the Eastern) side, the following circumstances going together: a politically (military) unified territory; rare population movements; imperial (military) autocracy having command over religious matters; the emperor being the source of the law; the practice of the law being in the hands of laypersons, not of ecclesiastics, and the presence of well-developed hierarchical lay civil service; ecclesiastical ecumenism (prevalence of the religious assemblies over the incumbents of ecclesiastical offices); communitarian liturgy (popular participation as a part of the ritual), marriage of priests and their full membership in the community; worship more decisive than belief as a criterion for establishing orthodoxy; "materiality" of the liturgy (real bread and wine, real immersion in water, real oil, etc.), linked with the idea that spirit and matter were not two separate and opposed entities but rather manifestations of the same ultimate reality, and that matter was "spirit-bearing" no less than the soul of the individual. And, most importantly, salvation seen as a collective, not an individual, process; sin considered as a separation from the community and penance as reconciliation with it – not an institution for individual guilt and punishment, the priest acting as witness rather than as judge.

On the Western side we may construct an ideal type opposed to the Eastern one almost on each item. A continuously divided territory, scene of vast movements of populations; divided military authorities; unified, autocratic ecclesiastical government; the pope acting as the source of the law; the practice of the law in the hands of the ecclesiastical class, which virtually monopolized any type of knowledge; a "specialized" (if this term is allowed) rather than communitarian liturgy, highly symbolic, fleshless (pouring of water instead of immersion, unleavened bread, etc.; the individual soul, not material objects, being the repository of spirituality); priests required to exert a higher degree of sexual asceticism than normal humanity; the content of belief more important than the modes of worship; salvation considered an *individual* conquest; penance considered atonement for sin, while the priest sat as judge, rather than simple witness, of the individual failure sin was considered to consist in.

It is on this latter set of circumstances that a politics of transcendence is likely to be waged. Here, as it were, the earthly weight of the past and of the traditional customs of the community are much less incumbent. The new spirituality, the spirit of reform, is taken more seriously. The achievement of a desired future state of the Christian world seems not out of reach.[23]

It would be obviously ill-advised, if not extravagant, to conceive of all the traits of the two ideal types I have described as linked coherently among them, or all derived by some common factor. But at least two suggestions are worth considering. An increase in the autonomy of the spiritual apparatus seems to go together with an increase in the individualization of society. Moreover, the autonomy and the authority of the spiritual apparatus seem to grow stronger during periods of territorial fragmentation. Let us take these two hypotheses in succession.

1. A process of individualization of society enhances the opportunities and the ambitions of an apparatus of "spiritual specialists." The spiritual direction can be exercised directly upon the individual, independently from the role obligations he receives from his position

in society. Thus, the claims of the ecclesiastical hierarchy were based on their right to control the souls of the individual members of the Christian society, among which the souls of kings and emperors obviously must be also counted. Souls of powerful men, souls of rulers, but souls nonetheless, fully belonging to the jurisdiction of the spiritual. A grounding of the distinction between office ("role") and person became therefore paramount to the establishment of a spiritual jurisdiction, autonomous from other "social" powers as well as from other specialized areas of social life. An entirely new type of social relationship was thence introduced, the direct relationship of the ecclesiastical organization – as the organization which is specialized in spiritual resources – with persons *as such*, not as incumbents of roles. The new form of penance (sanctioned by the Lateran Council of 1215 but clearly emerging in the same period as the ecclesiastical revolution), with its direct relationship between priest and sinner, with inner contrition (grounded in feelings of *individual* guilt) replacing the process of communitarian reconciliation, is to be seen as one of the most striking manifestations of this direct, nonmediated, relationship between the individual as such (that is, not in his social capacities) and the provision of spiritual services by the ecclesiastical organization. Penance, together with the contemporary diffusion of the idea of Purgatory and hence of a measurable and, as it were, negotiable future destiny of the individual soul, also shows the double meaning of this new object of specialized service.[24] Being in charge of the direct, person-to-person control of the soul of the individual, the ecclesiastical class will penetrate into the process of determination of what has to be done by each person to move toward his or her ultimate ends. Ultimate ends are more important than proximate ends. This fact will lend supremacy to the ecclesiastical office. But the couple within which the way toward ultimate ends is determined has two poles: One is the priest, but the other is the individual. In this process the individual is helped to become autonomous from immediate social ties and role obligations. The door is open toward some wider autonomy.

2. The second hypothesis indicates that the strength of the spiritual apparatus increases in cases of territorial fragmentation. When the politico-military boundaries of a population are the same, the "territorial other," the military enemy, will coincide with the religious infidel. The military and the ecclesiastical class will, as it were, construct social reality in a unified way. Religious symbols will then be needed as a mere auxiliary device to strengthen a collective identity that is already well-defined by territorial or cultural boundaries. Cae-

saropapism – in the extended meaning of a military authority being in command over the spiritual apparatus – will then be the logical institutional consequence.[25]

But when the case is the opposite – as in the Western Christianity – and the population professing one religion is divided among several military authorities, and the possible enemies in temporal wars do not coincide with the eternal infidel, then the spiritual apparatus has a difficult and controversial, but exalting, task.[26] Out of the potentialities of this task the projects of a politics of transcendence may emerge, which attempts to solve the inherent contradiction between spiritual and territorial identities by subjecting the latter to the former. The scope and then the failure of this attempt in the West left room for the grounding of the modern state upon the principle of territorial contiguity. This entailed a series of consequences.

One is the consequence just hinted at. If a society is territorially defined, there is no longer a need for a spiritual class to define who and what the enemies should be. Interaction with them, moreover, will not be seen as manifesting spiritual, hence nonnegotiable, antagonisms. Coexistence and therefore an international system of independent states become possible and politics not religion, territorial interest not ultimate belief will govern foreign policy.

Another consequence derives from the particular nature of the territorial social bond. It is different from the associational bond, since in the associational bond the individual voluntarily chooses to enter, whereas it is not so, or only very exceptionally, in the case of the territorial one. It is different from the kinship bond, which predetermines not only membership but also its hierarchical ordering. And it is different from the religious bond, where membership is optional and not predetermined – at least in principle. But the hierarchical ordering, insofar as it is of divine origin, is predetermined. The territorial bond is to be contrasted, therefore, on two dimensions to the religious one: The individual is born into it, but then no other string comes attached to it, since the social structure, as in the case of voluntary associations, does not receive any preordained form.[27]

When territorial identity becomes relevant, impediments are minimized for any type of individualistic course of action – and one thinks here of the advantages the market system received from having developed on the background of territorial instead of kinship or spiritual collectivities. Moreover, social control can take a complete different form than in previous societies. Territorial boundaries make possible the definition in individual terms of the conditions for the observance of norms and hence clearly entail the universality of their application. In other words, territorial identity is one of the conditions for the emergence of the modern legal systems.

We may now decide that the analysis of our case needs not proceed further. I have chosen to refer to the Gregorian moment because I needed a case in which the emergence of a politics of transcendence, the mobilization of spiritual resources in the struggle for the autonomy and power of an apparatus monopolizing the means of knowledge and the means of salvation, and then the attempt to use this power for the transformation of the structure of social relations, could best be seen in their naked features. It was the first appearance of a style of politics, unique to the West, whose potentiality was then planted in the European political institutions. Out of this episode, a series of unexpected outcomes will derive, which cannot obviously be discussed here. Some of them will only be hinted at in the concluding section. But the analysis has produced a few generalizable hypotheses, which I will now sum up.

When the loosening of a territorial jurisdiction gives rise to forms of administrative and military fragmentation, and the concept of the enemy tends to be dissociated from the concept of the religious infidel, a politics of transcendence is likely to be waged, to keep intact the supraterritorial identity and make sure that the infidel will still be the real enemy. The same is likely to happen when traditional loyalties weaken and the members of a population tend to conceive of their destiny in individual terms. The customary controls will then work less effectively, individuals will easily move and be free to choose between alternatives, whereas the face-to-face relations, the small group or the local society, will cease to produce sufficiently cogent and easily enforceable norms for the conduct of the individual. A politics of transcendence should then provide the ingredients for new modes of control. One is the universalistic system of norms which tends to define the rights and duties of the individual qua individual; and modern law emerged to meet the need for this type of control. The other is the direct form of control of the individual soul; and here the resources mobilized by a politics of transcendence are employed to control the proximate ends of daily life by applying to them the principles dictated by some ultimate end.

What has been here called a politics of transcendence is a mode of absolute politics which occurred before the formation of the modern territorial state and whose protagonists belonged to an organized transcendent religion. The same fundamental ingredients will be there, however, in the more modern cases of absolute politics.

Failure and irony

"Like all victories, the victory of the Church in the Investiture Conflict had unforeseen consequences. By asserting its unique character, by separating itself so clearly from lay governments, the Church unwittingly sharpened concepts about the nature of secular authority. . . . the Gregorian concept of the Church almost demanded the invention of the concept of the State."[28] This is certainly one of the possible meanings of the overall phenomenon. But it is only one, and it has to be more clearly spelled out in its components.

The ecclesiastical apparatus mobilized the social resources it controlled monopolistically, or semimonopolistically, in order to assert its supremacy. It needed to do so because the new forms of territorial loyalties that were emerging threatened to subordinate its position. As in other periods, territorial fragmentation of the Christian temporal authorities induced projects of ecclesiastical centralization and supremacy. As in other cases, a relative weakness of one social actor – in this case, the church – provokes this actor into a project of overexpansion,[29] based on an ideological rationalization of its role, and hence in an ideological reconstruction of the desirable form of society. But the process of formation of this new society brings about new separate actors that come to control the resources originally mobilized for the goals of the reformers. This is what happened with the ecclesiastical revolution. The social resources mobilized by the church in her project were subtracted one by one from her control. I will rapidly show this by reviewing what happened to the four type of resources that I have described as components of the original "spiritual power."

Social knowledge was one of these and it was securely placed in the hands of the church. Wherever knowledge was needed, a portion of the ecclesiastical apparatus was present.[30] The fervor of the reformers, and the increasing demand for administrative, legal, and theological expertise (this last to counter the threat of the new heresies), led to a great expansion of knowledge. The universities, under the new Scholastic enthusiasms, were among the products of this process of expansion. The number of educated men rapidly grew during the twelfth century. Written documents multiplied. Thousands of young men flocked to the schools and then took service with lay or ecclesiastical officials. "By the end of the twelfth century the shortage of clerks and accountants was almost overcome; by the end of the thirteen century there was probably a surplus of men who could do this kind of work."[31] This surplus made the recruiting of intellectuals easier for the new secular authorities. Even if these intellectuals wore the robe of the clergy, and some threat of double allegiance lingered on for some centuries and was not dispelled completely until the times of Reformation, still it could be said that the ties of the intellectual with the Mother Church soon began to wear thin.

When a social actor that covers a particular position in the intellectual functions of society enters into a conflict with other agencies of society, it develops an ideology that helps define and justify its goals and coordinate its actions. For such a task, intellectual forces are needed. The status of the intellectuals is enhanced and their number grows. They are then to be found in greater numbers on the market, and in most divergent forms and postures. This makes them ready to serve other groups and projects, and to propose new and diverse ideologies. This is the type of situation that more and more became prevalent in the West, and that can be considered a premise for absolute politics, since intellectuals are needed to propose and present the projects that make the stuff of it.

The "control of rules" is another of the resources I have described as composing the spiritual power. I use this generic term to cover the production of norms, their enforcement, adjudication, conciliation, and so on. In a society dominated by custom, intervention by normative agencies was rare; but if one agency intervened, that was the church. When the church attempted a systematization of the world of norms, it aimed at strengthening and sanctioning this monopoly. And its ideology was geared toward that aim. "The theology of the Papal Revolution was a theology of judgment. . . . This theology underlay the church's establishment for the first time of an 'external forum' for the trial of crimes, as contrasted with the 'internal forum' of the confessional and the sacrament of penance."[32]

But the consequences, here again, were unexpected. When a separate autonomous body of law, the canon law of the church, was brought into being, a series of equally autonomous secular bodies of law were bound to appear. Indeed, the idea that the lay ruler had to be the guarantor of justice was implied in the new ecclesiastical conception of the law.[33]

Because the lay ruler "no longer shared responsibility for the guidance and governance of the Church . . . then their only excuse for existence was to enforce justice."[34] This conception corresponded to the reality of the process of state formation that was then taking place. Adjudication was the main activity through which the rulers, by involving the free population of a country in the work of the law courts, as either litigants or jurors (this last, in England), built a network of allegiances. This service was reciprocated in terms of fiscal duties; taxation and adjudication were then the stuff the new states were made of.[35] But if the law, thanks to the new theology, was becoming a new manifestation of the "sacred," then administering the law acquired the characters of sacrality. This was the ground out of which the ideology of the new state, and its potentiality for absoluteness, could grow. Sacrality was transferred to territorial authority. This was certainly not what the Gregorians had meant.

This transfer manifested itself for instance in attributing "eternity" (immortality), that is, immutability in time, to the body politic. "The body politic of Kingship appears as a likeness of the 'holy sprites and angels' because it represents like the angels, the immutable within Time."[36] Continuity in time of an object, of a "body," is the necessary attribute of a lastingly recognizable identity. The territorial state possessing a *body politic* could now take the succession of the church in performing the function of lending ultimate identity to its subjects, and therefore become "an object of political devotion and semi-religious emotion."[37] The idea of *corpus mysticum* having been transferred to the territorial identity, the notion of fatherland, of *patria*, emerges. Death for one's own territorial identity – as defined by the boundaries within which the *laws of the fatherland* are valid – becomes sacred. The words of the Maccabees (3:20), "We will fight for our *souls* and *laws*," preached by a French cleric in 1302 during the fight between France and the papacy, become a central theme of political propaganda.[38] Laws are for the collective body, what the soul is for the individual: spiritual, hence eternal, hence identity defining. And there was no more question of inflicting penance for killing territorial enemies.[39]

This spiritual-eternal nature of the state became an attribute not only of its law-producing activity but also of one of its apparently more material, but crucial, activities: taxation. The perpetuality and impersonality of the fisc was obviously a condition for the perpetuality and impersonality of the state. Thus the sempiternity of the fisc was even compared, in thirteenth-century texts, to the eternity of God and Christ.[40] What more telling evidence of a full transfer of spirituality!

A further aspect of the same process was the transfer of the principle of the impersonality of the office from ecclesiastical to state institutions. The first recipient of this transfer was the office of the king itself. The strategy of individualization of the church – aimed at controlling on a direct, secret (within the confessional), and hence "private" relation the souls of the powerful individuals – backfired. The soul of the person became the subject of the ecclesiastical control only thanks to the creation of a second body, this one escaping any individual ecclesiastical control. It was the body of the king. There lay the real seat of the new territorial authority. There one could also discover the emergence of the impersonality of public offices and hence of the autonomy of a new "public" sphere.[41]

Being in control of the operations of the law meant, for the territorial authorities, possessing a tool for social change. And a powerful one. In fact, the idea of a willful transformation of society (the realization of a "Christian" society) was already present in the Gregorian movement. The state, by inheriting the control of the law, inherited also the potentiality of transforming existing society, or aiming at transforming it, or part of it, following conceptions of what a good society should be. It was a new and far-reaching condition of government.

The centrality, within the new territorial state, of the idea and of the practice of the law, the idea of the sacrality and hence of the perpetuality of a "body of law," as "body politic," constituted the premises for some absoluteness in the conception of what the activities having to do with administering the population of a territory were about. But the supremacy of the law in the medieval polity bore ambivalent consequences. If it strengthened the hand of the territorial administrator, it also constituted in itself a higher authority than the state. Indeed, it was the highest authority imaginable. "Law had been conceived as existing independently of the will of any ruler, independently even of the will of God; God himself was obedient to Law ... so the king, he is below the Law, though he is below no man."[42] The idea of a *Rechtsstaat*, of a "law state," of the rule of law is already there in essence.[43] If this aspect is considered, the victory of the territorial state was far from being complete. And this was not only because the church, and through it a normative order which had to be essentially pluralistic, still remained embedded in the Western polity, nor because temporal lords other than the king were able to to muster enough power to successfully appeal to that superior authority, but because the idea of some superior ("natural") right paved the way to the entry of a new actor on the scene where the possessors of rights play their act following identifiable interests and according to rules. This actor was the individual; not as such, at first, but as a proprietor. Property indeed represented the only sufficiently durable identity to parallel the durable identity of the soul as a criterion for the recognition of an individual.

The construction of a body of law and its supremacy, therefore, was the ground for the introduction of two new types of political identities: those of the territorial states and those of the individuals as proprietors. If the first could conceive, at the extreme reach of the pursuit of their interest, the possibility of absolute politics, the second would obviously stand at the other extreme. The two alternatives, *of absolute politics* aiming at molding society, and of *minimal politics*, leaving the structure of power intact as it emerged from the social dealings and exchanges, were present in the legal nature of the state.

The road that a state had to tread to approach the conditions of absolute politics was, then, paved by the transfer of the other resources that had formed the power spiritual, the capacity for inducing collective devotion and the function of defining the enemies. Very much thanks to its growing involvement in the law – in the organization of the ecclesiastical apparatus and in the "ceaseless petty round of business and litigation" that this activity generated[44] – the church lost its monopoly in the control of devotion. After the Gregorian revolution the heretical movements exploded in the West. They had their ups and downs, but never ceased until the great breakdown in the unity of the church. Obviously, the church fought back in astute or heroic ways, and never lost its capacity to induce forms of devotion; it simply lost its monopoly. The sects on the one side, the state on the other side were the beneficiaries of this new opening on the market of devotion.

We have already seen that war is a great producer of devotion. It can be "personal" or "group" devotion – and in the reality of battle it is often of that nature. But when the identity of the sides in the battles is repeatedly the same, and territorially defined, devotion cannot escape being, in some form, referred to the state. On this basis the state became capable of defining the ultimate ends of its citizen. It was a short step to the emerging of the temptation to propose some ideology of its own. Whether in texts, oaths, ceremonies, music, or monuments, all the Western states did that to some extent. Some did it more explicitly and intensely. With the previous general scheme in mind we would say that the weakest states needed an overt ideology most. The weakest states are those which are most dangerously threatened by external or internal enemies or by the strong presence of an alternative spiritual apparatus. These had difficulties in recovering the spiritual autonomy that the ecclesiastical apparatus had taken away. The strongest states (France, Spain) did it by applying the strength of their bureaucratic apparatuses. They were capable of abolishing the privileges of the clerical estate, the tax exemption of the clergy, the church's legal immunities – in a word, the interference of an external spiritual jurisdiction on their territory.[45] The weakest states, which could not do the same bureaucratic-political means alone, had to mobilize the devotion of their own citizens through some sort of spiritual, transformative project. The religious reform could be used to that end, and so it was, becoming another example of transcendent politics. Only, this time the spiritual apparatus acted not for itself. And when it seemed to be at the head of the movement, at its inception, this was in the territorially weakest states and the autonomous spiritual leadership was destined soon to abdicate all kinds of territorial power. During the period in which the identity of the political collectivity still needed to be shored up by the presence of common ideas about salvation, the political enemy again tended to coincide with the religious one. But a European system of territorial powers could not be grounded on this coincidence. When the religious justification of war and violence could not be tolerated any more, the territorial principle came to monopolize the production of ultimate collective identities. The Hobbesian moment seemed to be the definitive response to the Gregorian one.

But history again was being ironical. The previously least autonomous state got rid of superterritorial authorities and recovered the undivided devotion of their subjects with the corroborating help of the new religions separate from Rome. The states that had not adopted the transcendent politics of the Reformation had still to accommodate the presence on their territory of a spiritual antagonist, or at least of an alternative apparatus of spiritual control, whose power and privileges had only in part been reduced by concordats. These states found themselves often in need of explicitly proposing and imposing some course toward long-term ends and of defining for their subjects some ultimate identities, thus ideologically dressing up the territorial bond. Absolute politics and intellectually formulated ideology, then, marked the style of governments and oppositions in those countries where the church apparatus kept at least a partial grasp on the soul of the subjects.

Not less ironical were the consequences of establishing individual ties between the apparatus of spiritual control and the souls of the believers. The control of the church over the collectivity, and chiefly over its most powerful members, was certainly strengthened, at first, from such untying of the individuals from its traditional collective memberships. The new allegiances and bequests could thus be addressed directly to the church. But if the stress on the individual bargaining of the means of salvation emancipated the individual from the traditional structures, it also set the premises for a further emancipation. The church soon became incapable of solving the problem of the social control of an individualistic society. A new series of disciplining structures emerged out of the civil society itself. But when civil society was weak or insufficient, the possibility of absolute politics was there to shore up social self-discipline and meet the need for general control. In this case, enemies were more sharply defined, or simply evoked. And only the territorial state could now perform that operation.

Finally, the traditional "ritual power of the weak" also underwent some unexpected transformation: We may recognize it in the representational rituals of the mass democracy of today.

The ingredients of absolute politics have been here exposed as they have emerged from the original dissociation of the spiritual and the temporal realms. These have been shown to correspond to the realms of ultimate or proximate ends, at a certain moment of Western religious and political history. The process of their dissociation has not been a process of secularization of politics. Rather, throughout that process, first, the spiritual apparatus has sought freedom from its dependence on the territorial rulers, in an attempt to conquer direct ascendence over the administration of society; thereafter, the territorial apparatus has retrieved, in different ways and degrees, some influence over the formation of ultimate ends. This reappropriation of the right of defining ultimate ends is more radical for those weak nations that fight to overcome their disadvantages. It meets less resistance when a weak civil society is unable to propose alternative identifications to satisfy the need for long-term certainties. Similarly, groups, classes, or movements, when they are weak, need to explicitly and forcefully propose long-term ends, to overcome their weakness. Thus, at times, the means of absolute politics (the capacity to induce devotion, self-sacrifice, long-term commitment, hopes or illusions of transforming reality) are in the hands of movements or groups. At times they are in the hands of states or other collectivities controlling the use of force. This is a most threatening case.

Notes

1 J. L. Talmon, *The Rise of Totalitarian Democracy* (Boston:Beacon, 1952), pp. 1–2.

2 Ibid., p. 11.

3 Ibid., p. 4.

4 "Quand sous l'effet de la sécularisation le sacré est refoulé de son domaine naturel qui consiste en la sphère religieuse, il trouve un refuge dans d'autres spheres, au prix, s'il le faut, d'une altération, par exemple dans la sphere du politique" (in the Preface to J. P. Sironneau, *Sécularisation et religions politiques* (La Haye: Mouton, 1982), p. x).

Like Talmon, Freund, throughout his work, places in the eighteenth century the process through which political power acquired "prerogatives, functions, procedures, aspirations, ideas" which up to that moment had been specifically religious. These positions are criticized by H. Blumenberg, *Säkularisierung und Selbstbehauptung* (Frankfurt, 1974), who shows the fallacy of equating working-class ethics with monastic asceticism, a philosophy of history with a doctrine of salvation, and so on.

5 Ibid., p. 6.

6 W. Ullmann, *Principles of Government and Politics in the Middle Ages* (London: Methuen, 1974).

7 Q. Skinner, *The Foundations of Modern Political Thought* (Cambridge: Cambridge University Press, 1978), vol. 2, pp. 349–52.

8 G. Tellenbach, *Church, State and Christian Society* (Atlantic Highlands, N.J.: Humanities, 1979), p. 186. The difference between the original Cluniac movement and the Gregorians can be better expressed by the Weberian dichotomy of religious orientations: *ascetic/hierocratic*. Asceticism implies abolition of present concerns, isolation from the world, and rational and exclusive orientation toward the future (salvation). Hierocratic orientation implies the recognition of the charisma of office (refused by the ascetic), of the need for specialization and professionalization, hence of a permanent ecclesiastical apparatus. Weber's observation that ascetic religion is compatible with Caesaropapism can account for Cluny's willingness to make alliances with the empire. The hierocratic Gregorians, instead, were doomed to clash with it.

9 This is the thesis repeated throughout the work of Harold Berman, *Law and Revolution: The Formation of the Western Legal Tradition* (Cambridge, Mass.: Harvard University Press, 1983). This thesis tends to receive now the consensus of the historians.

10 Georges Duby, *The Three Orders: Feudal Society Imagined*, Arthur Goldhammer, trans. (Chicago: University of Chicago Press, 1980), p. 276.

11 For a development of this argument, see A. Pizzorno, "Some other kind of otherness," in A. Foxley et al., *Development, Democracy and the Art of Trespassing* (South Bend, Ind.: University of Notre Dame Press, 1986).

12 Duby, *The Three Orders*, p. 15.

13 "The discovery, exposition and fixation of the norms of conduct for the Christian, or what was called the *norma recte vivendi*, could not be undertaken by the untrained who lacked adequate knowledge: this was a task that presupposed special training, hence knowledge. The demand for *scientia*, that is, expert knowledge, stands in closest proximity to the character of the Church as a corporate body that must be directed according to Christian norms deducible from the Christian faith" (Ullman, *Principles of Government*, p. 35). See also Duby, *The Three Orders*, pp. 14–15. Berman, *Law and Revolution*, pp. 73ff., shows that the clergy administered also the criminal law.

14 " 'Secular' crimes were also sins; in fact, the words 'crime' and 'sin' were used interchangeably" (Berman, *Law and Revolution*, p. 70). This is true wherever religions of salvation have not yet appeared, or where they are not autonomous enough and the definition of the "sacred" remains the task of the territorial-military authorities. It was true, for instance, in Japanese, until very recently.

15 The meaning of the appearance of the individual will in the late Middle Ages is obviously complex. On the one side, the church promotes the individualization of the will for the obvious reason that this type of will allows it to receive at least part of the inheritance of the deceased. And, indeed, the priests were expected to ensure that the faithful did not die intestate. On the other side, the "pious gifts" were not just made out of an individualistic calculation of advantages to be received by the soul of the deceased in Purgatory. Even if often the will's opening clauses dealt with the ecclesiastical steps taken to liberate the soul of the testator from Purgatory, the will could include arrangements for having people participate in the funeral, and similar communitarian or "earthly status" concerns. Bequests could be made toward repairs of roads or bridges, toward charitable purposes, and the paid-for prayers were not limited to the testator's needs but were offered for the good of friends, of the community, or of "all Christian souls." (See J. C. Dickinson, *The Later Middle Ages* (London: Adam & Charles Black, 1979), pp. 348–359. See also Berman, *Law and Revolution*, pp. 234–236.) In other words, the long-term identity of the testator, at the moment in which he calculated the best allocation for his earthly riches, consisted not simply in the identity of his soul in Purgatory, but in some identity of himself as defined by the memory he would leave in his community. Or his family: "Le XII siècle voit l'enrichissement de

la mémoire . . . les familles aristocratiques dressent et allongent leurs généalogies" (J. Le Goff, *La Naissance du Purgatoire* [Paris: Gallimard, 1981], p. 315). In other words, his identity was finally defined in circles of other persons, which had some *lasting* power to recognize and value him.

This is probably still a too "secular" description of what was taking place in that critical moment. "Les suffrages pour les morts supposent la constitution de longues solidarités de part et d'autres de la mort, de relations étroites entre vivants et défunts" (Le Goff, *La Naissance du Purgatoire*, p. 315). The community which was supposed to last, and whose recognition therefore allowed this individual to make calculations, was composed, one would say, of those who surrounded the individual in life and would join him afterlife and of those who followed the currently living individuals, and would follow them later in afterlife. It was a community that made possible both a horizontal (in space) and a vertical (in time) system of recognition and retribution. These are indeed the premises for any type of individualistic calculation. See Pizzorno, "Some other kind of otherness."

16 One may see the inadequacy of the use of categories like "religious" or "economic" for the definition of decisions having to do with the "long term," that is with the formation or preservation of a collective and, at the same time, individual, durable identity. They were decisions "snatching a small portion from the world of meaningless change to make it a replica of eternity" (R. W. Southern, *Western Society and the Church in the Middle Ages* [London, 1970], p. 28); or, simply, to confirm the existence of a durable collectivity capable of assuring its members a continuous recognition: "quel renforcement de la cohésion des communautés – familles charnelles, familles artificielles, religieuses ou confraternelles – que l'extension après la mort de solidarités efficaces" (Le Goff, *La Naissance du Purgatoire*, p. 24).

17 "The Frankish bishops in 923 imposed three years' penance on everyone who had been present at the battle of Soissons. . . . Similarly the Norman bishops after the battle of Hastings enjoined a penance of one year for each man killed by any member of the victorious army" (Southern, *Western Society and the Church in the Middle Ages*, p. 226). Of course, such harsh punishments were fictitious. Given the system of substitution that allowed the sinners to redeem their misdeeds by alms, or by engaging other persons to undertake the penance, the net result consisted not in the spiritual costs for the sinner but in the material benefits for the church. But the symbolic value, of strengthening the superterritorial jurisdiction of the church and keeping subordinated the territorial or personal allegiances, remained intact. Consider also that the Norman bishops enjoined that penance to the soldiers of the army they (and the pope) had favored.

18 V. Turner, *The Ritual Process* (Ithaca: N.Y.: Cornell University Press, 1969), p. 107. The consciousness of representing the powerless, and *therefore* being able to uphold a higher ethical standard, was very clear in the ecclesiastical conception of the separate functions within a Christian community. From that consciousness the idea followed that the ruler is accountable to the long-term identity of the people, symbolized and interpreted by the church, and therefore that the church is entitled to provide the competence of an established judicial authority to potentially recognize the ruler's guilt. For a classical analysis of these points, see F. Kern, *Kingship and Law in the Middle Ages* (New York: Harper & Row, 1970), pp. 97–110.

19 Turner leans, at least implicitly, toward this second interpretation. The most explicit statements about the tension toward the future as characterizing the powerless and the unsuccessful are to be found in Weber (under the influence of Nietzsche). Religions of salvation represent the solution of the problem of theo-

dicy for the powerless classes. Tension toward the future is a function of power-lessness in the present.

20 Cf. Duby, *The Three Orders*, chap. 2.

21 Ullman, *Principles of Government*, p. 41.

22 The idea of considering the difference between the Eastern and the Western Christian world as a sort of "control experiment" for determining the factors influencing the relations between church and state is implicitly contained in several analyses of this theme, and explicitly in T. M. Parker, *Christianity and the State in the Light of History* (London: Adam & Charles Black, 1955), pp. 66ff. See also S. Runciman, *The Eastern Schism* (Oxford: Oxford University Press, 1955), and N. Zernow, *The Church of the Eastern Christians* (London: S.P.C.K., 1942).I pursue here, however, an interest slightly different than that of those authors.

23 One may think that in terms of environmental conditions, Rome would show features more akin to the Eastern than to the Western type. This was indeed true. But the reform movement, Hildebrand, and most of his followers had their roots in the Germanic (or Frankish) regions of Christianity. Here, the organization of the church, its ideology, and its relationship with the environment were what the ideal typical description would have had them to be. The fundamental circumstance is probably the one described, for two centuries later, by R. Brentano in his comparative analysis of the church in England and Italy (R. Brentano, *Two Churches – England and Italy in the Thirteenth Century* (Princeton, N.J.: Princeton University Press, 1968). In Italy, the church (not differently from in Byzantium) was not isolated or monopolistic in its intellectual functions. Notaries, lawyers, were at work everywhere and laymen participated in the ecclesiastical administration. In a word, no strong boundaries of a "Gothic" style separated the church from society. In England, the ecclesiastical apparatus, which monopolized teaching and writing, was formed as a very distinct organization, with specific sets of functions, and these were subordinated to the central function of pastoral care. It was a sort of corporation, an enterprise of teaching and leading toward a better society. The triumph of spirituality was the true inspiring ideology.

24 The new form and new institutionalization of the practice of penance is central to understanding the process of social change we are here dealing with, and in particular the change in the position of the clergy in society. It is an expression and an instrument of shifting the control on the individual from the techniques of shame to the techniques of guilt. It institutionalizes the idea of morality as intention and will, away from morality as conformity to social customs – which Abelard first introduced into philosophical thinking. And it helps to separate the idea of sin from the idea of crime, therefore performing a function parallel to that of the contemporary institutionalization of the legal systems. See M. Hepworth and B. Turner, *Confession: Studies in Deviance and Religion* (London: Routledge & Kegan Paul, 1982); and also C. Vogel, ed., *Le Pécheur et la Pénitance au Moyen-Age* (Paris: Cerf, 1969), and Berman, *Law and Revolution*, pp. 68–76; 172–173.

The element of calculation was already present in the preauricular confession, the so-called Irish confession, common between the seventh and eleventh centuries, which was based on precise taxation for each category of sin. But only the construction of the idea of Purgatory involved in the calculation the whole long-term identity of the person. See J. Le Goff, *La Naissance du Purgatoire*; also J. Chiffoleau, *La comptabilité de l'au-délà* (Ecole Française de Rome, 1980).

Of course, it must not be forgotten that the institutionalization of penance was also seen as an important weapon in the fight against the heretics. But this circumstance strengthens the previous interpretation of the general meaning of the new phenomenon. Against collective movements threatening the loyalty of the individual to the official collectivity, the church used a technique of individualization.

25 It will be noted that this interpretation of the reasons for Caesaropapism is different from the Weberian one. In fact, Weber (*Economy and Society* [Berkeley and Los Angeles: University of California Press, 1978], pp. 1161ff.) simply gives a description of Caesaropapism and notes how its emergence is more probable when religiosity is based on the magical charisma of the priest and not on a bureaucratized and rational apparatus possessing its own doctrinal system – and less likely when religiosity is based on an ethics of salvation. But this association is either a tautology (needing, moreover, several qualifications if one must include Eastern Orthodox Christianity among the nonbureaucratized, nondoctrinal religions) or implicitly points to the circumstances that religion of salvation tends to expand beyond political boundaries and hence comprises populations belonging to different political units. This last circumstance should be seen as the real factor that makes Caesaropapism unlikely.

At the same time, one should observe that Caesaropapism has a tendency to reestablish itself because it is in the interest of every political authority to control the spiritual apparatus by imposing political boundaries to religious identity de facto if not by way of doctrine (Gallicanism and Anglicanism express processes of such a nature, with different intensity).

26 It would be interesting to control this hypothesis on a larger set of comparative cases; the hypothesis, in short, being that the coincidence, or not, of the religious and the military boundaries has an impact on the relative power of the religious apparatus. One would have to consider, for instance, the case of the complete subordination of Shinto in Japan, where the boundaries of the military and the religious community have for so long exactly coincided. (The longest lasting case of a "traditional" political religion, or, rather, the artful and skillful refabrication of one, when needed, by the Meji?) Of, on the other side, the case of the Islam under the Caliphate. There the subordination, although with peculiar autonomy, of the religious specialists, was rather due to a situation in which the boundaries of the military community were wider than the boundaries of the religious one. That is, several religions coexisted within the same political collectivity. This accounts for the exceptional – for the times – religious tolerance of those regimes.

In Christianity the ecclesiastical apparatus has always enjoyed some *libertas* and was never subordinated to the military and administrative apparatus. Nor, before Hildebrand, had the church ever tried to conquer hierocratic supremacy. Even with Gelasius – the highest doctrinal moment of ecclesiastical aspirations – the full *potestas* of the emperor was clearly recognized by the church and only the superiority of the pope in matters spiritual was forcefully asserted. There were, however, throughout history, variations in the relative power of the ecclesiastical apparatus. There were, one might say, "Gelasian" moments (close to hierocracy) and "Constantinian" (or "Carolingian" or "Ottonian") moments (close to Caesaropapism). A cursory overview seems to find the former taking place in periods of territorial fragmentation of the Christian world; the latter, in periods of unification. The validation of this hypothesis could contribute toward pacifying the diverging views about the nature of the relations between church and state in Catholic Christianity. (For a neat summary of these views, see B. Tierney, *The Crisis of Church and State 1050–1300* [Englewood Cliffs, N.J.: Prentice-Hall, 1964], pp. 3ff.)

27 These four types of bonds can be considered covering the main possibilities of

macrosocial organization. The way I have classified them can be pictured in the following fourfold table:

		Type of Membership	
		Predetermined	Optional
Type of hierarchical ordering	Predetermined	kinship	religious
	Optional (outcome of an internal process)	territorial	associational

28 J. Strayer, *On the Medieval Origins of the Modern State* (Princeton, N.J.: Princeton University Press, 1970), p. 22.

29 "The Pope's power over princes could only be effective by being over- effective." (Southern, *Western Society and the Church*, p. 125).

30 "The new techniques of government depended increasingly on expert knowledge, and this enhanced the practical importance of those who were equipped by intellectual training to provide this commodity. As it happened, the long process whereby the laity had relinquished all claim to participate in scholastic training above an elementary level was virtually complete by the end of the eleventh century – the very moment when the practical importance of advanced scholastic training first became apparent in medieval Europe. This gave the clergy a monopoly of all those disciplines which not only determined the theoretical structure of society but provided the instruments of government" (ibid., p. 38).

31 J. Strayer, *On the Medieval Origins*, pp. 24–25. Cf. also A. R. Myers, *Parliaments and Estates in Europe* (San Diego, Calif.: Harcourt Brace Jovanovich, 1975), p. 16.

32 Berman, *Law and Revolution*, p. 529.

33 Ibid., p. 83.

34 Strayer, *On the Medieval Origins*, p. 23.

35 Ibid., pp. 28–41.

36 E. Kantorowicz, *The King's Two Bodies: A Study in Medieval Political Theology* (Princeton, N.J.: Princeton University Press, 1957), p. 8.

37 Ibid., p. 232.

38 Quoted ibid., p. 251. This whole point is dealt with classically in Kantorowicz's chapter "Pro Patria Mori," ibid., pp. 232–272.

39 On the contrary, the mobilization for a national war even suspended the privileges and immunities of the territorial clergy. According to Nogaret (an exceptional view, however), "in defense of the fatherland it was a merit rather than a crime if a man killed his own father" (ibid., pp. 250–251). One can grasp here the change in the nature of the conception of the enemy, between this situation and that described in note 17, above.

40 Ibid., p. 191. An analogous point is made by Strayer, *On the Medieval Origins*, pp. 26ff. In this case, it is interesting to see a validation of the hypothesis that ideology is mainly needed in conditions of weakness. When the sacrality and hence the perpetuality of the fisc was compared to the sacrality of the body of Christ, the real

stability of the fiscal system was all but assured. At that time permanent taxes were very seldom imposed, so that the continuity of revenue was made possible only by the periodic summoning of parliaments. (Cf. F. W. Maitland, *The Constitutional History of England* [Cambridge: Cambridge University Press, 1963], pp. 179ff.). The perpetuity of the state, and of its main institutions, is first ideologically constructed (couched in the terms of a previous ideology) and then gradually realized.

41 This is the well-known central thesis of the Kings Two Bodies.

42 Maitland, *The Constitutional History*, p. 101. See also ibid., p. 195, and Myers, *Parliaments and Estates*, p. 19.

43 Berman, *Law and Revolution*, pp. 292–294.

44 Southern, *Western Society and the Church*, p. 111.

45 For a clear assessment of the state of knowledge on this connection, cf. Skinner (*The Foundation*, II, p. 60), who summarizes it in the following way: "Where it proved possible to arrange such Concordats, the Government involved – as in France and Spain – tended to remain faithful to the Catholic Church throughout the Reformation. But where the disputes over Annates, appointments and appeals remained unresolved – as in England, Germany and Scandinavia – the pressures on the Papacy continued to build up."

2

Challenging the boundaries of institutional politics: social movements since the 1960s

CLAUS OFFE

Political sociologists and political scientists who analyze Western European politics have made it a commonplace since the 1970s to emphasize the fusion of political and nonpolitical spheres of social life. They have seriously questioned the usefulness of the conventional dichotomy of "state" and "civil society." Processes of fusion are evident not only on the level of global sociopolitical arrangements, but also among citizens as elementary political actors. The delineation between "political" and "private" (in other words, moral or economic concerns and modes of action) is becoming blurred.

This diagnosis is based on at least three phenomena: (1) the rise of "participatory" moods and ideologies, which lead people to exercise the repertoire of existing democratic rights more extensively; (2) the increased use of noninstitutional or nonconventional forms of political participation, such as protest, demonstrations, and unofficial strikes; and (3) political demands and conflicts concerning issues that used to be considered moral (such as abortion) or economic (such as the humanization of work). Not only are the institutional channels of communication between the citizenry and the state used more often and more intensely by a greater number of citizens and for a wider range of issues; in addition, their adequacy as a framework for political communication is being challenged.

We thus see a rather dramatic model of political development in the advanced Western societies: As public policies exert a more direct and visible impact on citizens, citizens in turn try to win a more immediate and inclusive control over political elites by means fre-

Thanks for extensive comments and criticism are due to John Keane, Herbert Kitschelt, Peter Lange, Dieter Rucht, Bart von Steenberge, and Helmut Wiesenthal. Most of this study was written while the author was a Fellow at the Netherlands Institute for Advanced Study, Wassenaar, in 1982–83.

quently seen as incompatible with maintaining the institutional order of the polity. Since the mid-1970s, a number of mostly conservative analysts have described this as a dangerous cycle that must lead to erosion of political authority and even of the capacity to govern.[1] They would shield the economy from overly detailed and ambitious political intervention and would also insulate political elites from citizens. Their proposed solution, the neoconservative project, is thus a restrictive redefinition of what can and should be considered political, and a corresponding elimination from government agendas of all issues, practices, demands, and responsibilities defined as "outside" the proper sphere of politics.

Central to this project is the image of a breakdown or implosion of the autonomy and authority of nonpolitical institutional spheres and hence their increasing dependence on political support and regulation. In this sense, one can argue that the "autonomous" cultural and structural foundations of aesthetic production, science and technology, the family, religion, and the labor market have been so eroded that only the political provision of rules and resources can keep these subsystems alive. But, according to the neoconservative analysis, the extended reach of public policy into formerly more independent areas means both a gain and a loss of state authority: More variables and parameters of civil society can and must be manipulated, but there are fewer and fewer nonpolitical – and hence noncontroversial – foundations of action to which claims can be referred or from which metapolitical (natural or given) premises for politics can be derived. As the functions of the state expand, its authority (capacity to make binding decisions) is debased. Rather than growing stronger by greater comprehensiveness, political authority subverts its nonpolitical underpinnings, which appear increasingly as mere artifacts of the political process.

It is the undermining that the neoconservative project is trying to reverse in a sometimes desperate search for nonpolitical bases of order and stability. What is needed, according to the neoconservatives, is the restoration of uncontestable economic, moral, and cognitive standards. They hope to reprivatize conflicts and issues that public authority cannot deal with properly. As a consequence, the concept and practice of politics turn reflexive; politics comes to center on the question of what it is – and is not – about.

The new social movements obviously oppose the substantive content of this project. Nonetheless, they share an important analytical insight with the neoconservatives: The conflicts and contradictions of advanced industrial society can no longer be meaningfully resolved through etatism, political regulation, and the inclusion of ever more issues on the agendas of bureaucratic authorities. Only beyond this premise do neoconservative and movement politics diverge. The new social movements seek to politicize civil society in ways that are not constrained by representative-bureaucratic political institutions and thereby to reconstitute a civil society independent from increasing control and intervention. To emancipate itself from the state, the new movements claim, civil society itself – its institutions and its very standards of rationality and progress – must employ practices that belong to an intermediate sphere between private pursuits and concerns and institutional, state-sanctioned modes of politics.

The "new politics" of the new social movements can be analyzed, as can any politics, in terms of a *political paradigm*, which identifies its social base (or actors), issues, values, and modes of action.[2] In this context I will first describe the "old" paradigm, which was dominant throughout the post–World War II era. Next, I will discuss the "new" paradigm. Then I will explore how the rise of the new paradigm has been explained. In this section I will also consider why we are justified in speaking of new (rather than a revived form of old) political cleavages. Next I will offer some means of assessing the strength of the new social movements and their potential future impact. Finally, I will outline a new model of political cleavages and examine the alliances that might emerge from them. Most of the material on which this discussion is based is taken from West Germany, with occasional comparative references to other Western European countries.

The central problem of democratic politics in modern society is to maintain the diversity within civil society while creating some measure of unity, or bindingness, of political authority: *E pluribus unum*. This problem is more easily solved in political systems whose underlying diversity remains one of *interests*; it becomes more difficult when *values* or cultural models must also be mediated.[3] In the first case, the individual and collective political actors share an evaluative framework. They differ in their interests but agree on the values (for example, control over economic resources) in terms of which those interests are defined. A conflict over values creates a more complex situation. Society must resolve not only the distribution of rewards but the more fundamental question of whether the rewards allocated *count* as valuable. This second-order conflict over the *criteria* of goodness of public policy is the key to understanding current conflicts over the proper scope and boundaries of the political in some Western European polities.

The old paradigm

It is probably right to insist, following Max Weber, that no substantive definition of the realm of the political can be given, and that any *general* attempt to define "the political" must be satisfied with a formal concept (such as coercive, collective regulation or territorial sovereignty, or the authoritative allocation of values). Nevertheless it is possible to specify which substantive concerns are politicized at any given moment in a particular society. If everything can be the object of political transaction at some point, not everything can be political at the same time. In a given polity there is always a relatively stable evaluative framework according to which interests are recognized as such. There is, furthermore, a "hegemonic" configuration of issues that seem to deserve priority and in respect to which political success or progress is primarily measured, while others are marginal or "outside" of politics. Modernization theory, for instance, has tried to construct developmental sequences, according to which issues such as nation building, citizenship, participation, or redistribution move in and out of the center of politics in a certain temporal sequence.

In this sense, the core items on the agenda of Western European politics in the period from the immediate postwar years until the early seventies were issues of economic growth, distribution, and security. These central concerns of "old politics"[4] are reflected on the level of survey data on "what people believe are the most important issues facing society." After World War II and the resolution of colonial issues, questions of nation-state identity (the particular West German case aside) played only a small political role. Conflicts over the constitutional institutions were even more conspicuously absent. The social, economic, and political order adopted in the late 1940s and early 1950s was built on a highly encompassing liberal-democratic welfare state consensus that remained unchallenged through the late 1960s by any significant forces on the political Right or Left.

This is true at least of three central elements of the constitutional postwar accords, all of which were adopted and defended in terms of their conduciveness to economic growth and welfare. First, despite some marginal elements of indicative planning, codetermination, or nationalization, investment decisions were left as the prerogative of owners and managers acting in free markets and according to criteria of profitability. Second, the acceptance of capitalism as a machine for growth was complemented by organized labor's acceptance of it as a means for income distribution and social security. The prevalent concern with growth and real income led working-class spokesmen to renounce more extensive projects of societal change, in exchange for a firmly established status in the process of income distribution, while it made investors more willing to accept the new status of organized labor. The third element of the postwar design (adopted in the German case from the Weimar Republic) was a form of political democracy predominantly mediated through party competition. This arrangement was well suited to limit the conflicts transferred from the sphere of civil society into the arena of public policy, especially where, as in West Germany, there was a significant separation between the organizations representing *societal* interests (unions, employers, churches, etc.) and the *political* parties concerned with winning votes and office according to the model of the "catch-all-party."[5]

The implicit sociological assumption underlying the constitutional arrangements of the liberal welfare state was that "privatistic" family-, work- and consumption-centered patterns of life would absorb most citizens' energies and aspirations. Conflict over public policy would for that reason be of no more than marginal significance. This constitutional definition of the respective spaces of action of capital and labor, of the state and civil society, was a correlate of the centrality of the values of growth, prosperity, and distribution.

Since the 1950s, "security" has been the term most often used in electoral campaigns and slogans by both major parties in West Germany. It has three important aspects. First, it refers to the *welfare state*, that is, to the issues of providing an adequate income and standard of living for all citizens and protecting them in cases of illness, unemployment, old age, or general indigence. Second, it refers to diplomacy and *defense*. Third, security involves an aspect of *social control* as it concerns the issues of dealing with and preventing all sorts of "deviant" behavior (including illness as deviance of one's own body), especially as its consequences might affect the viability of the family, the legal, economic, and political order, and the individual's ability to participate in these institutions.

The two postwar decades in which the "old politics," that is, the paradigm of a comprehensive growth and security alliance, prevailed were, of course, not a period devoid of social and political conflict. But there was a remarkably broad and undisputed agreement about the "interests," issues, actors, and institutional modes of resolving conflict. Economic growth, advances in individual and collective distributional positions, and legal protection of social status were the central concerns. Collective bargaining, party competition, and representative party government were the virtually exclusive mechanisms for resolving social and political conflict. Specialized, comprehensive, and highly institutionalized interest organizations and political parties were the dominant actors. All of this was endorsed by a "civic culture" that emphasized the values of social mobility, private life, consumption, instrumental rationality, authority, and order, and which deemphasized political participation. Alternative modes of conflict resolution, or collective actors not easily accommodated within the framework, were marginalized by the end of the fifties, and the issues and proponents of socialism, neutralism, national unity, citizenship, and economic democracy were reduced to virtual insignificance. Not only the "end of ideology" thesis imported from American social science but even diagnoses amounting to an "end of political conflict"[6] were acclaimed widely as plausible sociological interpretations of sociopolitical reality. And the partly reactionary, partly progressive critique of the values of consumer society failed to make any impact on the solid cultural foundations of postwar, post-totalitarian welfare capitalism.

The new paradigm

Raschke has made one of the few attempts to formulate a substantive concept for the new paradigm; he speaks of an emerging *Paradigma der Lebensweise* (paradigm of way of life or mode of life).[7] Most of the social scientific literature on the subject either emphasizes rupture and discontinuity – by using terms like *new protest movements*, *new politics*, *new populism*, *neoromanticism*, *antipolitics*, *unorthodox political behavior*, and *disorderly politics* – or describes the new paradigm's means of conflict as "unconventional."[8] The most encompassing, although still less than inclusive, label used by activists themselves is *alternative movements*, a term as void of positive content as *countereconomy*, *counterinstitutions*, and *counterpublic (Gegenöffentlichkeit)*.

The vagueness of these negative conceptualizations – which is, incidentally, paralleled by recent macrosociological designations of contemporary Western society as *postindustrial society* – makes it difficult to determine which concerns and issues can be subsumed under this category. Even enumerations aiming at completeness are rare in the literature. Melucci has given one such list: "the student movement, feminism, sexual liberation, urban movements, ecology struggles, the mobilization of consumers and users of services, of ethnic and linguistic minorities, communitarian and countercultural movements, the struggles around health issues, and others."[9] But some movements are missing from this compilation – most obviously the peace movement.

The new social movements politicize themes that cannot easily be classified in the binary code of social action that underlies liberal political theory. They locate themselves in a third, intermediate cat-

Table 2.1. *Forms of noninstitutional action*

		Ends	
		Not binding for wider community if accomplished	Binding
Means	Not recognized by political community as legitimate	private criminals 1	terrorists 2
	Recognized as legitimate	sociocultural movements 3	sociopolitical movements 4

egory, and claim a type of issue that is neither private (in the sense of being of no legitimate concern to others) nor public (in the sense of being recognized as the legitimate object of official political institutions and actors). But these issues consist of collectively relevant results and side effects of the actions of either private or institutional-political actors for which the actors cannot be held responsible or made responsive by available legal or institutional means. The new movements' space of action is *noninstitutional politics*, which is not provided for in liberal democracy and the welfare state.

This raises a conceptual problem: What do we mean by *noninstitutional politics*? Precision about this definition appears particularly relevant because the term *new social movements* is often used in a way that includes, for instance, religious or economic concerns. A minimum requirement for employing the word *political* for a mode of action is that the actor make some explicit claim that the *means* of action can be recognized as legitimate and the *ends* of action can become binding for the wider community. Only social movements that share both these characteristics have a political quality and will therefore interest me here. Two interesting limiting cases, represented by new religious sects and by terrorism, are thus not included. The distinctions are illustrated in Table 2.1. Purely *social* or religious movements make use of perfectly legitimate means of action, such as the legally guaranteed freedom of religious practice. They do not intend to enforce their specific values and ends on everyone, but simply claim to be allowed to enjoy their rights and freedoms, and in the case of a diametrical opposition between their values and those of the wider community, they retreat to private spaces, such as many rural communes. There is no attempt to use these rights for collectively binding purposes.

Terrorist groups, in contrast, cannot expect their violent means to be recognized as legitimate and rightful by the wider community. On the other hand, their objectives are quite conventionally (if absurdly and unrealistically) political. They consist – to take the aims of, say, the West German Rote Armee Fraktion (RAF) or the Italian Brigate Rosse (BR) – of an anti-imperialist revolutionary war, the outcomes of which would clearly be binding upon the entire community in quite an elementary way.

In contrast to either the sects or the terrorists, politically relevant new social movements do make a claim to *be* recognized as political actors by the wider community. Their means are defended as legitimate even when their forms of action do not enjoy the legitimacy conferred by established political institutions. And they aim at objectives that would bind society as a whole, rather than just the group itself.

Diverse as these concerns appear, they have a common root in certain values that, as I will argue later, are not in themselves new but are given a different emphasis and urgency. Most prominent among these values are autonomy and identity (with their organizational correlates, such as decentralization, self-government, and self-help), and opposition to manipulation, control, dependence, bureaucratization, regulation, and so on. Frequently used (although problematic) ways to describe the difference between the old and new values include classifying them by dimensions such as concerns with scarcity versus concerns with alienation, zero-sum games versus non-zero-sum games, quantitative versus qualitative demands, the pursuit of interest versus the pursuit of identity, having versus being, material equality versus freedom, and the like.

Modes of action typically involve two aspects: the way individuals act together to constitute a collectivity (*internal mode of action*), and the way they confront the outside world and their political opponents (*external mode of action*). The internal mode is already referred to by the term *social movements*; the process by which multitudes of individuals become collective actors is highly informal, ad hoc, discontinuous, context sensitive, and egalitarian. In other words, while they have at best rudimentary membership roles, programs, platforms, representatives, officials, staffs, and membership dues, the new social movements consist of participants, campaigns, spokespersons, networks, voluntary helpers, and donations. Typically, in contrast to traditional forms of political organizations, they do not employ the organizational principle of differentiation in either the horizontal (insider versus outsider) or the vertical (leader versus rank-and-file members) dimension. On the contrary, they seem to have a strong reliance on synthesis – the fusion of public and private roles, instrumental and expressive behavior, and community organization – and, in particular, a poor and at best transient demarcation between "members" and formal "leaders."

Concerning the external mode of action, demonstrations and other protest tactics use the physical presence of large numbers of people. These tactics intend to mobilize public attention by mostly legal, although unconventional, means. They are paralleled by demands whose positive aspects are articulated mostly in negative logical and grammatical forms, such as *never*, *freeze*, and *ban*. Such tactics and demands indicate that the actually or potentially mobilized group conceives of itself as an ad hoc and often single-issue veto alliance (rather than an organizationally or even ideologically integrated entity). This conception leaves room for a wide variety of legitimations and beliefs.

The external mode of action also emphasizes the principled and nonnegotiable nature of concerns, which can be seen both as a virtue and a necessity imposed by relatively primitive organizational structures. Social movements relate to other political actors and opponents in terms of sharp antinomies, such as them/us, the desirable and the intolerable, victory or defeat, now or never. This logic of thresholds obviously leaves little room for political exchange or gradualist tactics.

The new social movements' insistence on the nonnegotiability of their concerns frequently provokes a vehement reaction from political forces operating in the old paradigm. Critics often see their action flowing from irrational, politically incompetent, and irresponsible dispositions and consider their tactics counterproductive – even if some of their concerns are recognized as legitimate.

These accusations are partly accurate. The new social movements cannot negotiate because they do not have anything to offer in exchange for concessions. They cannot promise, for instance, less energy consumption in return for the discontinuation of nuclear energy projects the way trade unions can promise (or at least practice) wage restraint in return for employment guarantees. This is because the movements lack some of the properties of formal organizations, most important, the internal bindingness of representative decisions, which can assure to some extent the terms of a political deal will be honored. They also typically lack a coherent set of ideological principles from which to derive an image of a desirable society and to deduce the steps toward achieving it. Only if such a theory were available to the movements could they exchange long-term gains for short-term losses and undertake tactical rationality and alliance formation. Movements are also unwilling to negotiate because they often consider their concern to be of such high and universal priority that no part of it can be meaningfully sacrificed without negating the concern itself.

But these structural limitations do not necessarily justify charges of blindness, parochialism, and *Gesinnungsethik* because, from the point of view of the new social movements, institutional modes of political rationality and collective decision making involve selectivities and nondecisions that tend to filter out the central concerns of the new paradigm.

Finally, the most striking characteristic of the actors in the new social movements is that they do not rely for self-identification on either established political codes (Left or Right, liberal or conservative, and so on) or on the partially corresponding socioeconomic codes (such as working class or middle class, poor or wealthy, rural or urban). Instead, they classify the universe of political conflict in categories taken from their issues, such as gender, age, and locality, or even, in the case of environmental and pacifist movements, the human race as a whole.

To summarize, the new paradigm forsakes the dichotomous concepts of social action that were central to the old paradigm. The opposition of the public-political to the private has been superseded by three spheres: the private, the noninstitutional political, and the institutionalized political. So too the contrast of state and civil society is superseded as the new movements claim the space of "political action within civil society" as the terrain from which to challenge both private and institutional-political practices. (Table 2.2 provides a scheme of these contrasts.) The new paradigm thus demands that the categories legitimating the old politics themselves be recast.

The phenomenology of the new paradigm

Although the new paradigm insists that the old political and socioeconomic categories are irrelevant, this by no means implies that the social base of the new movements is in fact so amorphous and heterogenous. As I will argue below, it consists of three rather sharply circumscribed segments of the social structure: the new middle class, especially those who work in the human service professions and/or the public sector; elements of the old middle class; and those people outside the labor market or only peripherally involved, such as the unemployed, students, housewives, and the retired.

While it is hardly self-evident what change in social variables might

Table 2.2. *Main characteristics of the old and new paradigms*

	Old paradigm	New paradigm
Issues	economic growth and distribution; military and social security; social control	preservation of the environment, human rights, peace, and unalienated forms of work
Values	freedom and security of private consumption and material progress	personal autonomy and identity, as opposed to centralized control
Modes of action	internal: formal organization, large-scale representative associations	internal: informality, spontaneity, low degree of horizontal and vertical differentiation
	external: pluralist or corporatist interest intermediation, political party competition, majority rule	external: protest politics based on demands formulated in predominantly negative terms
Actors	socioeconomic groups acting as groups (in the group's interest) and involved in distributive conflict	socioeconomic groups acting not as such, but on behalf of ascriptive collectivities

lead from the old to the new paradigm, it does seem to make intuitive sense to search for stages of societal differentiation. Thus the old paradigm would correspond to a social structure of relatively durable and distinctive collectivities, such as classes, that is, groupings of status, professional relationships, and economic interest, or cultural communities and families. The new paradigm would correspond to greater individuation, namely, to a type of social structure in which the collectivities of the old paradigm have become both less distinctive and less durable as points of reference.

In the course of their lives citizens of advanced Western societies typically "migrate" through a sequence of professions, occupations, and jobs that includes phases of training and unemployment; belong to more than the "normal" two families and experience increasingly frequent periods in which they belong to no family at all; and partake (or at least have the option of participating in) a variety of cultural communities, aesthetic contexts, and styles of life and consumption all of which are transforming more rapidly than generational change and are increasingly stratified by age-group (as the youth cultures). This seems to suggest that, while functional and institutional collectivities do certainly continue to exist, they do so in ways that are less easily perceived by highly mobile populations and that consequently undermine the subjective bindingness of temporary "belonging."

Of the many likely consequences of this kind of structural change, only one is of interest here: the resulting mode of self-categorization that emerges under a virtually permanent "crisis of adolescence" (in other words, a continuous looseness of the ties that connect individuals with structural or cultural collectivities). The subjectively most durable and distinctive parameters of social identity are defined by age and sex; perhaps determined by language and regional or ethnic origin and present place of residence; and, of course, characterized by one's existence as a human being with its attendant anxieties and vulnerabilities. This suggests that the greater one's experience of contingency and mobility (often involuntary and unpredictable), the greater one's propensity to choose "permanent" parameters of social identity around which to form.

Comparison with traditional politico-ideological formations

Although there are probably no strict analogues to the new social movements' configuration of issues, values, modes of action, and actors in the political history of industrial capitalist societies, a number of parallels with past political ideas and ideologies are striking. They have often been referred to as keys to interpreting the politics of new social movements. Thus, use of the term *neopopulism* in connection with these movements suggests an affinity with *populist* movements.[10] The parallel, however, ends when we come to issues, which for traditional populism are mainly ensuring the economic status and viability of small producers through state intervention and protective regulation.

There is also a clear, although again limited, affinity between the paradigm of the new politics and *liberal* and libertarian political traditions. The obvious parallel is the emphasis on limiting state power through strengthening civil rights and liberties. The major difference is that the new social movements' demand for autonomy focuses not on economic liberties but on the protection and preservation of values, identities, and modes of life in the face of the political and bureaucratic imposition of some kind of "rational" order.

Partial analogies as well as crucial differences also exist with respect to *conservative* parties and ideologies. A dilemma of conservatism is that to resist effectively the weakening of conservative values (such as property, authority, the family, and traditional culture), it must support the modernization of economic and political structures: Continuity presupposes change. This uneasy equation, not necessarily the conservative impulse itself, is exploded by the new social movements. Although these movements often strongly emphasize the preservation of traditional communities, identities, and social as well as physical environments, preservation is often seen to be incompatible with technical, political, economic, and military modernization. Any designation of the new social movements as "conservative" is meaningful only if the concept is given important qualifications.[11] It is true that one of their basic impulses is to protect and maintain "valuable" conditions. But the new social movements consider ongoing economic, political, military, and technological modernization a means not of preserving, but of destroying such conditions.

Finally, convergences as well as divergences with respect to the *socialist* tradition of political ideas must be noted. The obvious parallel is a shared insight into the destructive, anarchic, irrational, and dehumanizing impact of capitalist industrialization on all aspects of human life. The divergence starts with the new movements' radicalized and no longer dialectical critique of the forces of production and its further development, and their consequent turn into "antiproductivist" views of technology and industry. It continues with the denial of any privileged role in the process of social transformation for the industrial working class, which sometimes is suspected of being the class on which the system has its firmest economic, political, and ideological grip. Finally, the new social movements regard etatist forms – in both Eastern and Western Europe – in a highly negative way.

The new paradigm poses a challenge to a notion common to all the political ideologies listed above: namely, that politics evolves toward the fuller realization of some value – be it recognition of rights and liberties, growth of wealth, equality, or the approximation of social life to some moral order – and that this realization is brought about by specifically political roles and institutions. The new social movements differ with this notion on two counts. First, their concerns do not fit the assumption of "progress" toward some idealized social order. To be more precise, what they see as progress is not the continuation of hitherto known trajectories of modernization but rather the introduction of social arrangements less dependent on such technical-bureaucratic modernization.

The new social movements seek values and identities which they consider utterly threatened by the social and political forces that offer a deceptive version of progress. They formulate causes in terms of recognition of existing identities rather than gain, maintenance of what is (or full restoration of what is not yet entirely lost, such as ecological balance, and cultural symbols providing identities) rather than what is desirable in terms of past experience. This antiprogressivist, defensive notion of causes and concerns is well expressed in the antithesis of progress and survival, and it is because of such logic that terms like *Prinzip Leben*, *Lebenswelt*, and *Lebensweise* have been central to both political self-interpretations and philosophical and sociological analysis of the new paradigm.[12]

Abandoning the idea of progress and perfection in favor of tenaciously defending present values and identities is a model of politics that can and does exist without a theoretically construed "project." Hence the often-commented-on piecemeal, ad hoc, pluralist, and selective nature of the views and demands of the new social movements, as well as their conspicuous rejection of totalizing ideologies. Furthermore, it follows from this challenge to the views underlying the old paradigm that the criteria of progress are not likely to be changed within the institutional forms and procedures geared to promoting conventional progress. The political sphere must be "reappropriated" from the institutions that have come to monopolize it and given back to the societal forces and their institutionally unconstrained action. Thus, the new social movements' rejection of the notion of progress as well as of totalizing ideologies is complemented by a challenge to the institutional forms in which progress has occurred.

Assessing the new paradigm: political results and sociostructural potential

We must now assess the strength of the social and political forces behind the new paradigm. Any attempt to answer questions of absolute or relative strength, or to make intertemporal and cross-sectional comparisons, has to overcome substantial methodological difficulties. For, in contrast to the political actors of the old paradigm, those of the new paradigm do not have institutionalized modes of gauging success, performance, and growth; consequently, any measure adopted by the observer may be grossly misrepresentative. A system of social bookkeeping exists for dominant values – national and individual income statistics, election results, military and social security – but it is always difficult to measure institutionally unrecognized values, both absolutely and in relation to other social systems or to the system's own past.

The absence of official procedures for monitoring extrainstitutional political forces renders contestable any statement about their status and development. Consider, for example, violent confrontations between demonstrators and the police: Because of an uncertain mixture of "technical" and "social" reasons, the number of policemen wounded in such conflicts seems always to be recorded much more easily, quickly, reliably, and visibly than the number of demonstrators wounded. The institutions of cognitive culture, beginning with government statistical offices and not excluding the empirical social sciences, often discriminate against oppositional values by failing to measure them in standardized and easily accessible ways.

One needs a good political theory from which to derive valid measurement instruments, leading in turn to data on which a good political theory can be built. In spite of this circularity, there can be little doubt that the issues, values, forms of action, and actors that make up the new paradigm have expanded both its social base and political impact, whether strength is measured on the individual or collective level, in terms of noninstitutional or institutional forms of action, or in terms of political inputs or outputs.

Whatever their theoretical perspectives and value judgments, social scientists find themselves in a broad (and rare) agreement that, from the late 1960s on, "the idea of unconventional political participation as a legitimate resource of democratic citizenship has spread out into the wider political community" in Western European countries; that there exists today a "widely spread constituency for radical political action"; and that these politics are "full of young, well-educated men and women who do not accept that their political efficacy is bounded by officially sanctioned channels of representative democracy."[13] Not only has this potential for action grown as a fact, but it has been widely recognized as legitimate (or morally defendable) in spite of the absence of institutions that could accommodate it.

We could obtain an even more reliable assessment of the strength and potential of the new paradigm's social base by combining findings about its sociostructural locations with theories about likely further transformations in the social structure. Much of what is known about the new social movements' sociostructural composition suggests that they are rooted in major segments of the new middle class. One primary characteristic of these segments is that they are, according to Giddens, "class-aware" but not "class-conscious."[14] That is to say, there appear to be relatively clear structural determinants of agents, those likely to participate in the new politics, but the *demands* (and thus the beneficiaries) are not at all class-specific; they are highly dispersed and either universalistic or heavily concentrated in particular groups (defined, for instance, by locality, age, or interaction with certain state practices, laws, or institutions). New-middle-class politics is, in contrast to most working-class politics as well as old-middle-class politics, typically a politics *of* a class, but not *on behalf of* a class.

Structural characteristics of the new-middle-class core of the new social movements include high educational status, relative economic security (and, in particular, experience of such security in the formative years),[15] and employment in personal service occupations. The preponderance of people sharing these attributes has been well documented for both the various "issue movements,"[16] and the "green" coalitions of these movements. But most new social movements also include elements from other groups and strata with whom they tend to form a more or less stable alliance. Most important among these are peripheral or decommodified groups and elements from the old middle class.

By *decommodified* or *peripheral groups* I mean social categories whose members' social situation is not presently defined directly by the labor market and whose time, consequently, is more flexible; examples include middle-class housewives, high school and university students, retired people, and unemployed or marginally employed youths. One common characteristic of these groups is that their conditions and life chances are shaped by direct, highly visible, and often extremely authoritarian and restrictive mechanisms of supervision, exclusion, and social control, as well as by the absence of even nominal "exit" options. They are in this sense trapped and this has often led them to revolt against the bureaucratic or patriarchal regime. Peripheral groups, like many middle-class professionals, can afford to spend considerable amounts of time on political activities. These two segments also sometimes share institutional environments, as in the cases of teachers and their students, social workers and their clients, and so on.[17]

Finally, the immediate economic interests of the old middle class – independent and self-employed people such as farmers, shop owners, and artisan-producers – often coincide with or at least do not diverge from the concerns voiced by the new social movements.[18] On the other side, the principal classes of capitalist societies, namely the industrial working class and the holders and agents of economic and administrative power, are least easily penetrated by the new paradigm.

In several senses, it can therefore be said that the new social movements' pattern of social and political conflict is the polar opposite of the class-conflict model. First, the conflict is staged not by one class but by a social alliance that consists, in varying proportions, of elements from different classes and "nonclasses." Second, it is not a conflict between the principal economic agents of the mode of production, but an alliance that includes virtually every element *except* these agents. Third, the demands are not class-specific, but rather strongly universalistic or highly particularistic, and thus either more or less "categorical" than class issues.

This configuration of class forces and class politics can be interpreted as the outcome of a long process of divergence between what Parkin has called "working class conservatism" and "middle class radicalism."[19] This is the reverse side of the development of the welfare state, in which the working class as a whole is granted institutionalized political and economic representation and some legal claim to security. But the price of this success (restricted and fragile as it remains) has generally been the limitation of working-class movements' political goals and the specialization of their organizational forms. More concretely, struggles won on behalf of people as workers, employees, and recipients of social security transfers were accompanied by a cumulative deemphasis of their interests as citizens, consumers, clients of state-provided services, and human beings in general.

According to some logic of political compromise and interclass accord, the broadening of the welfare state *inclusion* involves the *exclusion* of important dimensions of class conflict and a corresponding narrowing of the state's agenda. However, the issue areas from which working-class organizations have largely withdrawn, and which they often had to abandon in their struggles for institutional recognition and improved social and economic conditions of their core constituency, tend now to be occupied by middle-class radicals. The middle-class radicals, again partially because of the accomplishments of the fully developed welfare state, are sufficiently numerous and economically secure to afford to reemphasize some "forgotten" working-class issues and revitalize some of the noninstitutional forms of politics used earlier by the working-class movement itself.

Virtually all projections and speculations about the future social structure of Western European democratic welfare states seem to suggest that at least two components of the new paradigm's social base – the new middle class and the peripheral segments – are much more likely to increase than to disappear. Although some interesting doubts have been raised concerning the further growth of personal and social services and the number of new-middle-class people providing them,[20] there is little prospect that the major social functions of new-middle-class occupations (such as teaching and the distribution of information; provision of health service; social control; and administration) can be replaced. Replacement is unlikely because of the complexities of these services and the demand for them. This demand, in turn, is determined largely by the labor market's shrinking ability to organize and absorb the entire volume of labor power. Especially under conditions of economic crisis, more and more people are transformed from workers into clients for longer and longer periods of time. Thus, the relative growth of the decommodified segment guarantees the social existence of large parts of the new middle class and may even pave the way for new forms of political alliance between these elements.

It is perhaps less obvious that the old middle class can be expected to be stable. This element, however, enjoys the interest and support of diverse forces such as conservative economic policymakers (who are aware that it is the only likely source of additional employment) and alternative or "dualist" models of economic reorganization bidding farewell to the proletariat[21] and observing favorably the rise of new forms of self-employment.

In sum, there can be little doubt that at least two elements of the social base typically supporting the new paradigm are rising in terms of numbers and strategic resources. This constitutes an important difference between new and old social movements, because old social movements regularly consisted of forces unlikely to survive the impact of the economic and cultural modernization they desperately resisted. It also parallels the early period of the working-class movement, which was inspired by its well-founded prophecy that its numbers and strengths were increased by the very system against which it struggled.

Of course, numbers do not tell the whole story. If there is reason to expect that the issues around which people are mobilized will be resolved easily or that they can be kept off the political agenda, then lasting political conflicts and alliances are unlikely to emerge from them. However, the opposite would be the case if the non-class issues politicized by the new social movements could be considered the intrinsic and continuously reproduced outcomes of established modes of rationality of production and domination in the institutional, economic, and international environment of Western European capitalist democracies. We must therefore now examine the issues and concerns of the new social movements – and their likely future relevance to the agendas of the advanced Western societies.

Structural issues or psychic discomfort? The agenda and the critics

The theories of "unconventional," "mass," or "deviant" political behavior widely accepted in the 1950s and early 1960s maintained that mobilization for noninstitutional political action was the consequence of the loss of economic status, access to political power, integration into intermediary forms of social organization, and recognition of traditional cultural values inflicted on certain parts of the population by modernization.[22] If modernization of societies means, above all, the disarticulation of spheres of action (such as the private and the public), then antimodernist movements insist on preserving a traditional "wholeness" of life.[23] Social "uprootedness" of the alienated and the marginal was the key explanation in these theories. Collective behavior, according to Smelser, is an irrational, exceptional, hysterical, wishfully thinking, or otherwise cognitively inadequate response to structural strains emerging from modernization. This response was said to be based on negative and/or positive myths or highly simplistic interpretations of tension.

The implicit message of this sort of theorizing – which often appears to have been politically preoccupied with preventing a rise of fascist and authoritarian mass movements – is evident and often highly self-assured: First, the backward, marginal, and alienated elements of society form the basis of noninstitutional politics. Second, expressive resistance against modernization is irrational, and thus, if the modernizing elites are not overwhelmed by it and institutions are defended by repressive means of social control and other mechanisms, the resistance is bound to fail. Third, resistance is a transitory phenomenon, because modernization will eventually provide the benefits of progress to all.

Little if any of this sort of theorizing finds support in analyses of the new social movements. The new middle class constituting the most important part of these movements can hardly be said to be uprooted; it is connected rather closely with, and experienced in the use of, established political and economic institutions. Participants in protest movements such as the British Campaign for Nuclear Disarmament in the late 1960s "appear well integrated into a broad range of social activities and institutions."[24] In addition, "higher levels of protest potential are not associated with an estrangement from orthodox politics, but are part of a parallel, dualist attitude toward the use of political action."[25] The strata that most support protest politics are generally economically secure, and some of them, such as middle-class undergraduates, are often among the most advantaged members of the community."[26]

Neither do these segments advocate, as the "romanticist" interpretation would have it, premodern, prescientific, undifferentiated patterns of social organization; they espouse arrangements that would allow specifically modern values (such as individual freedom and humanistic and universalistic principles) to be realized more fully than it seems they could be in centralized, bureaucratized, and technology-intensive forms of organization. The models for these arrangements are as a rule pragmatically designed and proposed, and they often make selective use of the accomplishments of technical, economic, and political modernization. For instance, the call for decentralization is derived not from an irrational longing for premodern small communities, but from an understanding of both the destructive side effects of centralization and the potential for decentralization made available by, among other things, information and communication technologies.

Nor could these movements be described plausibly as "irrational," because their social base participates to an above-average extent in the cognitive culture of society. As a consequence, we often find complex, pragmatically limited, and nonideological accounts of social reality and its dilemmas as well as a relatively high level of tolerance for ambiguity and divergence of ideological principles. The new movements can perhaps best be described, in the words of Galtung, as "a federation of issue-movements that work out the level of integration they find justifiable, supporting each other in many things, perhaps not in all."[27] Within this framework cognitive skills and intellectual tools (such as technology assessment, social and economic forecasting, ecological and strategic application of systems analysis, and the elaborate use of legal tactics) are often employed to defend the demands made by the new social movements, and the core activists and informal leaders of, for instance, German citizens' initiatives are often teachers, lawyers, journalists, and other professionals.

It seems already clear that the new movements are different from those analyzed by the older theories. But can this also be said of their issues?

Social issues
One well-known difficulty in any analysis of political issues derives from the dual reference made whenever this concept is employed. A question is said to be an issue if significant numbers of actors feel – according to their particular values, needs, wants, or interests – that the question must be resolved in ways that conflict with the interests of other actors, and events or developments cause needs to be considered salient enough to transform a hitherto unrecognized "problem." Thus, "issue-ness" is the joint effect of values and facts, interests and events. Accordingly, the rise of new issues can be explained by emphasizing either subjective or objective factors.

In predominantly subjective or, more precisely, psychologizing and reductionist explanations, the major weight is given to a change in actors' values, motivations, subjective dispositions, and resources of action, even though changes in these variables may themselves be related to prior objective factors such as political and general socialization, or developments within the welfare state. On the other side, predominantly objective explanations rely primarily on independent

Table 2.3. *Approaches to analysis of the new social movements*

Dimension	Psychologizing approach	Structural approach
constitution of object of analysis ("issue-ness")	emphasis on push of new values and preferences ("rising demands")	emphasis on perception of and knowledge about events and developmental tendencies: *pull* of interpreted facts ("need defense")
major independent variables	formation of motives	formation of cognitions and cognitive competence
research methods	survey research	historical and institutional macroanalysis
location of observer	neutral outside observer; emphasis on attitudes	participant-observer, exploring interaction between events and understanding
likely prediction	spasmodic action	institutional results and changes

variables such as events, conditions changing, structural problems, and so on, although more subjective intervening or mediating mechanisms (for instance, the actors' cognitive capacity to perceive events) may be inserted in the model. Ultimately, each approach is tied to an opposing school of thought in social theory, namely, "actor-centered" psychologizing individualists and "structuralist" or "functionalist" thinkers (see Table 2.3).

Of course, this dichotomy should not suggest naively that, within the structural approach, there is a direct link between events and the behavior of collectivities and individuals. But, contrary to the subjective approach, the structural perspective does imply that actors do not act solely on the basis of the *inner reality* of their feelings, preferences, needs, and wants; they also respond to pressure from *outer reality*, as represented by their implicit patterns of perception and interpretation. According to the structuralist model, although inner reality may be *caused* by objective circumstances, such circumstances are mediated through a conscious *cognitive* process rather than being a passive reflection of external conditions of the new social movements and unconventional modes of political participation.

Existing research and interpretation are overwhelmingly inspired by the psychologizing approach. That is to say, there has been more interest in the *push* of new values, demands, and actors that provides an agenda than in the pull of objective events, developments, or systemic imperatives. For the most part, researchers have assumed that new issues or forms of action reflect rising demands of actors, as opposed to a rising urgency to defend *existing* needs whose conditions of fulfillment have deteriorated. Similarly, explanatory variables have more often been motivational than cognitive. The methods employed have much more often been particularly suited for the study of individual actors (such as survey research) than for the study of systemic variables (such as historical methods or institutional macroanalysis).

Further, the psychologizing approach is more often favored by outside observers of movements; such movements' self-theorizations tend to refer to objective conditions as the major generators of issueness; and thus to action as the rational response to the perceived nature of the problems. Similarly, the psychologizing approach would rather conceive of the long-term perspective of movements in terms of oscillating waves or transient "moods," while a more structural approach is inclined to think in terms of basic discontinuities and changes of axial principles. Perhaps one could even say that the psychologizing approach is committed intellectually to forming theories *about* social movements, while the structural approach is interested in building theories *of* or *for* the social movements.

The well-known research of Inglehart clearly belongs to the psychologizing approach because it suggests the spread of value changes as the major variable in the rise of the new politics.[28] This explanation, which also integrated structural variables such as economic prosperity, as well as ahistorical psychic mechanisms, consists of two conditions. First, the new middle class can *afford* to be critical of the old values because they already enjoy, to a large extent, prosperity and security. Second, they *tend* to be critical because, according to Maslow's hierarchy of needs, prosperous people will seek self-actualization, for which both the goals and forms of action of the new politics provide ample opportunities.

There are, however, at least two difficulties with this explanation. First, it is highly unspecific; the supposedly predominant need for self-actualization could equally well lead to new and unconventional, but entirely *private*, life-styles and consumption patterns rather than to new *politics*. Second, this explanation remains contingent on the age cohort that experiences prosperity and security; it is unable to account for either the spread of the politics into strata that have not participated in these conditions, or the stability of such movements even after the generation that initiated them ceases to be active.

An explanation that depends exclusively or predominantly on conditions of socialization and the norms and values of a particular stratum is therefore inadequate *if* the phenomenon turns out to be a new political paradigm that could be generalized in time and through the social structure.[29] In other words, if we are interested in new social movements as the potential protagonists of a new paradigm, Inglehart's explanation clearly cannot account for their hypothetical significance; it needs to be amended by a less psychologizing interpretation.

Such an alternative approach traces the origin of issues to circumstances, changes, and events that take place "outside of actors," or as the unintended by-products of their actions and the workings of institutions. This more structural argument (which is clearly favored by authors who look on the new movements more in terms of their potential for structural change than in terms of their political deviance and potential for disturbing institutional process) refers to three interrelated aspects of postindustrial societies.[30]

First, the negative side effects of established modes of economic and political rationality are no longer concentrated and class-specific; they are dispersed in time, space, and kind so as to affect virtually every member of society in a variety of ways (*broadening*). Second, there is a qualitative change in the methods of domination, making their efforts more comprehensive and inescapable, and disrupting even those spheres of life that so far have remained outside the realm of rational and explicit social control (*deepening*). Third, both political and economic institutions have lost any self-corrective or self-limiting capacity; they are caught within a vicious circle that can be broken only from outside the official political institutions (*irreversibility*).

These are sweeping propositions concerning contemporary Western European societies, and they require some elaboration.

In terms of *broadening*, Habermas has argued most consistently and cogently that in late capitalist societies the work role is neither the exclusive nor the basic focus of deprivation, which equally affects the roles of citizen, client of administrative decisions, and consumer.[31]

Foucault had presented an even more radical portrayal of power and powerlessness that can no longer be attributed to any central causal mechanism, least of all industrial production.[32] This type of argument obtains great plausibility if we consider two characteristics of modern political economies and the technological systems, both military and civilian, on which they depend: their enormous capacity for conflict displacement, and the increasing scope of the impact of failures (in other words, their growing proneness to catastrophe).

The first characteristic concerns the extent to which concrete conflicts can be solved by imposing the costs of their solutions on external actors or shifting them to new dimensions of privilege and deprivation. In this sense, the resolution of a wage conflict may result in regional imbalances, new health hazards at work, inflation, or cuts in social programs for certain groups. Interconnectedness and interchangeability also extend the scope of the effects of failures or errors. Any number of illustrations come to mind, from large-scale technological systems (industrialized agriculture, atomic energy, urban transportation, military defense, and so on) or from large-scale economic and administrative organizations (world markets, national social security systems, and so on). Both kinds of society-wide spillover lead to a "classlessness" or an increasingly "social" character of deprivation, a fact that would render plainly inadequate any traditional Marxist view of core conflicts and contradictions.

The *deepening* of deprivation affects fundamental levels of physical, personal, and social existence. This aspect of modern forms of control is often referred to by metaphors such as the "invasion" or "colonization of the life-world."[33] That is to say, economic and political regulation is no longer limited to external constraints on individual behavior.

This pervasive social control is often described as a functional requirement of a new stage of production: "The mechanisms of accumulation are no longer fed by the simple exploitation of the labor force, but rather by the manipulation of complex organizational systems, by control over information and over processes and institutions of symbol-formation, and by intervention in interpersonal relations. Production . . . is becoming the production of social relations and social systems . . . it is even becoming the production of the individual's biological and interpersonal identity."[34] Such vague and global propositions might be clarified by exploring the idea that large-scale social and technological systems tend to become, as they grow, exponentially more sensitive and vulnerable to, and hence intolerant of, unpredictable, irregular, or "deviant" modes of behavior among their component actors. Therefore, they come to rely on ever greater modes and more detailed preventive and coordinated measures of surveillance and control.[35]

The third point, *irreversibility*, refers to the structural incapacity of existing economic and political institutions to perceive and deal effectively with the global risks and deprivations they cause. The rather paradoxical image one receives from current theories of both economic failure and "state failure"[36] is that these institutions are all-powerful in controlling, exploiting, and dominating their social and physical environments, and at the same time largely helpless to address the self-paralyzing consequences of their use of such power. This blocked learning capacity (the inability to undertake self-transformation or even self-limitation) has led to protest directed "not against the failure of the state and society to provide for economic growth and material prosperity, but against their all-too-considerable success in having done so, and against the price of this success."[37]

To be sure, some of these more structural and objectivist accounts of the political, economic, and technical dynamics of advanced industrial, and not always exclusively capitalist, societies may be influenced strongly and even distorted by a partisan perspective on the new social movements and their emancipatory potential. From the point of view of sociology of knowledge, one would hardly be surprised to find a circular relationship between social actors and the prevailing interpretation of the social reality within and upon which they act. This would constitute a serious problem, however, only if such theories could be shown to be nothing but ideological projections of those with whose practical concerns they coincide. This is clearly not true of the critique I have just summarized; there is broad agreement among structural analysts of Western industrial societies on the three trends just enumerated.[38]

The validity of the sociological interpretations

These proposed trends might be looked upon as tendentious views made up to legitimate deviant political subcultures. On the other hand, their demonstrable validity would provide a sociological interpretation of the rise of the new social movements, whose mode of political action would then appear as a rational response to a specific problem environment. This interpretation would be more compelling, the more the following conditions were demonstrated:

1. These propositions are shared by a wider community of informed and competent contemporaries who do not themselves become involved in movement politics.
2. The values advocated and defended by the new social movements are not "new," but part of the repertory of dominant modern culture. This condition obviously would make it difficult to think of the movements as flowing from either premodern or postmodern subcultures.
3. The constituency of these movements as well as their pool of activists are drawn from the social groups who have easiest cognitive access to the workings of institutional processes or those most likely to be affected by their negative consequences.
4. The issues central to the new social movements are those, and only those, whose predominance and urgency are caused by the objective trends just outlined.
5. The new social movements' extrainstitutional forms of action are explicitly used and justified by reference to learning incapacities and a structural lack of responsiveness of established institutions, rather than in the name of some revolutionary political doctrine.

To start with the question of "new" values, it could very well be claimed that what is *least* new in today's social movements is their values. There is certainly nothing new in moral demands such as the dignity and autonomy of the individual, integrity of the physical conditions of life, equality and participation, and peaceful and solidaristic forms of social organization. All these values are firmly rooted in political philosophies (as well as aesthetic theories) of the last two centuries, and they are inherited from the progressive movements of both the bourgeoisie and the working class. This continuity suggests that the new social movements are, in their basic normative orientations, neither *postmodern*, emphasizing values not yet shared by the wider society, nor *premodern*, adhering to the remnants of a romanticized prerational past. They are rather the contemporaries of the societies in which they live and whose institutional embodiments of economic and political rationality they oppose.

The opposition is primarily not between old and new values but between conflicting views of the extent to which different elements of modern values are satisfied. The values themselves, such as autonomy, identity, authenticity – but also human rights, peace, and the desirability of balanced physical environment – are largely noncontroversial. This fact is what either leaves the new social movements' intellectual and political opponents rather defenseless or leads them to misrepresent and often caricature these values as romantic or as the predilections of privileged groups who have lost contact with social "realities." What we observe is an awareness of the disaggregation and partial incompatibility among modern values. The ties of logical implication *between* values, such as links between technical progress and the satisfaction of human needs, property and autonomy, income and identity, and most generally, the rationality of processes and the desirability of outcomes, are perceived to have disintegrated. This cognitive awareness may lead to a selective emphasis on some values, but this is still different from a value change.

If we turn to the actors of the new paradigm, the structural explanation leads us to expect that they are most likely to be those who can most easily understand the nature of systematic irrationalities, or those who are the most likely victims of cumulative deprivations. The first part of this expectation is supported by the fact that levels of education (and possibly the recency of educational experience as indicated by age) are the most important condition of the new movements' activism. Two factors may contribute to this direct correlation. One is that more schooling leads to some perceived competence to make judgments about complicated and abstract economic, military, legal, technical, and environmental matters. The other is that higher education increases the capacity to think (and conceivably even to act) independently, and the preparedness to question received interpretations of the world.

Moreover, cognitive access to systematic irrationalities, especially their deepening aspects, might be supposed to be greatest for those who work in personal social services or in administration because they are confronted most immediately with those irrationalities. Also, people can be expected to be least inhibited in developing and expressing favorable attitudes toward the concerns of the new movements if they are secure in their economic position. In most European countries such relative prosperity and, most of all, security are enjoyed by public sector employees. If we combine these four variables (educational attainment, age, personal services, public sector employment) we get very close to the social category that, according to all quantitative evidence, has the highest proportion of people favoring the concerns and practices of the new social movements. This category also consists of the groups described by various neoconservatives as a "new class" and to be typical proponents of an "adversary culture."[39] The fit of the structural explanation to peripheral or decommodified groups is less obvious.[40] One possible congruence would be the experience, shared by the various elements in this heterogeneous category, of exclusion from modes of participation in society and polity that are mediated through active and stable labor-market participation and large-scale formal organization. Another answer would be the substantially lower degree of personal autonomy that most members of peripheral groups (especially middle-class housewives and adolescents) enjoy. Finally, one might speculate that these groups are relatively less constrained by norms and institutions in a society in which more and more of the life span is spent outside formal work roles but in which widely accepted models of how to spend *non*-work life have not yet been established. This might lead to an anomic condition in which a shrinking proportion of the societal map is charted by the institutions.

The structural explanation is least able to account for a sizable mobilization of the old middle class, as in environmentalist and regionalist movements. They are responding to the violation of traditional values, and their actions could therefore be analyzed more adequately in terms of the old social movements.

The issues of the new paradigm are also clearly connected to the view of a social reality characterized previously. All major concerns of the new social movements converge on the idea that life itself, and the minimal standards of "good life" as defined and sanctioned by modern values, are threatened by the blind dynamics of military, economic, technological, and political rationalization; and that there are no sufficient and reliable barriers within dominant political and economic institutions to prevent disaster.

This view also provides the basis for the adoption and legitimation of unconventional modes of action. This is so for two reasons. First, if life and survival are at stake, formal faithfulness to any established "rules of the game" is easily discredited as insignificant. Second, if institutional mechanisms are seen to be too rigid to recognize and absorb the problems of advanced industrial societies, it would be inconsistent to rely on them for a solution.[41]

That the values on which the new social movements are based must be understood as a selective radicalization of modern values, rather than a comprehensive rejection of them, is also evident from the dynamics of the new paradigm of extrainstitutional politics. This paradigm depends as much on the accomplishments of political and economic modernization as on criticisms of its unfulfilled promises and perverse effects. For instance, the two decades preceding the rise of the new feminist movement in the second half of the 1960s probably brought the most rapid and far-reaching advances in women's social position within the last century: easier access to higher education and the labor market, smaller families and a reduced work load in increasingly mechanized households, less rigid attitudes as well as liberalizing legislation concerning birth control, abortion, and divorce. Similarly, ecological movements can invoke testimonies from the centers of scientific, economic, and political institutions that point out vividly the possibly catastrophic consequences of an unmodified continuation of current modes of rationality. Likewise, the new peace movements often only popularize and radicalize doubts that already exist among some military and strategic experts concerning the dilemma, risks, and contradictions built into current defense plans. In these as well as other cases, proponents of the new paradigm rely on structural changes, pieces of knowledge, and standards of legitimation provided by dissenting minorities within ruling elites.

The contemporary, integrated, and in that sense modern nature of at least the middle-class component of the new social movements is further highlighted by the well-documented fact that those who use nonconventional political action do not lack experience with or awareness of available conventional forms of political participation.[42] On the contrary, these actors are relatively well experienced in, and often frustrated with, conventional practices. Accordingly, the new social movements' critique of political parties, parliamentary government, public bureaucracies, majority rule, and centralization always appears to concentrate on the limitations, partial rigidities, instances of malfunctioning, and empirical evidence of deterioration of political institutions rather than on their global and principled rejection.

Finally, the modern character of the new social movements is underlined by their evident belief that the course of history and society can be created and changed by people and social forces determined to do so. This methodical assumption even allows, as a rule, for contingency concerning the areas in and means by which such change might be accomplished. It thus differs fundamentally from the doctrines of classic Marxism (as well as some other earlier modern social movements), which relied on ontological assumptions about the predetermined, privileged, of even "correct" social groups, points in time, organizational forms, and tactics by which change could be brought about.

The potential impact of the new social movements

I have organized this discussion of the potential impact of the new social movements along three thresholds that they can either pass or fail sequentially. The first threshold concerns the survival or disintegration of highly amoebic forms of collective political action typical of the new social movements. If continuity is achieved, the second threshold concerns *success*, which could be nil (with a likely negative implication for survival), limited and permanently constrained, or cumulative and increasing. Finally, the social and political impact of relatively successful new social movements could amount to an effective challenge to and eventual abolition of the dominant old paradigm or it could at least result in a gain of "territory" by the new social movements. Although much comparative research, on both individual movements and movements in different countries, is still needed, some hypothetical generalizations about each of these thresholds can be suggested.

Survival

The fact that social movements are by definition informal in their mode of action makes their continuity always precarious. They are directly dependent on events in their social environment to provide the impetus for action. In contrast, formal organizations are able to exist for a while even if nothing happens. Social movements have often tried to overcome this difficulty by defining certain days as occasions for collective action (May Day, Women's Day, the Easter marches of the European peace demonstrations in the late 1950s and early 1960s, the Solidarity strikes in Poland in 1982, and so on). But this technique presupposes a sufficiently abstract and inclusive definition of the collective identity of actors and their causes. Where such a definition is absent, certain locations are often charged with symbolic meaning and made the focuses of collective action. Such has been the case in West Germany with occupied houses and urban renewal areas in urban struggles and with certain well-known construction sites of nuclear energy plants and airports. However, these are obviously weak and primitive methods for securing survival.

Slightly more ambitious means are national congresses, conferences, and organized central demonstrations, such as the peace rallies in Italy, France, the Netherlands, England, Belgium, and West Germany in the fall of 1981. In terms of numbers of participants, these demonstrations were enormously successful. But this success only highlights the difficulties of continuity; any future demonstrations failing to achieve comparable turnouts would certainly be considered signs of decline by all sides. Thus, organizers of informal mass action are trapped by their own accomplishments: Either they try to repeat them with a considerable risk of failing, or they do not, inviting the often largely accurate supposition that their former success was only a result of skillful exploitation of transient circumstances as well as some initially generous but subsequently declining media coverage.

Moreover, the frail organizational infrastructure behind such centralized events is exposed to two structural difficulties. Because its leadership is usually self-appointed and based on volunteer work, its legitimacy or representativeness is likely to be questioned. And because it has no recognized formal procedure by which dissent can be overcome, there is only the harsh alternative of reaching unanimity or separating.

As partial functional substitutes for formal organization, social movements have often developed charismatic leaders or clearly formulated "theories" from which leaders can derive their legitimacy and interpret the world. In contrast to student movements of the 1960s, the new European social movements of the late 1970s and early 1980s conspicuously lack these substitutes. Any claim to speak "for" the movement, or even to be the interpreter of a generally accepted ideology, is met with suspicion and resistance. This is the case for more than contingent reasons or a "mood" favoring pragmatism, pluralism, and experimentation.

The new social movements' nonideological nature is rather the result of a structural dilemma. Mobilization for protest usually takes place relatively late in the life history of a political issue, that is, only after the major alternatives have already been defined and the consequences have become clearly visible to the wider public. Because of their lack of institutional status and reliance on protest tactics, the movements have little chance to intervene in an earlier and still relatively open stage of the political process. Thus, they must give absolute priority to the broadest possible negative coalition of forces. Under such time pressure, and given a widespread distrust of totalizing ideological claims, ideological debate tends to get pushed aside, and any insistence on particular ideological points of view is discredited as violating norms of solidarity and effectiveness. This means, however, that the movements fail to develop more than rudimentary strategic perspectives on positive solutions to policy problems, and that they do not put protest issues in context with one another to develop a coherent political program. Hence we find within the new social movements numerous and fundamental unresolved or repressed ideological antimonies.[43]

In sum, to the extent that survival of the new social movements can be assumed to depend on formalized and explicit organizational or ideological mechanisms, their prospects for continuity appear far from certain. On the other side, the rational model of political organization underlying this assumption can itself be questioned. Rather than building their own organizational infrastructures, the new social movements have been very successful in utilizing institutionalized public spaces and modes of communication *outside* the core political institutions. Failure to build political forms of their own has facilitated this use of the nonpolitical forms of others. Most prominent among the public spaces being used or created are organized religion and, to a lesser extent, art (popular music as well as literature and theater), science, and sports. Under these roofs the ideas of the new social movements have often been formulated, made visible, and given institutional protection and legitimacy; and large groups of people who think of themselves as parts of the movements have been able to come together. Other nonpolitical means of symbolizing political allegiance have similarly been used, such as life-styles, aesthetic preferences, consumption patterns, and clothing. All these "cultural" sources of continuity and coherence tend to escape our view if we concentrate exclusively on the more traditional properties of political organizations.

A further example of the ways the new social movements make up for lack of formal organization is the close affinity and transferability of efforts among individual issue movements. Conscious reliance on a common cultural background makes it quite likely, for instance, that ecological activists can be mobilized for peace issues, or that feminist groups will support urban movements. Such cooperative networks and ad hoc alliances may well provide a measure of continuity and stability equivalent to what formal organization can achieve. This is also likely in view of the fact that minimal formalization, the fusion of social movements with cultural institutions, and the connection of the social bases of different issue movements guarantee maximum immunity from countermeasures ranging from selective concessions to repression.

From this point of view, the rationalistic requirements of a consistent and elaborate program, a totalizing understanding of the world, and a unification of economic, cultural, and political currents within the new social movements (such as is presupposed by Touraine and his method of sociological intervention)[44] could be considered a mixed blessing, even if it were realistic. A loosely connected set of issue movements that does not strive for ideological or organizational integration might turn out to be superior for both survival and success. This would depend, of course, on the validity of two assumptions introduced previously: that the destructive consequences of the dominant modes of political and economic rationality remain visible and provocative enough to provide continual specific focuses of protest; and that the social and political foundations of the middle-class radicalism that responds to such provocation remain what they are.

Success
There are three types of success that the new social movements can achieve. *Substantive* success refers to a positive or (more often) negative decision made by economic and political elites that conforms to the demands of a new social movement: A protested construction project is stopped or abortion legislation is liberalized. *Procedural* success includes changes on the level not of decisions but of the mode of decision making: Referenda are permitted or arrangements for participation, representation, and consultation are introduced where the rationality of the administration, courts, or investors had prevailed. *Political* success means that recognition (by opponents) and support (by present potential allies) are granted by institutional actors such as associations, political parties, and the media: The movements are incorporated into the programmatic declarations and platforms of unions and parties, and individuals representing these demands may be co-opted.

All these categories of success have been accomplished by urban, ecological, antinuclear, peace, and feminist movements, but there appears to be some correlation between general economic conditions and the political agenda's penetrability. Increased international tension, stagnating or negative growth rates, skyrocketing unemployment rates, and the rapidly deteriorating fiscal base of social security systems have largely foreclosed the political agenda and the objective possibility that elites will respond favorably to the new social movements' demands. But the effect of these conditions of crisis appears to be dual and polarizing. On the one side, they revitalize the corporatist alliance of forces that give almost unconditional priority to the restoration of growth and social as well as military security. On the other hand, the crisis and, even more, prevailing responses to it are taken by increasing numbers of people as compelling evidence of the likely disastrous effects of restoring traditional patterns.

As the space for compromise shrinks under the impact of crisis, the peace formulas so successfully designed by reformist coalitions such as the German Social Democratic–Liberal government of the late 1960s and early 1970s (economic growth *and* quality of life, economic and technical modernization *and* protection of the environment, detente *and* faithful compliance to American defense hegemony, and so on) break down. So, too, does the alliance of the industrial working class and the progressive elements of the new middle class. The new emphasis on unrestrained growth and modernization does not provide the resources by which both sets of policy objectives could be reached and both constituencies of reformism satisfied. This breakup of earlier formulas and alliances leaves the new-middle-class proponents of the new paradigm as politically frustrated as growing numbers of peripheral groups are economically frustrated.

Alliances

I wish to conclude with a discussion of the proposition that whether the forces representing the new paradigm transcend their presently marginal, although highly visible, power position, and thus whether they can challenge the dominant old paradigm, will depend most of all on whether and how the cleavages and inconsistencies that exist between the new middle class, peripheral groups, and the old middle class within the new social movements can be resolved.

Until the mid-1970s the traditional Left–Right continuum was an approximately adequate model in which all relevant political and societal collective actors could be located. The underlying dimension, manifestly reflected in the West German party system, ran from conservative economic liberalism to reforms and redistributive etatism, with a liberal-reformist position in between. This linear model is clearly no longer adequate. In terms of both individual value dispositions [45] and collective action and actors, a new cross-cutting dimension must be added. It depicts the contrast between the old paradigm and the new. We thus get a *triangular* model of the political universe: the forces of the traditional Left, the traditional Right (liberals and conservatives), and the new social movements (including their ex-

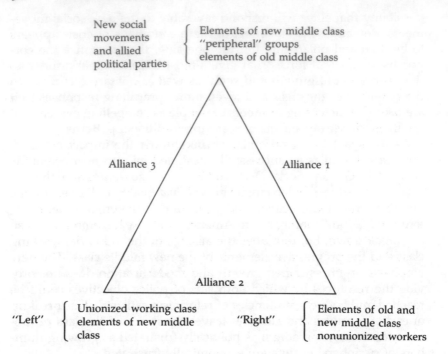

New social
movements
and allied
political parties
{
Elements of new middle class
"peripheral" groups
elements of old middle class

Alliance 3   Alliance 1

Alliance 2

"Left" {
Unionized working class
elements of new middle
class

"Right" {
Elements of old and
new middle class
nonunionized workers

Figure 2.1. A triangular model of political cleavages and potential alliances.

periments with "green" or "alternative" parliamentary politics). The resulting configuration is represented in Figure 2.1.

Such arrangements are, however, basically unstable, at least if equal distance is assumed between the three polar points. Final choices and decisions can only be made after the alternatives have been reduced to two, which implies the need for coalitions or at least ad hoc alliances. I will now try to assess the relative probability of three possible alliances: the proponents of the new paradigm with the traditional Right (Alliance 1); the "great coalition" corporatist alliance, which would largely exclude the new paradigm (Alliance 2); and the new paradigm with the traditional Left (Alliance 3).

I propose that which alliance will emerge depends on which of the three groups making up the forces of the new paradigm will come to be seen as dominant. This by no means hinges primarily on the numerical strength of the groups within a given new social movement or within the new social movement as a whole. To a large extent it depends on the policies by which political elites make positive or negative symbolic reference to, and establish selective relations with, one of these groups and on the extent to which they refer specifically to any one of them. For all the possible alliances, there are clearly visible policy initiatives in the issue areas of each major new social movement that can be utilized effectively to consolidate the respective alliance. A matrix representing these connections between issue movements, selective references to constituent components of the new social movements, corresponding policy proposals, and each of the three alliances is presented in Table 2.4.

To begin with, let us consider the policies that might lead to the formation of Alliance 1, between the traditional Right and the new social movements, the target group of which is the old-middle-class elements in the movements. In relation to the ecology movement, proponents of this alliance are well equipped to respond by traditional conservationist strategies, emphasizing the ethical, religious, and aesthetic values of unspoiled nature, creating national parks, and relying largely on market mechanisms for implementation. The neopopulist approach is even able to offer some selective support to the feminist movement. Certainly, there is little agreement on abortion or the egalitarian treatment of women in the labor market; but there is much more affinity concerning the opposition to pornography, some family-related social policy, and symbolic recognition of women's special role in society. Substantial convergence also exists between some of the new movements' experiments in alternative economies and liberal-conservative economic doctrines. This includes a vehement rejection of the legitimacy of working-class organizations. Not only have neo-liberals from Friedman to Dahrendorf hailed the rise of "shadow work" and the informal economy but Catholic conservatives have proposed "self-help" (based on voluntary unpaid work in the family and local community) as the solution to the fiscal and functional deficiencies of established forms of social policy. These doctrines, as well as support for tax subsidies for small businesses, obviously have much in common with the communitarian approaches of alternative movements.

Finally, limited agreements also exist between some segments of the peace movement and conservative forces. As with the civilian use of nuclear technology, much of the protest has to do with choice of sites rather than decisions about overall strategy. Thus, conservatives can easily join local protests against the location of nuclear warheads. Moreover, recent technological condemnations of nuclear weapons as immoral in themselves can be converted easily into a plea for large-scale increases in conventional defenses. Finally, both groups would favor appeals for national self-reliance in defense policy.

Here, two conclusions must suffice. First, and contrary to assumptions frequently made in the media and some of the social science

Table 2.4. *Issues/movements, alliances, and component groups: policy proposals and initiatives*

	Selective emphasis on role of . . . within new movements	Feminism and human rights	Issue/movement Peace	Environmental protection	Alternative or "dual" economy
Alliance 1 (Conservative–liberal Right plus new movements)	Old middle-class (positive reference)	Antipornography initiatives	Shift to conventional defense strategies	Conservationism	Support for communal and self-help forms of social services
		Family-centered social policies for women	Appeals to national self-reliance in defense policy	Concentration of industrial locations plus natural parks	Tax subsidies for small business
		Symbolic recognition of the special role of women and minorities in society		Environmental regulation through market mechanisms (fines and incentives)	
	General characteristics: (symbolic) invocation of premodern communal values: critique of bureaucracy and regulation, centralization and welfare state egalitarianism				
Alliance 2 (Conservative–liberal Right plus social democratic, etc., Left)	Peripheral groups (negative reference)	Increasing labor market flexibility and mobility	Reliance on supranational arenas and nuclear deterrence strategies of defense policy	Promotion of environmental protection and new energy resources as a high-technology growth industry	Promotion of part-time employment for peripheral groups
		Improving access of women and minorities			
	General characteristics: active depoliticization of concerns of new social movements; emphasis upon the illegality of their means and irrationality/irresponsibility of their aims				
Alliance 3 (Social democratic Left and new movements)	New middle-class (positive reference)	Preferential living and quota systems	(Conditional) proposals for unilateral disarmament	Inclusion of environmental and Third World–related criteria in industrial policy	Support for cooperatives, protected, and "parallel" labor markets
		Redistribution of work within production and household			Economic democracy
	General characteristics: increase compatibility between demands of new movements and traditional working-class concerns and interests				

literature, there is by no means a natural or unchangeable tendency for the new social movements to align with the Left. Second, actual consolidation of the frequently proposed alignment between the new politics and liberal-conservative forces would not constitute any serious challenge to the operational reality of the old paradigm. By being absorbed into this alliance, the new politics would stop aspiring to power positions in state and society. It might allow itself to be co-opted in exchange for concessions that would preserve some premodern protected territories of the natural environment, sex roles, forms of work, communities, and defense strategies.

Important segments of political elites are currently attempting to design policies that could lead to Alliance 2, between the traditional Left and traditional Right. Implicit in this project is a negative reference to the peripheral groups in the new social movements. These movements are perceived primarily as expressing the needs and values of those who neither contribute to industrial production nor conform to its values and standards of rationality. Because of failures in the processes of material and cultural reproduction and subversion by some of their intellectual mentors, the peripheral groups (such as the squatters' movements in various German and Dutch cities) have escaped the basic discipline presupposed for orderly functioning of a complex society. They have adopted a fundamentally hostile attitude toward the institutions of private property and the state without being able to develop a workable political alternative. Their attitude toward the welfare state is taken to be basically cynical and exploitative. The logical public policy consequences of this assumption are repression and surveillance, exclusion and nondecisions, and, at best, a measure of symbolic politics aimed at preventing the peripheral elements from winning support among the old or new middle classes.

A broad Left–Right coalition supporting this type of response can be brought about by capitalizing on the parallel fears that the new social movements provoke in both camps: In the Left, fears of unemployment and declining standards of social security; and in the Right, fears of violence and the prospect of communist infiltration of peripheral groups. Both sorts of apprehensions are accentuated by the general economic and international crisis.

This type of policy response to the new social movements again illustrates their interaction with public policy: These movements are shaped not just by what they are but by how they are perceived, interpreted, and symbolically treated by political elites, and by the extent to which these elite responses determine the relative weight of components within the movements. In this sense, the attempt to define the new social movements as embodiments of criminal or deviant political behavior can well become self-fulfilling by excluding their more reformist elements and thereby defining protest politics' space of action as primarily for those willing to engage in militant anti-etatist acts. This strategy does not, of course, omit the possibility that concerns of the movements will be addressed in a technocratic matter (for instance, environmental issues in terms of the preservation of strategic economic resources such as water; feminist issues in terms of the labor market and demographic planning; alternative forms of economic organization in terms of more effective and efficient provision of services; peace issues in terms of arms control strategies). But in spite of such responses, Alliance 2 is as unlikely to change the dominant paradigm of politics as Alliance 1 is. However, this confrontation approach is more likely to lead to a relatively high and permanent (albeit fluctuating) level of violent extrainstitutional conflict.

Alliance 3 is based on a strategy that links the traditional Left and the new social movements by focusing on the new-middle-class core of these movements. To a significant extent, it also relies on an opening of traditional organizations of the Left (communist and social democratic parties and unions) to youth, women, and the unemployed, in other words, a positive relation to peripheral segments. Such an attempt to transcend the limits of the industrial proletariat in both directions and thereby to absorb some of the new movements' concerns has been proclaimed most clearly by the Italian Communist Party and, in a somewhat different way, by the French socialist trade-union confederation, the CFDT. But it would be premature to conclude that this kind of alliance is most likely to emerge within working-class organizations that have, comparatively speaking, least abandoned their traditional socialist aspirations.

On the contrary, one could speculate about a U-shaped relationship between the degree of "revisionism" or "modernism" of working-class political organizations and their responsiveness to the new social movements by the fact that the German Social Democratic Party (SPD) has, since 1959, increasingly abandoned its identity as a classic working-class party and consequently relied on, and electorally benefited from, the new middle class. It also has made considerable efforts to demonstrate its openness to the concerns of the new social movements (a tendency which, since the late 1960s, has been effectively symbolized by party chairman Willy Brandt). Thus, a highly "modern" social democratic party may hope to compensate for the losses resulting from its weakening roots in the working class by establishing links with the new-middle-class constituency of the new social movements.[46] As demonstrated by the debates and controversies within

German social democracy in the early 1980s, and particularly after the fall of the Schmidt government in September 1982, such an electoral realignment is not easy to accomplish unless social democratic parties adopt changes on a strategic (rather than tactical, electoral, or ad hoc) level. Such a reorientation is, for structural reasons, least probable under conditions of economic crisis. On the other hand, the force of these economic imperatives may not preclude such reorientation (particularly for a Left party out of government office). They may even contribute to its accelerated adoption if a general "Gestalt switch" concerning the future of growth-and-security-based industrial systems occurs.

Three conceivable factors would allow Alliance 3 between the traditional Left and the new social movements. First, the new-middle-class-element within social democratic parties may already be sufficiently entrenched to resist effectively any unconditional retreat of policies to the "productivist" philosophy of economic growth and to traditional conceptions of military security. Second, the very nature of the economic crisis and defense dilemmas may render the prospects for renormalization (full employment, free international trade, the welfare state, and an effective and balanced nuclear deterrence) sufficiently unrealistic to weaken the more traditional resistance to such a reorientation. These two factors alone would explain the rise of priorities such as "selective" or "qualitative" growth, skepticism about technical change, basic doubts about conventional measures of labor productivity and productivity increases, and proposals for unilateral strategies of disarmament. All these priorities have become increasingly popular in the northwest European countries, where there are strong social democratic parties (especially where these parties have experienced electoral defeats since the mid-1970s, as in Great Britain, Norway, Sweden, Denmark, the Netherlands, Austria, and West Germany).

A third fact that may be of some relevance is that all the major social movements can make positive references to and even draw on more or less defunct, forgotten, or repressed aspects of the past ideological traditions of today's Socialist, Social Democratic, and Communist parties and other working-class organizations. Such parallels are most obvious between the new peace movements and the traditions of European socialist pacifism before World War I, and in the demands for an end to political and economic discrimination against women.

Similar parallels are being drawn between today's experiments with alternative economic organizations and the tradition of working-class production and consumer cooperatives. Furthermore, the concern not only with production, wages, and the worker but also with the product, its use values, and the consumer is a traditional (if often marginal) element in the demands of classic working-class organizations that overlaps with the demands of modern environmentalist movements. Such affinities seem to suggest that not just the "postrevisionist" social structure and present policy dilemmas of modern Social Democratic parties but also their "prerevisionist" heritage could become instrumental in an alliance between them and the new social movements.

This third possible alliance is obviously the only one that could lead to an effective and successful challenge of the old paradigm of politics.

Common to the three scenarios and, for that matter, the patterns of political conflict in Western European states during the late 1970s and early 1980s, is the collision between forces within and forces outside the conventional definitions of politics, its legitimate collective actors, and its forms of action.

Notes

1 Samuel P. Huntington, "The United States," in M. Crozier et al., eds., *The Crisis of Democracy* (New York: New York University Press, 1975).

2 The term *political paradigm* (as I borrow and redefine it from J. Raschke, "Politik und Wertwandel in den westlichen Demokratien," *Aus Politik und Zeitgeschichte* 36 [1980]:23–45; and K. W. Brand, D. Büsser, and D. Rucht, *Protestbewegungen in der Bundesrepublik* [Frankfurt: Campus, 1983] refers to a comprehensive model of what politics is about.

3 On the basis of the distinction between interest cleavage and the cleavages of cultural models, one would predict that culturally highly homogeneous societies encounter the fewest difficulties in establishing stable and effective arrangements for dealing with even severe interest cleavages. The European country that best supports this hypothesis is, of course, Sweden.

4 K. L. Baker, R. J. Dalton, and K. Hildebrandt, *Germany Transformed: Political Culture and the New Politics* (Cambridge, Mass.: Harvard University Press, 1981), pp. 136ff.

5 O. Kirchheimer, "Der Wandel des westeuropäischen Parteisystems," in *Politische Vierteljahresschrift* 6 (1965):20–41.

6 H. Schelsky, *Der Mensch in der wissenschaftlichen Zivilisation* (Opladen: Westdeutscher Verlag, 1961); E. Forsthoff, *Der Staat der Industriegesellschaft* (Munich: Beck, 1971).

7 Raschke, "Politik und Wertwandel."

8 *New protest movements* is used by K. W. Brand, *Neue Soziale Bewegungen* (Opladen: Westdeutscher Verlag, 1982); *new politics* by K. Hildebrandt and R. J. Dalton, "Die neue Politik," *Politische Vierteljahresschrift* 18, 2/3 (1977); *new populism* by Jürgen Habermas, *Strukturwandel der Öffentlichkeit: Untersuchungen über eine Kategorie der bürgerlichen Gesellschaft* (Neuwied: Luchterhand, 1962); J. Habermas, *Theorie des Kommunikativen Handelns*, vol. 2 (Frankfurt: Suhrkamp, 1981); and Bernd Marin, "Neuer Populismus und

'Wirtschaftspartnerschaft,' " *Österreichische Zeitschrift für Politikwissenschaft* 9,2 (1980): 157–170; *neoromanticism* by U. Schimank, *Neoromantischer Protest im Spätkapitalismus: Der Widerstand gegen Stadt- und Landschaftsverödung* (Bielefeld: AJZ, 1983); *antipolitics* by Suzanne Berger,"Politics and Anti-Politics in Western Europe in the Seventies," *Daedalus* 108, 2 (1979): 27–50; and *unorthodox political behavior* and *disorderly politics* by A. Marsh, *Protest and Political Consciousness* (London: Sage, 1977).

The description "unconventional" is employed by M.Kaase, "Bedingungen unkonventionellen politischen Verhaltens in der Bundesrepublik Deutschland", in P. Graf Kielmansegg, ed., *Legitimationsprobleme politischer Systeme*, Sonderheft 7 der Politischen Vierteljahresschrift (PVS) (Opladen: Westdeutscher Verlag, 1976), pp. 184ff.

9 A. Melucci, "New Movements, Terrorism, and the Political System," *Socialist Review* 56 (March-April 1981):98.

10 H. C. Boyte, "The Populist Challenge: Anatomy of an Emerging Movement," *Socialist Revolution* 8, 32 (1977).

11 Cf. Claus Offe, " 'Reaching for the Brake,': The Greens in Germany," *New Political Science* (Spring 1983):45–52

12 *Prinzip Leben* is used by P. Kelly and J. Leinen, eds., *Prinzip Leben: Ökopax – die neue Kraft* (Berlin: Olle u. Wolter, 1982); *Lebenswelt*, by Jürgen Habermas, *Theorie des Kommunikativen Handelns*, vol. 2 (Frankfurt: Suhrkamp, 1981); and *Lebensweise*, by Raschke, "Politik und Wertwandel."

13 Samuel H. Barnes and M. Kaase, eds., *Political Action: Mass Participation in Five Western Democracies* (London: Sage, 1979), pp. 59, 106, 135.

14 Anthony Giddens, *The Class Structure of the Advanced Societies* (London: Hutchinson, 1973).

15 Ronald Inglehart, *The Silent Revolution: Changing Values and Political Styles Among Western Publics* (Princeton, N.J.: Princeton University Press, 1977).

16 On the peace movement, see F. Parkin, *Middle Class Radicalism* (Manchester: Manchester University Press, 1968); on the environmental movements, see S. Cotgrove and A. Duff, "Environmentalism, Class, and Politics" (University of Bath: Science Studies Centre, n.d., Mimeographed); on various civil rights and feminist movements, see H. Schenk, *Die feministische Herausforderung: 150 Jahre Frauenbewegungen in Deustchland* (Munich: Beck, 1980), pp. 108–18.

17 It is worth noting that many of the movements and revolts since the mid–1960s originated from institutions *outside* the labor market or the firm; examples include the patriarchal family and the status and role it assigns to women, children, and youth; the university and school systems; "total" institutions such as prisons and armies; and the more custodial and oppressive parts of the welfare state apparatus.

18 For instance, in the antinuclear movement the local old middle class has often joined protests against building new power plants (see Herbert Kitschelt, *Kernenergiepolitik* [Frankfurt: Campus, 1980]). Strong old-middle-class elements usually support regionalist movements such as the Occitan movement in the hope of winning more economic subsidies from the central state (see A. Touraine, *Le pays contre l'Etat* [Paris: Seuil, 1981]). Movements resisting urban renewal find a natural ally in local merchants, who fear that large-scale commercial capital will move in as soon as city centers have been modernized.

19 Parkin, *Middle Class Radicalism*.

20 J. Gershuny, *After Industrial Society: The Emerging Self-service Economy* (London: Macmillan, 1978).

21 André Gorz, *Adieu au Prolétariat: Au-délà du Socialisme* (Paris: Editions Galilée, 1980).

22 W. Kornhauser, *The Politics of Mass Society* (New York: Free Press, 1976); N. J. Smelser, *Theory of Collective Behavior* (New York: Free Press, 1963).

23 Cf. Brigitta Berger, Peter L. Berger, and H. Kellner, *The Homeless Mind: Modernization and Consciousness* (New York: Random House, 1973).

24 Parkin, *Middle Class Radicalism*, p. 16.

25 Marsh, *Protest and Political Consciousness*, p. 87; cf. J. P. Olsen, *Organized Democracy: Political Institutions in a Welfare State – the Case of Norway* (Bergen: Universitetsforlaget, 1983), chap. 1.

26 Marsh, *Protest and Political Consciousness*, p. 165.

27 Johann Galtung, "The Blue and the Red, the Green and the Brown: A Guide to Movements and Countermovements" (Geneva: Institut Universitaire d'Etude du Développement, 1981, Mimeographed), p. 18.

28 Inglehart, *The Silent Revolution*.

29 This is suggested by Marsh and Kaase.

30 This approach is clearly favored by Brand (*Neue Soziale Bewegungen*); Brand, Büsser, and Rucht, *Protestbewegungen in der Bundesrepublik*; J. Hirsch, *Der Sicherheitsstaat: Das 'Modell Deutschland,' seine Krise und die neuen Bewegungen* (Frankfurt: Europäische Verlagsanstalt, 1980); and Raschke ("Politik und Wertwandel"), in Germany; and A. Melucci, *L'invenzione del presente: Movimenti, identità, bisogni individuali* (Bologna: Il Mulino, 1982), in Italy.

31 Habermas, *Theorie des kommunikativen Handelns*, p. 513.

32 Cf. M. Morris, P. Patton, eds., *Michel Foucault: Power, Truth, Strategy* (Sidney: Feral Publications, 1979).

33 Habermas, *Theorie des kommunikativen Handelns*.

34 A. Melucci, "The New Social Movements: A Theoretical Approach," *Social Science Information* 19, 2 (1980): 217–18.

35 Cf. Hirsch, *Der Sicherheitsstaat*.

36 M. Jänicke, *Wie das Industriesystem von seinen Missständen profitiert: Kosten und Nutzen technokratischer Symptombekämpfung; Umweltschutz, Gesundheitswesen, innere Sicherheit* (Opladen: Westdeutscher Verlag, 1979).

37 Berger, "Politics and Anti-Politics," p. 32.

38 Cf. Offe, "Reaching for the Brake."

39 On the new class cf. B. Bruce-Briggs, ed., *The New Class?* (New York: Transaction Books, 1979); and H. Schelsky, *Die Arbeit tun die anderen: Klassenkampf und Priesterherrschaft der Intellektuellen* (Opladen: Westdeutscher Verlag, 1975). On *adversary culture*, see Daniel Bell, *The Cultural Contradictions of Capitalism* (New York: Basic Books, 1976).

40 The new middle class and peripheral groups seem to share two structural characteristics. First, most of the peripheral groups are past, present, or potential clients of providers of social and personal services, and this clientage can often be supposed to affect their central life interests. Second, and probably more important, both groups share the condition of decommodification: The economic logic of efficiency, of thinking in terms of costs and returns, is far less applicable to the use of one's own labor power and efforts.

41 Cf. D. Rucht, *Planung und Partizipation* (Munich: Tuduv, 1982), p. 277.

42 Cf. Marsh, *Protest and Political Consciousness*; Olsen, *Organized Democracy*.

43 Herbert Kitschelt, *Der ökologische Diskurs, Eine Analyse von Gesellschaftskonzeptionen in der Energiedebatte* (Frankfurt: Campus, 1984).

44 A. Touraine, *La prophétie antinucléaire* (Paris: Seuil, 1980).

45 Barnes and Kaase, *Political Action*; Baker, Dalton, and Hildebrandt, *Germany Transformed*.

46 Cf. U. Himmelstrand et al., *Beyond Welfare Capitalism: Issues, Actors and Forces in Societal Change* (London: Heinemann, 1981), for a similar argument concerning the Swedish SAP.

3

Religious transformation and the future of politics

SUZANNE BERGER

Over the past three decades in Western Europe, the Catholic church, a bulwark of social and political order, has developed the cracks and fissures of advanced decay. Complex networks of values, beliefs, practices, and organizations built up by the church over centuries are disintegrating. In France where the dimensions of religious change have been the most striking, weekly mass attendance dropped from about one-third of all Catholics in the 1950s to about 15 percent at the end of the seventies.[1] The numbers of those taking confession, communion, and confirmation fell. Ordinations declined from over 600 a year to about 150 between the mid-sixties and mid-seventies.[2] Surveys of the faithful find growing pockets of doubt and resistance to central tenets of doctrine.[3] The subcultural institutions which sheltered the Catholic community from the onslaught of secular culture and from the Republic are in ruin. Catholic Action associations, among the largest mass movements of the postwar period, have become sects with small audiences beyond the immediate participants.

These phenomena appear in all Catholic Western Europe, more advanced in France, the Netherlands, and Germany than in Spain, Italy, or Portugal; but everywhere the trends seem to move in the same directions. There are, to be sure, countertendencies: an upsurge of charismatic religious practice, some revival of monastic recruitment, continued mass support for private – that is, Catholic – schools, the success of new styles of Catholic politics, particularly in the Italian

I am grateful for the support of a Guggenheim Fellowship during 1979–80 and for the helpful comments of Renaud Dulong, Peter Gourevitch, David Laitin, Peter Lange, Gary Meyers, and Charles Sabel. All translations in the text, except that of Tocqueville, are mine. A shorter version of this chapter appeared in the *European Sociological Review* I, no. 1 (1985).

Comunione e Liberazione movement. The dominant fact, however, is the collapse of old patterns of religious practice and of long-established religious institutions. It may well be, as some historians argue, that what we conventionally regard as traditional Catholicism is a religious edifice of fairly recent creation, one dating to the Counter-Reformation and even, in some of its wings, to nineteenth-century construction.[4] But the critical issue for politics is that this is the religious order on which and against which modern Western European politics emerged. The massive transformation of this church in its institutional, ritual, and creedal dimensions thus alters in many ways the territory of politics.

The decay of religion, we argue here, has worked to change politics by releasing fragments of this Catholic socioreligious order to travel along trajectories no longer determined by the centripetal pulls of the church. Even as they break away from their original moorings, the fragments of the old Catholic world retain considerable internal coherence and vitality. As they venture now onto terrain outside the influence of the church, as they move into alliance and combination with groups of entirely different genesis and history, the Catholic fragments adapt to new circumstances by reworking and reordering the load of historical experience, transcendent aspirations, and political visions they bring with them from the Catholic past. As they approach novel situations and strike new alliances, the fragments change by internal recombination of their original stock of resources and expectations. At the same time, the Catholics also modify their new allies, by disrupting within them old balances of force and interest, material and ideal. The reworking of the original components of the Western European Catholic legacy, the insertion of the elements of an old religious tradition into the political movements of lay, secular, and socialist politics, and the ferment within these latter groups created by the injection of the new Catholic materials are producing major ideological renewal.

In exploring the routes by which religious transformation shapes the new politics of Western Europe, the approach laid out here starts from the discovery of the survival and continuing vitality of political orientations forged in a Catholic matrix, now at work outside their original territory. Against this view, which emphasizes the efficacy of traditional religious elements in the ideological recomposition of European politics, two other ways of conceiving the role of religious decline in political change ought to be signaled, for they have dominated contemporary thought about this process.

The secularization hypothesis

One important body of scholarship emphasizes the relationship between the decomposition of old religious institutions and a concurrent series of political changes described as a crisis of governability. For those who draw connections between the waning of traditional religion and the unraveling of long-accepted notions of what is possible and desirable in politics, the main process at work is secularization. Modernization makes faith a private affair and thereby destroys a major source of social constraint.

In this analysis modernization implies, first, secularization in the specific sense, that is, the eviction of the church from social, political, and economic life and the restriction of its authority to the regulation of the special business of religion.[5] Secularization is also broadly understood to involve detaching and disengaging faith from a cluster of political, social, and economic attitudes and practices with which religious beliefs had formerly been tightly entangled. The consequence of secularization, conceived in this broad sense, is thus to reduce the sway of collective norms over individual interests and desires. Without compelling collective norms, public life deteriorates into a struggle of wills; the deference that once supported authority in the workplace and in the state dissolves, and groups seek to "punch their weight in the marketplace," in John Goldthorpe's sense.[6] Conceptions of the public interest disappear in the clamor of corporatist claims.

This view of how religion, understood as the linchpin of a traditional social order, might in its decline bring down a liberal-democratic order rejoins Joseph Schumpeter's notion that capitalism is incapable of generating values that legitimate its social order.[7] The operative constraints on individuals in modern societies thus remain those rooted in preindustrial beliefs and attitudes. Weaken this traditional legacy and the consequences will be the undermining of contemporary power relations. Thus the disappearance of religious fidelities, one of the principal elements in the reservoir of traditional attitudes and beliefs, diminishes social compliance. The privatization of religious beliefs destabilizes politics by disjoining faith from social and political consequences. Whether religion as a private concern persists or not, then, is not the main issue. Rather it is unraveling a traditional nexus of social, political, and religious attitudes and institutions that unleashes (or, alternatively, liberates) individual behavior from old constraints and thereby endangers social stability.

The debate over the moral and religious bases of modern societies is a classic one in social theory. Historically, many have rejected the view that the sources of cohesion and legitimacy in modern society are principally rooted in an earlier social order and are somehow inherently determined by what can be preserved from a traditional, religious heritage. They argue that the curbs on individual and group selfishness that a conservative religious outlook once provided are or could be supplanted by constraints of another kind. The solidarities of workplace and neighborhood might draw individuals into identification with larger communities, and not only into group corporatism and chauvinism. Civic morality may develop as an autonomous political phenomenon, without need of religious sustenance. Or, in another view, people may cooperate and obey for reasons that have little to do with the legitimacy of authority. Men and women may not live by bread alone, but that may be as much as they expect from the state. The material affluence that industrial societies create may provide legitimation enough for the political and economic order of capitalism. Indeed, once religious convictions are dissociated from politics, the poisonous conflicts over church–state relations that nourished antisystem politics over the past two centuries should abate. Thus the stability and legitimacy of liberal democracy might well be strengthened by the final disappearance of a traditional religious order.

Whatever the merit of these views, today those who hold them and conclude that the consequences of secularization for politics are benign are in retreat. The evident inability of liberal states to elicit from their citizens the discipline and sacrifices conceived of as necessary for moving out of a deep economic crisis lends support to the other camp of social theorists. The pessimistic view is that none of the checks that democratic societies themselves generate and bring into play are powerful enough to hold individuals and groups back from a socially destructive pursuit of material interest and self-expression. The decline in stable partisan attachments, political mobilization outside the major parties and interest groups, the rise of new single-issue movements, and increased conflictuality in all spheres of life are seen as aspects of the same process: the weakening of authority, as its traditional underpinnings are eroded by secularization, and the affirmation of particularistic interests. A dwindling supply of authority, an excess of demand, and, finally, a deficit of collective loyalties and trust, without which political solutions for the economic crisis that involve redistribution, deferral of rewards, or sacrifice will not work – these are the elements of the "ungovernability" problem.[8] And each of these elements can be seen as directly linked to the disappearance of a traditional order with the decline of religion.

The political religion hypothesis

In the darker version of the secularization thesis, the outlook for politics is an increasingly unruly society, with a greatly reduced capacity for collective endeavors of any sort. There is, however, another school of thought about the consequences of the decline of traditional religion for politics that concludes that the most likely outcome is not secularization but a radicalization and collectivization of public life. This second broad line of speculation about religion and politics starts from the premise that religious needs are a permanent part of human nature; or, in Daniel Bell's phrase, that religion is "a constitutive aspect of human experience."[9] Individuals seek not only for a private faith but also for an overarching sense to life that can answer their questions about the larger meaning of everyday life and that can encompass all aspects of their social existence. Modernization and industrialization do not, in this perspective, diminish the force of human yearnings to integrate religious, social, and political life in a single totality of meaning. What has changed in modern society is not human nature, as the secularization theorists would have it, but rather the religious institutions that channel and condition social life. When religious hopes and passions flow into well-established institutions, as they once did in Western Europe, as they still do in the United States and Britain, then religion and liberal values are compatible and mutually supportive. When, however, the churches fall prey to seductive appeals to adapt themselves to the times and abandon their traditional activities and mission, then they lose their followings, as people go elsewhere for the religious sustenance they no longer find in established religion. They may look to new cults, to charismatic reworkings of traditional faith, or to politics.[10]

The search to satisfy religious needs outside the church is, in this view, extremely dangerous for political and social stability. There is no process of secularization or disenchantment at work in modern societies. The religious commitments that once were linked to conservative political and social behavior have not disappeared, but are redirected. There is a transfer of religious commitment into politics, a shift of passions, religious intensity and a sense of transcendent mission and faith from the God of Christian belief onto the gods of secular political religions. Thus, for example, Stalinism appears in this perspective as "the most extraordinary displacement of religious faith since the Crusades. A gigantesque effort to compensate for the absence of God, to give a sense to life, to console those who suffer and help those who are dying."[11]

The decline of traditional religion, then, threatens liberal democracy by producing religious politics. When religious energies and aspirations are directed into politics, the result is the intolerant, ultimately totalitarian creed of the Jacobins, the Bolsheviks, the Maoists. The contemporary transformations of religion promise an intensification of political passions and a resurgence of revolutionary ideologies that demand the concentration of all power in the state. Those individuals whose break with traditional religion is motivated by unsatisfied yearnings to realize transcendent aims on earth and to achieve a unity between religious belief and everyday life are the most likely recruits for totalitarian politics. As expressed in a joke of the seventies, the notion is that the last Marxist-Leninist in Europe will be a disaffected Breton priest.

The politics of declining practice: France

How well do any of these views account for changes in the course of politics over the last three decades of erosion of conventional religious beliefs and practices in Western Europe?[12] France represents a kind of critical case for these theories, for there, rapid religious decline has been occurring in a political context strongly constrained by religion. In France religious practice predicts voters' choices far better than class, occupation, income, schooling, or region. The political parties choose allies and enemies from camps originally formed over conflicts about the role of the church in the modern state. On the grounds of that battle, there developed a subcultural segmentation of collective life that continues in much of rural and small-town France to reproduce in every community a "red" and a "white" world, each with its own social organizations, schools, values, and orientations to politics. The strength and scope of religious impact on politics, the massiveness of the recent changes in religious behavior together make it likely that the issues these theories identify as significant will arise in France with special force.

In France, the weakening of traditional religious patterns has apparently set in motion along different political trajectories fragments of the old Catholic world that once had the same politics. Through the Third, Fourth, and Fifth Republics, practicing Catholics of all social classes, income groups, and occupations provided massive support for the Right. The alliance of the church and the Right was born along with modern French politics.[13] In France, as in all Western European nations with significant Catholic populations, the modern democratic state had to defend its existence from the beginning against the church. What was specific to the French case, however, was the extent to which the terms of battle between church and state came to define the axes of partisan alignment and the persistence of these axes, long after the virtual disappearance of the original conflicts.

The mass entry of the French into politics – universal manhood suffrage, the emergence of the party system – took place at a time when the central issue on the political agenda was the secularization crisis. The French began to perceive the links between everyday life and politics at a point when the most salient of the state's interventions in society were those concerning the church. These intrusions arose around three conflicts. First, the church figured as one of the main elements in the feudal system destroyed by the Revolution and then as the principal force in antirepublican politics to restore the ancien régime. Like the nobility and the monarchy, the church was dispossessed of jurisdiction over substantial spheres of social and economic life by the Republic. In the struggles of the nineteenth century between conservatives and republicans, the church was the base on which the entire defense of the ancien régime coalition came to rest, for the church's legitimacy and influence extended over far larger sectors of the population than did the monarchy's or the nobility's.

The second range of conflicts between church and state arose over the church's international position. In a nationalist and patriotic democracy, the church's relationship to the Vatican, the ambiguities about the ultimate loyalties of church personnel, and the suspicion that on certain foreign policy questions French Catholics were a kind of "fifth column" generated problems that neither the Civil Constitution of the Clergy during the Revolution nor the Napoleonic Concordat put to rest.

Finally, there was a bitter conflict between the church and state over the values, beliefs, and loyalties of the French. The republicans believed that in order to make citizens, the state had to inculcate the same values in all men and women. This transmission had to take place in a common institution: the public school. The church, on the other side, believed that forming Christians required the acquisition of certain ways of understanding the world that could only be communicated in schools under Catholic control. The battle over the souls of French children and between republican and Catholic ideals of authority, of citizenship, and of the good society thus came to be fought out as a battle between *l'école laïque et unique* and *l'école libre*. The tensions over the first two church–state conflicts largely abated after the separation law of 1905. The passions over the school question, in ebb over the last fifteen years, have resurged after the Socialist victory of 1981. The largest political demonstrations since François Mitterrand's election have been those called by the proponents of nationalizing the Catholic schools and integrating them into a single public system and on the other side, by the partisans of the private Catholic school system.

Church–state conflict provided the grid which oriented the system of political parties that emerged in the nineteenth century. The terms of this battle came to define Left and Right in politics. When socialism appeared as a significant political force in the last quarter of the nineteenth century, the alliances and lines of battle it generated were superimposed upon, but never effaced, the partisan alignments of the earlier struggle. The resilience of political commitments formed in this first mass politicization is strikingly demonstrated in the consistently high correlations between religious practice and votes for the Right. Historically, the link between the two was reinforced by the pressure of the clergy and its explicit instructions to the faithful on the eve of elections. But the hierarchy's electoral role disappeared after World War II, and still the high correlations between practice and Right voting continued.

Only with the rapid collapse of religious structures over the past two decades has the political homogeneity of the Catholic world finally begun to crumble. Out of the old camp of the Catholic Right have emerged three different populations, each identifiable by a point of departure within the Catholic world and a point of arrival within the politics of the national community.

The redistributed Right

Catholics with a past of high rates of religious observance but no special involvement in the organizational network of the Catholic subculture have now begun to change their politics. In the 1970s when the Socialist Party began to make important gains in the once massively conservative strongholds of the Catholic West and elsewhere in France where regular practice was general, the connections between churchgoing and Right politics appeared to be dissolving. But what actually was in process in these regions was a rapid decline in practice, and with it, a realignment of once observant populations into political behavior more typical of the French community at large. Evidence is still sparse, but studies like Philippe Braud's in Brittany suggest that as religious practice drops in old Catholic areas, the population redistributes itself electorally among the parties in proportions close to national averages.[14] The gains of the Left among the Catholic populations of the West are thus gains realized among that part of the population which is less and less practicing. Because this group was once disproportionately right-wing, its shift toward national patterns automatically benefits the Left.

The faithful

Catholics who continue to practice regularly remain politically conservative. A 1977 survey of Catholics found that of those who practiced regularly (i.e., attended mass at least once or twice a month) 67 percent voted for the Right; in contrast, of those who are not churchgoers, only 37 percent chose a Right party.[15] In the 1981 presidential elections, 81 percent of the practicing Catholics voted on the first round for a candidate of the Right in contrast to 49 percent of French citizens overall.[16] (In 1974, 90 percent of the practicing Catholics had chosen a Right presidential candidate.)

Catholic militants

Finally, there is a population of Catholics that has shifted massively to the Left, bringing new electors and members to Socialist and Communist parties and unions and to the antinuclear, regional ethnic, ecology, and other single-issue movements that gravitate in the Left's orbit. Many of these Left Catholics have ceased religious practice or at least no longer practice in traditional modes. What is common in the past of these Catholics is a history of militance in either the social action movement of the Catholic subculture, or in the Catholic trade-union movement. For those activists who come to the Left from Catholic Action (and also from Catholic groups like La Route, the older Scouts branch), the typical personal itinerary is a transfer into politics after a period of socialization in a Catholic movement.[17] The links between experience in Catholic Action and support for the Left hold for priests as well as laymen: The largest group of clerical supporters of the Left work in specialized Catholic Action organizations.[18] For those Catholics who come from the trade-union movement (the *Confédération française démocratique du travail*, CFDT), participation in politics has not meant abandoning the organization in which the militants were first engaged in public life.[19] The CFDT activists continue to participate in politics primarily through the union; while those brought into collective action by Catholic Action usually leave these associations behind when they move to the Left.

The former Catholic Action participants and the CFDT members constitute a reserve of potential political activists, important both because of absolute numbers and because older reservoirs of political militants are drying up. Practicing Catholics are far more likely to belong to associations than are either Left or Right non-churchgoers.[20] But though Catholics have participated more in associations, in the past they have not been active in political parties. Until recent years, even Catholics with Left inclinations avoided membership in political parties. For example, a survey in early 1968 of members of the predominantly Left-Catholic communitarian movement Vie Nouvelle found that reforming politics in France (*"formation d'un vrai parti de la gauche non-communiste"*) ranked low in their priorities, far behind international issues like the Vietnam War and Third World development.[21] Of these Vie Nouvelle Catholics, only 13 percent belonged to political parties while 27 percent were members of "sociocultural organizations" (for literacy, against famine, for UNESCO, and so forth) and 31 percent participated in religious groups.[22] Since Catholics vote at rates higher than those of the population at large, the unwillingness to participate in political parties needs special explanation. But whatever its causes, the impact in the past of a participation limited to voting was to strengthen the Right.

The benefits to the Left, therefore, of a breakdown both of the constraints that once bound Catholics to the Right and of Catholic reluctance to participate in parties go well beyond any electoral advantages. The real significance lies in an increased capacity for mobilization and the enlarged organizational resources that accrue to the Left as it taps a reservoir of militants whose formative collective experiences include intense participation in Catholic subcultural associations and who retain a high propensity for activism. As militants within Left parties and movements, as highly visible models for Catholics still moving away from old religious-political moorings, these recruits are, if nothing else, important new troops for all groups on the Left. And this is a resource of no small significance in a period in which party participation and membership are on the decline. But do these new activists bring anything more to the Left than reinforcement for the old ideas and institutions?

The theories confronted

Neither of the two general views of religious decline and political change laid out above can account for the trajectories of all three Catholic populations, though each of them explains some part of the picture. The secularization hypothesis seems confirmed for those groups in which declining religious practice is associated with new Left voting. And for these groups, the notion that those who abandon faith in traditional religion reinvest it in extremist politics appears refuted, since the leveling-off of high rates of religious observance in once conservative Catholic regions has only evened out to national patterns the rates of electoral support for the Left. The decline of religion has not provided any extra premium for the Left, nor has it reinforced extremist factions within the Left or Right. Indeed, in the

1984 elections to the European Parliament in which Jean-Marie Le Pen's Front National made major gains, the former Catholic bastions of western and eastern France were among the regions in which this extreme Right party did least well. For those French citizens who no longer go to church regularly and who participate in politics mainly by voting, the political effects of religious decline apparently are to align behavior with that of the rest of the nation, as the secularization theorists had foreseen.

The weakness of the secularization thesis emerges, however, when one considers two other sets of Catholics: the faithful, who continue to practice regularly, and the militants. For devout Catholics, there has been no separation of the affairs of religion and politics, since those who "keep the faith," or at least keep going to church with the same frequency, have barely modified their political behavior. The numbers of practicing Catholics who vote for the Left have not risen significantly. Apparently what is happening is not primarily a dissociation of faith and politics, as the secularization thesis predicts, but rather the disappearance of religion (or at least of its external manifestations) and a subsequent shift in political behavior. The notion that religious faith and practice are compatible with virtually any politics is not confirmed by the patterns of change and continuity in mass politics in France. There is little evidence at the mass level for the proposition that religious commitment can be detached from specific political consequences.

Finally, the secularization explanation sheds little light on the political evolution of a third population: the Catholic activists, whose first experiences of militancy and participation took place within the associations of the Catholic subculture and who have now shifted en masse into Left politics. If the secularization hypothesis cannot account for why the most participant members of the Catholic community have not evenly distributed themselves over the entire political spectrum but rather have clustered on the Left, does the political religion hypothesis provide a better understanding? Alain Besançon, Juan Miguel Garrigues, and other conservative intellectuals in their wake, have claimed that the shift of Catholics to the Left represents a kind of conversion, in which transcendent hopes and faith that once had been channeled into religion are poured into political commitments. They draw parallels between the two churches, Catholic and communist, and between the modes of authority, membership, and salvation that the convert seeks in each.[23] The passionate embrace of the new political religion in this view requires turning against the old faith. Of the convert they say, as Sainte-Beuve, paraphrasing Racine, did of the Jansenists, "The church angers him, for his impiety would annihilate the God he has rejected."[24] From this perspective, it is not surprising that those who now vote for the Left are no longer religiously observant. The critical phenomenon is not the dissociation of religion and politics but the loss of religious faith and its reinvestment in politics.

The political religion hypothesis predicts that the migration of Catholic activists into politics will feed into a *particular* set of Left groups, those of extremist, illiberal, and totalitarian cast. The specificities of political recruits from Catholic backgrounds are supposed to propel them toward political groups that propose wholesale social and political transformation, that demand high degrees of discipline and self-abnegation, and hold liberty in contempt. In one sense, this view directly challenges the secularization thesis, which foresees a redistribution of Catholics over all the political spectrum and, within the Left, evenly across all factions. But there is a deeper point of agreement between the two hypotheses, for they both conclude that the Catholics will be absorbed into existing political organizations and the Catholic political legacy dissolved in existing political categories. New wine can be poured into old bottles without bursting them; the integration of Catholics into the political community will not transform it.

And yet, this assimilation is what appears least certain as one considers the impact of the understandings of the world and transformative visions that the militants of Catholic origin have brought with them into Left parties and social movements. The ideas and behavior of these activists express a determined advocacy of distinctive values, priorities, and orientations. Some of these overlap with the views of the secularist Left; others diverge widely. The entry of these political ideas into the French Left has provoked new tensions and stirred up old controversies. On issues such as decentralization and worker self-management, the new Left militants have reopened old battles by rediscovering and championing causes long ago defeated in internecine Left conflicts. The activists of Catholic origins have also, paradoxically, played a part in the revival of the church–state issue. It was in large measure to resist the new currents in Left politics that other Socialists and Communists pushed the Mitterrand government so hard to make the nationalization of Catholic schools a high priority. In order to reassert the secularist republican tradition of the Left against the new politics, to rally the Left on familiar battle lines under banners proclaiming the Republic's right to educate all its children, and thereby to marginalize the supporters of a new Left, the old anticlerical battle was once again joined. The result was a wave of protest against governmental intervention in private schools more massive than any mobilization since May-June 1968. The government retreated in defeat.

In the clash between the ideas and expectations that the Catholics bring with them into Left politics and the objectives and practices that now prevail within these organizations arise opportunities for change in ideology and institutions. To understand the origins and internal dynamic of the orientations borne into politics by the new militants, one must return to the organizations and worldview from which these agents of ferment set forth.

The original matrix

The common point of departure for the Catholic militants is participation in organizations shaped by the great struggle of the second half of the nineteenth century within the church over its survival in a liberal, democratic society. This controversy within the church produced, broadly speaking, two camps, the liberals and the integralists. The main organizational heirs on the integralist side are the Catholic Action movements, founded in 1886 and then reorganized as "specialized" associations in the 1920s. The organizational heir on the liberal side is the Confédération française démocratique du travail (CFDT), founded in 1919 as a Catholic trade-union confederation, the Confédération française des travailleurs chrétiens (CFTC), and deconfessionalized and renamed in 1964. The descendant that has failed to establish its claims in this line of succession is the Christian-Democratic political party, Mouvement Républicain Populaire (MRP), founded in 1944. Of this current there remained after the mid-sixties only several small parties living off the vestiges of MRP cadres and electorate.

Christian democracy

Before laying out the worldviews of integralist and liberal camps and their distinctive contributions to contemporary politics, it is worth considering the case of the "failed heir," if only to note that Christian Democracy has played a minor role in mediating the politico-religious transformations of the past three decades in France.[25] The fact of this "absence" is an intriguing one: As Jean-Marie Mayeur notes, the MRP has been the only one of the great Christian-Democratic parties founded in the surge of postwar political reconstruction in Europe to have disappeared. The immediate cause of the MRP's demise was the victory of a strong Gaullist party that absorbed much of the MRP electorate. But why was the MRP, the largest party in France in June

1946, with 28 percent of the vote, so vulnerable to raids on its cadres and electors by a new center-right party?

In retrospect, the real weakness of the MRP was its inability to attract the generations of Catholics who came to public life with the institutional experience and political vision of either the integralist or the liberal traditions. Politically conservative integralists kept away from the MRP, their old antipathy for party politics having been strongly reinforced by experiences of Vichy, the Occupation, and the intense political polarization of the immediate postwar. Individuals of this generation sometimes voted for the MRP, but as a group they did not rally to the party. Many of them turned their efforts to the reconstruction of the corporatist associations which had been the strongholds of conservative integralism in the Third Republic.[26] In contrast, the interwar generation of integralist militants who had passed through Third Republic Catholic Action movements were for a time an important pool for the MRP. Half of the MRP legislators chosen in the 1945 and 1946 elections were former Catholic Action participants.[27] But the great wave of Catholic Action members of the postwar years would never regard the MRP as the natural destination of their militant lives. By the mid-fifties this group considered the MRP a party like the others, perhaps even worse – after the MRP sabotage of the Mendès-France government and its equivocation over decolonization. Large numbers of postwar generations of Catholic Action militants would remain outside party politics until the late sixties, when successive experience with protest against the Algerian War, then participation in the May-June 1968 movement brought them into Left politics.[28]

The MRP also failed to channel into politics the militants who had been organizationally socialized by the liberal Catholic tradition. The Catholic trade-union movement (*Confédération française des travailleurs chrétiens*, CFTC) in 1946 asserted its "total independence" of the party, refused to support MRP governments or any other, and decided that union leaders should not hold political offices.[29] This early and decisive turn against links between the union and the Christian-Democratic Party was all the more telling of the MRP's incapacity to exploit the materials provided by the Catholic past because of the apparent affinities between the two organizations: Major CFTC leaders had figured in the top ranks of the early MRP, and the CFTC would retain its "Christian" attachments and label until the end of 1964.

The measure of the MRP's failure can best be gauged by comparison with Christian-Democratic party politics elsewhere in Europe. In Italy, for example, *Democrazia cristiana* has been able to appeal to both the liberals and the integralists.[30] It has exploited to the full the ambiguities of being at the same time (1) a *party of Catholics*, the formula of the interwar *popolari*, which expresses political independence of the hierarchy; (2) a *Catholic party*, that is, one with objectives determined by the church, which it serves as a kind of political arm; and (3) the largest conservative party in the country. Oscillating among these political formulas for organizing Catholics, the DC has been able to pull in an extremely broad sweep of the electorate. A large stream of Catholic Action leaders continues to flow into DC party organizations. And until the early 1970s, relations between the Catholic trade union and the party remained close enough that unionists held party positions and elective offices. In achieving this hegemony within the Catholic political community, the DC profited from two indisputable advantages that the French did not have. In Italy, the hierarchy retained tight control over Catholic Action movements and this greatly facilitated the channeling of its elites into the party. Secondly, the experience of fascism had left an organizational vacuum on the Right and center-Right that the DC occupied rather easily. The handicaps of other contenders for this space were so great that although the DC could not entirely disregard them, it could maintain a strong Left faction within the party leadership without losing favor and influence with rightist voters.

Thus, unlike the MRP, the DC's strategies and the favorable historical circumstances in which it was founded made it possible for the Italian party to draw support from all segments of the Catholic political community. The original and fatal weakness of the MRP was, precisely, a corresponding incapacity to attract the masses and the activists of the major political currents of French Catholicism. There was an earlier tradition of Christian Democracy that fed into the MRP, but this tradition was not itself broad enough to support a major party. Christian Democracy's prewar bases had been rather narrow, and they only partially overlapped with the "natural constituency" of a Christian-Democratic party, that is, with the population of religiously faithful mass-attending Catholics. Indeed, by 1956 the MRP could attract only about one-third of this "natural constituency."[31] With thin roots in Catholic terrain, with conservative credentials less reliable than those of the old center and moderate parties, the MRP was condemned, once the Gaullists organized as a party, for the Gaullist party combined centrist politics with a leader capable of winning a mass following in all social classes. The MRP refused to be a Catholic party; it failed to become a party of Catholics; it was bested as a conservative party.

The liberals

In the great debates among Catholics in the nineteenth century over religion and politics, liberalism referred to a heterogeneous mix of doctrines and sentiments that were internally neither consistent nor coherent.[32] Their considerable ambiguities allowed for the coexistence within the same person of quite contradictory ideas. What defeated Catholic liberalism in the nineteenth century, however, was papal interdiction, not internal confusion. And when liberalism of Catholic origin came into its own in the mid-twentieth century, with the transformation and triumphant expansion of the CFDT, it was not because liberalism had acquired a coherent ideological substance; rather, it was because the political orientations and values of one part of the old Catholic liberal program had been embodied in an organization successful in identifying and formulating new political demands.

The dominant ideas in Catholic liberalism until the middle of the century were only in minor part those of the classic liberal. Lamennais, Montalembert, and Lacordaire did seek liberty in the sense of a limitation of the powers of the state, at least with respect to religion. But they also imagined as the highest ideal a society in which religion and politics would be reunited. Such a program required regrounding politics on the basis of an essentially religious morality and reconciling religion with modern politics by transfusing the church itself with democratic values and condemning the alliance between the ancien régime and the church, an alliance the liberals regarded as circumstantial, mistaken, and *contre nature*. A series of papal condemnations of these views and of those who professed them culminated in the *Syllabus of Errors* (Pius IX) in 1864, which decisively cut the ground out from under those Catholics who believed that liberalism in any sense represented a possible bridge between modern society and the Catholic church.

What survived of Catholic liberalism was a conception of the proper spheres of religion, politics, and society and of the norms and institutions that could maintain the boundaries between the spheres. This set of notions was the de facto basis for the politics of the many Catholics who rejected integralist theses, rather than an explicitly articulated view. When justification for such a separation of spheres was formulated, stress was usually laid on its importance for the survival of religion in a modern society. This was the kind of argument that Tocqueville had laid out already in *Democracy in America*:

I am so much alive to the almost inevitable dangers which beset religious belief whenever the clergy take part in public affairs, and I am so convinced that Christianity must be maintained at any cost in the bosom of modern democracies, that I had rather shut up the priesthood within the sanctuary than allow them to step beyond it.[33]

But neither the climate of French Catholicism nor, indeed, that of postrevolutionary France was favorable to the flourishing of political ideas that were liberal in this sense.

The institutional expansion of the liberal current in French Catholicism came only when a set of ideas about the autonomy of politics and the separation of economic, religious, and social spheres of life were associated with a particular set of organizational strategies in the syndical practice of the CFDT. In the early postwar years, the reformers of the reconstruction current of the CFTC explicitly espoused a view of politics which distinguished its moral basis from that of religion and which sharply rejected all notions, theological or Marxist, about the absolute character of the interests and values at stake in politics.[34] They wrote that political choices reflect the nature of "political reality, which despite certain elements of determinism, mainly is shaped by events, by wills, and by the unpredictable exercise of freedom."

Neither as knowledge nor as action can politics ever be certain and complete. Politics is a mix of knowledge of facts and adherence to particular values. It oscillates constantly between an analysis of the present and a surge towards the future. What distinguishes politics in this sense from simple pragmatism is a concern for a better future; what distinguishes it from dogmatism is the conviction that the future will always exceed our predictions.[35]

However important this intellectual formulation for the reformers' self-clarification and evolution, its broad political influence in French society derived not from its presentation as a set of ideas but from its "enactment" in a set of CFDT organizational orientations and strategies. As Paul Vignaux has described, the organizational changes advocated by the reformers of liberal pragmatic persuasion extracted the union from party and church affiliations. The construction of an autonomous sphere for syndical activity – in a country in which the dominant union, the CGT, was tightly linked to the Communist Party – was enormously important for the political space it offered to dissident, defeated, but still vital syndical traditions. CFDT autonomy provided a shelter where, alongside the trade unionists of old Catholic CFTC stamp, there prospered and multiplied in new mutations the remnants of earlier syndical traditions that had been driven out of main-line Left organizations by the SFIO and the Communists. Some of the most important new leaders of the CFDT were men like Albert Detraz and Marcel Gonin, whose political roots lay not in the traditional Catholic matrix but in anarcho-syndicalism and in a variety of socialist minority cultures.

A haven for political syndical traditions in exile from a Left dominated by anticlericalism and Marxism of rigidly orthodox persuasion, the CFDT also has provided fertile terrain for the germination of new ideas. Some of these resulted from grafting perceptions of new social needs and observations of syndical practices in other countries onto older, half-forgotten elements in the French syndical tradition, as in the case of *autogestion* (worker self-management). Fruitful intuitions that 1968 confirmed about new demands in French society for more flexible and informal exercise of authority and growing resistance to the old work hierarchies and disciplines, a sympathetic curiosity about experiences of worker control elsewhere, and the rediscovery within the ideological baggage that some of their own members brought along with them of anticentralist and antistatist orientations – all these elements led to the CFDT "discovery" of *autogestion*. What is significant here, as in the CFDT's discoveries of democratic planning or of solidarity as a distributive principle, was not so much the substance of the doctrinal innovation in itself. Most of these ideas were eclectic: powerful not for their theoretical coherence or radicality but because they combined old and enduring values from previously isolated or mutually hostile subcultures of the French political community and put them together to identify new issues and demands. Some of the doctrines thus generated were indeed rather short-lived. What is most important is that the organization provided space and encouragement for a tolerant, pragmatic, even opportunistic experimentation with new political ideas.

These features survived the organization's move to the Left, that is, its move to closer cooperation with the Socialists, after the *Assises du socialisme* in 1974. They have come to be seen as constituting an alternative model, a "second Left," one without the ideological rigidities of the traditional Left, one that practices a more open, democratic, pragmatic mode of representation, one that might even be considered liberal, in a society where that term was less tightly associated with bourgeois interests and politics than it has been in France.[36]

The integralists

Liberal and integralist Catholicism do not translate into Left and Right politics. Indeed, most Left Catholics are determinedly antiliberal, having, as René Rémond has put it, "skipped the liberal, democratic phase" in their move to socialism.[37] When, for example, Socialist leaders met with heads of Catholic organizations to discuss problems likely to arise over the fate of Catholic schools were the Left to win the 1978 elections, virtually the only defenders of the liberal thesis were the nonbelievers.[38] The most hostile to liberal views of those present at the meeting were the Left Catholics. A Socialist freemason, Roger Fajardie, argued for a simple division of labor between socialism and religion with "religion responding to the problem of the origins and final ends of life, and socialism seeking to provide men with the best possible life in the interval between birth and death." The Socialists' mission would be to transform daily life and "all the rest belongs to the realm of each person's own private life."[39] Thus, there are no grounds on which Socialists and Catholics should ever meet, let alone come into conflict. The Catholics present violently attacked this view. They denied that religion is a personal fact and argued that as good Catholics, they were obliged to bring their religious convictions to bear in their politics, that is, in their evaluation of socialist political practice, and that as good Socialists, they were obliged to bring the political insights they derived from Marxism to bear in their religious practice and in their participation within the church. The Vie Nouvelle leader Philippe Warnier, a Socialist, summarized: "For me, a Christian, nothing in politics should escape the judgement that faith, evangelical criticism and religious meaning suggest. Similarly, it seems to me that nothing that comes from faith and the Church ought to escape a political judgement. Since we are members of a political party, this is our business."[40]

What is at stake between liberal and integralist Catholic traditions is not Left or Right politics but entirely opposed conceptions of the relation between religion and politics. As Emile Poulat has expressed it, a liberal Catholic might be socialist *and* Catholic; an integralist would be socialist *because* he was Catholic. For the integralist, it is "not that faith unites those whom politics divides, but that faith is the ultimate judge of all, even where men cannot agree on what that judgement is. Politics is justified or condemned by faith; it is submitted to a higher principle instead of being left autonomous."[41]

Vatican II dealt mortal blows to the theological bases of integralism; the crumbling of the walls that protected the Catholic subculture from the outside community undermined the organizational solutions of integralism; and participation in Left parties has destroyed its political foundations. But the map that integralism provided for understanding society and the state and for charting a course of action within politics continues invisibly to orient much in the ideas and behavior of Left Catholic militants. The peculiar features of this legacy account for the specificities of the Catholics' contributions to Left politics.

The fundamental integralist objectives that were laid out in the last half of the nineteenth century were a reconquest of society and an "integral" application to it of principles derived from Catholic belief. Integralism rejected the notion that any spheres of life lay beyond the reach of religious regulation. The doctrines of Social Catholicism, then, far from reflecting any liberalization of the church, were central to the integralist definition of the church's role in modern democratic societies, for they were blueprints for the restructuring of all social relationships within a Catholic world.[42]

The implementation of the integralist project involved enormous transformation within the church: major theological shifts, the development of a Catholic subculture, the adaptation for "domestic" purposes of ways of dealing with outsiders that had been pioneered in missionary work in underdeveloped countries, and new relations between clerics and laymen. The amplitude of these shifts was magnified in France, for as a result of the Revolution and the continuing hostilities between republicans and Catholics, the French church had become quite dependent upon Rome. Under the control of an ultramontane hierarchy, the French church launched into the reform of practice, doctrine, and institutions with a vengeance.

The changes introduced in the half-century following the *Syllabus of Errors* responded to the modern world by building walls to shield the church from "progress, liberalism, and recent civilization." At the heart of this operation were theological shifts that sharply demarcated the church and the faithful from the outside world. An institutional vision of the church, in Avery Dulles's suggestive analysis, had been strong in Catholicism since the Counter-Reformation, and in the second part of the nineteenth century achieved a kind of hegemony that obliterated other visions of the church.[43] Its central understanding was of the church as a perfect, complete society, analogous to – indeed, coterminous with – civil society and the state. Reinforcing this emphasis was a powerfully enunciated return to Thomism.[44]

Critical to the institutional conception was the "visibility" both of the structures and hierarchy of the church and of its membership. The practical implementation of this thrust in the ultramontane reforms of the nineteenth century was a tightening up of all those rules that distinguished religion from profane activity and a continual pressure for more frequent participation in the rites of the church. The shift in emphasis from a definition of the community of the faithful as the broad community of the baptized to one in which the faithful are those who confess and take communion frequently; the downgrading of popular religion and the attack on "superstitious" utilization of church symbols and rituals; the segregation by dress and life-style of the clergy, as the wearing of the cassock and special garb became required – these and many other accompanying changes in the life of the church served to draw sharp lines between who was in and who was out. As documented in local and regional histories, these new rules had a profound impact on Catholic communities.[45]

Such efforts at self-preservation moved the church closer to the model of the Protestant churches. In Paul Tillich's terms, the Catholic church shifted from a sacramental toward a theocratic type of church.[46] Tillich argued that the critical test of whether a church is sacramental or theocratic is the principle of membership: birthright membership through infant baptism signifies sacramentalism in Catholicism; elective membership of adults signifies theocracy in Protestantism.[47] The new stress in late-nineteenth-century Catholicism on the regular performance of the rites and the tendency to regard those who were baptized but did not partake frequently of the sacraments as "dechristianized" or even "pagan" brought the church closer to the Protestant view of a religious community.

The second major way in which integralist reforms broke with the sacramental mode was in their ambition to reorder society in accordance with God's law. Tillich finds such an objective characteristic of theocracy and foreign to sacramentalism:

> Sacramental churches have the character of a mother, who carries and includes her children. You belong to such a church, from birth to death, without a real decision on your own part. It is not your willing and acting that constitute the church, but the church constitutes you and your will and your activity. Holiness is a reality and only in the second place is it a commandment. . . .
>
> Sin and error do not separate you from it. Moral and social perfection do not unite you with it. Just as the relation between mother and child is incapable of being destroyed by good or bad activities on the part of the children, so a sacramental religion has a social function only by consequence, not by intention. . . .[48]
>
> In contrast to this attitude, theocracy deals with the problem of realizing the will of God. . . . [It] uses political power in order to change social institutions and individual morality in obedience to the divine commandments. Prophetic religion is the highest form of a theocratic attempt to subject a nation, its social and individual morality to the justice of the Kingdom of God.[49]

In the absence of any prospects for a reconquest of all society, the Church reformers proposed to build a world for the faithful within which social relations would be ordered in accordance with Catholic teachings. The integralists sought to Christianize the world by carving out in it a protected sphere within which Catholic social doctrines would organize collective life. They tried to incarnate religious beliefs in the values and institutions of a Catholic subculture. Rather than seeking for signs of God's will in the world at large and in its changes, they sought to anticipate the coming of the Kingdom of God by hunkering down in a closed society which they barricaded against the world.

The church built a dense and wide-ranging network of associations to draw in Catholics at all stages of life and from all social categories. This interlocking series of organizations included groups with specifically religious aims, like the Enfants de Marie; groups with professional objectives that paralleled associations with similar constituencies in the "outside world," for instance, Catholic sports teams, Catholic lawyers' associations; and finally, and most important in the network of Catholic organizations of the past fifty years, groups with the objective of penetrating and transforming classes (*milieux*) and their distinctive social environments. The specialized Catholic Action associations were founded in the 1920s, for workers, students, peasants, professionals, and so forth.

This cluster of organizations constituted a closed Catholic world or subculture, with sharply defined and well-protected frontiers between members and outsiders.[50] The comprehensiveness of the organizational range within the Catholic subculture, the importance of doctrine and the defense of orthodoxy, the tight mesh between doctrine and organizational embodiment, the relationships between the core of lay and clerical militants at the center of the system and the outer circle of passive believers – all this resembles the patterns of subcultural development that took place in roughly the same period on the extreme Left.[51] The Catholic subculture, like the Communist subculture, worked to encircle and protect believers, to instill a particular set of values and behaviors, and to build in microcosm the kind of society that the church hoped to establish for the nation as a whole one day.

The subcultural structures that French Catholicism set in place in the effort to survive and protect its world in an unfriendly environment withdrew large numbers of Catholics from the political community. Hostile to the Republic, opposed to the emerging liberal capitalist order, and organized in institutions that duplicated republican associations in a parallel but self-contained network, Catholics in the subculture participated little – beyond voting – in national politics. And yet, paradoxically, despite the church's hostility to the state and its attempts to encapsulate Catholics in a world as impermeable as possible to the influences of a secular and liberal society, the impact of this subcultural development was in many ways to consolidate and stabilize the political and social order. The church did so not only by electoral support for the Right, but also by channeling the activism of the faithful into participation in social movements within the subculture.

The strong distinctions in Catholic social doctrines between society and the state and between social activism and political militance were translated organizationally into sharp distinctions between participation in institutions within the subculture and participation in politics outside it. Catholic militants were engaged from youth in channels which fed them at each of life's professional and private junctures into the next set of subcultural associations. The young Scout naturally progressed into the Jeunesse Etudiante Chrétienne (JEC) and then into Action Catholique Indépendante (ACI). The young worker when he married moved from the Jeunesse Ouvrière Chrétienne (JOC) into Action Catholique Ouvrière (ACO). Although in the early postwar period many Christian-Democratic leaders were former Catholic Action activists, there was no organic link between the interlocking networks of subcultural organizations and the MRP party, as there was in Italy. The integralist conceptions of collective activity to refashion society by militance in social movements were counterposed to notions of political action in a fashion so radical as to block attempts to harness the subculture to a political party.

As Catholics gathered within the confines of a community redefined by integralist reforms, the outside world came to seem strange, menacing, and pagan. As Emile Poulat has recorded in *Naissance des prêtres-ouvriers*, the discovery that France was no longer a country of Christians was one made regularly after the last quarter of the nineteenth century.[52] The infrequency of church attendance among urban workers focused debate over how to Christianize society on a more specific issue: how to reconquer the working class. Priests noted with horror a "rampant paganism"; workers "as strange to us as savages living on beaches, savannas, in forests. . . . [Ivry-Port, a working-class suburb of Paris] is a barbarian land, with savages, pagans; for them Christ has never come."[53] Watching the long procession that transported the remains of Anatole France and Jean Jaurès to the Pantheon in 1924, Père Lhande saw the workers marching in the parade as "hybrid, amorphous beings that only come out on the eve of great earthquakes, just as some kinds of toads and night animals come out only in the heavy hours before a storm. There were all those pariahs, the undesirables, men with the crooked faces of degenerates, followed by women of even more sinister aspect."[54] "The greatest scandal of the nineteenth century," proclaimed Joseph Cardijn, the founder of the Jeunesse Ouvrière Chrétienne, "is that the Catholic Church has lost the working class."[55]

Once shaped by a vision of a Catholic world enclosed within sharply defined boundaries with a pagan world outside, the problem appeared as one familiar from the church's long missionary experience in non-European societies.[56] The two great missionary efforts that grew out of this analysis were the Catholic Action movement that appeared in France in the 1920s and the worker-priest movement founded after World War II. The first relied on organizing lay Catholics under the direct supervision of clerical advisors (*aumoniers*) to bring back to Christianity men and women from the same social group (*milieu*) as the missionary's. Peasants would go to peasants; workers to workers; students to students. "We will make our brothers Christian again, by Jesus Christ we swear it," sang the young workers in the JOC. These associations were to be mass movements of ordinary people, replacing the study and prayer groups of small elites that the church had promoted in the nineteenth century. Catholic Action movements made explicit one of the principal tenets of integralist belief: that religion should not be simply a matter of private life, but a commitment to collective action.

There was significant resistance within the clergy to this discrediting of faith lived out as private belief and worship within the community of practicing Catholics.[57] But the mass conceptions of Catholic Action triumphed within the French church, and with them, the notion that the best Catholic is not the one who tends his own faith and tries to order his private life in accordance with it, but rather the person whose faith leads to militance beyond the frontiers of the regularly practicing Catholic parish. Given the rigorous distinctions that operated in integralist thought between society and the state and between activism within subcultural organizations and participation in the despised political parties, the shift from private faith and practice to public commitment did not yet spill over into politics. But the ground was laid here for a significant absorption into the bounds of the political of activities and sentiments that previously had been conceived of as part of private life. As the Belgian founder of Catholic Action for workers, Abbé Cardijn, put it: "No more apostolate on the side-lines of life, but all of life becoming apostolic again in order to conquer the masses; the whole real context of life becoming once again a field for the extension of the Kingdom of God."[58]

The Catholic Action movements were set to studying their own conditions of life: to "see, evaluate, and act on" (*voir–juger–agir*) everything that diminished the possibilities for a full development of the human being (ACJF, 1964). All forms of oppression, exploitation, and servitude were to be identified and eradicated. How they were to be eliminated remained rather vague. What was critical – both for the expansion of Catholic Action and for its ultimate influence on politics beyond the Catholic community – was the application of the integralist grid to the task of identifying an extremely wide range of kinds of exploitation and suffering that impoverished and diminished human beings. It would be through the extended application of this integralist grid that Catholics discovered north–south relations, foreign workers, torture at home and abroad, French colonialism in Algeria, the problems of Palestinians, Biafrans, Cambodians, of hunger in the world.

The second great missionary movement was the worker-priests.[59] Starting after World War II from the same notion of a pagan working class that the church (including, now, the Catholic Action movements) had failed to reach, the worker-priests concluded that the missionaries before them had not grasped the radical and irreversible alienation of the working class from existing Christian institutions. Missionary effort would succeed only when the missionary stripped himself completely of his original culture and assimilated himself entirely to the working-class world.[60] The missionary comes to the workers not to uplift them but to join them and become one of them. The missionary must divest himself of his old way of life, his culture, his values, for they are parts of a bourgeois world that separate him from working-class life. As the head of the worker-priest group, the superior of the Mission de Paris, expressed it:

> We are the *francs-tireurs* of the clergy, parachuted into pagan territory, not to blow anything up, but simply to bear witness. To do so, we desire to incarnate ourselves as fully as possible in the heart of the working masses. We never forget that the priest is a consecrated, not an isolated person; that he ought to work in the setting in which he lives. We desire to incarnate everything, except sin. We think constantly of the words of Saint Paul: "Christ emptied himself and took the form of a slave, being born in the likeness of men." (Phil.II, 7.) In living like workers we must sacrifice the traditional priestly way of life; if necessary, sacrifice health and even reputation, in order to be wholly one with the human communities of neighborhood, work, and leisure.[61]

The working class is so alien to the condition of civilized man that the priest's sacrifice in becoming a worker was compared to Christ's sacrifice.

> Some callings mutilate. . . . A missionary usually cannot readapt himself to his own country. If a man has really thrown himself into the Mission de Paris, he may never be capable of anything else again. There may be a certain regression on the personal level. One may abandon as much in remaining as a missionary in Paris as in going off to Africa.[62]

The vision of a priest who converts the heathen "by sharing their collective fate [*communauté de destin*], by becoming one with them"[63] expressed in the most powerful way old and deep currents in Catholic thought: that the Christian is unified with those who suffer, that the Christian changes the world by incarnating the new in his own life and works. Incarnation would become a mode of political militance as the result of successive efforts to carry out the integralist project in the working class. For Catholics who would move into Left politics after the 1960s, incarnation shaped a special understanding of democracy and a specific set of expectations about the agencies of social change.

First, in the sense most fully developed by the worker-priests, incarnation suggested solidarity and fusion with the most suffering groups in society as the highest form of political commitment. In the two decades after World War II, it was the industrial workers who absorbed the commitment of Catholic militants motivated by this solidaristic vision of political action. The workers seemed to these Catholics to have been condemned for life to unremittingly harsh, poorly paid, and unrespected labor and isolated by indestructible barriers from French bourgeois society. Later, the same reflexes of thought worked to propel the activists into solidaristic identification with immigrants and other subproletarian groups at home and with the poor of the underdeveloped world.

The Catholics saw themselves neither as intellectuals with some specialized knowledge that would make them an avant-garde of the masses nor as the possessors of special experience or education that would make them natural representatives of the people. The militant act is one of personal solidarity. From that act of solidarity and fusion *follow* various views about the world and historical change that the militant acquires along with the other distinguishing marks of his new milieu. From that may follow a role as a representative or leader. But political theories and leadership roles are the consequence of a completely assumed solidarity, and not its motivation. One of the worker-priests who defied the church's order to leave the factory and went on to high office in the CGT metalworkers' union and to Communist Party membership remembers going into the plant with the idea that "the real form of love is solidarity, in life and in death."[64] Entering the factory in order to become part of the "very body of the working class," the man then found it "logical" to pursue this identification to the end, that is, to join the CGT and the Party. Ideas about building a new society, Marxist conceptions of economy and history came later, a consequence, as he explained, of belonging to the working class. Asked whether he had become a syndicalist and a Communist in order to make the revolution, he reflected that his original idea had been to change relations among men, but that changing social structures was a notion he acquired very soon after: "The revolution seemed a normal thing. It was the goal of the workers with whom I was. And I would go even that far to be with them."

A fundamental Catholic doctrine, incarnation derives its full force as a template for political thought from its association with the sacramentalism of Catholic ecclesiology. Richard P. McBrien explains the sacramentalism of the Catholic as one which " 'sees' the divine in the human" and finds God's purposes at work in the material stuff of everyday life.[65] Sacramentality in this sense encompasses incarnation and provides a template not only for models of personal action in politics but also for conceptions of how the world is changing and for the connections between action in the present and longterm objectives.

The Kingdom of God is built in part of human accomplishments in the present. In the Catholic view, McBrien explains, "The history of the world is, at the same time, the history of salvation. This means for the Catholic that authentic human progress and the struggle for justice, peace, freedom, human rights, and so forth, is part of the movement of and toward the Kingdom of God (Vatican II, Pastoral Constitution on the Church in the Modern World, n.39.) To be involved in the transformation of the world is to be collaboratively involved in God's own revolutionary and transforming activity."[66]

The notion that human beings participate in bringing about the Kingdom of God has nourished diverse political visions in the Catholic community. The sociological and political ambiguities of this religious doctrine allow even the same group of Catholics to shift rather rapidly among different interpretations. Danièle Hervieu-Léger has, for example, shown how, under the combined pressures of internal debate and ferment and the events of the May-June 1968 student revolt, a group of Catholic university students moved from a proselytizing concept of collaboration in the construction of the Kingdom of God, to a notion of bearing witness with one's own life and values, to prophetic, even millennarian visions.[67] These alternative religious views implied very different forms of politics; and, in fact, the students in the group Hervieu-Léger studied went off in all directions.

The variations in the political interpretations militants draw from the template laid out by the principle of sacramentality and the doctrines associated with the Kingdom of God are, however, constrained by an ancillary principle about means and ends, a kind of religious corollary of sacramentality. This notion is critical for understanding how the militants would transpose the religious template onto the field of political action. First, as McBrien explains, "a sacrament not only signifies; it also causes what it signifies. [The Church] 'causes' grace (i.e., effectively moves the world toward its final destiny in the

Kingdom of God) to the extent that it signifies the reality toward which it presumes to direct the world."[68]

To participate in the creation of the Kingdom of God, men and women must consider their actions and commitments not as instrumental toward a final goal but as part of that final goal. The notion of efficacy at work here is not so much that of choosing means which are rational for obtaining particular ends as that of identifying and collaborating in current works that signify and thus embody the Kingdom of God.[69]

The militants who started from this religious template were led to particular understandings of the relationship between means and ends in politics. First, and most obvious, if means are part of the end, "one cannot collaborate in the Kingdom of God regardless of the means," as, for example, one of the clerical advisors to the Scouts movement warned, at a point when the leaders in that group were moving toward support for the Algerian nationalists.[70] Later, in the same sense, many of the activists of Catholic origins who saw *autogestion* as the heart of the Socialist program would argue against the view that a major extension of state control via nationalizations had to precede *autogestion*. As one man who had been a leader of the JEC in 1968 and later became the editor of a socialist review put it, "Means that are contradictory to an objective destroy the objective."[71]

Beyond the notion that certain means are in and of themselves unacceptable or else contrary to the ends they purport to serve, the transposition of religious principles about means and ends into politics led Catholic militants to regard the values, institutions, and ways of life they were presently developing as pieces of the future.[72] In the ideas of Catholic militants of virtually all political persuasions, there is a recurrent focus on what can be created now, whether in small "total" communities, or social experiments in schools, local government, and hospitals, or in work.[73] Thus one militant, a CERES Socialist, the manager of what remained of the Lip watch factory, described his principal political activity as "keep Lip alive."[74] Once the heroic days of *autogestion* at Lip were over; when the Lip workers were no longer the shining example of what a fraternal community of producers could do, even under capitalism; once even the CFDT and the Socialists had given up on Lip, why did this militant continue? "Partly out of outrage at the violation of human dignity and trust when all the promises to the workers were broken; partly because of friendship and respect for them. But also, though I believe that in the long run our society has to be completely transformed, and Christianity, too, has this long-term hope and faith, I also believe *we must incarnate this hope right now*."[75] The political translation of religious views about how to build the Kingdom of God is the conviction that the concrete accomplishments that hope and faith inspire in the present are truly valuable, and not simply reformist compromises that ameliorate life under capitalism, while real politics works for the revolution.

Integralist ideas enter Left politics

I tell you, most solemnly, unless a wheat grain fall on the ground and dies it remains only a single grain; but if it dies, it yields a rich harvest. (John 12:24)

None of the integralist projects for reconquering a world made pagan by secularism, democracy, and industrialization succeeded. Indeed, in the effort to rechristianize French society, the church set in motion forces that would progressively erode its own strongest subcultural bases. The centrifugal disintegration of the Catholic world has been attributed to two different but concurrent processes. First, the center did not hold. Drastic changes in church doctrine, organization, and practices destroyed old modes of religious regulation without putting new stable relations into place. Many of these shifts have come to be associated with Vatican II reforms. In fact, the loosening of old connections between hierarchy and followers and among doctrine, belief, and practice went far beyond anything envisaged or sanctioned by the Council. At the center, from which a rigid and coherent set of rules had once emanated, there now seemed to be confusion and loss of direction. The center's new commands were imperfectly transmitted by the hierarchical relays. The faithful paid less and less attention to word from above, and the behavior of Catholics became more and more deviant, as, for example, in the widespread disobedience of papal decrees on birth control.

Secondly, the subcultural organizations that had been mandated to do the church's work in the outside world came under increasingly strong pulls from this world. They were, to put it simply, assimilated by the natives they had come to convert. The attractive power of the larger community has been explained in various ways: as secularization that progressively penetrated and weakened the religious commitment of the missionaries; as the triumph of affluence, which made consumerism so irresistible that missionaries and natives alike abandoned their old rites and were absorbed in the new material pleasures of private life; or, more simply, as the erosion of those features of French society, such as anticlericalism and Jacobinism, that had been specific obstacles to the integration of Catholics into republican France. In whichever combinations, these tides tugged at subcultural organizations that were no longer securely moored to an immovable anchor. The result was the centrifugal dispersion into Left parties and movements of people whose formative political experiences had been those of trying to change the world by implementing in it objectives and strategies elaborated within an integralist frame.

Nothing in the experiences that propelled Catholic Action militants into Left politics eradicated the original integralist urge to implement religiously derived principles in present political, social, and economic realities. The collapse of the walls between the subculture and the larger society allowed Catholic Action militants to move into Left parties and social movements without ever renouncing the integralist ambition of integrating one's political and spiritual hopes and expectations in a single coherent set of beliefs. This passage to politics stands in sharp contrast to the experience of the CFDT militants, whose shift from Christian trade unionism to deconfessional syndicalism and toward involvement in party politics started from an acceptance of liberalism, that is, of the notion that religion and politics constitute two distinct and separable realms of human experience requiring different modes of thought and action. In principle, at least, the Catholic liberals left religion out of their politics, while the militants socialized in the integralist traditions of Catholic Action took with them into politics a highly elaborated set of interpretations and aspirations that originate in a religious vision. In considering, then, what Catholics have brought into Left politics, it is above all the orientations of the activists of subcultural/Catholic Action origins that are at issue. While remnants of religious values and of the CFTC past are not entirely absent in the approach to politics of Catholics of liberal and CFDT origins, they persist here as vestiges. The religiously derived political predispositions are not, as they are for the ex-Catholic Action militants, still vital parts of a whole structure of beliefs and understandings that support basic commitments to political action on the Left.

Much in the Catholic Left ideas about politics coincides with the understandings of the secular and Marxist Left. There is in common a rejection of pragmatism, of the notion that the path to a good society lies through a set of partial solutions, arrived at through successive approaches to discrete problems or through the negotiation of compromises among divergent interests. There is a common conviction that contemporary societies are based on exploitation and injustice and that changes of a revolutionary, not reformist, sort will be needed to uproot this order. There is a fundamental commitment to political action, not to defend men as they are, but man as he could be. As one former Catholic militant reflected when asked why he remained active in his union, despite the cost to his professional career: "Because of hope: a faith that there's something in people beyond the pettiness and stupidity I see every day. I wouldn't be doing all this just to get people higher wages or better working conditions, though they deserve them! Even if there were a more equal distribution of incomes or people got more to eat, *so what*! So what – unless there's something beyond that. I did see something of what people can really be in May-June 1968, and in that kind of collective experience, everyone gets his own. If I didn't believe that something like that was possible, I wouldn't go on, especially when you think how little all our political efforts have amounted to, how little has really changed."[76]

Another former Catholic Action militant, whose political itinerary went from the JEC to UNEF during the Algerian war to the PSU and then into the top leadership ranks of the Socialist Party, described his fundamental commitment to the belief that "man can be better and more than he is today"; that the "American model of man" is unacceptable; that "human beings can relate to each other in ways other than those prescribed by the dominant ideology of today." Our generation of activists, he said, resembles the Jansenists, who, contrary to conventional wisdom, had faith in men, that is, believed that they could become other and better than they were.[77]

The conviction that the fundamental objectives of politics require transforming human beings rejoins some of the most important tenets of belief of the Jacobin and Marxist French Left. But this common conclusion is attached to entirely different chains of assumptions about society and politics in the worldviews of the Left of Catholic integralist origins, on one hand, and the Left of secular, republican origins, on the other. In the world view of the Jacobins and the Marxists, the principal agencies of collective action are political parties and the state. Society is seen as the locus of resistance to change. Social groups are regarded as the crystallization of individual interest. Social diversity and heterogeneity are considered obstacles to progress toward equality and justice. In contrast, the Left Catholics regard civil society as the locus of collective dynamism and creation. They see human beings as capable of self-realization and change through free association with others. Their vision is of a society with an enormous potential for self-organization and collective action. And they see forces of social transformation as straining against the deadening weights of political parties and the state. This revolutionary project thus remains attached to the sharp distinctions between society and state of nineteenth-century French Catholicism. The special attentiveness to the transformative forces at work within society builds on the sensitivities of those educated to look for "the signs of the times," as Pope John XXIII exhorted, in the everyday struggles of ordinary human beings for more dignity.

These political predispositions have found a strong and natural expression in the *autogestionnaire* currents of the Left. They are also remarkably persistent in the politics of Catholics in organizations far less hospitable to such orientations, for example, the Communist Party. Of all French political organizations on the Left, the Communist Party is perhaps the most suspicious of autonomous social groups and the most hostile to recognizing that significant change may come about through spontaneous social movements. This resistance was amply demonstrated in the party's reactions to mass demonstrations against the Algerian War, to May-June 1968, and to the new protest movements of the seventies and eighties. It is all the more striking, then, to find Communists of Catholic origin emphasizing the potential of autonomous social forces and attempting to reconcile this view with more orthodox positions on democratic centralism. An exemplary case of such an effort was presented by Jean-Louis Moynot, a confederal secretary of the CGT and a Communist Party member, whose militancy began in Catholic organizations.[78] Moynot (in 1979) wrote about *autogestion* that while worker demands for more control over the productive process and over working conditions might be co-opted by employers, still there was a possibility of giving a revolutionary thrust to this movement. Similarly, the antinuclear movement, women's liberation, ecologists, tenants' organizations, consumer associations, all express

problems that arise as contradictions in society and between the social base and an invasive oppressive capitalist state, which is less and less able to respond to social needs.... A revolutionary *autogestionnaire* strategy consists of supporting these phenomena and being ready, not to channel them in an authoritarian or paternalist way, but ready and available as an instrument of dialogue and of synthesis: in sum, present as a revolutionary ferment.[79]

Moynot argued that many of the questions raised by the new single-issue movements, by 1968, by Italian trade unionism, indeed, even by Rocard and the *autogestionnaire* currents of the Socialists were not reformist evasions of class struggle. Rather, they identified significant social conflicts that could be brought to a revolutionary issue. Moynot urged in his writings and apparently also within the CGT and the party that the party neither ignore nor take over the new social protest movements, but try to push them beyond their original demands and beyond corporatist formulations. The party is necessary as an agency of synthesis, as an organization that promotes a vision of the social whole and of the long perspective, he acknowledged. But one reads in Moynot and in the statements of other Communists of Catholic origin the persistent conviction that the real sources of political dynamism lie in social movements and that the party's positions threaten to suffocate them rather than to move them on to a wider vision of political action.

Moynot's high rank in the CGT and in the party made his resignation from the confederal bureau in October 1981, after protest over Afghanistan and Poland and over a hardening within the CGT, a special event, but his reactions were not idiosyncratic. Poland in particular was a major crisis of conscience for many Communists of Catholic origin, even those who had "digested" Hungary and Czechoslovakia. In the eyes of these militants, Solidarity was a massive social movement whose genesis and spread clearly owed nothing to political machinations or dissident party elites. It seemed that in repressing the working class the Polish state and party were trying to wipe out the elements of a new society that had spontaneously burst forth in the confines of the old order. The doubts these militants had stored up about how the French Communist Party (PCF) had ignored or tried to sabotage the 1968 demonstrations of students and workers, about how it had dismissed the social protest movements of the seventies, and about how it had reversed an apparent shift toward greater democratization and decentralization in party and CGT structures, were all crystallized by Poland. The fate of Solidarity seemed to exemplify in the large the deficiencies of a model of politics based on a hegemonic party and a centralized state. The conflicts generated within the CGT and the Communist Party by the political orientations of the militants of Catholic origins have hardly transformed these organizations, though convergence of this current with other, wider streams of Communist dissent has contributed to the present ideological turmoil in the party.

Within the Socialist Party (PS), in contrast, the political predispositions of the activists of Catholic organizational origin have had far greater impact: because the party's structures are looser and power less concentrated than in the PCF; because of the very large numbers of militants of Catholic provenience; and finally, because in the PS, the two major streams, liberal and integralist, that came out of the church's nineteenth-century travail converge on the same side of the party's great ideological divide. In conflicts of a kind parallel to those described above for the Communist Party, Socialists who believe that major social and economic transformations depend on using the leverage that party dominance and control of the state provide are arrayed against Socialists who look to autonomous decentralized social forces as the source of change.

At the core of the second group are Socialists of Catholic Action origins and Socialists from the CFDT.[80] Where Socialists of Jacobin inspiration, like Jean-Pierre Chevènement, explain the failures of the Mitterrand government by the weakness of the state – a lack of coherence, will, and ambition – the Socialists on the other side, the "second Left," see the strength of the centralized state and the reflex to call it into action on all occasions as the principal problem. They argue, as Edmond Maire, secretary-general of the CFDT recently did, that hope lies in a new "subterranean ferment that is starting to revive the social fabric" and in "favoring development from the bottom up, from the interplay of multiple initiatives."[81]

Such views – sometimes stigmatized as "la gauche américaine" [the American Left] – are completely rejected by the other Socialist camp. As Jean-Pierre Chevènement explained in a 1980 interview in Témoignage Chrétien:

> Consider the refusal to mobilize for the conquest of state power . . . and, at the same time, the justifications for social experimentation and for "local democracy": do they not correspond already to a kind of new "historic compromise" between the grand bourgeoisie, to whom is left serious business [capital accumulation] while the new petite bourgeoisie fools around with its new gadget, "quality of life"?
> Believe me: "la gauche américaine" really exists. In the name of "civil society" and under the cover of a battle against the state, in fact, the way is being prepared for an extension of the market, for the commercialization of everything, for a clearance-sale of all the values that constitute the civilization and dignity of the nation.[82]

The process of ideological renewal does not, however, proceed only by the head-on collision of opposing conceptions. The ideas that the Socialists of Catholic origins bring into the party also promote change by expanding categories already present in the socialist vision. Consider, for example, exploitation, a concept central to socialist analyses of contemporary societies. For Socialists coming to Marxist analysis from secular republican origins, exploitation is the product of a particular economic system and its principal victims are identified in relation to the dominant mode of production in capitalism: the industrial workers. For Socialists of Catholic origins, a wider conception of exploitation remains operative under the Marxist grid of analysis. The old orientation of personal militancy toward "the most suffering" pushes these Socialists beyond the proletariat to the Third World poor and the discovery of north–south relations in world politics; to immigrant workers in France and the identification of a cleavage between the privileged and the excluded that cuts across the proletariat; and to the groups hit hardest by the economic crisis and a program of social solidarity and redistribution, and not simply cranking up the growth machine again.[83] These understandings of exploitation come close enough to conventional socialist sentiments to be able to slip into and stretch Marxist categories. The new expanded notions of exploitation thus become part of the view of the world of a far larger group of Socialists than those with organizational experience in the Catholic subculture.

A rebirth of ideology?

The disintegration of old religious beliefs and structures in France has had, then, two contradictory sets of consequences for politics. For the large population of French Catholics whose practice has been declining, the effect has been to align their politics with those of their fellow citizens. With the collapse of the Catholic subculture, one of the main reservoirs of antisystem politics is disappearing. For this population, one whose political participation is largely confined to voting, religious change has apparently diminished the resonance of ideological politics of the old kind.

But at the same time, the collapse of the Catholic subculture has destroyed a network of institutions and beliefs that once had worked to preserve the limited nature of French politics. The militants whose activism had previously been confined to associations within the Catholic subculture have been propelled into political parties and single-issue social movements. The effect of this mass entry of Catholics with organizational experience in Catholic Action or in the CFDT has been to revive and expand the range of ideological conflicts in French politics. As these militants brought new ideas and expectations about politics into the parties and defended them by amalgamation with old Left categories, the scope of ideological politics has been widened. The inclusion of new political subjects under the aegis of old political formulas has given new life to old ideas and has also meant that the new issues will be approached as matters of fundamental principle.

To return to the example of exploitation: As long as exploitation retained its original Marxist sense and was used primarily to defend the primacy of the working class and of workplace-based struggles, it seemed likely to have less and less political purchase. The growing affluence of French industrial workers, their relatively stable numbers as a proportion of the French work force, changes in technology and labor markets, and, finally, changes in the workers' own conceptions of the relation between work and the rest of life – all made exploitation in its original and specific Marxist sense less and less useful for identifying new political problems or even for mobilizing the old Left constituencies. But when exploitation was expanded to include a variety of new subjects (the urban subproletariat, women, immigrant workers, for example), fresh life was given to the concept and novel political possibilities arose. At the same time, this ideological expansion meant that the parties (and an eventual Left government) would be likely to perceive these political problems not as susceptible to pragmatic, gradual, or technocratic resolutions, but as issues in which the very nature of socialism was at stake. The inclusion of new subjects in old categories, an ideologization of new political issues, and, as a consequence of these two phenomena, an intense struggle over ideas within the political parties; these are the constituent elements of the process by which the entry of new participants has revived ideological politics.

The processes of ideological transformation that have been explored here are rooted in institutional disintegration and recomposition and in the formative militant experiences of elites. The massive economic and socio-structural changes of the four postwar decades and of the crisis now in progress in France have cast up formidable problems and opportunities, but these have no inherent meaning or natural resolution. Political understandings of these issues arise not out of intrinsic features of the problems, but out of unstable, dynamic constellations of old and new worldviews. What role will the Catholic legacy play in shaping these new understandings? The argument laid out here suggests that the answer over the long term depends mainly on two complex issues: on the one side, the resistance of other militant traditions to the new ideas propelled by former Catholic activists; and on the other side, the exhaustion or renewal of religious institutions and belief systems that might nourish new generations of militants.

A host of imponderables surrounds both of these lines of inquiry. The ways in which French politics remain constrained by old patterns of partisan alignment was made clear again over the last five years as the vast mobilizations over the schools again arrayed anticlericals and Catholics on the old battle lines. As Louis Mexandeau, the author of the Socialist party platform on nationalization of the church schools explained, what is at stake "are not philosophical judgments on the nature of schools, but a political battle on the very nature of power."[84] It is hardly surprising that the forces straining for ideological change within the French Left aroused the somnolent troops of the old anticlerical coalition. What is principally at issue, after all, is the whole collective understanding of political parties, the state, and society that was forged in the battle for the Republic. But now the old slogans are brandished, not to unite the Left against a reactionary alliance of church and ancien régime, but to wage war within the Left: to rally the anticlerical and secular Marxist groups against the others. To halt the transformation of Left politics, new ideas are revealed to be "Catholic." Once the old enemy has been smoked out again, there is an appeal to familiar political reflexes and a call to return to Republican politics. The immediate consequence within the country has been to revive old definitions of Left and Right, and within the Left, to diminish the influence of the ideas and personnel of Catholic origin. But how enduring will this revival of old alignments be?

As for the church and the Catholic subculture, the trends of the postwar period raise the prospect that the institutional infrastructure that socialized generations of militants may be on the verge of collapse. If religious practice and the authority of Catholic norms and doctrines continue to shrink, if the sources that fed into the new streams of political activism dry up, the groups that now press for political renewal may find no successors. But need we consider the religious decline of the postwar years irreversible?

Notes

1 *Radioscopie de l'église en France, 1980* (Paris: Diffusion Bayard-Press, 1980), 33–4; surveys by SOFRES cited in *Témoignage Chrétien*, July 3, 1975:20. Statistics on practice vary somewhat from survey to survey and by how the questions are phrased: See François A. Isambert, "Le Sociologue, le prêtre et le fidèle," in Henri Mendras, ed., *La Sagesse et le désordre, France 1980*, (Paris: Gallimard, 1980); and Pierre Bourdieu, Monique de Sainte-Martin, "La Sainte famille: L'épiscopat français dans le champ du pouvoir," *Actes de la recherche en sciences sociales*, especially 18–20. The classic work on practice in France is Gabriel Le Bras, *Introduction à l'Histoire de la pratique religieuse en France* (Paris: Presses Universitaires de France, 1945). On statistics of Catholic practice and decline in various Western European countries, see David Martin, *A General Theory of Secularization* (Oxford: Blackwell, 1978), and John H. Whyte, *Catholics in Western Democracies* (Dublin: Gill & Macmillan, 1981).

2 Raymond Deville, "Situation des grands séminaires en France," *Etudes* (June 1978):803.

3 The most important surveys of changing religious attitudes in France are summarized and discussed in Jacques Gellard, "Marginalité de l'Eglise en France?" *Etudes* (January 1979 and February 1979). A 1973 SOFRES survey cited in these articles (p. 93) found, for example, that despite papal injunctions, 51 percent of practicing Catholics considered use of contraceptive devices "not wrong."

4 See, for example, Jean Delumeau, *Le Christianisme va-t-il mourir?* (Paris: Hachette, 1978). New edition with discussion and debate of the main thesis by critics in appendix.

5 On secularization, see Peter L. Berger, *The Social Reality of Religion* (London: Faber & Faber, 1969), and Bryan R. Wilson, *Religion in a Secular Society* (London: C. A. Watts, 1966). For provocative and important discussions of the literature on modernization and religion, see Daniel Bell, "The Return of the Sacred? The Argument on the Future of Religion," *British Journal of Sociology* 28, no. 4 (December 1977), and Mary Douglas, "The Effects of Modernization on Religious Change," *Daedalus* (Winter 1982). See also Martin, *A General Theory of Secularization*, and François-André Isambert, "La Secularisation interne du christianisme," *Revue française de sociologie* 17 (1976).

6 Goldthorpe's argument is laid out in "The Current Inflation: Towards a Socio-logical Account," in Fred Hirsch and John H. Goldthorpe, eds., *The Political Economy of Inflation* (London: Martin Robertson, 1978).

7 Joseph Schumpeter, *Capitalism, Socialism and Democracy*, 3rd ed. (New York: Harper, 1949). See especially chaps. 11, 12, and 13.

8 See, for example, Samuel P. Huntington, *American Politics: The Promise of Disharmony* (Cambridge, Mass.: Harvard University Press, 1981); also his contribution and those of Crozier and Watanuki on governability, in *The Crisis of Democracy*, Report on the Governability of Democracies to the Trilateral Commission (New York: New York University Press, 1975).

9 Bell, "The Return of the Sacred?," p. 442.

10 In France, powerful, though polemical, expressions of this view are provided by Alain Besançon in *La Confusion des langues* (Paris: Calmann-Lévy, 1978) and Juan Miguel Garrigues, "L'Eglise catholique et l'Etat libéral," *Commentaire*, no. 8 (Winter 1979–80).

11 Jean-Marie Domenach, *Ce que je crois* (Paris: Grasset, 1978), p. 193.

12 A useful comparative analysis of religion, class, and party in Western European politics is Richard Rose and Derek Unwin, "Social Cohesion, Political Parties and Strains in Regimes," *Comparative Political Studies* 2, no. 1 (April 1969). For France, see Guy Michelat and Michel Simon, *Classe, religion, et comportement politique* (Paris: Presses de la Fondation Nationale des Sciences Politiques/Editions Sociales, 1977); Guy Michelat and Michel Simon, "Religion, Class and Politics," *Comparative Politics* 10, no. 1 (October 1977); and Christel Peyrefitte, "Religion et politique," in *L'Opinion française en 1977* (Paris: Presses de la Fondation Nationale des Sciences Politiques, 1978); for local and regional studies: Suzanne Berger, *Peasants Against Politics* (Cambridge, Mass.: Harvard University Press, 1972); Edgar Morin, *Commune en France* (Paris: Fayard, 1967); Serge Bonnet, *Sociologie politique et religieuse de la Lorraine*, Cahiers de la Fondation Nationale des Sciences Politiques (Paris: A. Colin, 1972).

13 The argument that follows summarizes one I have laid out in *The French Political System* (New York: Random House, 1974), pp. 18–25, 59–68; and in "Monde catholique, pratique religieuse et vie politique," in Jean-Daniel Reynaud and Yves Grafmeyer, eds., *Français, qui êtes-vous?* (Paris: Documentation française, 1981).

14 Philippe Braud, "Les Elections législatives de mars 1978 dans la région Bretagne," *Revue française de science politique* 28, no. 6 (December 1978); also Peyrefitte, "Religion et politique".

15 The Right here includes the *Centre democrate*, the *Parti républicain*, the Gaullists (R.P.R.), and an extreme Right group (Forces Nouvelles). From a SOFRES survey (October-November 1977) for the DGRST of declared Catholics (unpublished). I am grateful to Jerôme Jaffré for allowing me to consult the SOFRES surveys.

16 Calculated from survey reported in Jacques Julliard, "Comment la France a basculé," *Le Nouvel Observateur* (June 1–7, 1981):40.

17 Among the many biographical and autobiographical accounts of militant trajectories from Catholic Action to the Left, the following are especially useful: Robert Chapuis, *Les Chrétiens et le socialisme* (Paris: Calmann-Lévy, 1976); Eugene Descamps, *Militer* (Paris: Fayard, 1971); Fredo Krumnow, *Croire* (Paris: Editions Ouvrières, 1974); Michel Rocard, *Des Militants du P.S.U.* (Paris: Epi, 1971); Danièle Hervieu-Léger, *De la mission à la protestation* (Paris: Cerf, 1973); Jean-Marie Donegani, "Itineraire politique et cheminement religieux," *Revue française de science politique* 29, no. 4–5 (August-October 1979); Renaud Dulong, "Christian Militants in the French Left," in S. Berger, ed., *Religion in West European Politics* (London: Cass, 1982); and two collective works: "Les Militants d'origine chrétienne," *Esprit*, no. 4–5 (April-May 1977), and "A Gauche, ces chrétiens . . . ," *Autrement*, no. 8 (February 1977).

18 SOFRES 1977 survey results reported and analyzed in Christel Peyrefitte, "Le Clergé français, est-il en crise?" *Commentaire*, no. 2 (Summer 1978), p. 168.

19 On militants in the CFDT, see Hervé Hamon and Patrick Rotman, *La Deuxième gauche* (Paris: Ramsey, 1982).

20 SOFRES 1977 survey for the DGRST (unpublished), p. 89: 39 percent of all religiously observant Left Catholics belong to one or more voluntary associations, as do 37 percent of all religiously observant Right Catholics. In contrast, only 27 percent of nonpracticing Left identifiers (and 26 percent of nonpracticing Right) belong to one or more voluntary associations. [Voluntary associations were defined to include parties and unions as well as PTAs, neighborhood groups, and so forth.]

21 Marie-Aude Poisson, "La Vie nouvelle et la politique (1968–1971)," memoire, Institut d'Etudes Politiques (1972), pp. 130–1, 140.

22 There are similar findings for other groups of Left Catholics: A 1954 survey of readers of *Témoignage Chrétien* showed that 50 percent belonged to some Catholic Action association but only 15 percent to a party. Jean-Pierre Gault, *Histoire d'une fidelité, Témoignage Chrétien 1944–56* (Paris: Editions Témoignage Chrétien, n.d.), pp. 76–78, 81. In the Catholic workers organization (Action Catholique Ouvrière), André Rousseau found that party membership rose from 8 percent in 1968 to 18 percent in 1976. [More than 95 percent of these workers belong to unions; more than a third also belong to other voluntary associations.] André Rousseau, "L'Action Catholique Ouvrière," in *Actes de la recherche en sciences sociales*, no. 44–45 (November 1982):70–1.

23 For recent statements in the same tradition, see Besançon, *La Confusion des langues*, and Garrigues, "L'Eglise catholique et l'Etat libéral."

24 Sainte-Beuve, *Port-Royal*, Book I, p. 17.

25 See Michael Fogarty, *Christian Democracy in Western Europe, 1820–1953* (London: Routledge & Kegan Paul, 1957); R. E. M. Irving, "Christian Democracy in Post-War Europe: Conservatism Writ-Large or Distinctive Political Phenomenon?" in *West European Politics* 2, no. 1 (January 1979); Jean-Marie Mayeur, *Des Parties catholiques à la democratie chrétienne, XIXe–XXe siècles* (Paris: A. Colin, 1980); R. William Rauch, Jr., *Politics and Belief in Contemporary France: Emmanuel Mounier and Christian Democracy, 1932–1950* (The Hague: Martinus Nijhoff, 1972).

26 On the conservative corporatists, see Berger, *Peasants Against Politics*; Pierre Barral, *Les Agrariens français de Méline à Pisani* (Paris: Presses de la Fondation Nationale des Sciences Politiques, 1968); and Isabel Boussard, *Vichy et la Corporation Paysanne* (Paris: Presses de la Fondation Nationale des Sciences Politiques, 1980).

27 From F. Bazin thesis, cited in Mayeur, *Des Partis catholiques*, p. 167.

28 On Catholic militants in protest against the Algerian War, see especially Hervé Hamon and Patrick Rotman, *Les Porteurs de valises* (Paris: Albin Michel, 1979).

29 Hamon and Rotman, *La Deuxième gauche*, p. 36; Paul Vignaux, *De la CFTC à la CFDT. Syndicalisme et socialisme, "Reconstruction" (1946–1972)* (Paris: Editions ouvrières, 1980), pp. 7–40.

30 In the large literature on the DC, Arturo Parisi, ed., *Democristiani* (Bologna: Il Mulino, 1979), is perhaps the single most relevant work for comparisons with contemporary French developments. See also Douglas A. Wertman, "The Catholic Church and Italian Politics: The Impact of Secularization," in S. Berger, ed., *Religion in West European Politics* (London: Cass, 1982); and Jean-Marie Mayeur, *Des Partis catholiques*, chap., 14. For an excellent brief discussion of the origins and current fortunes of different conceptions of the relations between the DC and the church, see articles by Jacques Nobécourt and Philippe Pons in *Le Monde*, July 10–11, 1983.

31 Mayeur, *Des Partis catholiques*, p. 168.

32 For useful overviews of Catholic liberalism in the nineteenth century, see Roger

Aubert, ed., *L'Eglise dans le monde moderne*, vol. 5 (Paris: Seuil, 1957), chaps. 1 and 2; and Roger Soltau, *French Political Thought in the 19th Century* (New York: Russell & Russell, 1959), chaps. 3 and 4. See also Emmanuel Barbier, *Histoire du catholicisme libéral et du catholicisme social en France*, 4 vols. (Bordeaux: Cadoret, 1924), and in the more recent literature, the remarkable work of Paul Bénichou, *Le Temps des prophètes* (Paris: Gallimard, 1977); José Cabanis, *Lacordaire et quelques autres. Politique et religion* (Paris: Gallimard, 1982); and Mayeur, *Des Partis catholiques*. The distinction developed in the text between liberalism and integralism has been most fully explored in the works of Emile Poulat; see especially his *Eglise contre bourgeoisie* (Paris: Casterman, 1977).

33 Alexis de Tocqueville, *Democracy in America* (New York: Random House, Vintage, 1945) vol. 2, Book 2, chap. 15, p. 156.

34 See Hamon and Rotman, *La Deuxième gauche*; Paul Vignaux, *De la CFTC à la CGDT* (1980); and Paul Vignaux, "Un Catholicisme républicain," in *Esprit*, nos. 4–5 (April-May 1977); Pierre Rosanvallon, "La C.F.D.T. et la laïcité," in *Esprit*, nos. 4–5 (April-May 1977).

35 From Georgette Berault [Georgette Paul Vignaux], "Conscience politique et conscience religieuse" (1957), as cited in Vignaux, *De la CFTC à la CFDT*, p. 38.

36 On the "second Left," see Hamon and Rotman, *La Deuxième gauche*, and debate on the book in Marcel Gauchet, "La Deuxième gauche," *Intervention*, no. 2 (January-February 1983); Alain Bergounioux, "La Deuxième gauche contre l'esprit de 89?" and Michel Crozier, "La Deuxième gauche s'est-elle trompée?," *Intervention*, no. 3 (March-April 1983). The best account of the historical origins of the "two Lefts" [written from the perspective of the "second"] is Pierre Rosanvallon and Patrick Viveret, *Pour une nouvelle culture politique* (Paris: Seuil, 1977). For criticism of the "second Left" by others from similar political origins, see articles in *Esprit* (December 1983).

37 René Rémond in roundtable discussion cited in François Bédarida and Jean Maitron, eds., *Christianisme et monde ouvrier*: Cahier de Mouvement Social, no. 1 (Paris: Editions ouvrières, 1975), p. 16. See also René Rémond, "Droite et gauche dans le catholicisme français contemporain," *Revue française de science politique*, no. 8 (September-December 1958).

38 Meeting organized by La Brèche, a Catholic association, with the Socialists on the theme "Des chrétiens interrogent des socialistes," November 23, 1977. I have consulted a corrected copy of verbatim minutes.

39 Minutes of La Brèche–Parti Socialiste meeting, p. 8.

40 Minutes of La Brèche–Parti Socialiste meeting, p. 32.

41 Emile Poulat, *Eglise contre bourgeoisie* (Paris: Casterman, 1977), p. 197. See also Emile Poulat, "'Modernisme' et 'intégrisme.' Du concept polémique a l'irénisme critique," *Archives de sociologie des religions* 27 (January-June 1969).

42 This interpretation draws heavily on the previously cited work of Emile Poulat.

43 Avery Dulles, *Models of the Church* (New York: Doubleday, 1978), especially chap. 2 on the church as institution.

44 On the uses of Thomism, see Emile Poulat, "L'Eglise romaine, le savoir et le pouvoir," *Archives de sciences sociales des religions* 19, no. 37 (January-June 1974); also Poulat's summary statement in the roundtable discussion, Bedarida and Maitron, eds., *Christianisme et monde ouvrier*, p. 13; the church never resigned itself to "modern society" and developed a counterproposal of a global society, a blueprint for which was laid out by the *Syllabus* of 1864; the Catholic social movement was the instrument designed to reconquer society; and Thomism was the fundamental ideology on which this global project was based.

45 An excellent account of the implementation of these reforms is Yves-Marie Hilaire, *Une chrétienté au XIXe siècle? La Vie religieuse des populations du diocèse d'Arras (1840–*

1914), 2 vols. (Villeneuve-d'Asq: Publications de l'Université de Lille III, 1977). A fundamental bibliographic source for French religious history in the nineteenth and twentieth centuries is Jean-Marie Mayeur, ed., *L'Histoire religieuse de la France, Problèmes et méthodes*. (Paris: Beauchesne, 1975).

46 Paul J. Tillich, "The Social Functions of the Churches in Europe and America," *Social Research* 3, no. 1 (1936).

47 Ibid., p. 95.

48 Ibid., p. 93–4.

49 Ibid., p. 94.

50 For a review of the literature on subcultures and critical analysis of the concept, see Gary Alan Fine and Sherryl Kleinman, "Rethinking Subculture: An Interactionist Analysis," *American Journal of Sociology* 85, no. 1 (July 1979).

51 For the French Communists, see Annie Kriegel, *Les Communistes* (Paris: Seuil, 1968); on communist and Catholic subcultures in an Italian city, David I. Kertzer, *Comrades and Christians* (Cambridge: Cambridge University Press, 1980). For a fascinating account of Catholic subcultural organization in a working-class French parish, see Antoine Delestre, *35 Ans de mission au Petit-Colombes, 1939–1974* (Paris: Cerf, 1977).

52 Emile Poulat, *Naissance des prêtres-ouvriers* (Paris: Casterman, 1965).

53 Henry Cochin, "Rapport à L'Assemblée générale de l'Oeuvre des chapelles de secours, *Semaine religieuse de Paris*, May 17, 1913, pp. 749–751, cited in Poulat, *Naissance des prêtres-ouvriers*, p. 138.

54 Cited in ibid., p. 133.

55 Cardijn speaking to Belgian *jocistes* in 1929, cited in ibid., p. 138.

56 In the seminars that prepared the future worker-priests for their assignments, there was virtually no discussion of economics or of the sociology of working-class life; but there were lengthy presentations on the church's experience in converting the barbarians in early Christian times. See ibid., p. 114.

57 See, for example, the resistance to the organization of the *Jeunesse Agricole Chrétienne* in Brittany, Berger, *Peasants Against Politics*, pp. 90–8. One major argument against specialized Catholic Action was that it weakened the parish-based territorial organization of Catholic life.

58 Quoted in Poulat, *Naissance des prêtres-ouvriers*, p. 148.

59 See ibid.; *Les Prêtres-Ouvriers Documents* (Paris: Editions de Minuit, 1954); Jean Lacroix, "L'Eglise et la Mission," *Esprit* (December 1953).

60 See Poulat, *Naissance des prêtres-ouvriers*, p. 93.

61 Hollande, as cited in ibid., p. 412.

62 Abbé Godin, author of *La France, pays de mission?* the work that "launched" the worker-priest movement, cited in Poulat, *Naissance des prêtres-ouvriers*, p. 393.

63 A worker-priest quoted in Poulat, *Naissance des prêtres-ouvriers*, p. 398.

64 Interview, November 9, 1979. The militants I interviewed in 1979–80 for this research will here be identified only by their organizational memberships and political "itineraries." About two dozen militants were interviewed, in sessions ranging from an hour to eight hours; some I saw several times. The interviews were open-ended. The profiles of the militants drawn from the interviews have been supplemented by a large autobiographical and biographical literature produced by political activists of Catholic origin [see note 8] and by unpublished autobiographical essays.

65 Richard P. McBrien, "Roman Catholicism: E Pluribus Unum," *Daedalus* 111, no. 1 (Winter 1982):76.

66 Ibid., p. 77.

67 Danièle Hervieu-Léger, *De la mission à la protestation* (Paris: Cerf, 1973), pp. 158–203.

68 McBrien, p. 77.

69 Ibid.

70 Frater, "La B.A. BA du militant," in *Dialogues*, no. 1 (March 1958), a journal started by former members of La Route. I am grateful to Jean-Louis Moynot for making available a collection of periodicals from this group.

71 Interview, May 22, 1980.

72 One ex-Catholic militant who had joined the Maoists after 1968 explained that he left the Maoists because of the a priori, theoretical views of reality. What he is looking for is "a revolutionary group that prefigures the future society, because, in the end, today's choices determine the future and shape the human beings who incarnate these choices; the 'means' prefigure the end; events count for more than theory; the expression of the real aspirations of men weighs heavier than the strength of a revolutionary groupuscule." This autobiographical "testimony" is presented in Jean-Paul Ciret and Jean-Pierre Sueur, *Les Etudiants, la politique et l'Eglise* (Paris: Fayard, 1970), pp. 132–3.

73 On the role of Catholics in local voluntary associations and social experimentation, see Gary G. Meyers, "Villeneuve: A Community Study in French Political Subculture and Public Policy," 2 vols., unpublished doctoral dissertation, Stanford University, 1982.

74 Interview, May 20, 1980.

75 The emphasis was there in speech.

76 Interview, February 2, 1980, with a manager, a graduate of one of the *grandes écoles*, who as a student had worked with the Petits Frères des Pauvres; had been "galvanized" by May-June 1968; then participated in a communitarian experimental parish (at Antony); and now was a CFDT *délégué du personnel* in a large private firm.

77 Interview, June 11, 1980.

78 Jean-Louis Moynot started in the Scouts movement (La Route); moved into *Jeunesse-Loisir, Mouvement de Libération des Peuples* (1955) and UNEF (1957); and then into the CGT (where he became *secrétaire confédéral* in 1967) and the Communist Party. See Jean-Louis Moynot, "Base sociale et révolutionnaire d'une démocratie de masse," *La Pensée*, no. 205 (June 1979); "Quelle réponse à la crise peut changer la vie?" *Le Monde*, July 3, 1981; "Jean-Louis Moynot s'explique," *Témoignage Chrétien*, no. 1946 (October 26, 1981); and *Au milieu du gué CGT, syndicalisme et démocratie de masse* (Paris: Presses Universitaires de France, 1982). This account draws also on interviews with Moynot (January 30, February 26, May 29, 1980) and on his unpublished article "Où est le rôle de la foi?" (written 1968–69), and articles and reports he wrote for La Route.

79 Moynot, "Base sociale," p. 102.

80 Roland Cayrol's survey of delegates to the 1973 Socialist Party Congress showed that practicing Catholics in the party were far more inclined than others to consider issues like *autogestion* and foreign workers as very important and were less interested than other delegates in questions of wages, pensions, the Middle East conflict, abortion, and wiretapping. Roland Cayrol, "L'Univers politique des militants socialistes," *Revue française de science politique* 25, no. 1 (February 1975), pp. 32–3.

81 Edmond Maire, "Vive l'initiative," *Libération*, September 5, 1983.

82 Jean-Pierre Chevènement, interviewed in *Témoignage Chrétien*, no. 1871 (May 19–25, 1980), p. 10.

83 For an analysis of the economic crisis as a fundamental divide in industrial societies, resulting from the illusions and excesses of the previous decades of rapid growth and affluence, and requiring radically new patterns of distribution and solidarity, see the September 22, 1982, statement of the Catholic Bishops Conference, *Pour de nouveaux*

modes de vie. Déclaration du Conseil permanent de l'Episcopat sur la conjoncture économique et sociale. Much in this view is shared by the CFDT and by the Rocardian current of the PS.

84 Minutes of La Brèche–Parti Socialiste meeting, November 23, 1977, p. 38.

4

The politics of time: changing paradigms of collective time and private time in the modern era

CHARLES S. MAIER

What is the politics of time?

"Can one tell – that is to say, narrate – time, time itself, as such, for its own sake?" Thomas Mann asked sixty years ago in *The Magic Mountain*. "That would surely be an absurd undertaking. A story which read: 'Time passed, it ran on, the time flowed onward' and so forth – no one in his senses would consider that a narrative." Is it similarly absurd to inquire into the politics of "time, time itself, as such for its own sake"? Mann, after all, reconsidered. Because time within the story, like time in a dream, ran at a different experiential pace than it did for the author, "it is clear that time, while the medium of the narrative, can also become its subject. Therefore, if it is too much to say that one can tell a tale of time, it is none the less true that a desire to tell a tale about time is not such an absurd idea as it just now seemed."[1] In the same cautious sense, this chapter takes up the question how politics is about time, and how the time presupposed by politics has changed in the course of history.

Politics concerns time in at least two ways. The first is ideological. Politics comprises one of the fundamental means by which all societies resolve and carry out the decisions that order their collective life. A political decision establishes a rule that will be enforced by the state; community officers can legally invoke physical compulsion if necessary.[2] Thus the sphere of politics differs from the economic sphere, in which social transactions allegedly rest upon voluntary exchanges of goods, services, and claims on value. It also differs from the religious sphere, in which nonworldly sanctions and motivations lead to desired behavior. Nonetheless, politics rests upon vision as well

This essay is dedicated to Franklin L. Ford – historian whose interests have ranged in time and through time and teacher whose encouragement has extended over time – on the occasion of his sixty-fifth birthday.

as compulsion. It is based on shared or competing concepts of collective purpose. It envisages a desired future; it invokes a formative past. To act in the political domain is to propose a view of how society should progress through history. Political action must posit some underlying notions of time.

Thus, in the first instance, there is a politics of time because those who govern or want to govern advance characteristic ideas of how society should reproduce itself through time. They also advance a concept of how time itself is constructed as a medium for history.[3] Nineteenth-century bourgeois or liberal society presupposed a linear and constant time as the matrix for history. Twentieth-century political systems – either communist and fascist, or our own contemporary Western regimes that we might term "postliberal" – envisage time as more plastic. Mussolini's enthusiasts painted "Better a day as a lion than a year as a jackal," on Italian housewalls in the 1930s. A windy slogan, it still fit in with a whole fascist challenge to "liberal" time. Contemporary postliberal society also looses the constraints of linear time. Its entrepreneurs sell time-shares in vacation resorts as property; its hard-pressed parents insist that "quality time" makes up for just plain time with children; employers experiment with "flex-time" schedules; owners of video recorders can make simultaneous events sequential; physicists and artists challenge the intuitive one-way flow of time with reversible sequences. In effect, bourgeois society served time; fascist regimes (and in some respects, which shall be only touched upon in this chapter, Stalinism as well) denied time; and postliberal communities tend to decouple collective and individual, public and private, time, renouncing the coordination and alignment that was earlier sought.

There is a second dimension to the politics of time. This involves its allocation. Besides suggesting characteristic images of history and temporal order, political leaders also propose different uses for time considered as a scarce social resource. Indeed, in one vision that recurs from antiquity to recent cultural conservatives, political activity itself presupposes time freed from claims of work or necessity.[4] But even when leisure is not postulated as the condition of politics, political communities seek to influence or constrain the balance between "free time" and work, or private life and public commitments. They often hope to privilege some stages of the life cycle above others, rewarding age or youth. Sometimes they intervene in the generational cycles for the transmission of power and property.

Recent scholars have now recognized time as an important, explicit theme for the social sciences except, curiously, in the study of contemporary politics. There it has been treated indirectly at best, as in such issues as the political business cycle.[5] There are two probable reasons why historical or social science discussion has not chosen to ponder the contemporary politics of time. First, time is the ultimate scarce commodity, but it is irrevocably limited for everyone. Rulers, subjects, scholars, workers, athletes, lovers, are subject to its constraints. Philosophers have understood that the finitude imposed by time helps define us as a species. Time, wrote Hegel, "is the externally perceived pure self that is not grasped by the self, the concept [of the self] only looked upon. . . . time thus appears as the destiny and the necessity of spirit that cannot be complete in itself, [as] the necessity of enriching the portion of unconsciousness within consciousness."[6] Precisely this universal finitude must make time seem more basic than politics. If each of us recedes into a future of fading memories and dust, how could time possibly be subject to politics? Politics involves mobilizing community resources of constraint to allocate scarce goods or to privilege some values above others. Time as an existential quality cannot be distributed and therefore has been often treated as politically unproblematic.[7]

Still, time is a scarce collective as well as individual resource. If a society needs its citizens' time, it must purchase or commandeer it against alternative claims. Even if a nation does not face absolute shortages of time, as it does, say, during modern warfare, leaving time at the disposition of individuals or under the control of the economically powerful still amounts to an important collective choice. Nonetheless, social scientists have rarely grappled with the issue of how a community mobilizes time or leaves it to the individual and family as a political question. When they have considered time as a constraint – that is, in terms of its scarcity – they have tended to apply the intellectual framework they customarily use for analyzing scarcity in general: economic analysis. Even Marx presupposed the underlying concepts of classical economics when he asked, "What is a working day? What is the length of time during which capital may consume the labor-power whose daily value it buys?" But he understood there was a political dimension and added that the normal working day was "the product of a protracted civil war, more or less dissembled, between the capitalist class and the working-class."[8] Most social science, however, has concentrated on the market transaction, not the political pressure that may lie behind it. Time is conceived of as a commodity but hardly as a stake of political regulation.[9] This chapter tries to remedy such neglect. If politics must concern time, the question now is how.

Time and the liberal political order

The history of the politics of time can begin with a schema that is rigid and unshaded but remains useful as a first approximation. In the nineteenth and twentieth centuries, we can identify for Western societies not just one but three political concepts of time. They are labeled here liberal, fascist, and postliberal. Each has rested upon a characteristic vision of social time and a characteristic approach to control of individual time.

What is termed here the "politics of liberal time" has its roots in the general development of Western rationalism since the High Middle Ages, the advent of clocks, and the standardization of hourly intervals independent of the length of daylight. If such measures were first sought by churchmen to call their monks to devotions, the new pattern of hours came to regulate urban labor and activity.[10] The Reformation, or at least the advent of Calvinism, was a further victory for those governing their work and prayer by a homogeneous and measurable linear time. Protestant time flattened out the seasonal texture of Catholic time, punctuated by feast days and recurrent processions.[11]

The advent of Protestant time, linear and untextured, contrasted not only with Catholic liturgical seasons but also with Stoic and Renaissance perceptions of historical cycles and ineluctable decline. (Indeed, Catholic time and Renaissance time shared the ancient, Mediterranean sense of vicissitude and fall.) The classical legacy transmitted a pessimistic conviction of historical decay. The public commitments needed to maintain a republican commonwealth were always subject to political and moral entropy. Corruption and demagogy undermined the virtues of the civic fathers. "Fortune," like the tides, lapped at the sand castles of the city-state.

As Pocock has stressed, the poignant awareness of republican decline was transplanted from the Mediterranean to the Anglo-American political world.[12] But conservative defenders of an agrarian commonwealth, republican or aristocratic, no longer attributed decay to inescapable fortune. They lamented the growing corruption of commerce and interest groups. Protestant time – the ascetic rationalization of the calendar on behalf of accumulation and industry, the triumph of diligence over decay – helped animate later Whig celebrations of progress in eighteenth-century England. But Stoic and Renaissance time contributed to the critical countercurrent, the fear of moral declension and political vulgarity.

Whether partisans of cycles or progress, the early modern philosophers understood that time entered crucially into politics. Duration was the critical component of institutional existence. War, wrote Thomas Hobbes, "consisteth not in battle only, or the act of fighting; but in a tract of time, wherein the will to contend by battle is sufficiently known: and therefore the notion of time is to be considered in the nature of war; as it is in the nature of weather."[13] Civil government was established to remedy not occasional violence but the continuing war of all against all; security hinged upon expectation of duration. Similarly for Locke, civil society presupposed property, and property depended upon the capacity for persistence through time. Otherwise, "if the fruits rotted or the venison putrified before [the hunter] could spend it, he offended against the common law of nature and was liable to be punished; he invaded his neighbor's share."[14] Money, however, furnished a means of storing value, thus sanctioned accumulation and inequality, and finally required the formation of government to protect property. For both these theorists of the social contract, therefore, time could no longer just be taken for granted. For Hobbes, war, and for Locke, wealth, required establishment of the state; and neither war nor wealth could be specified without a concept of continuity across time.

The new awareness of time was reinforced, logically enough, by the rationalization of space that distinguished the seventeenth and eighteenth centuries. Space and time became the twin concerns of rulers and philosophers. Sovereigns sought the consolidation of cohesive territorial states out of the dispersed dynastic fragments of the Spanish and Holy Roman Empires. To symbolize their power they turned to builders who no longer accepted architectural space as a classical realm of repose, but as a plastic material to be shaped and displayed. The designers created grand palaces, *trompe l'oeil* decoration, and formal gardens as microcosms of the vaster realms their patrons claimed to order and control. Natural philosophers, from Galileo and Kepler through Descartes, Leibniz, and Newton, worked out the laws of motion that coordinated space and time through unified laws. Development of the differential calculus allowed thinkers to overcome the paradoxes of infinitesimals and continuous motion bequeathed by the Greeks. The new sense of mastery did not initially diminish what was felt to be the intuitive framework of continuous time and infinite space: "Absolute, true, and mathematical time, of itself, and from its nature, flows equally without relation to anything external," Newton insisted.[15] Faced with the difficulty of specifying the nature of space and time, Hume, however, proposed they could only be talked about as the residual gaps between physical objects or separated events. For Kant this radical empiricism was frustrating; he responded with his celebrated "Copernican revolution" that argued space and time were universal conceptual categories, synthetic a prioris by means of which the human intellect had to order perception. Space and time inhered in our mental constitution; there was no possibility of experience without them.

The ordering of space and time, an observer might have easily believed, became an obsession of the emerging liberal era. It was fitting that the railroad, the great nineteenth-century invention for knitting together vast spaces, demanded the standardization of time. Before the trains ran between them, London time remained four minutes ahead of Reading's; New York City time, four minutes ahead of Philadelphia's. Every city enjoyed its own zenith and set its proper hour. The railroad lines now imposed their own standard time until in 1884 an international conference finally demarcated the hourly zones of 15 degrees of longitude that we have today.[16]

More generally, bourgeois society devoted intense energy to establishing frontiers, real and figurative. It drew boundaries not only between geographical territories, but between public and private, state and society, executive and legislative, politics and market, childhood and maturity, workplace and home, and between present and future. That last dichotomization required heroic renunciation: the legacy of Weber's Calvinist asceticism. No matter what the reality of Victorian sexual practice, the ideology of deferred gratification was awesome. Just as striking was the capacity to defer material consumption, which cannot be explained only by lower levels of income. The transmission of wealth to children, the willingness to invest in annuities at 3 percent even on the eve of World War I, testified to a confidence in the future and the willingness to wait for it. When Laurence Wylie went to Roussillon in the early 1950s, he learned that the local farmers at the turn of the century planted oak orchards which at the earliest would nurture truffles in six years. When urged to plant apricot orchards in 1950, they resisted: "'We know we should plant trees, but what's the use? Who knows if we and our children would be here by the time they started to bear?'"[17]

On the other hand, these patterns also revealed how reluctant liberal society was to provide for the future of individuals through collective provisions. Dealing with the privations of old age and illness remained a task primarily for the family, individual foresight, and perhaps church or local charity. Doubtless this had always been the case. Nonetheless what earlier had been just the accepted fact now became glorified as positive ideology; for the private networks and institutions that had sustained the old were undermined by liberal rulers. Indeed there seems to have been a positive effort to decollectivize the risks of the life cycle. The risks of the future would fortify the enterprise of the present. If finally toward the end of the century statesmen came to believe, first in Bismarck's Germany, then in post-Victorian Britain, that it was necessary to intervene to assure minimal old-age provisions, they still sought to link individual thrift in the present with welfare in the future by virtue of the insurance principle.[18]

Insofar as there was an allocative politics of time in the liberal era, it lay in this effort to construe time as a marketable commodity. Recent historical work has shown that the notion of rational labor markets caricatures the transactions between employers and employees persisting throughout much of the nineteenth century. At best, William Reddy argues, there was a market culture, not a market society.[19] But culture, in the sense of the discourse of politics, is what is of interest here. Managers at least would endeavor to enforce labor market conditions according to the doctrines of liberal political economy. These suggested that an individual's time was his fundamental property. Time endowed everyone with a minimal asset that he could bring to the market; the expectation of old-age needs provided individuals with a minimal incentive for productive accumulation. But was there not a certain self-contradiction in the liberal approach? On the one hand, government disinterested itself in the allocation of time, as it allegedly did with property. On the other hand, nineteenth-century civilization sought to standardize the measurement of time, to establish uniform units of time, and eventually to coordinate time signals (culminating in the 1913 broadcasting of standard Greenwich time from the Eiffel Tower) so that society might be made more subject to its impartial discipline. In these latter instances, however, government moved to supply standards as a sort of infrastructure, much as in France the state would run the Ecole des Mines, or elsewhere subsidize turnpikes and bridges and guarantee the regulations of the market that single firms wanted enforced to discipline unscrupulous competition. The state intervened as the servant of technological entrepreneurship. This did not preclude its effort to keep the allocation of time an affair of the market.

If nineteenth-century society and its ruling groups wanted to enhance time as a commodity, they had to encourage the rationalization of temporal commitments. The process began earliest with the army, where the state's interests were clearest. The patchwork of company recruitment, or locally based levies for long terms, gave way to universal obligations fixed for a brief but predictable period. In the Prussian system, the draftee knew that a series of diminishing obligations would mark the progress of his aging. To be sure, short-term conscription allowed mass armies to a degree that the eighteenth century had not mustered. The obligation went hand in hand with the diffusion of ideas of universal citizenship in the wake of the French Revolution and its wars. Conscription also allowed states to expropriate time and labor directly rather than to hire it, and it was often easier to raise men than taxes. But the fixing of the length of military service also responded to the general impulse to rationalize a labor market, which amounted to a market for commitments of time. As Foucault has written: Adam Smith "unearths labour, that is, toil and time, the working-day that at once patterns and uses up man's life. . . . if there is an order regulating the forms of wealth, if this can buy that, if gold is worth twice as much as silver . . . it is because [men] are all subject to time, to toil, to weariness, and, in the last resort, to death itself."[20]

Governments and entrepreneurs thus moved more generally to diminish indefinite commitments of labor duration. The abolition of slavery and then of indenture, the infringement of apprenticeship, and the spread of salaried and wage labor were part of this process. Certainly these reforms beckoned as moves toward liberty and away from arbitrary control. The liberal program was deemed emancipatory even as it served to rationalize time as a commodity. The shorter the unit of time sold, the more theoretically independent was the vendor. At the same time, however, the less encumbered and the more flexible was the labor market. Workers themselves absorbed the new mentality as they learned to bargain for hours and not for the price of the cloth they sold their employers. "Laborers had learned to think of time and effort as underlying variables in relating work to pay, instead of concentrating all their attention on the tangible product."[21] They did not always gain vis-à-vis their employers. By 1900, American steelmasters had extracted a seven-day work week from their largely immigrant labor force, an achievement that patriarchal residues precluded in industrial Europe.[22] Commodifying time thus did not always mean winning shorter hours; nonetheless, labor representatives still understood it as the starting point for greater autonomy. In the words of one British working-class spokesman, labor's "great motto" was "The Master's right in the Master's time, and the workman's right in his own time."[23]

On the one hand, nineteenth-century civilization brought the greatest self-subjection to supposedly absolute standards of time. "Serving time" meant a prison term now fixed in years; but all of bourgeois culture was involved in serving time. Serving time, however, required mastering time. The very effort to impose control over time (and space), the perfervid demarcation of private and public spaces, family time and work time, the discipline involved in granting to the future the same immediacy as the present (and with the growth of the historical sciences, the same immediacy now rendered to past time as well) – these exertions were intended only to adjust human life more rationally to the constraints of an absolute time and space. In fact they subverted Newtonian time and suggested that society might impose its own schedules on its supposedly absolute flow.

Denying time: from the liberal to fascist paradigm

Two impulses tended to dissolve the absolute time that marked the bourgeois era. The tendency for time to be brought under control and thus to be stripped of its allegedly immutable quality can be described as an intrinsic development. Time took on the character of a plastic medium by the very process of being measured, equipartitioned, and packaged. Certainly scientists and philosophers undertook some radical redefinitions. In his 1898 paper "La mesure du temps," the French mathematician Henri Poincaré pointed out, "we have no direct intuition about the equality of two time intervals."[24] Like the physicist Ernst Mach before him, Poincaré argued that we could know only local times, no single absolute time valid for all the universe. In the Newtonian universe velocities were simply additive; the man walking in a moving train combined two speeds relative to the ground. How could this condition hold, however, when, as experiments suggested, the motion of the earth did not alter the observed speed of light? Einstein's 1905 Special Theory of Relativity resolved these puzzles and calculated how the various times of different coordinate systems in space would relate to each other. Nor were the physical sciences the only intellectual arena for the overhaul of nineteenth-century concepts of time and sequence. In the same years, Freud suggested that different stages of development from infantile desire on were preserved in the layers of the mind. Novelists, too, would experiment with the dissolution of linear narrative. Time as a Newtonian flow might persist intuitively, but intellectually it no longer served so exclusively as the matrix for science or art.

At the same historical moment, control of industrial time became a large stake in the class rivalry that still preoccupied bourgeois civilization. The factory became a major battleground, even if the struggle was no longer just the raw, exploitative contest over the length of the working day that Marx had described. Instead, the organization of the production process became the more refined stake. Despite the advance of industrial discipline, skilled labor still managed as of 1900 to preserve a large degree of control of factory time. Artisans and unions governed the pace of the shop floor and initiated new workers

into the elaborate routines and articulated pace of work even in mechanized halls. This sphere of autonomy underneath the factory roof
was resented by management as a form of malingering, "soldiering"
or "ca'canny." Scientific management involved an effort to reduce
the laborer's remaining control of factory time in the very name of
making time the arbiter of industrial discipline. Scientific management
was based upon differentiating job tasks after careful stopwatch analysis or measurement of physical activity. Schemes such as Taylorism
and the spread of the assembly line allowed management a chance
to reappropriate factory time from their work force. When summer,
or daylight saving, time was instituted in World War I, labor further
resented the manipulation of what they saw as their customary day.
Antagonism culminated in Turin with the strike of the clockhands in
April 1920, when a massive walkout was triggered by the FIAT management's insistence on holding the clock tower to daylight saving
against efforts by the workers' commission to return it to the standard
hour.[25] Class conflict meant a struggle to control time. But making
time itself a stake had to undermine the earlier sense of its sovereign
objectivity.

In short, while nineteenth-century society yoked family and work,
sexual morality, forms of fictional representation, and the compara-
bility of economic values all to an iron sense of time, this very discipline eroded the fixity that became so stressed. The very energy
applied to staple institutional life upon a rigid temporal frame could
be turned toward making the perceived structures of time themselves
more malleable. On a political and economic level this evolution meant
the increasing infringement of jurisdictions over time that had been
earlier unchallenged. By the late nineteenth century, the degree to
which individuals might simply rent or sell claims on their own time
became increasingly contested. On the one side, entrepreneurs demanded increasing control of the use of time when they hired labor.
They were no longer content to engage a worker's energy by the hour
and allow his labor organizations still to prescribe the patterns and
uses of the time they nominally controlled. Industrialists and engi-
neers wanted real control and developed concepts of scientific management and efficiency to justify the claim. On the other side, even
before the advent of scientific management the state had felt compelled to intervene in questions of time. It kept children out of factories, was asked to supervise the length of the working day first in
mining and then in all industry. Scientific, philosophical, artistic experiments all suggested by the advent of the new century that time
was not so absolute, not so objectively measured, and not so readily

made a standard for transactions in terms of its quantitative parameters.[26] With this awareness, the politics of time moved from a "liberal" phase – in which control was supposedly allocated primarily to the market – into an authoritarian era in which public authorities sought to reclaim temporal control and redefine the nature of historical time. Time was to be repoliticized – on the Left by an enthusiasm for planning, on the Right by fascist themes of subjecting its flow to heroic control.

Planning probably involved the less grandiose conception. It meant an effort to subject economic decisions to political control and to organize the flow of resources for the future. Instead of allocating time as a commodity, time along with other collective goods would be decommodified. In the Soviet Union, where after 1928 the Plans became emblematic of the regime, they became known informally by their duration: the Pyatiletka or the Five-Years. In effect, however, the regime merely took over the subordination of present consumption to future production that bourgeois society had itself demanded, changing the mechanism for influencing time preferences from the market to the state. The invocation of utopia, and the resort to regimentation, replaced the payment of interest. The claim of the future over the present, the justification of sacrifice on behalf of a socialism and industrial development to come became the motivating vision of the regime.

No would-be totalitarian state can afford to let time remain a private resource or market commodity. But the way in which time might be nationalized or woven into the metaphors of power varied. If the Soviet discourse about time required subordinating the private present to the collective future, the fascist themes were less institutional and more primitive. Moscow propagandists envisaged history less as the record of the past than as the generator of a socialist future. Berlin's spokesmen, in contrast, sought less to subordinate the present than to perpetuate it. If the Soviet metaphors stressed social immortality – "Lenin lives!" – German political imagery consecrated national mausoleums. As the labor battalions intoned at the grandiose commemorations of the Munich Putsch, "We are building the eternal Feldherrnhallen of the Reich, the marches which lead into eternity until the hammers fall out of our hands. Then let us wall ourselves into the breast of these altars."[27] Here was a vision that denied death even while glorifying it. "Into eternity arises the cathedral/Which towers darkly over all Germans/A restless sepulchre to the world."[28] Today's reader might best recapture the atmospherics by visiting Franco's vast underground cemetery in the mountains outside Madrid, the Valley of the Fallen. The thematic of fascist or Nazi time consisted precisely of its juxtaposition of permanency with its transfiguration of death.

Of course, to select the mass choruses of the Nuremberg congresses or outdoor dramas (*Thingspiele*) must overemphasize Nazi ritual morbidity. What made such motifs acceptable was their simultaneous fusion with themes of modernization and industrial progress. Fascist Italy, as much as Germany, combined these discordant elements, foreshadowed even before World War I in the Futurist celebration of velocity and death, as incarnated in fast motorcars or armored trains. Hitler purposely punctuated his 1932 campaign for the Weimar presidency with airplane flights; the Duce's enthusiasts cheered as Italo Balbo's squadron returned from their transatlantic flight in 1935. Such efforts clearly sought to affirm the fascist conquest of time.[29] Nevertheless, in the German case, above all, the identification with modernity remained uneasy. If bourgeois time was linear and continuous, Nazi temporality attempted to transfigure and perpetuate selected moments. Nazi time (like the time of earlier Romantic poets, but unlike the Victorian emphasis on maturity) celebrated youth, but youth to be consigned to the pyre, for which SS recruits trained by jumping through the solstice fire.[30] The melding of youth, vigor, and death remained a major element of what Friedländer and J. P. Stern have both termed "Nazi kitsch." It attracted the French fascist Robert Brasillach, who recorded his horrified, homoerotic fascination with the disciplined young party members tented together for the Nuremberg rally.[31] The emphasis on youth promised the denial of aging. The dead hero never decayed; he remained immune to the universal entropy that afflicted the living. As the spirit of the dead war volunteers intoned in Richard Euringer's *Thingspiel*: "What use is it to live on and to mature? Those who survived will never grasp it; those who survived will never know it. Bliss was it to burn to death."[32] The intensity of momentary experience, preeminently that of the trenches where Hitler matured and from which the Arditi stormed, became the existential payoff, not mere duration. Fascism was the revolt of the young – "*Giovinezza, giovinezza*" in the words of its Italian hymn; and the myth, despite all the evidence of growing paunches straining brown or black shirts, was that fascism remained the movement of the young.

On the other hand, fascism was the triumph of the permanent. If the moment of collective heroism was the individual's highest destiny within the movement, the party and regime were to be eternal, hence monumentalized within the Egyptic structures that Hitler contemplated endlessly in the basement of the Chancellery. The National

Socialist Party program, the Twenty-five Points of 1920, was to remain unaltered no matter how transgressed in practice. The election of March 1933 was to be Germany's last election; the Reich would last a thousand years. Mussolini's *impero* resumed where the Romans had left off. On the individual level aging and mortality were to be transcended by climactic sacrificial intensity. On the collective level institutional decay was simply negated.

But all this, it will be protested, was propaganda and pretension. On one level yes, but it accompanied a pervasive effort to reverse liberal concepts and to decommodify time once again. If the flowing unilinear paradigm of nineteenth-century time was supplanted in favor of eternally present heroes, immutable party programs, and marble monuments, so too fascist initiatives sought to remove from the marketplace the principles for allocation of individual and collective time. How was this program to be carried out? Most obviously, the liberal labor market – more precisely, the pluralist evolution of the liberal labor market characterized by unions and collective bargaining – was to be decisively transformed. Both Italian and German regimes replaced free trade unions with new "corporations" or labor fronts, and combined new state-controlled arbitration with the prevailing enforcement of employers' control. The process culminated most brutally during the war with the importation of foreign workers and the assignment of tasks to the death camps. Labor time went from a resource to be distributed by market exchange to one that had to submit to political command.[33]

The demands of the two world wars led even liberal societies such as Britain to impose political constraints on labor and leisure time. But Britain and the United States generally sought a voluntary, patriotically motivated commitment from labor spokesmen in the form of no-strike pledges and wage restraint. Likewise, capitalist systems in general would embody some of the trends toward control of leisure time that the fascist regimes sought to encompass and control. As the historian of the Italian fascist Dopolavoro has written, "For large-scale enterprise there was nothing especially novel, much less 'fascist,' about setting up facilities to regulate the leisure of workers."[34] Moreover, the problem of workers' dissipation worried bourgeois moralists throughout industrial society as hours became limited; the saloon or café seemed to beckon perilously outside the factory gate. But for the state or party to take in hand free time as a potential political resource was a new claim. In the wake of the Italian fascist Dopolavoro, the Nazis organized Kraft durch Freude, and the other authoritarian regimes of interwar Europe followed with their workers' associations. When the International Labor Organization's board convened in 1935 to discuss leisure, no one "suggested that workers' spare time was a purely personal matter."[35]

To be sure, social democratic and labor organizations had earlier sponsored leisure activities, emphasizing sports and fraternal gatherings. But they sought to offer a workers' counterculture, to build an encompassing movement to subsist within a world of opportunities from which they felt excluded. Behind the fascist structures lay the intent to wrest control of the workers from these earlier organizations and to claim control of time. The organization of leisure was part of an embracing network of formations that were to encadre the child, youth, and adult. Balila or Hitlerjugend would prepare for party membership. Girls and women were now given organizational roles, sent to regional and national meetings, and brought into the public sphere, but one kept effectively under control by the regimes. Germans would later remember that the traditional time devoted to family activity succumbed to the various group claims as family members had to run off to one meeting or another. The demarcation of private and collective time that underlay nineteenth-century notions was eroded as much as possible.

Fascist time lasted only a historical moment. The implications of the Nazi temporal concepts hardly had the chance to be instituted. They remained claims inherent in propaganda and secular rituals. "It is clear that the trajectory of time here is not linear but circular," notes the uncanny protagonist of Michel Tournier's fictional but penetrating evocation of an SS training school. "You live not in history but in the calendar. . . . Hitlerism is resistant to any idea of progress, creation, discovery, or imagination of an unknown future. Its virtue is not rupture but restoration: hence the cult of race, ancestors, the dead, the soil."[36] Fascist time remained a psychological alignment, a longing for permanence or for a frozen moment: "The world will hold its breath."[37] And as the Nazi vision crumbled, as its architects were forced to confront their failure, they welcomed the destruction of the bourgeois past as a surrogate for the perpetuation of the fascist future: "Under the debris of our shattered cities the last so-called achievements of the middle-class nineteenth century have been finally buried. . . . Now that everything is in ruins, we are forced to rebuild Europe. . . . In trying to destroy Europe's future, the enemy has only succeeded in smashing its past; and with that everything old and outworn has gone."[38]

Decoupling time: the postliberal paradigm

To recapitulate, bourgeois concepts of time were linear and intuitive. Societies progressed through history, and the anticipated reality of future time was a vivid one. It motivated saving, investment, and family continuity. The allocation of time could be left to the market. The bourgeois family, it was assumed, would clearly delineate private from public uses of time, and this articulation of family time and work time structured much working-class experience as well. The very stress upon control and mastery of time, however, led to far more relativist concepts. Dividing time, alloting time, weighing the future against the present, finally made time appear more plastic. From being measurable it became malleable. The new consciousness of time extended from the physicists' insistence that measurable time must be "local time" to political intrusions upon leisure and private time. The new political doctrines of the twentieth century thus demanded that the party or the state control time and that the community claim more total temporal commitments from its citizens. For the Left, planning overcame the market and the market's regulation of time. Fascism and Nazism wrenched away private control of time to glorify patriotic intensity as an experience of immortal moments. Totalitarian time thus sought to transcend the linear flow inherent in liberal and bourgeois temporal consciousness. It also rejected subjecting time to market allocation.

Nonetheless, a nontotalitarian path also led away from the temporal consciousness of the nineteenth century. As time became more plastic and less of a commodity, it could be entrusted either to the state or to the individual. Totalitarian concepts resisted private, individual time. Fascism entailed a political *Gleichschaltung* of temporal commitments, not the surrender of time to subjectivity. On the level of abstract science, the partisans of "German physics" of the 1930s rejected the theory of relativity. They did not find official favor merely because Einstein was Jewish or because they promised a takeover of the scientific establishment from within. In effect, the Nazi spokesman sought to dominate the constraints of time and space through politics. This required reaffirming intuitive concepts against the epistemological sophistication of post-Newtonian physical theories. Lenin's distrust of Ernst Mach's epistemology partook of comparable misgivings: in each case recent mathematical physics seemed to undercut claims to master space and time on behalf of politics. Critics on Left and Right felt that science, rightly applied, should be able to mold the future on behalf of the community. Hence the appeal of eugenics in the Third Reich and of Lysenkan genetics under Stalin. Both totalitarian regimes favored those scientific doctrines that bestowed on politics the capacity to transcend present constraints and construct a future history through biology. But scientific ideas that seemed to privilege subjectivity were suspect.[39]

The concepts of time that have come to prevail in contemporary

Western European and American society, however, have remained relativist. Nonetheless, abandoning state efforts to restructure the public meaning of time, efforts to nationalize, in effect, the past and future, has not meant a simple return to market regulation. If nineteenth-century liberalism entrusted the market with coordinating commitments of individual time, and if fascism politicized time, postliberal society has largely renounced either recourse. It has acquiesced in the decoupling of private and collective time.

On one level, such a claim must seem paradoxical. Every individual today can own an inexpensive quartz watch that provides more accurate measures of the hour than the most expensive mechanical chronometer. Each of us can set the watch by time signals keyed to atomic clocks. The regulation of airlines, or television broadcasting, or computer time-sharing requires the alignment of time slots more intensively and carefully than ever before. But this very precision allows a customizing of time for individual consumption that could not earlier be tolerated. Measuring the flow of time with such ubiquity and accuracy makes possible oases of temporal commitment that were not earlier tolerated. If society coordinates the measurement of time, it renounces collective claims upon the uses of time. In effect we carry around our own temporality as if it were a Walkman. We are tuned in to a standard repertory but immersed in a private universe.

Postliberal time has thus become experienced as a more plastic and malleable image of time. It has continued the erosion of bourgeois time's clear articulation of past, present, and future. T. S. Eliot's painstaking effort half a century ago to dismantle sequential time and to render convincing the perception of simultaneity and recurrence, the intuition that time present encapsulates time past and time future, has tended to become so commonplace a component of postliberal sensibility that its power is hard to recover:

> Quick now, here, now, always –
> Ridiculous the waste sad time
> Stretching before and after.[40]

Critics will object, here if not earlier, that this stage theory of temporal consciousness – the transition from liberal time, through totalitarian time, to postliberal time – is too complex. Rather than stages, might it not just be the case that we have witnessed the recurring life cycle of social movements? Every historical era, it could be argued, starts with the formation of a new collective identity, the positing of a new utopia, which by its very nature demands the collapse of present and future and the forging of a long-term vision transcending personal mortality. This experience allows the renewal of social purpose and energy, what Sorel, borrowing from Vico, envisaged as a process of *ricorso*, what Durkheim labeled "collective effervescence," and what the contemporary sociologist Alberoni terms the *"stato nascente."*[41] Such moments of collective enthusiasm cannot last, however; and part of their decomposition must be the reassertion of private spaces, reemphasis on the household and property, and private time. The liberal discourse of time, in such a perspective, thus represented a reaction or detente after the era of revolution, while contemporary decoupled time follows upon the feverish ideological commitments of the earlier twentieth century. In short, rather than stages of temporal consciousness, we confront recurring political cycles. Periods of utopian construction stress public time, transcending individual mortality, collective rituals, and the constituting of new communities. Periods of reaction reaffirm privacy, the search for individual or family fulfillment, and produce a decomposition of public roles.

We need not deny such a cyclical view of temporal awareness, depending in turn upon a natural history of social movements, but we can still claim that concepts of time and the politics of time also change from cycle to cycle. What is termed here "postliberal time" corresponds to a period of postideological fervor, just as bourgeois time developed most clearly after the age of revolution in the late eighteenth century. However, decoupled postliberal time varies significantly from nineteenth-century liberal time. It remains more subjective, less disciplined, and less publicly coordinated. It possesses far less compelling a sense of future. Liberal time was still a public framework for history, family, and enterprise. Contemporary decoupled time offers more of a presentist sanctuary.

The new balance of past and future is perhaps most evident in terms of economic life. One key is the intergenerational transmission of wealth and the role of inflation. The accumulation of assets to secure family continuity was a major private concern of the middle-class family. Acquisition of a home or a postal savings account or a life insurance policy represented respectability and social anchorage for the middle class. Investment in *rentes* and consols to provide an income for children was prevalent at the higher strata. For the well-to-do, property was passed on at clearly defined occasions that marked the transit of family life, primarily at death, but also via dowries when children were married. The process of capital formation might be slow and laborious, but the moments of transmission were distinct and episodic, often eagerly awaited, and sometimes the occasion for great quarrels. Novelists such as Samuel Butler and John Galsworthy suggested, in fact, that the family was merely the host organism for property, as if wealth like some parasite cell remained immortal and merely chose successive carriers.

Intergenerational transmission of capital is still important, perhaps even more so in quantitative terms, but the mechanisms have changed so as to reduce the sense of epochal family transitions. Instead, one may speculate, a continuous two-way flow of income and assets has succeeded lump-sum donations. Social security or occupational group pension plans diminish the urgency of individual accumulation of assets. Social security, in fact, represents little more than an income transfer from those actively employed to the elderly with the promise that those who now pay will some day benefit. It establishes a counter-current of income from young to old that continuously equilibrates the transfer of assets from old to young. It weakens the conceptual link between present saving and future consumption, and it may make the older generation more willing to transfer their assets piece-meal over the long term of parenthood instead of at their own deaths or their children's marriages. Dowries disappear, but investment in children's education has become a far greater form of intergenerational capital transfer. Nonetheless, it is keyed less to any sacramental renewal of family life than to a more functional acquisition of skills. Recent twentieth-century experience has thus separated the tangibility of wealth from the major life stations that conveyed the reality of future time.[42]

The testimony of prices and interest rates suggests a similar devaluing of the future. On the threshold of World War I, prevailing interest rates were 2.5 to 3 percent; deep into the 1960s, they rarely surpassed 5 to 6 percent. The investor who laid away savings on the eve of World War I would have waited a quarter century to double his money. Today such a time horizon is inconceivable. Inflation, too, testifies to a foreshortening of the future, a preference for income in hand rather than promises of greater wealth in the future. Rapid inflation suggests that a community just does not have confidence in the preservation of assets through time, and, of course, the failure to believe there is a meaningful economic future must only stimulate inflation. Obviously inflation rates of 3 to 5 percent in 1984–85 reflect more stability than the double-digit experiences of the 1970s. Nonetheless, control of inflation has been achieved less by taxation than by capital imports in the United States and by the diffusion of high interest rates throughout the OECD economies. If the foreshortening of the future appears reversed as inflation ebbs, the precariousness of the economic sense of the future is still attested to by high interest rates. Either case amounts to a flagging capacity to credit the future and to endow it with substantial persuasiveness.

Such a fading must restrict the capacity for market coordination of claims on time. On the one hand, claims on present time are increasingly subjected to market allocation. Indeed, we have been witnessing a saturation of marketed time: whether for psychiatric hours, weekly slots of resort property, memberships in athletic clubs. But the saturation of present claims is compensated for by the weakening of intertemporal market coordination. The future is less credible and less sellable. Nor can the faltering of intertemporal commitment be overcome by democratic politics. The state can coerce present time but not future time. It cannot conscript the twenty-year-olds of the year 2000 in 1984. Perhaps it does not want to. The conditions of contemporary democratic politics – the role of the television public, the high premium on momentary economic performance, the devaluation of history that politicians themselves must respond to even when they do not encourage it – intensify the presentist preoccupations.

Contemporary society has reached a point where it may actually require less coordination of private and public time. During the heroic age of economic growth and accumulation, market incentives that rendered future rewards a convincing alternative to present consumption or leisure had to play an important role. During the bleak interwar years when many Western nations turned to authoritarian regimes, the coordination of private time was likewise important. The authoritarian regimes perceived private time as a resource for political opposition. But if the collective project of a society is precisely to have no collective project, then its role should be only that of "servicing," so to speak, the exploitations of private time. The nightwatchman state becomes the state that winds the clocks. Moreover, it is precisely the "customization" of time – the creation of everyone's temporal oasis – that helps to define this new state role.[43]

To be sure there are countercurrents. When Laurence Wylie returned to Roussillon in 1961, a decade after being told that trees were too long-term an investment, he could see "fruit orchards in every direction" and even olive trees that would not bear for twenty years.[44] It is unclear whether the attrition of public time is a trend that marks an epoch or is just part of the general impatience with state intervention in civil society that has characterized the electoral politics of the 1980s in Britain, the United States, West Germany, and elsewhere. Many of the political "movements" discussed by Claus Offe in this volume rebel against this flattening of time. When such movements worry about the arms race or about ecology, they protest the devaluation of the future; they have long-term horizons. Yet to a degree they must thereby represent the past as well as the future. For environmentalism offers a notion of public allocation of time and space – it frets about future forests – which is certainly not the fascist rejection of time as a commodity but does express a dissatisfaction with decoupled time. Environmentalism yearns for the reintroduction of the collective future into the public agenda.

Whether feminism and the women's movement have a similar preoccupation seems more ambiguous. To be sure, women's spokesmen often claim to speak for the nurturing priorities of society, the concern for human needs through the life cycle. On the other hand, societies that earlier imposed great collective projects often did so at the expense of women's aspirations for public-sphere participation. Fascism assigned women the task of continuing the race through physical reproduction and family tasks. Democracies that have stressed the historical future have often insisted on the compartmentalization of family life from public participation. Such a legacy has necessarily made feminism distrustful of public projects in which women were to play restricted roles. In contrast, decoupled time has largely responded to women's needs for flexibility of family and work roles in the life cycle and even in the working day. The women's movement, in short, involves less of a collective nostalgia for the future than environmentalism or the disarmament movement.

Recent indications suggest, however, that a new balance of collective and individual time may be sought. American politicians talk about work and family, values that presuppose a basis in private time but that also entail a commitment to a long-range future. European leaders demand present sacrifices to restructure their economies for long-term viability. The principles on which to reassert the future, to propose a collective agenda, remain unclear. Bourgeois Europe had one coherent approach. It treated the control of time and space as property rights so that they might be exchanged for others of value. To commodify space and time, liberal Europe had to mark out clearer frontiers, build better walls and clearer work schedules. In so doing, it implicitly stressed the values of privacy and leisure. There may be no equally robust normative principles for the allocation of time today. The liberal willingness to trade the present for the future has dissipated; the Christian vision of the future no longer compels; and no sufficient political consensus exists to make imperative allocations. Nor should we necessarily desire them. European history has suffered too greatly at the hands of those, on one side, who were intoxicated with the future, and those, on the other side, who dreaded that it might depart from the past. Still, as Albert Hirschman has written, Western societies oscillate between private and public commitments, between an atrophy and an orgy of civic commitment. "What is to be done about this atrophy and subsequent spasm? How can we learn to take up public causes with enthusiasm, yet without the frenzy and the millennarian expectations that guarantee failure and massive disappointment?"[45] Certainly one component of that lesson must be the recovery of time as a theme of politics. This requires in turn the re-creation of a public agenda based upon the long-term, one that validates earlier civic achievements and envisions our collective future as history.

Notes

1 Thomas Mann, *The Magic Mountain* [1924], H. T. Lowe-Porter, trans. (New York: Knopf, 1960), pp. 541–542.

2 Weber stresses, of course, the resources of politics, that is, constraint. Kelsen emphasizes the conjunction of norm and enforcement. The tough-minded stress on constraint can also oversimplify the political. Carl Schmitt's insistence on friend versus foe (much like Lenin's idea of who [dominates] whom, *kto-kovo*) virtually makes all political life into civil war. Elements of trust, legitimacy, law, and reciprocity should also remain crucial to the idea of the political. See the Introduction to this volume.

3 An analogy might be sought in the physics of General Relativity and subsequent unification theories. These models have reinterpreted forces originally envisaged as the properties of bodies in space as aspects of the geometry of space–time in its own right.

4 Sebastian de Grazia, *Of Time Work and Leisure* (New York: Twentieth Century Fund, 1962), pp. 408–437, in which it is argued that leisure frankly postulates inequality, that politics should help foster the conditions for leisure, but true leisure cannot be construed as functional for the state. Benjamin Constant, on the other hand, maintained that the direct democracy of the polis often amounted just to a way to fill time and fend off *inquiétude*, while modern representation was a desirable expedient for citizens with crowded schedules: Modern liberty allowed autonomy and time to oneself. See Stephen Holmes, *Benjamin Constant and the Making of Modern Liberalism* (New Haven, Conn.: Yale University Press, 1984), pp. 59–60, 73–74. For a recent sample of the large literature on leisure and its definition as the "freedom from the basic primary obligations derived from the basic units of society" (p. 74), whether work or collective ritual, see Joffre Dumazedier, *Sociology of Leisure* (Amsterdam and New York: Elsevier, 1974).

5 In addition to writing extensively on people's use of time, sociologists have traced how individuals' personal sense of time changes under stress. See, for instance, the questionnaires cited by Marie Jahoda, Paul F. Lazarsfeld, and Hans Zeisel in *Die Arbeitslosen von Marienthal* (Leipzig, 1932), which revealed that unemployed workers could not account for their allocation of time during idle days; hours vanished in the recalling. Anthropologists explore the implications of temporal concepts, and Pierre Bourdieu has insisted that the observer's awareness of how a society deals with time – whether in delaying revenge, reciprocating gifts, or constructing ritual calendars – allows the social scientist to overcome the rigid epistemological separation between the society's actual practice and the structural patterns posited by the observer. See Bourdieu, *Outline of a Theory of Practice*, Richard Nice, trans. (Cambridge: Cambridge University Press, 1977), pp. 3–9, 97–107. Theorists such as Max Weber and, following him, Alfred Schutz, identified time as an underlying dimension of meaningful social action, which is based upon memory of the past and expectations of fulfillment in the future. Cf. Talcott Parsons, *The Structure of Social Action* (New York: Free Press, 1968): "The time category is basic to the scheme [of purposive social action]. The concept end always implies a future reference" (p. 45; and cf. p. 732).

Economists now debate the significance of time for their theories. Classical economics always balanced future enjoyment against present restraint in concepts of investment and interest rates. Post-Keynesians, however, insist more radically that a concept of historical time undermines the very possibility of economic equilibrium. See Basil Moore's argument that the concept of general equilibrium is vitiated by acceptance of historical time (i.e., time as a one-way vector in contrast to the physicists' potentially reversible time), in Alfred S. Eichner, ed., *A Guide to Post-Keynesian Economics* (White Plains, N.Y.: M. E. Sharpe, 1979), pp. 120–122. Paul Davidson argues similarly that general equilibrium models cannot deal with calendar time because they allow for no intervening shocks after the stipulation of initial parameters. See his article in Daniel Bell and Irving Kristol, eds., *The Crisis of Economic Theory: The Public Interest* (Special Edition, 1980):156–159. For an applied discussion of economic behavior where duration becomes a major variable in its own right, see Tibor Scitowsky, *The Joyless Economy: An Inquiry into Human Satisfaction and Consumer Dissatisfaction* (New York: Oxford University Press, 1976). On the issue of allocating scarce present time, see Gary S. Becker, "A Theory of Allocation of Time," *Economic Journal* 75 (1965):493–517.

Historians, too, have turned to time as a subject in its own right, and not merely as a medium they have generally taken for granted, much as swimmers do with water. A large historical literature now presents the transition from premodern notions of time – irregular, compressed into variable segments according to seasons and needs – to modern or industrial time, allegedly expropriated by the entrepreneur to discipline an emerging capitalist work force. Thus the history of regulating time has now become familiar, made all the more so with David S. Landes's recent *Revolution in Time: Clocks and the Making of the Modern World* (Cambridge, Mass.: Harvard University Press, 1983). For some aspects of the medieval meaning of time, see Jacques Le Goff, "Merchant's Time and Church's Time in the Middle Ages," in *Time, Work, and Culture in the Middle Ages*, Arthur Goldhammer, trans. (Chicago: University of Chicago Press, 1980), pp. 29–42. Also Edward P. Thompson, "Time Work-Discipline, and Industrial Capitalism," *Past & Present* 38 (1967):56–97; Tamara Hareven, *Family Time and Industrial Time* (Cambridge: Cambridge University Press, 1982); also the recent synthesis of Stephen Kern, *The Culture of Time and Space 1880–1918* (Cambridge, Mass.: Harvard University Press, 1983). Perhaps the most profound historical treatment of time as a category of political thinking is J. G. A. Pocock, *The Machiavellian Moment: Florentine Political Thought and the Atlantic Republican Tradition* (Princeton, N.J.: Princeton University Press, 1975), which I draw upon below. For a revealing contrast between European, Christian "one-directional time of apotheosis and fulfillment" and Mesoamerican "cyclical repetitive time frozen in an unalterable sequence," see Tzvetan Todorov, *The Conquest of America*, Richard Howard, trans. (New York: Harper & Row, 1984), pp. 86–87. And for a recent survey of concepts of time in philosophy and history, see Krzysztov Pomian, *L'ordre du temps* (Paris: Gallimard, 1984).

6 Georg Friedrich Wilhelm Hegel, *Phänomenologie des Geistes* (Frankfurt am Main: Suhrkamp, 1975). Cf. Martin Heidegger's critique in *Sein und Zeit*, 14th ed. (Tübingen: Max Niemeyer Verlag, 1977), para. 82. For Heidegger, temporality is the prior condition that allows existence to "fall away" from being-as-such into the realms of everyday life and historicity. Cf., too, Heidegger's discussion of "world time" as the time we measure publicly through clocks, calendars, and significant events (para. 81) – all of which represent, in some sense, our unsuccessful effort to evade an awareness of death and the limits of being.

7 Modern medicine forces some shading of this generalization, but only at the margin. Societies may have to make a choice over how to use scarce resources that can now prolong life. They also decide between investing in prevention for the many or high-tech medicine for the few: Pap tests or CT scans. Hence there is a politics of

triage, but that will not be treated here. There are also political discussions concerning the *uses* of time. Traditionally, the celebration of leisure, or the concern for its proper use, has marked conservative social critiques.

8 Karl Mark, *Capital*, vol. 1 (Moscow: Foreign Languages Publishing House, 1959), chap. 10, section 5, p. 264, and section 7, p. 299. Cf. also p. 271.

9 This does not hold for political efforts to establish legislative limits on the working day. The struggle for the eight-hour day in Europe in the aftermath of World War I provoked many discussions of the uses of time. So, too, has the recent movement for further reduction of labor. A good sample is found in the publications of the French group Echanges et Projets. See their volume *La révolution du temps choisi* (Paris: Albin Michel, 1980), calling for a *"politique globale"* of time (p. 251) that would cut down on work, break the lockstep of schooling and labor, and enhance labor.

10 Le Goff, "Labor Time in the 'Crisis' of the Fourteenth Century: From Medieval Time to Modern Time," in *Time, Work, and Culture*, pp. 43–57; Landes, *Revolution in Time*, pp. 58–78.

11 On the different textures of Catholic and Protestant time, see Natalie Davis, "The Sacred and the Body Social in Sixteenth-Century Lyon," *Past and Present* 90 (February 1981):40–70. For the connection of time and ritual, see Emile Durkheim, *The Elementary Forms of the Religious Life* [1912], 2nd ed. (London: George Allen & Unwin, 1976), pp. 209–19. And, of course, ritual-punctuated time was not wiped out all of a piece. See Laurence Wylie's evocation of the pre-1914 village life in "Peyrane," in *Village in the Vaucluse* (New York: Harper & Row, 1964), chap. 13.

12 See Pocock, *Machiavellian Moment*, esp. pp. 78–80, 423–505.

13 Thomas Hobbes, *Leviathan*, Part I, chap. 13.

14 John Locke, *The Second Treatise of Government*, chap. 5, paras. 37, 45–50.

15 Cited in Kern, *Culture of Time and Space*, p. 11.

16 See Wolfgang Schivelbusch, "Railroad Space and Railroad Time," *New German Critique* 14 (1978):31–40.

17 Wylie, *Village in the Vaucluse*, p. 33.

18 For extensive bibliographies and exploration of the influences between the two societies, see the essays collected in W. J. Mommsen, ed., *The Emergence of the Welfare State in Britain and Germany, 1850–1950* (London: Croom Helm and the German Historical Institute, 1981).

19 William M. Reddy, *The Rise of Market Culture: The Textile Trade and French Society, 1750–1900* (Cambridge: Cambridge University Press, 1984). "Market society was a mirage. Market culture was the social order that emerged when the language of this mirage insinuated its assumptions into the everyday practice of European society" (pp. 1–2).

20 Michel Foucault, *The Order of Things: An Archeology of the Human Sciences* (New York: Random House, Vintage 1973), p. 225.

21 Reddy, *The Rise of Market Culture*, p. 244.

22 David Brody, *Steelworkers: the Non-Union Era* (New York: Harper Torchbooks, 1969), pp. 37–39.

23 Cited by Peter Bailey, *Leisure and Class in Victorian England* (London: Routledge & Kegan Paul, 1978), p. 180.

24 Cited in Abraham Pais, *The Science and the Life of Albert Einstein* (New York: Oxford University Press, 1983), pp. 126–128. Cf. also Arthur I. Miller, *Imagery in Scientific Thought: Creating 20th Century Physics* (Boston and Basel: Birkhäuser, 1984), pp. 99ff.

25 The literature on scientific management and work processes is now a large one. For a now classic Marxian critique, Harry Braverman, *Labor and Monopoly Capital: The Degradation of Work in the Twentieth Century* (New York: Monthly Review Press, 1974),

and for an important critique, see Michael Burawoy, *The Politics of Production* (London: Verso, 1985), pp. 21–84; for the impact of American concepts in Europe, see Charles S. Maier, "Between Taylorism and Technocracy: European Ideologies and the Vision of Industrial Productivity in the 1920's," *Journal of Contemporary History* 5, no. 2 (1970):27–61; for a recent assessment stressing indigenous sources, and a useful bibliography, see Robert Boyer, "L'introduction du Taylorisme en France à la lumière de recherches récentes" (Paris: CEPREMAP, 1983). For this and other useful essays by Heidrun Homburg, Aimée Moutet, and others, see the "Colloque International sur le Taylorisme. Université Paris XIII, May, 2–4, 1983. For the question of "summer time," see Ian Bartky and E. Harrison, "Standard and Daylight Saving Time," *Scientific American* 240, no. 5 (May 1979). For the strike of the clockhands, see Giuseppe Maione, "Il biennio rosso: lo sciopero delle lancette," *Storia Contemporanea* 3, no. 2 (1972):239–304.

26 One philosophical reaction was to celebrate time, in effect, as infralinguistic – to be really understood only intuitively as the underlay of existence. Cf. Henri Bergson's notion of *durée* in *An Introduction to Metaphysics* [1903], T. A. Goudge, ed., T. E. Hulme, trans., (New York: Liberal Arts Press, 1949), and the discussion in Kern, *Culture of Time and Space*, chap. 3, "The Present," which documents diverse literary and philosophical efforts to "thicken" the present and overcome its separation from the past or history.

27 Cited in Klaus Vondung, *Magie und Manipulation. Ideologischer Kult und politische Religion des Nationalsozialismus* (Göttingen: Vandenhoeck & Ruprecht, 1971), p. 31. I have drawn this quote from Saul Friedländer, *Reflections of Nazism: An Essay on Kitsch and Death* (New York: Harper & Row, 1983), p. 51, a suggestive, albeit allusive, work. For the Soviet celebration of Leninist immortality, see Nina Tomarkin, *Lenin Lives!* (Cambridge, Mass.: Harvard University Press, 1982).

28 Gerhard Schumann, "Ins Ungeheur steigt die Kathedrale," cited by Ernst Loewy, *Literatur unterm Hakenkreuz* (Frankfurt am Main, 1966), p. 239, and by Richard Grunberger, *A Social History of the Third Reich* (Harmondsworth: Penguin, 1974), p. 447. Cf. Elia Canetti's description of Speer's monumental architectural plans that would perpetuate Hitler's dominance over the masses, in "Hitler, nach Speer," in *Das Geswissen der Worte* (Munich: Hansen Verlag, n.d.), esp. pp. 163–170.

29 See most recently Jeffrey Herf, *Reactionary Modernism* (Cambridge: Cambridge University Press, 1984); and for an evocation of Italian fascist emphasis on technology, see the 1984 Colosseum exhibit, *L'economia italiana tra le due guerre 1919–1939* (Rome: IPSOA and Comune di Roma, 1984).

30 Michel Tournier, *The Ogre*, Barbara Bray, trans. (New York: Pantheon, c. 1972), pp. 282–284; cf. Friedländer, *Reflections of Nazism*, p. 31.

31 Robert Brasillach, *Notre avant-guerre* [1941], in Maurice Bardèche, ed., *Oeuvres Complètes de Robert Brasillach*, vol. 6 (Paris: Club de l'Honnête Homme, 1964), pp. 257–274 – a section taken from "Cent heures chez Hitler," *Revue Universelle*, October 1, 1937.

32 Cited by Grunberger, *A Social History of the Third Reich*, p. 459. *Thingspiele* were allegedly *urdeutsch* amphitheater melanges of patriotic drama and choral recitation. Cf. Rainer Strommer, "'Da oben versinkt der Alltag. . . .' Thingstätten im Dritten Reich als Demonstration der Volksgemeinschaftsideologie," in Detlev Peukert and Jürgen Reulecke, eds., *Die Reihen fast Geschlossen: Beiträge zur Geschichte des Alltags unterm Nationalsozialismus* (Wuppertal: Hammer, 1981).

33 For the best recent discussions of the control of labor in the Third Reich, see Carola Sachse, Tilla Siegel, Hasso Spode, and Wolfgang Spohn (with an introduction by Timothy W. Mason), *Angst, Belohnung, Zucht und Ordnung* (Opladen: Westdeutscher Verlag, 1982).

34 Victoria de Grazia, *The Culture of Consent: Mass Organization of Leisure in Fascist Italy* (Cambridge: Cambridge University Press, 1981), p. 60.

35 Cited ibid., p. 240.

36 Michel Tournier, *The Ogre*, pp. 265–266.

37 Cited as a chapter title by Alan Bullock in *Hitler: A Study in Tyranny* (London, 1952).

38 Joseph Goebbels's address on Radio Werewolf, cited by H. R. Trevor-Roper, *The Last Days of Hitler* (London, 1971), p. 58, and by J. P. Stern, *Hitler: The Führer and the People* (Berkeley and Los Angeles: University of California Press, 1975), p. 34.

39 See Alan Beyerchen, *Scientists Under Hitler: Politics and the Physics Community in the Third Reich* (New Haven, Conn.: Yale University Press, 1977); Herbert Mertens and Steffen Richter, *Naturwissenschaft, Technik, und NS-Ideologie. Beiträge zur Wissenschaftsgeschichte des Dritten Reichs* (Frankfurt am Main: Suhrkamp, 1980); and David Joravsky, *The Lysenko Affair* (Cambridge, Mass.: Harvard University Press, 1970).

40 "Burnt Norton," the first of "The Four Quartets," in *The Complete Poems and Plays* (New York: Harcourt Brace, 1952), p. 122.

41 See Franco Alberoni, *Movimento e Istituzione* (Bologna: Mulino, 1977), pp. 35, 45–103; cf. Georges Sorel, *Reflections on Violence* [1908] (Paris: Marcel Rivière, 1950), pp. 129–30; Emile Durkheim, *The Elementary Forms of the Religious Life*, 2nd ed. (London: George Allen & Unwin, 1976), pp. 9–10, 209–219, 439–440, on the collective definitions of time through ritual and moments of collective enthusiasm; Victor Turner's discussion of "liminal states" in *Drama, Fields and Metaphors* (Ithaca, N.Y.: Cornell University Press, 1975), chap. 6.

42 Jack Goody has summarized the relationship of landholding patterns on the structure of marriage and child-rearing in "Strategies of Heirship," *Comparative Studies in Society and History* 15, no. 1 (1973):3–20.

43 The result, however, may not simply be the renunciation of collective time, the loss of a community awareness of history and of a collective future. It can also be the devaluation of the private time that becomes available in larger doses. Between 1934 and 1966, American salaried and wage-earning men reduced their time at meals, movies, card playing, reading books, and traveling, to devote at least half of the hours saved to television. See Scitovsky, *The Joyless Economy*, p. 163, summarizing a paper by J. P. Robinson, "Social Change as Measured by Time Budgets." Other laments in the same vein include S. B. Linder, *The Harried Leisure Class* (New York: Columbia University Press, 1970).

44 Wylie, *Village in the Vaucluse*, p. 364.

45 Albert O. Hirschman, *Shifting Involvements: Private Interest and Public Action* (Princeton, N.J.: Princeton University Press, 1982), pp. 132–133.

Part II
Changing boundaries of political activity

5

Long waves in the development of welfare systems

MASSIMO PACI

> Historical research must force open the gates of the present. The paradox is
> that the best means to that end seems to me an immersion in what I have
> called the historical *longue durée*.
>
> Fernand Braudel

Dimensions of social protection and welfare

The overwhelming public support for government intervention in the
social field and for the welfare state has been gradually but surely
weakening. As one official observer has pointed out:

In the early 1960's it would have been very difficult to find any long-term
forecast not based on the assumption that the growth of the welfare state
was just as long lasting – and for that matter just as desirable – a process as
economic growth itself. Since then, however, general attitudes have changed
considerably and the ruling thought nowadays is more probably that the
continued growth of the welfare state is neither likely nor even desirable.[1]

Indeed, both neoliberal and neo-Marxist analyses of the crisis of
the welfare state converge. They argue that the spectacular growth
of public expenditures in Western countries in the last decades endangers the accumulation process. The burden imposed upon business to finance welfare programs together with the rise in the interest
rates resulting from deficit financing induce a scarcity in the supply
of capital for productive investment. Albert Hirschmann reminds us
that this argument was advanced long ago by Colin Clark, who "alleged that in the nature of the capitalist system a fairly rigid limit was
set to the ability to divert factor income for purposes of expanding
social services and other public expenditures."[2]

Growing awareness of the limits of the welfare state has led to a
reappraisal of the role of the market, of the family, and of voluntary
organizations as alternative mechanisms of resource allocation for the

179

provision of social protection and welfare. In the words of Emile Van Lennep, Secretary General of the Organization for Economic Cooperation and Development (OECD), "New relationships between action by the state and private action must be sought; new agents for welfare and well-being developed; the responsibilities of individuals for themselves and others reinforced. It is in this sense that the emergence of the Welfare Society is both inevitable and desirable."[3]

In the United States advocates of less government and more competition in matters of welfare are gaining influence in the health field of policy. The Stockman–Gephart bill, for instance, introduced in the Congress in 1981, calls for elimination of federal regulatory programs in health care, with the argument that "The American people, not a regulatory superstructure, should determine how they will obtain health care and at what cost. *This can be done only if economic competition replaces government control and if customer responsibility replaces government regulation.* What is needed is a fundamental change in the structure of the system."[4]

In Western Europe this promarket and procompetition policy thrust remains less prominent, at least with respect to the provision of public services. Still, there is growing attention to the welfare role played by family and voluntary organizations. One important policy option is to reverse the trend toward bureaucratization by a system of incentives designed to encourage provision within the family. Signs of this "resocialization of social welfare" have appeared in many countries with schemes to encourage families to look after handicapped members, to take on foster children, and so on.[5] Similarly, the World Health Organization (WHO) has recently called for

a new type of health education . . . starting from consumer demands and building on existing skills and knowledge rather than replacing them through hard interventionist measures. Well developed self-care programs could transfer many technical skills to lay persons while at the same time making use of traditional health practices in the family . . . The appeal of self-care and self-help can be expected to grow as self-diagnostic and self-treatment technology is developed, as the demand for caring services supersedes demand for curative services.[6]

These new policy concepts imply a major revision in the conventional wisdom of social science. In the new view an extensive, mature welfare state no longer represents the most progressive historical response to needs for social protection as compared with that offered by market or voluntary organizations. Many cultural developments have contributed to altering the conventional, "evolutionist" view, from neoliberal and neo-Marxist analyses of the fiscal burdens of the welfare state to the social critique of custodialism developed by authors as diverse as Michel Foucault, Thomas Szasz, Ivan Illich, Erving Goffman, and others, all of whom demand enfranchisement of the consumers (the poor, the sick, the aged) and their liberation from bureaucratic, even totalitarian, institutions.[7]

But if the evolutionary or unilinear model has failed, we still lack a new model that explains how and why the boundaries between market, state, and voluntary agencies in the provision of social welfare change over time and across countries. To attempt to construct such a model today is probably an impossible undertaking. Here I will limit myself to a description of some crucial moments in the history of social policy in the hope of contributing some elements to a much needed formal analysis of the main factors and processes in the search for an appropriate balance among market, welfare state policies, and voluntary organizations. Before taking on this task, however, a discussion of some essential analytical perspectives is useful.

Marxists approach these issues with a "two-sector" model, that is, one describing only the relationships between the state and the capitalist market, leaving aside the "third sector" represented by family, traditional institutions, and voluntary organizations. This restrictive focus probably derives from Marx's own emphasis on the process of "commodification" of social relations under capitalism and on the subservience of all moral and private relations to the "cash nexus." Of course, the social and economic processes that Marx observed were quite congruent with his theory: Rapid industrialization and uncontrolled urbanization were weakening traditional family and community ties. But we know now that those years, the heyday of market capitalism, were historical anomalies; before and after the family, mutual aid and voluntary organizations played important roles in the distribution of resources and particularly in the provision of social protection. Yet even if developed to explain a particular historical moment, Marxist theory today still retains the original vision of "commodification" of personal and community relations through capitalism.[8]

Marxists today focus on the question of the "functional" or "dysfunctional" (or "contradictory") relationship between welfare measures and market capitalism. Until recently, prevailing interpretation on the Left has been that social welfare programs are "functional" to capitalism since they assure the reproduction of a healthy and skilled labor force, thus keeping down wage costs. Without these social overhead programs, higher wages would be required to make wage labor more acceptable and to assure a supply of labor. This kind of functionalist explanation was embedded in the general view of the welfare state as an instrument of social control in a capitalist society, arising from the need to quiet the discontent generated by surplus labor.[9]

But a different view now emerging on the Left suggests that the very expansion of social welfare has contributed to increasing the power of workers in the labor market. Bowles and Gintis demonstrate, for example, that during the last thirty years the growth of the "social wage" in the United States has been five times as rapid as the growth of labor's direct compensation, and they conclude that the expansion of social policies curtails the mechanism of the "industrial reserve army" and results in a partial "deproletarianization" of labor.[10] Similarly, Piven and Cloward recall that almost half of the aggregate income of the bottom fifth of the American population is derived from social welfare benefits, so that "the poorest people in this country are now as much dependent on government for their subsistence as they are dependent on the market," and they point out that "an industrial reserve army of labor with unemployment benefits and food stamps is less effective as an instrument by which to deflate wages and workplace demands."[11]

In this new Marxist interpretation such weakening of the mechanism of the "industrial reserve army" is part of a general process of "decommodification" of labor and wants induced by expansion of the welfare state.[12] If we agree with this new radical interpretation that contemporary social policies have not turned out to be functional for capitalism at all, it would still be a mistake to conclude that they are necessarily dysfunctional. Indeed, the relationship between welfare policies and the capitalist market seems much like the one that the market, according to Fred Hirsch, maintains with "precontractual" or "preindustrial" values: These last need to remain strong enough to provide a moral basis for the legitimation of capitalism, but not so strong as to curtail the development and functioning of the market.[13] The same can be said of public welfare: Too much of it leads to rigidity of employment and wages and curtails profits, but too little drives up wages as the only means left to assure the "social reproduction" of the working class. From this point of view, the functional versus dysfunctional nature of the relationship between capitalism and the welfare state seems more a matter of historical circumstances and vicissitudes than a "structural" attribute defined once and for all.

Thus the differential development of social policies over time and across countries can be broadly described as an experimental process of defining boundaries between three different resource-allocation mechanisms: the market, voluntary or traditional nonprofit institutions, and the welfare state. Karl Polanyi's classic distinctions among three alternative processes of allocating values in society is apposite here. Polanyi contends that markets dominated resource allocation for only a brief era in the nineteenth century. Before and after two other allocation systems or "transactional modes" characterized the distribution of resources in society: "reciprocity," that is, obligatory gift-giving between kin and friends, and "redistribution," or obligatory payments to a central political authority that uses the receipts for its own maintenance to provide community services and as an emergency stock in case of individual or community disaster.[14]

Polanyi's typology of resource allocation, however, cannot in its own right explain historically why one allocative means assumes primacy over the others. As Douglass North has pointed out, it is unclear how the boundaries between the three "transactional modes" are established and how or why they shift over time.[15] Others, however, have attempted an explanation. R. Mishra, for example, has analyzed state-provided social services (and fiscal benefits), "occupational welfare" provided by the market through the firm, and charitable assistance provided by traditional or voluntary associations. For Mishra these are alternative provisions: Where statutory assistance remains low, mutual aid and occupational welfare are high, and he cites the Japanese case "where occupational welfare forms a part of the traditional (feudal) paternalistic relation ('familialism') between the employer and the employee," and the case of the United States where "the absence of a public health-care system and the low level of state pensions have encouraged the development of occupational benefits to fill the gap."[16]

In his recent work, Albert Hirschman has offered a more important contribution to the problem of explaining long-term changes in welfare systems.[17] He believes it is possible to specify in the capitalist countries a long-term cycle of collective behavior moving along the public-private axis as individuals make the "critical evaluation of their own choices and experiences . . . an important factor behind new and different choices."[18] For Hirschman citizen-consumers oscillate between preferences for the private and the public sectors, impelled back and forth as their expectations about the quality of goods and services each sector can provide are continually disappointed. Public services, according to Hirschman, are particularly vulnerable to the danger of disappointing consumers, especially when, as occurred in recent decades, they have undergone rapid expansion with a deterioration of inputs such as untrained personnel and technical and organizational deficiencies.

Thus this analysis would suggest that the expansion of the welfare state, more than representing the apex of a unilinear historical process, is part of a long cycle of demands, whose turning points constitute realignments between private and public sectors. To be sure, Hirschman's notion that the deterioration of public services leads more to discontent within the public sector (*voice*) and not to defections (or *exit*) on the part of dissatisfied citizen-consumers outside remains puzzling (and is hardly elaborated in his analysis). That idea forms a strange presupposition in an analysis designed to account for the shifts of demand along the private–public axis. Moreover, this interpretation is burdened by a presumption of a monopoly provision of public goods that is hardly realistic. As several authors, especially Burton Weisbrod, have shown, the private and nonprofit sectors are prepared to offer substitutes for public services even if not perfect equivalents. From the point of view of our concerns, the private–public axis that Hirschman focuses on is insufficient to describe the varieties of social protection we find in historical experience. For this we must take into account as well the "third sector."

As Weisbrod contends, the conventional two-sector model, public versus private, for provision of collective goods is inadequate. Consumers may find themselves in a "suboptimal" position both in the private sector, by making socially inefficient choices, and in the public one, by having to accept too much or too little. Thus a third, the "voluntary nonprofit," sector develops to accommodate the behavior of consumers. Changes over time and across countries in the substitution ratios among the three sectors can thus be explained in terms of political demand and changes in per capita income levels. Until a political majority is able to demand public provision of a collective good, the minority will have to remain satisfied with voluntary organizations. As sufficiently coherent political demand emerges and as a society generates sufficient national income, it moves to supplant traditional family or charitable provisions with public welfare. Once per capita income reaches a relatively high level, however, consumers develop diversified needs and seek market substitutes for the public provision of goods, thus making the long-term relationship between income levels and the size of the public sector resemble an inverted U curve.[19]

Roughly speaking, this kind of model fits the long-term development of Western European social policies. In the case of health policy, philanthropic care and voluntary hospitals preceded the development of public institutions in the first half of the nineteenth century, just as friendly societies were developed before national health insurance during the second half of the century.

Still, to study the long-term change in the boundaries between the welfare state, the market, and voluntary organizations, Weisbrod's model has to be supplemented in at least two respects. On the supply side, one must take into account variables such as technology with its impact on the ability of private providers to substitute for public services. (The shift from public health to private medicine at the beginning of this century depended in part on the "therapeutic revolution" and the availability of new marketable drugs.) On the demand side, Weisbrod's model also requires greater shading. Public intervention in welfare matters has not always depended on the emergence of a homogeneous majority constituency. Indeed, the role of the political mobilization of the working class in the development of social legislation is strong only in those European societies that introduced social insurance schemes relatively late.[20] Impulses promoting welfare measures elsewhere came from political leaders, such as Bismarck, who were intrinsically conservative and hardly pressured by a homogeneous majority.[21]

Thus, to summarize, evolutionary and dichotomous schemes must be supplemented in two major respects. The first major amendment must be to emphasize the analytical importance of the so-called third sector, in addition to that of state and market, in which social protection is provided by reciprocity, whether within such traditional frameworks as the extended family, local communities, charities, and corporate fraternities, or within modern frameworks based on voluntary association. The second amendment is to substitute a long-term cyclical scheme for the idea of a unilinear welfare-system development characterized by the progressive growth of state intervention. In fact, it is a question of emphasizing the plausibility of several historical recurrences in long-term welfare history rather than a real cycle as such in the forms of social protection. As Hirschman has observed, any persuasive cyclical theory must be endogenous, that is, it must demonstrate that every phase is driven necessarily by the "internal contradictions" of the prior phase.[22] But we are still far from being able to demonstrate this. Even a casual glance at the evolution of national welfare systems reveals the importance of exogenous variables such as war or technical innovation, with decisive discoveries and inventions. Nonetheless, the idea of a long cycle allows us to read afresh the historical and comparative material and to offer a new framework for judging the contemporary debate on the "crisis of the welfare state." For these purposes I will try to apply the cyclical and three-sector scheme to the long-term evolution of British welfare, aware, of course, of the deficiencies in this initial application.

Self-help, mutual aid, public relief

In preindustrial societies, care of the poor and sick was left to the household and to private charity. The organization of poor relief was in the hands of the clergy, who provided assistance through the parishes. As Rimlinger notes, "A production process based on peasant and artisan household provided for the cost of maintaining the household over its life cycle: most of the costs of social and economic insecurity were internalized."[23] The period from the early sixteenth to the late eighteenth century was a time of transition. Poverty and public health problems were treated in much the same way as in the medieval community, and the administrative patterns were hardly altered. Nonetheless, the increased perception of beggars and vagrants in the seventeenth century, the apparent inadequacy of family and private charities, increasingly drew in central public authorities. The rationale for state intervention was less public assistance per se than social control and security. The legislation relating to the poor began with measures to repress beggars and kept this character until the mid-nineteenth century and, in many countries, even later. As Sydney and Beatrice Webb argued, the British system up to the early nineteenth century was "relief for the poor within a framework of repression."[24]

The early transition in Britain from a kinship and charity-based tradition to the "public assistance system," in which intervention complemented market forces, was related in part to Britain's early industrialization. But the shift had other reasons as well. The "peculiar pattern of secularization," characterized by the church's early withdrawal from welfare activity, and the multiplicity of sects also played a role.[25] Whether or not the extended family system ever existed in preindustrial Britain is a subject of lively debate; nonetheless, Michael Anderson has concluded that England, together with northern France, the United States, and perhaps the Netherlands, was exceptional for its low percentage of extended family aggregates. Within the cities, the industrial division of labor eroded family unity.[26] As Chiara Saraceno has written, "Neither a property holding unit nor a unit of labor, the working-class family was based on wages, but this condition, especially at the beginnings of industrialization (roughly 1750 to 1850), was precisely the condition that prevented it from being a living community"[27] – a condition aggravated by the loss of domestic capacity on the part of women whose childhood and adolescence had to be dedicated to factory labor.

Given the weakening of kinship and religious networks, the traditional landed classes responded to growing landed poverty by introducing the so-called Speenhamland system to southern counties in 1795. Created in the spirit of the old order, the aim of the Speenhamland system was to establish a living family wage by tying the income of the laborer to the price of bread and to family size. The enactment can be seen as the last attempt to keep the family and the village as the cadres of social welfare. But Speenhamland could not outlast the economic crisis engendered by the Napoleonic Wars, the subsequent tariff protection given to wheat producers, and a series of exceptionally poor harvests between 1811 and 1831. The increase of the family, the guaranteed minimal family income, put such a heavy burden on the local relief system that its costs began to undermine the economic base of the landed class. On the other side, by tying farm families to the parish, the system was a hindrance to the labor mobility increasingly required by the industrial economy.[28]

These pressures all led to a shift to the "public assistance system" embodied in the New Poor Law of 1834, which superseded the Speenhamland system of outdoor relief and was designed "to drive men to work or into the workhouse."[29] The new ideology of *laissez-faire* and *self-help* behind the 1834 act and other reforms conformed not only to middle-class attitudes but to the behavior of a growing part of the working class as well. The rise of real wages from 1820, and even more clearly after 1840, led to a demand for market-based services. The number of families with salaried live-in servants in British and North American cities rose to about 15 or 20 percent during the nineteenth century.[30] Another market expanded rapidly for medical services, whether the demand for regular consultations – these were the years that saw the rise of the family doctor or general practitioner – or the market for "remedies." But perhaps the most significant measure of self-help attitudes linked to the market was the development of savings banks. Even before the legislation of 1817 that placed these institutions under public control, they grew vigorously, with their greatest development to follow from 1830 or 1840, when they opened up to the less wealthy elements of the working class.[31]

Thus the new public assistance system with its emphasis on custodialism, its creation of a centralized system overseeing local providers of relief, meant the withering away of family welfare and a promarket policy option. Britain led, but the other European societies followed.

After a series of inconsistent experiments during the Revolution, France set in place a new system under the Directory and Napoleon. It was based on local boards for the distribution of relief and workhouses for institutional welfare. But outdoor relief – that is, outside the workhouse and based on the family – remained more important.

Towns had a charity office (bureau de bienfaisance) usually headed by the major, described as representative of the poor, and authorized to receive gifts and legacies on their behalf. The rule that relief should be given at home – as Marshall noted, "almost exactly the reverse of the British practice" – was widely accepted. "The idea was that, if the pauper remained at home his relatives would care for him; if he was put into an institution, they would wash their hands of all responsibility."[32] The sharp difference between British and French practice in the mid-nineteenth century stemmed principally from the maintenance in France of the household economy and the network of rural social relations. As Ashford summarizes, "The vast majority of Frenchmen lived in small communities where the sick, disabled and infirm could find a meager living or call on charity in manageable proportions. . . . Social assistance was not as pressing as in Britain nor did most Frenchmen want to see individual self-reliance (prévoyance) replaced by public programs."[33]

Nonetheless, the development of British welfare also began to change course as voluntary, solidaristic initiatives, after an eclipse of almost half a century, reemerged gradually in the face of the expansion of the market and the gaps in state provision. On the one hand, the working-class household reorganized itself as a modern "nuclear" family, as did the middle-class household, and resumed its role in decision making and task allocation for its members so as to guarantee them a minimal level of security.[34] On the other hand, voluntary action saw a new burgeoning above all in the form of private philanthropy. By the early 1870s, 880,000 poor were being assisted outside of institutions.[35] Even more vigorous was the surge of working-class clubs and friendly societies, up in membership from 648,000 in 1793 to 704,000 in 1803, 925,000 in 1815, above 4 million in 1870, and almost 5.5 million by the end of the century.[36] This imposing growth can be explained in part as a result of the growing insurance role that the friendly societies played as they lost their earlier syndical and religious or recreational functions to become a complement of the working-class nuclear family.[37] But the expansion also was symptomatic of the reaction, so to speak, of the solidaristic and voluntarist impulse in the face of the market and of state deficiencies.

Health policy and the market for medical services

The nineteenth-century shift of boundaries among the three basic mechanisms of poor relief, likewise took place in the sphere of medical care, where there was a long-term shift from a system based on traditional healing to one geared to public health and the market for health services. Aside from the small elite of university-trained physicians in the eighteenth century, who tended to and were recruited from the upper strata of society, health care was left mainly to the family and to women: "Healing was female, when it was a neighbourly service, based in stable communities, where skills could be passed on for generations and when the healer knew her patients and their families. . . . If she could not always cure, neither could she do much harm, and very often she was able to soothe."[38]

This healing role of women did not cease with the coming of industrial society. Women were systematically excluded from the profitable business of doctoring for many decades of the nineteenth century, but they continued to "watch" the sick, assist with traditional remedies, and deliver babies. The system seems to have been at least as widespread as today's health-care provisioning. In almost all countries of Europe, rural areas had a healer-dominated health system at least until the late nineteenth century or early twentieth century.[39] Efforts to suppress quackery by legislation generally proved unavailing in both Europe and the United States, where in the Jacksonian era the states relaxed restrictive licensing. In general, "there was no mass support for the idea of medical professionalism, much less for the particular set of healers who claimed it." Also, "By the 1840's medicine had largely become a layman's prerogative."[40]

The proliferation of patent medicines helped reinforce the traditional healing system. In both the United States and Great Britain, the wholesalers of the panaceas, the newspapers that earned substantial revenues advertising the remedies, and the local healers prospered together. As Magali Sarfatti-Larson notes, "until the end of the century, the fastest growing 'medical' market was that of patent medicines, produced outside of any respectable medical persuasion."[41] Throughout the nineteenth century professional health care had little to offer as a more promising alternative. Most therapies remained simply ameliorative as late as 1910; immunization and drug treatment contributed little to the reduction of death from infectious diseases until sulfonamides and then antibiotics came into use from the late 1930s.[42]

For many decades the best physicians were caught in a situation in which they were aware of the ineffectiveness of traditional remedies, but did not yet have any means with which to replace them. A spirit of "medical nihilism" pervaded the best centers. French clinicians became increasingly skeptical about most old drugs and treatments earlier taken for granted; while by the 1850s in Vienna pathology and diagnosis had far outstripped therapeutic means whose worthlessness was increasingly obvious.[43] This therapeutic gap between increasingly sophisticated diagnosis and the availability of scientific remedies was one influence that helped to divert attention from curative to preventive health services and from medical insurance to public health. Until the early 1800s the main objective of reformers had been to make medical care accessible to the poor through schemes of voluntary or national health insurance. This emphasis yielded, however, to the sanitary reform movement that emphasized prevention of disease. As Shyrock notes,

It was probably not an accident, then, that concern about health insurance – in either national or voluntary form – declined as interest in "public health" mounted. Even socialists do not seem to have returned to health insurance concepts until after 1860. The shift in interest was symbolized by the fact that Edwin Chadwick, the English leader, began his career with the study of voluntary insurance as provided by benefit societies, but subsequently gave all his attention to sanitary reform.[44]

Sanitary surveys also began to emphasize the contribution of poor living conditions to the death and illness rates of the urban poor and potentially to other city dwellers as well. "Death and disease seemed to lurk in the houses and haunts of the poor, ready to emerge as epidemics to threaten the health and life of their betters."[45] Overcoming initial resistance in Britain, elsewhere in Europe, and the United States, reformers established boards of health throughout the middle third of the century. Despite all hesitations, however, public health provisions still expanded more vigorously than the private medical sector.

It was the growth of moderate affluence that allowed the market for medical services to expand from the latter part of the nineteenth century on. In part this required an initial compromise with traditional healing and "quackery." Patients went to the family doctor less because cures were expected, than for "his parental attitude, his wisdom, his willingness to provide detached yet personalized help . . . to the reliance of rituals of help, he could add the prestige of middle-class status and at least the semblance of scientific capacity."[46] Doctors accepted the side-by-side existence of quacks and healers and the consolations of patent medicine. Nonetheless, from the beginning of the twentieth century the medical profession increasingly monopolized the market for medical services, convincing both governments and the public of its superior therapeutic effectiveness. Advances in bacteriology and modern surgery contributed to a rising confidence in scientific management. Moreover, the pioneering sanitary reforms of the prior generation finally began to have a payoff in reduced mortality and illness rates that could be attributed to the newly prominent physicians. The result was the introduction or reimposition of antiquack legislation and the reinstitution of licensing – now entrusted in the United States to the medical schools. The public health sector was to be confined to contagious diseases and sanitation, keeping it away from the areas of practice.[47]

In Britain the opposition between the two sectors was less clearcut than in the United States, but doctors managed to exploit state intervention to loosen the supervision of their consumers, who had organized collectively in friendly societies earlier than they had grouped themselves as producers of medical services. Many physicians already worked within a framework of "contract practice" for a club or friendly society on a salaried basis.[48] The alternative often was working as a public employee in rural districts or as a sanitary official. The result was that when Lloyd George proposed health insurance in 1911, the British Medical Association contested particular points, but on the whole remained favorable.[49] In return the physicians won capitation fees as a basis for remuneration and supervision by special insurance committees in which they themselves were represented. The friendly societies remained the major losers of the 1911 legislation as the powerful insurance companies prevailingly captured the administration committees of the new insurance program.[50] The physicians' strategy of compromise paid off again in 1946 with the National Health Service (when the private insurance companies were removed) and as late as the reorganization of 1974, which reinforced the centralized control of 1946, accenting the technical and medical voice over the National Health Service and preventing any reversion of influence to collective consumers or local supervisory boards that might have been harsher political adversaries.

In sum, the medical and hygiene sector, like the whole sphere of public assistance, more generally passed through major phases, each characterized by a diverse mix of three fundamental allocative mechanisms: An initial stage based primarily on traditional resources of the family and folk healers gave way to a more market-determined distribution, initially of "irregular" services provided by quacks and patent medicine suppliers, then of the "regular" services offered by physicians, which in Britain were both encouraged and constrained by the collective consumers of the friendly societies. The state long restricted its supervision to the field of public hygiene and hospitals. Under the impetus, however, of pressure from the working-class movement and modernization of the medical elite itself, public intervention increased through the instrumentality of national insurance – never to win a clear-cut supremacy of control, but in fact to reach a compromise with the medical profession and reinforce its technical power.

The parabola of the welfare state

Most of the social insurance legislation introduced in Western European countries from the last decades of the nineteenth century on did not threaten the logic of the market. The new provisions by and large were organized and administered throughout the market; they were often voluntary, and when made compulsory their coverage was usually limited to the active work force. The plans always insisted on the direct link between contribution and benefit, and entitlement was contingent on adequate contribution.[51] This implied further that only through participation in the labor market could the individual become eligible for protection. Social insurance schemes also buttressed the market ideologically as governments emphasized the "binding" or "contractual" nature of the insurance principal, especially in Germany and on the Continent, where the financial responsibility of the state remained implicit and insurance was treated primarily as a bipartite arrangement between employers and employees.[52] As Titmuss summarizes this "industrial achievement-performance model," it had no redistributive objectives but was "fundamentally based on work, rewards, productivity, and merit."[53]

To be sure, variations existed. The compulsory insurance schemes introduced in Germany during the 1880s relied on the traditional schemes of social protection based upon the guild and a corporative social stratification that liberalism had never completely erased. These vestiges – more than Bismarck's antisocialist strategy, according to Rimlinger – recommended the institution of broad public coverage.[54] The health insurance legislation of 1883 took joint worker–employer sickness funds, administered on a craft or plant basis, and endowed them with public-law status, enabling them to negotiate with new associations of insurance physicians likewise granted public-law recognition. Enrollment followed as a compulsory attribute of job holding. So, too, the 1889 general pension scheme for old age and invalidism was keyed to the level of the insured's earnings, as it fell into one of five income classes. Statutory provisions were thus grounded in a traditional framework of corporatist work relations and stratification.[55]

The British social insurance scheme introduced by the Liberals between 1908 and 1911, which shared many attributes with the German structure, nonetheless made significant departures. Lloyd George visited Germany when preparing the 1911 National Insurance Bill and was "tremendously impressed" by what he had seen. The British health insurance schemes incorporated the network of friendly societies and private insurance companies as "approved societies." But in other spheres Britain lacked the survivals of corporative and guild practices German reformers could draw upon. The compulsory insurance schemes had to accommodate themselves to the logic of the market – or interfere with it in a more explicit way than in Germany.[56] Old-age pensions were instituted on a noncontributory basis, financed out of general revenue, and providing equal payments regardless of the pensioner's previous status and earnings. (The French, in contrast, introduced a scheme analogous to the differentiated German pension plan in 1910.) In a further departure, the British Liberals instituted compulsory unemployment insurance, a provision that Bismarck had not inaugurated and that would have to wait for the Weimar Republic. Since compulsory unemployment insurance was financed by all employers and employees, it meant a subsidy by stable industries for the unstable, and openly went beyond the logic of the free market.

So, too, the British national health insurance scheme of 1911 went beyond German concepts. The role of state financing was visibly larger in Britain, and any sense that the "approved societies" were themselves meeting the bill was correspondingly attenuated. Premiums were levied on a flat-rate basis rather than graded by income, and every insured worker who collected received a uniform weekly amount. Every subscriber, moreover, could choose his own "approved" insurer, instead of having registration imposed as a consequence of the occupational group.[57] Thus the "social service state"[58] established during the liberals' tenure set the pattern for a more universal system of welfare. As Lloyd George noted in preparing the 1911 bill, "Insurance necessarily temporary expedient. At no distant date hope State will acknowledge full responsibility in the matter of making provision for sickness, breakdown and unemployment."[59]

Over the next thirty years, Lloyd George's hope was widely shared in Britain. The Depression and two world wars generalized the feeling, which Beveridge captured with his 1942 report, that everyone was vulnerable and that the statutory provision of welfare was needed not only for the deserving poor or the manual worker, but for the population as a whole. The postwar legislation, including the National Insurance and Family Allowance acts of 1946, substantially followed this mandate. Compulsory insurance was extended to include the entire population and every citizen was deemed to be entitled to a "universal national minimum" financed out of taxes. With entitlement perceived as a consequence of citizenship and given the reliance on general state revenues to finance welfare, the British legislation cut all connections between welfare provision and the market. In-kind services, such as public education and housing, were likewise augmented. Crowning the system was the National Health Service of 1948: "The Health Service had nothing to do with class relations, poverty, subsistence, or the defects of the capitalist system . . . it suppressed the economic market and replaced it by a calculus of need."[60]

But the legislation of the 1945 Labour government represented the high-water mark for state hegemony and public welfare. Although the social costs of the welfare state continued to rise under the Conservatives during the 1950s, the underlying universalistic principles began to weaken by the early 1960s. The flat-rate principle was modified, as the National Insurance Acts of 1959 and 1966 reintroduced the criterion of graduated contributions and payments into pensions, health insurance, and unemployment coverage. Payments for pharmaceuticals crept into the National Health Service while hospitals were permitted to set aside private beds and consulting rooms, with the result, according to one critic, of "a steady shift towards a highly differentiated, fragmented system of welfare rights and privileges."[61]

But the British trajectory was hardly unique. Throughout the Western countries welfare provisions became more oriented toward the labor market and increasingly seen as part of earnings, as

the benefits to be derived from the welfare state came to be regarded as a means for calculating differential gains. For every increase in one group's income and consumption, there were always other groups that could make a legitimate claim to keep pace. The alacrity with which basic pension systems created in the 1940s shifted into a variety of forms of constant updating was one expression of the more general tendency. Growth facilitated evaluations of comparative performance. Comparison facilitated identification of new individual and group inequities. New inequities facilitated expansion in social programs.[62]

Thus, if in the almost forty years from the National Insurance bill of 1911 and the postwar welfare legislation the state reduced the scope of the private economy in the provision of social protection, in the almost forty years since, we have witnessed a sort of "revenge of the market." But whereas many observers have commented upon the revival of market forces, it is harder to evaluate the comeback of the voluntary-solidaristic sector. Only recently has the tendency awakened the interest of students, including governments; and, in any case, information about informal, family, and voluntary activity remains elusive.

Even British commentators have recently contested the notion that family and primary-group assistance has progressively eroded, noting that such a diagnosis was made on the basis of newly settled communities where the role of informal social protection appears clearly lower than in older centers.[63] Certainly the family in Britain as else-where is undergoing radical transformations, with a divorce rate equal to one-third of marriages and a rapidly growing number of single-member households. Nonetheless, its role as a center of personal services seems to have increased; in effect, English families spend less today on services than twenty-five years ago, but spend much more to acquire the goods that can transform their domestic life into a "self-service economy."[64]

The weakening of family ties does not necessarily translate into a growth of demand for public assistance. As Jens Alber has recently observed, the sharp rise in divorce rates has been accompanied by a proliferation of self-help groups that tend to be substitutes for public programs.[65] The last years in Britain have seen a major expansion of self-help groups on the model of Alcoholics Anonymous, covering a large number of social needs. This trend is part of a larger growth of commitments to voluntary action. According to the *General Household Survey* people participating in voluntary action rose from 8.3 percent to 9.7 percent between 1973 and 1977, while the Wolfenden Committee found the number of voluntary organizations growing about two-thirds of a percent per year.[66] On the basis of such data as this, voices increase for a restructuring of the welfare state on the basis of decentralization of services and greater cooperation between public and voluntary sectors.

In sum, alongside the recovery of the market, the revival of the voluntary sector seems to confirm the hypothesis of a long-waved cyclical development of the complex system of social protection. The outline of this system at each moment of its historical evolution depends less on a mechanical addition of the three sectors than on a mix or interaction among them, one capable of giving life to complex institutional structures in which, so to speak, the scaffolding provided by the state is filled out by voluntary action and market transactions. The weight of each of the three components has apparently changed according to the long cyclical waves, whose persistence ultimately testifies to the fact that each constituent of the system cannot be reduced beyond a certain point. A given component may decline in importance during one phase but is destined to reemerge and in the final analysis cannot simply be "reduced" to the other two forms. Given this persistence, it seems legitimate to me, in conclusion, to recognize that behind contemporary appeals to revise the organizational form of the welfare state, which the current expansion of voluntary and market sectors tends to imply, there is a venerable impulse that cannot simply be denied. While the forces of conservatism are hardly likely to do so, this impulse must also be comprehended and supported by the progressive forces that have been traditionally identified with the welfare state and its conquests.

Notes

1 B. Cazes, "A Double Bind," in OECD, *The Welfare State in Crisis. An Account of the Conference on Social Policies in the 1980's* (Paris: OECD, 1981), p. 151.

2 Albert O. Hirschman, "The Welfare State in Trouble: Systemic Crisis or Growing Pains?," *American Economic Review* (May 1980):133.

3 E. Van Lennep, "Opening Address," in OECD, *The Welfare State in Crisis*, p. 12.

4 Quoted in M. E. Rushefsky, "A Political Critique of Competition in Health Care," paper presented at a meeting of the American Political Science Association, New York, September 1981, p. 10. Emphasis added.

5 R. Klein, "Values, Power and Policies," in OECD, *Welfare State in Crisis*, p. 12.

6 World Health Organization, Regional Office for Europe, Regional Programme in Health Education and Lifestyles, 31st Session (Berlin: September 15–19, 1981), p. 3.

7 An important challenge to welfare services emerged in the 1970s from the women's movements, which criticized male professional authority over women's lives in the medical area. Viewed as an institution of social control, medicine was assailed for perpetuating female dependency, and women's self-help groups and alternative clinics were organized. Similar developments occurred in education (from "free schools" to "educational alternatives") and in other fields of "social reproduction" (housing, food) where the self-help movement spread. For U.S. developments, see J. Case and R. C. Taylor, *Coops, Communes and Collectives. Experiments in Social Change in the 1960's and 1970's* (New York: Pantheon, 1979).

8 For an eloquent example, cf. Harry Braverman, *Labor and Monopoly Capital* (New York: Monthly Review Press, 1974), pp. 276, 279:

The population of cities, more or less completely cut off from a natural environment by the division between town and country, becomes totally dependent upon social artifice for its every need. But social artifice has been destroyed in all but its marketable forms. Thus the population no longer relies upon social organization in the form of family, friends, neighbors, community, elders, children, but with few exceptions must go to the market, and only to market, not only for food, clothing and shelter, but also for recreation, amusement, security, for the care of the young, the old, the sick, the handicapped. . . . As the family members . . . become less and less able to care for each other in time of need, and as the ties of neighborhood, community and friendship are reinterpreted on a narrower scale to exclude onerous responsibilities, the care of humans for each other becomes increasingly institutionalized.

9 Cf. James O'Connor, *The Fiscal Crisis of the State* (New York: St. Martin's, 1973); Frances Fox Piven and Richard A. Cloward, *Regulating the Poor: The Functions of Public Welfare* (New York: Pantheon, 1971).

10 Samuel Bowles and Herbert Gintis, "La crisi del capitalismo liberal-democratico. Il caso degli Stati Uniti," *Stato e Mercato* 1, no. 1 (1981):118.

11 Frances Fox Piven and Richard A. Cloward, *The New Class War. Reagan's Attack on the Welfare State and Its Consequences* (New York: Pantheon, 1982), p. 82.

12 Cf. Claus Offe, "Competitive Party Democracy and the Keynesian Welfare State. Some Reflections upon their Historical Limits," *Stato e Mercato* 1, no. 3 (1981):11. For interpretations that stress the strains the welfare state places on the availability of capital in general, see James O'Connor, *The Fiscal Crisis of the State* (New York: St.

Martin's, 1973); and Ian Gough, *The Political Economy of the Welfare State* (London: Macmillan, 1979).

13 Fred Hirsch, *The Social Limits to Growth* (Cambridge, Mass.: Harvard University Press, 1976).

14 Karl Polanyi, *The Great Transformation* (Boston: Beacon, 1944).

15 Douglass North, "Markets and other Allocation Systems in History: The Challenge of Karl Polanyi," *Journal of European Economic History*, 6 (1977):715.

16 R. Mishra, *Society and Social Policy: Theoretical Perspectives on Welfare* (London: Macmillan, 1977), p. 96. One of the main factors that – according to this author – accounts for different countries' differential expansion of state provision of welfare is the unionization of unskilled workers: "demands for a more general social policy – of which social services were a part – were not raised in Britain until after the influx of unskilled workers in the ranks of organized labor.... Indeed a part of the thesis advanced here is that a high density of workers' unionization leads to more collectivist social policy, partly because it transforms the less skilled workers, with a far more precarious position market in terms of wages and security of employment, into a pressure group" (pp. 106–107).

17 Hirschman, "Welfare State in Trouble," p. 133, and *Shifting Involvements – Private Interest and Public Action* (Princeton, N.J.: Princeton University Press, 1982).

18 Hirschman, *Shifting Involvements*, p. 6.

19 Burton Weisbrod, *The Voluntary Non-Profit Sector* (Lexington, Mass.: Lexington Books, 1977), pp. 244–251.

20 J. Alber and Peter Flora, "Modernization, Democratization and the Development of Welfare States in Europe and America," in P. Flora and Arnold J. Heidenheimer, eds., *The Development of Welfare States in Europe and America* (New Brunswick, N.J.: Transaction Books, 1981). See also M. Shalev, "Class Politics and the Western Welfare State," *Stato e Mercato* 6 (1982). Homogeneity of demand will also be a function of secularization. See Heidenheimer, "Secularization Patterns and the Western Extension of the Welfare State: 1881–1981" (unpublished manuscript, 1981).

21 Gaston V. Rimlinger, *Welfare Policy and Industrialization in Europe, America and Russia* (New York: Wiley, 1971), and Rimlinger, "The Historical Analysis of National Welfare Systems," in R. Ronson and R. Sytel, eds., *Explorations in the New Economic History*, (New York: Academic Press, 1982).

22 Hirschman, *Shifting Involvements*, p. 4.

23 Rimlinger, *Welfare Policy and Industrialization*, p. 149.

24 Ibid., p. 18. See also G. Rosen, *A History of Public Health* (New York: MD Publications, 1958).

25 See Heidenheimer, "Secularization Patterns"; also T. H. Marshall, *Social Policy* (London: Hutchinson, 1965), p. 15.

26 Michael Anderson, *Approaches to the History of the Western Family: 1500–1914* (New York: Macmillan, 1980) Italian translation: *Interpretazioni storiche della famiglia. L'Europa occidentale 1500–1914* (Turin: Rosenberg & Sellier, 1982), p. 52. On the urban family, Neil Smelser, *Social Change in the Industrial Revolution* (Chicago: University of Chicago Press, 1959), pp. 384ff.

27 Chiara Saraceno, *Anatomia della famiglia. Strutture sociali e forme familiari* (Bari: De Donato, 1975), p. 75. Cf. E. P. Thompson, *The Making of the English Working Class* (London: Gollancz, 1963), pp. 333–336.

28 This is the major point of Polanyi's class presentation of the Speenhamland system in *The Great Transformation*, pp. 77–110. Population in the half century from 1781 to 1831 increased from 9.25 to 16.54 million, or about 75 percent.

29 Piven and Cloward, *Regulating the Poor*, p. 33.

30 Real wages in Phyllis Deane, *The First Industrial Revolution* (Cambridge: Cambridge University Press, 1965); servant statistics in M. Anderson, *Approaches to the History of the Western Family*, p. 48.

31 Smelser, *Social Change*, pp. 370–372.

32 Marshall, *Social Policy*, p. 34. On the French system, cf. Rimlinger, *Welfare Policy*, p. 27.

33 Douglas E. Ashford, "The Growth of Social Security in Britain and France: Welfare States by Intent and Default," (Ithaca, N.Y.: Cornell University, September 1981, Mimeographed), pp. 13–14.

34 Saraceno, *Anatomia della famiglia*, pp. 81ff.

35 Cf. G. F. Ferrari, "La sicurezza sociale in Gran Bretagna," *La Ricerca Sociale* 25 (1981):944.

36 Thompson, *Making of the English Working Class*, p. 420, for the early figures; W. M. Frazer, *A History of English Public Health, 1834–1938* (London: Bailliere, Tindall & Cox, 1950), p. 99; William Beveridge, *Voluntary Action*, (London: Allen & Unwin, 1948), Appendix A.

37 Smelser, *Social Change*, chap. 13, pp. 342–383.

38 B. Ehrenreich and D. English, *For Her Own Good: 150 Years of the Experts' Advice to Women* (New York: Doubleday, Anchor, 1979), pp. 41, 44. Compare with Richard Carlisle's 1819 assessment to his own doctor: "Like those old ladies, with you it was 'hit and miss,' every case an experiment; if the patient is killed the fault is in the disease, if her recovers, wonderfully clever, doctor! There is much less chance of being killed by an old lady for a doctress, as she will not be so rash with her experiments" (cited in D. Widgery, *Health in Danger: The Crisis of the National Health Service* [London: MacMillan, 1979], p. 2.).

39 For the pervasiveness of healers in Scandinavia, see O. Berg, "The Modernization of Medical Care in Norway and Sweden," in Arnold Heidenheimer and N. Elvander, eds., *The Shaping of the Swedish Health System* (New York: St. Martin's, 1980), p. 27; for England, cf. Richard Titmuss, *Commitment to Welfare* (New York: Pantheon, 1968), pp. 234–235; and Brian Abel-Smith, *Hospitals, 1800–1948* (London: Heinemann, 1964), p. 212, for the statistic that as late as 1864, folk practitioners in Lincolnshire still outnumbered trained men by a 9:1 ratio.

40 Ehrenreich and English, *For Her Own Good*, p. 48. Cf. J. S. Haller, *American Medicine in Transition, 1840–1910* (Chicago: University of Illinois Press, 1981), p. 199.

41 Magali Sarfatti-Larson, *The Rise of Professionalism: A Sociological Analysis* (Berkeley and Los Angeles: University of California Press, 1977), p. 20. See also R. H. Shyrock, *Medicine and Society in America, 1661–1860* (New York: New York University Press, 1960), p. 143; and Titmuss, *Commitment to Welfare*, p. 236.

42 R. H. Shyrock, *Medicine in America: Historical Essays* (Baltimore: 1966), p. 25; Thomas McKeown, *The Role of Medicine. Dream, Mirage, or Nemesis?* (Princeton, N.J.: Princeton University Press, 1979), p. 76. On the therapeutic revolution, see also E. D. Pellegrino, "The Socio-cultural Impact of Twentieth Century Therapeutics," in M. J. Vogel and Charles E. Rosenberg, eds., *The Therapeutic Revolution* (Philadelphia: University of Pennsylvania Press, 1979), p. 235.

43 Carlo M. Cipolla, *Public Health and the Medical Profession in the Renaissance* (Cambridge: Cambridge University Press, 1980), p. 114, on Vienna; on Paris, see Shyrock, *Medicine and Society*, p. 131.

44 Shyrock, *Medicine and Society*, p. 163.

45 Rosen, *A History of Public Health*, p. 62. For the general disinterest of physicians in sanitary reform and its reliance on statistical and engineering rather than medical skills, see Shyrock, *Medicine and Society*, pp. 164–165; also Rosen, *A History*, pp. 66–67;

and Barbara Rosenkrantz, *Public Health and the State: Changing Views in Massachusetts, 1842–1936* (Cambridge, Mass.: Harvard University Press, 1972), pp. 75–76.

46 Sarfatti-Larson, *The Rise of Professionalism*, p. 22; cf. Cipolla, *Public Health*, p. 115.

47 Rosenkrantz, *Public Health and the State*, pp. 152–153, 166, 182; also Sarfatti-Larson, *Professionalism*, p. 37.

48 Brian Abel Smith, "The History of Medical Care"; Titmuss, *Commitment to Welfare*, pp. 232–236; F. Honigsbaum, *The Division in British Medicine – A History of the Separation of General Practice from Hospital Care 1911–1968* (New York: St. Martin's, 1980), p. 315.

49 See Harry Eckstein, *The British Health Service* (Cambridge, Mass.: Harvard University Press, 1958); and V. Navarro, *Class Struggle, the State and Medicine – An History and Contemporary Analysis of the Medical Sector in Great Britain* (New York: Prodist, 1978), pp. 126–127.

50 A. Heidenheimer, H. Heclo, C. T. Adams, *Comparative Public Policy: The Politics of Social Choice in Europe and America* (New York: St. Martin's, 1975.), p. 16.

51 G. Esping-Andersen, "Cittadinanza e socialismo nel welfare state," *Stato e Mercato* 14 (1985):254.

52 Marshall, *Social Policy*, pp. 48–50.

53 Titmuss, *Social Policy, An Introduction* (London: Allen & Unwin, 1974).

54 Rimlinger, "Historical Analysis of the Welfare State," pp. 2–3.

55 D. A. Stone, *The Limits of Professional Power, National Health Care in the Federal Republic of Germany* (Chicago: University of Chicago Press, 1980), pp. 20–28.

56 G. V. Rimlinger, *The Emergence of Social Insurgence: European Experience before 1914* (Mimeographed paper), 1982.

57 Honigsbaum, *The Division in British Medicine*, pp. 17–18; Eckstein, *The British Health Service*, p. 26. In fact, the decision of 1911 represented a triumph for the commercial assurance companies vis-à-vis the friendly societies.

58 Asa Briggs, "The Welfare State in Comparative Perspective," *Archives européens de sociologie*, 2, no. 2 (1961):234.

59 Quoted in Marshall, *Social Policy*, p. 59.

60 Marshall, *Class, Citizenship and Social Development* (New York: Doubleday Anchor, 1965), p. 320.

61 B. Jessup, "The Transformation of the State in Post-War Britain," in R. Scase, ed., *The State in Western Europe* (New York: St. Martin's, 1980), p. 67; cf. G. F. Ferrari, "La sicurezza sociale in Gran Bretagna," in *La ricersa sociale*, no. 25 (1981):991.

62 Hugh Heclo, "Toward a New Welfare State?" in Flora and Heidenheimer, *The Development of Welfare States*, p. 396.

63 M. Abrams, *Beyond Three-Score and Ten: A Just Report on a Survey of the Elderly* (London: Age Concern Publication, 1978), confirms the tendency for the reconstitution of primary social-welfare networks in the case of the aged living alone. Cf. A. Cartwright, et al., *Life Before Death* (London: Routledge & Kegan Paul, 1973).

64 J. L. Gershuny, *After Industrial Society* (London: Macmillan, 1978).

65 Jens Alber, "Some Causes and Consequences of Social Security Expenditure," *Stato e Mercato*, no. 7 (1983):30.

66 *The Future of Voluntary Organizations: Report of the Wolfenden Committee* (London: Croom Helm, 1975); S. Hatch, "The Voluntary Sector: A Larger Role?," in E. M. Goldberg and S. Hatch, *A New Look at the Personal Social Services* (London: Policy Studies Institute, Discussion Paper no. 4, 1981); also D. Robinson and S. Henry, *Self-Help and Health: Mutual Aid for Modern Problems* (London: Martin Robertson, 1977); and D. Robinson, *Talking Out Alcoholism: The Self-Help Process of Alcoholics Anonymous* (London: Croom Helm, 1979).

6

Family, women, and the state: notes toward a typology of family roles and public intervention

LAURA BALBO

Introduction: three interpretive scenarios

No matter how natural it is to depict the family as the nucleus of private life, in fact it has long been a concern of public authority. But the nature of this public impact has changed. This chapter proposes a historical typology for the relationship of state and family during the last two centuries. To be sure, this is a history of the conceptual bases of the relationship, for actual practice was far less clear-cut, and carried forward older as well as more recent concepts.

Three scenarios in the history of Western societies are especially relevant. The first is the scenario in which the modern state came into being in France in the eighteenth and nineteenth centuries. The second is the welfare state as it took shape in Britain from the 1940s through the 1960s. The third scenario comprises the present day. Sociologists have advanced and debated several hypotheses to analyze these stages in the history of contemporary society. The terms "modern state" and "welfare state" can be used to summarize the first two phases. The third scenario has no clear designation, but the ideas of pluralism and complexity may provide the best interpretive guidelines for understanding its evolving interaction of state and family. I shall consider all three scenarios briefly in this introduction to set out the main lines of the argument.

For the modern state, the term *bonheur public* ("welfare" may provide the closest modern equivalent) became an issue of concern in the eighteenth century. In fact, the emergence of the idea itself signaled the shifting concern of public administrators from the mere assertion of authority to a more paternalist conception. As one manual of cameralist administration summarized:

The goal of policy is to ensure the happiness of the state by the wisdom of its regulations and to increase its force and power as much as it can. The science of policy thus consists of regulating everything according to the present state of society, of affirming it, improving it, and of acting such that everything is conducive to the happiness of the members who compose it. Policy aims at using everything comprising the state to affirm and increase its power as well as that of the public welfare.[1]

This summary by von Justi signaled the shift from a situation in which issues of social reproduction and welfare were left entirely to individuals and family networks – or, if available, to the benevolent concern of charitable institutions, mutual-aid societies, and churches – to a milieu in which the state progressively took responsibility for *bonheur public*, for acting "in such a way that everything contributes to the well-being of its members."

The second relevant scenario was the welfare state, particularly as it became established in Great Britain in the 1950s and 1960s, its "golden age." In contrast with the earlier notion, which asserted state responsibility for the protection, and control, of the economically weakest social groups, the spokesmen for the welfare state emphasized that the state would become guarantor of what were now called "citizenship rights." It would ensure that all citizens enjoyed a certain minimum standard of life, economic welfare, and security as a matter of right; and in order to implement such rights a complex array of ideological propositions, financial provisions, and institutional arrangements were developed. In this transition the process through which basic needs became perceived as basic rights and guarantees was essential. The classic conceptualization of this development was that offered by T. H. Marshall. To cite Anthony Giddens's summary of his thinking:

Marshall argues that over the past two hundred years or so two sets of influences have been in opposition in capitalist society: class divisions on the one hand and rights of citizenship on the other. Class is a source – the source – of fundamental inequalities in society. Citizenship is a contrary influence – one toward equalisation.

In Marshall's analysis the foundation and expansion of the welfare state appeared as something like the natural accompaniment of the development of citizenship rights. The establishing of civil rights leads in turn to political rights, which then in their turn produce a concentration upon welfare rights. The welfare state is the outcome of this process.[2]

Whether watching out in paternalist fashion for the *bonheur public*, or providing modern welfare entitlements, the state role, however, was crucial. The state was legitimized not only to distribute resources but also to define standards and criteria for the delivery of such resources, and to establish priorities for whose needs were to be endowed with the status of rights. But this was only one side of the story. Others have made the point that the coming of the modern state and the bureaucratic form later assumed by the welfare state meant that individuals became simultaneously more oppressed, manipulated, and deprived of personal freedom. As Foucault has argued, "discipline and punish" become as much the watchwords of the modern state as *bonheur public*. Control, regulation, and oppression by means of law and customs, the hospital as well as the prison, school and family, the treatment of illness and sexuality – all established contemporary society as it now is, hierarchical, centralized, controlled. How to affect and control individual behavior through public action was a crucial issue for the leaders of the French Revolution, who, in Mirabeau's phrase, were gripped by *"la fureur de tout gouverner."* The modern regime they helped create sought to wipe out institutions and milieus outside the sphere of the state, rendering individuals in the process subordinate, powerless and passive.

Nothing in the literature on the British welfare state may be compared to Foucault's sweeping interpretation. Nevertheless, several scholars have undertaken to demonstrate how behind universalistic principles, democratic pledges, and egalitarian values, a process was set into motion that far from reducing inequality, actually created new dimensions of it. Patriarchy and racism, in this view, emerge as key components of the British welfare state; social policies are tools to create consensus; and the logic of state action is primarily a logic of crisis management.[3]

As for the present, such terms as "pluralism," "differentiation," and "fragmentation" hint at a transformed scenario once again. Common to many widely accepted analyses is a shift from an emphasis on centralization to a description of a system that has no center; from a denunciation of encroaching power to a concern with governability or, indeed, survival of the system as such; from an exclusive emphasis on the state to growing awareness of the potential of other actors.[4]

My purpose here is to review these scenarios, examining aspects to which little attention has been paid. It is not my goal to assess the truthfulness of what has been put forward, nor can I do more than hint at a few concepts and hypotheses that might open a more problematic and possibly more imaginative perspective on the topics under discussion. We are dealing here with a historical process of extraordinary creativity. Throughout this process, happiness and rights increasingly came to be legitimate issues in the political arena. They were acted upon and provided the basis for mobilization and conflict. It is no minor accident that the modern state enters the historical scene under such circumstances. Whatever the lag between formal pledges and actuality, just the redefinition of goals helped define society symbolically as well as materially.

Social policies were tried out, institutions were established, space was created for experimentation and discussion, practices and values were generated that are now taken for granted. Tens of thousands took an active role in this process – reformers, philanthropists, writers, politicians – and millions were affected. Women, I shall argue, were especially relevant. If the issues are social reproduction, the family, and social services, it is women who are primarily concerned. Or, as I prefer to say, adult women, by which I mean those whose roles and, indeed, lives are defined by responsibilities and activities involved in reproducing and caring for others as well as themselves.

My claim here is that although they have been in subordinate positions at different historical epochs and in all the political systems that we deal with, women have actually been gaining strength as a consequence of the establishment of the modern state. I will discuss aspects of the bourgeois state, the welfare state, and the contemporary situation from this perspective. I am, of course, aware of and agree with interpretations that stress the sexist, discriminatory mechanisms within the state as it has come to function in Western societies, likewise of the marginalization of women in the economy and "the feminization of poverty."[5] That said, I still propose to demonstrate that by addressing the situation of women a variety of institutional reforms and social policies have made them one pole of an extremely significant relationship with the state. Furthermore, because of their position in society and because of traits that make needs, rights, and services a crucial aspect of the functioning of the modern state, women have become progressively more central. And, finally, they have been, individually as well as collectively, active subjects in this relationship, moving from "resistance" to the development of a "needs-oriented culture."[6]

The modern "bourgeois" state and issues of "bonheur"

Throughout the eighteenth and nineteenth centuries, law and family, school and family, the city and the family, public health and the family, became areas of public debate and increasing state intervention. Looking at the French case in particular, one might say that the modern state took shape through a process of establishing, shifting, and redefining boundaries between state and individual via the family. The demand for public assistance, the disastrous health environment for the majority of the population, the number and conditions of illegitimate children, the widespread concern with the education of the working class – all these brought pressure on the state as well as opened debate as to how involved the state should become in social problems. Several issues were intertwined. Questions of social turmoil and social order, the problem of public finance and the growing burden of public assistance, the dilemma of chaotic urban growth, all accumulated. Uniting them was the strategy of creating a working class that would be loyal, disciplined, and productive: the "normalization of the working class," in Donzelot's term.[7] The very real threat of the *grandes revoltes populaires*, until the turning point of the suppression of the Commune, set the background for discussions of city life, family, education, and health, of *puissance paternelle*, the debates over philanthropy, the role of women and children. At stake underneath all these issues was the formation of the bourgeois state.

The effort to grapple with these problems continued from the ancien régime to the Restoration. As the state progressively intervened, several processes emerged. The first was legislative, the coming into being of a system of laws, administrative and judicial practices, and institutions aimed at regulating public welfare. The second was the emergence of professionals, experts, associations, and agencies that sought both to take responsibility for and to have a role in these emerging spheres of public interest. Third was the generation of specific policies that addressed the family as an institution or particular members of the family unit and sought to modify the existing status and rights or behavior of adult men, women, and children. What is noteworthy is that these provisions, whether cast as incentives or deterrents, became progressively applied to a far wider public than initially intended.

Although policies targeted at the bourgeoisie and their consequences differed from those for *les classes populaires*, I shall address only the latter here. Time and again, given the priority of preventing social instability, there was an increasing demand for assistance, protection, and order. Simultaneously, state agents became aware that the basic satisfaction of social welfare needs offered the most useful mechanism for more widespread consensus, greater homogeneity of values and behavior, and, finally, predictability and control. One of the most delicate issues, for example, was that of conditions of infants and children. The masses of illegitimate and abandoned children urgently required support. But this entailed an intolerable growth in the state's financial burden, as well as new pressures from those who were not provided for to win a share of what was now made available. Subsidies for unwed mothers, for example, designed to encourage them to keep their children, subsequently generated the expectation that all mothers receive some support from the state, lest "vice be rewarded."

A further move in the same direction involved making marriage more popular among the working-class population (between one-third and one-half of all couples were not formally married). This effort was accompanied by the attempt to *constituer la mère de famille populaire*, that is, to make it possible for working-class women to take care of their babies, to feed them properly, to become familiar with basic hygiene, to improve housing standards, to send children to school rather than to factory work, to put money aside as savings, and to enjoy a weekly holiday.

This strategy of strengthening family life [*familisation*] of the working classes in the second half of the 19th century thus pivoted on the woman and gave her a certain number of tools and allies: primary education, instruction in domestic hygiene, working-class garden allotments [*jardins ouvriers*], Sunday rest. But the principal instrumentality was "social housing." In practice this meant taking the woman out of the convent so she could take the man out of the cabaret, and for that end one gave her a weapon, housing.[8]

In retrospect such developments may appear obvious, since the kind of family organization that we today have embodies this century-long process of imparting middle-class patterns to the working class via state intervention. But these measures did not take place without resistance. Not only were there many opponents of the new measures, whether from ideological conviction or material interest, but a large number of unintended consequences had also to be handled. What is more, state and family could not simply interact directly. Family policies helped give rise to a host of intermediate institutions, both state-supported and voluntary. Philippe Meyer provides a long inventory of associations concerned with assistance to children and youth, such as the Union Française de Sauvetage de l'Enfance et de l'Adolescence, the Ligue des Enfants de France, the Société contre la Mendicité des Enfants, and the Société de Patronage de Jeunes Détenus et des Jeunes Libérés. Professionals and experts, including lawyers, teachers, and public officials, were given formal roles in family policy, leading, as Meyer says, to a double movement, one on the part of a professional body seeking a larger share of power and another on the part of a state that was outlining a model of society.[9] As Donzelot likewise points out, the legislation of 1889, 1898, and 1912 progressively transferred sovereignty from the allegedly "morally insufficient" family to a new corps of notables – philanthropists, judges, and doctors specializing in the supervision of childhood.[10]

How can one summarize what happened to the *famille populaire* during these transformations? Donzelot argues that it is too restrictive

to say that the modern liberal state rescued the family from its disarray – following industrialization and urbanization – to use it as an
agency for reproducing the established order. Nonetheless, the family
unit, its internal relationships and mechanisms, was reshaped and
redefined in light of more general political goals. As stated above,
intervention on behalf of children, whether concerning their health
or their education, gave increasing leverage to the state and public
agencies. Guaranteeing children's health and requiring schooling
meant moving fathers out of control. But women, too, were offered
new rights against husbands and partners, against employers, and
against the risks of prostitution, poverty, and destitution. They were
induced, so to speak, to become allies in policies designed to inculcate
middle-class values in the working class, such as a sense of family
responsibility.

Women won legal status and incentives so that marriage would
replace concubinage and mothers could raise their children instead
of abandoning them, take care of their homes instead of working in
factories. But state action also affected women by regulating previously uncontrolled working conditions. For great numbers of
women, industrialization had brought salaries so low that prostitution became their *cinquieme quart* of work.[11] Slow as they were,
legislation and administrative action did become relevant in the second half of the nineteenth century; some measures went so far as to
address some underlying causes such as inadequate female education and the exploitation of working-class girls in "industrial
convents."

Obviously this process did not emerge as a long, conscious strategy;
moreover, it left women subordinate within the patriarchal structure
of what the modern state came to be.[12] Nevertheless, in the particular
process through which the modern state sought to carry out its responsibilities for public happiness, unexpected consequences intervened. The interdependent functioning of professional bodies such
as schools and hospitals, the attempts at educating working-class
women – in particular, at teaching them home economics – clearly
made an enormous difference in the conditions of everyday life. In
addition, conditions were created for the first time that made adult
women specifically responsible for servicing work, that is, for work
involving care and nurture. That is to say, women came to be struc-
turally located in networks and institutions and were taken into legal
consideration as responsible for service-oriented functions. They were
supposedly capable of tasks unknown to men and assigned special
roles accordingly. This meant being called upon to deal with the state
and state agencies as "privileged" partners.

The British welfare state and "citizenship rights"

The ambitious project of making it the state's responsibility to guarantee all citizens "a certain minimum standard of life, economic welfare and security,"[13] meant a new definition of the boundaries between the state and the family. Feelings of national solidarity accompanied the early planning of the welfare state in the 1940s: The awareness of urgent needs that had gone unmet for a majority of the population prompted public intervention. Moreover, there was a clear ambition to make it a model experience. As H. Rose suggests, "Britain might have lost territory and material power, but she still emerged from the war with a strong nationalistic sense of superiority over other European peoples. What Titmuss and the theoreticians of the welfare state did was to offer a way of continuing to be 'top nation.' "[14] What came into being in the 1950s and 1960s was a historically new experiment of state intervention which expanded into a great range of areas affecting individual and collective conditions as programs shifted from the original statements of the 1942 Beveridge Report on full employment to the concern with "personal social services" of the Seebohm Report. In this development citizenship rights enlarged the earlier notion of public happiness. Universal education, protection from unemployment and poverty, and assistance in sickness and old age became a general expectation. In fact, from the early model that was basically grounded on the aim of full employment and income maintenance, the British welfare state became conceived of as a much more sophisticated institution, that is, as an agency providing personal social services to large numbers of its citizens: the welfare service society. This shift in emphasis appears to me as a most revealing element.

The welfare service society implied universal rights, claims to personal services, high expectations, and shared standards as to a new "quality of life." The establishment of political boundaries was different from the earlier pattern. The earlier bourgeois state sought recognition of its role as a central, legitimate, visible agency, and to this end it limited traditional freedom and restricted the autonomy of competing institutions. But the British welfare state, in order to maintain legitimacy on the basis of its principles, had to establish a precarious balance among the many existing agencies, all of which it badly needed to produce and deliver services. As to the family, and roles within the family in particular, there was a process of adjustments and feedbacks.

What was the family agenda for the British welfare state? I do not have in mind the hypothesis of an explicit plan or a conscious use of a given family pattern; on the contrary, when examining the legislative or administrative measures one is struck by how undefined objectives are, by the extent to which basic assumptions are hidden or even contradict one another, and how partial and inadequate certain decisions seem in light of their supposed objectives. On the other hand, the state was by no means neutral with regard to the family as an institution: a whole range of measures, from transfer payments to welfare provisions, were grounded on certain presuppositions about family functioning and attempted to create, strengthen, or modify the appropriate conditions. The original family model, in fact, was quite traditional. As the Beveridge Report stipulated, "In any measure of social policy in which regard is had to facts, the great majority of married women must be regarded as occupied on work which is vital though unpaid, without which their husbands could not do their paid work and without which the nation could not continue."[15]

Welfare state policies have largely followed this paradigm. No provisions were made for adults who might choose to organize their reproduction outside the family or according to roles that differed from the traditionally defined ones. Subsequent steps did not substantially alter this attitude: Fiscal legislation, social security provisions, and employment policies treated married women as "a special insurance class," that is, as dependent on their employed husbands, penalized as taxpayers, and entitled to only limited sickness and unemployment benefits.[16]

But I argue that the British welfare state, although it expressed patriarchal attitudes and conservative ideology about sex roles and family organization, needed women's services in the labor market as well as at home. The new model was for women to be both housewives and workers. It envisaged that the role of the adult woman would be one of both laborer and housewife, and it was this dual expectation, and accommodation, that allowed the welfare state to work as well as it did.[17] On the one hand, women were hired in large numbers to staff the expanding public sector or, more precisely, welfare work of all kinds. On the other, whatever inadequacies and disservices were to be found – that this was the case has been made clear by many students of the British situation – the family played a compensatory role. The pattern of family organization that became generalized in the postwar decades proved to be a crucial buttress for the British welfare state because it provided flexible adaptive mechanisms for new structural requirements and it contributed to overcoming contradictions in the system. The family absorbed some of the contradictions inherent in a system that promised increasing well-being but was afflicted with persisting inequality. To give a few examples:

If the state cannot avoid the burden of expanding certain collective services, these must still be supplemented by family services, without which the former could not be utilized or would be too costly. If women have been required in the expanding service sector, their family labor has also been needed. Formulas such as the institution-alization of part-time jobs combine the two, and at the same time prevent exploitation from becoming excessive, which would contra-dict the expectation and promise of universal well-being. In this light we can understand welfare policies that officially assumed "normal" mothers were at home full-time while their children were young but that made provision for part-time schooling once they had reached a certain age; political programs that were initiated to expand public services but that simultaneously tolerated private facilities insofar as they provided partial answers to rising female employment; and state provisions that provided old people with home services but only insofar as they were supplemented by family services. In short, the welfare state presupposed a classical differentiation of family roles even as it moved to enact citizenship rights supposedly defined in individualistic terms.

If we examine the British system, we can summarize living con-ditions as dependent on goods and services acquired by family units on the private market on the basis of either earnings or cash welfare provisions, and – increasingly in a welfare system – on social services provided free by a variety of public institutions in the areas of housing, education, health, municipalities, and the like. But a situation that channels resources to individuals, or rather families, from a variety of external social institutions, still requires that families perform a number of tasks. Families are still left to choose among alternatives, to "combine" the resources from different sources, to adjust them to the specific requirements of each family member, and to provide services that are not available from other institutions. And for adult women in particular, a quite different situation came into being com-pared to the norm of twenty years earlier or in the previous gener-ation.[18] What observers often failed to point out was that children, the old, and the handicapped were not capable of carrying out the complex tasks required by the welfare system and that adults must be assigned the responsibility of helping others to make use of the services as part of their family role. In practice, women perform these tasks and do all the servicing work in the society. To take two ex-amples: The great majority of old people, including those who are invalided or housebound, live in their own homes or with their chil-dren. In 1975, fewer than 2 percent of those over sixty-five in England and Wales were living in private or state-owned institutions. The others were looked after or helped by their own families, that is, by their wives or daughters or other female in-laws.[19] As a rule, moreover, whatever services are provided do not fully cover the needs of an elderly person living alone. Home visits are made, but not often enough. Meals are brought to the house only twice a week. The family remains essential just to make access to other services possible. The situation is similar with regard to child care. While there was consensus on the community's effort to educate the new generation, the provision of services for younger children has been scarce and controversial. State provision for children under three is utterly inadequate, not only so far as the number of children in the age-group has been concerned, but also in terms of the actual demand.

Thus, women's work within and outside the family appears to be a strategic link among available service-delivery institutions. Because of services provided by women either free or at low cost, an enormous number of needs, although recognized as legitimate demands in a welfare state or service society, do not compete for scarce resources. Therefore they do not become a political demand capable of generating pressures, strains, and conflict. To use a different language, the cost of social reproduction has been kept down because part of the social reproduction process takes place in the family with no cost for business or for the state. What has been called the "political economy of reproduction" must be viewed not only as a crucial part of the capitalist mode of production in its most general sense, but specifically as an extremely flexible element that facilitates the task of sustaining "accumulation" needs and that legitimates the welfare or service society as providing the necessary resources for individual well-being.

The exploitation of women is not the only relevant perspective. Their leading dual lives, so to speak, means that women enter spheres of activity other than those of their families or work, or, more basically, that they step outside of homes and families for part of their lives. Because they remain crucially involved with tasks of social reproduction women play roles in welfare institutions, work out strategies, and handle resources they might not otherwise do. But this also means that women cannot live up to widely shared expectations as to rights and happiness. Insofar as they share the expectations that they must satisfy human needs, women must fail. What is asked of them is impossible. Yet they keep trying, and to a lesser or greater degree they also succeed in their "impossible task." They expose the contradictions in the nature of the social system and to some extent overcome them in their own lives. In other words, women have no choice but to reinforce and resist the logic they are expected to submit to. But it is built into the objective circumstances of their position in society that this resistance must be worked out on an individualistic basis rather than collectively organized; must be carried on in isolation rather than in visible mass struggles; must be silent and subterranean rather than overt. I call attention to these forms of resistance behavior, which traditional approaches have overlooked, precisely because they do not fall under the prevailing categories of analysis. Even women themselves have paid more attention to their visible struggles, from the suffrage movement to contemporary forms of feminist opposition. But attention to both levels and to the different forms of resistance might make us more aware of processes of conflict and opposition in society as a whole, and not to women alone.

A needs-oriented culture

Specific to the third scenario is that issues of social reproduction are viewed in a perspective of increasing segmentation and pluralism in the society, of a highly differentiated and fragmented social system, and of "multiple realities."[20] No longer is the state at the center of the picture as a powerful, pervasive, all-encompassing agency. No longer do we conceive of social policies as regulating all aspects of individual and social life, or assume that actors other than the state are subordinated and voiceless.[21]

Issues of *"bonheur public"* and *"police,"* of citizenship rights and the state, must still be addressed, but we deal now with an emerging needs-oriented culture in which a plurality of subjects have their say and there is an open process for possible outcomes: Concepts such as the "service society" and "service economy,"[22] and the interest shown in the third sector of voluntaristic associations, testify to the inadequacy of the state–market dualism for describing the variety of institutions that affect social reproduction and social life in general. Family, neighborhood groups, voluntary associations, are not interpreted as residual elements from past society but are investigated in their present form as crucial to the overall process of production and allocation of services.[23] It is important however, to distinguish family, kinship, and other similar groups from voluntary associations, self-help, and mutual-aid groups or movements. The latter evolve practices for meeting personal needs, but in so doing they also generate values, models, and "subcultures," and it is this activity that underlies their identity. The same cannot be said about the family or market and state institutions.

Just as there has been a growing variety of household types, and as kinship groups have become differentiated and varied – single-parent families, couples without children, homosexual couples, singles in separate household, extended families[24] – so a growing body of literature shows the complex networks and relationships that have come to exist, be they in French towns, Scandinavian suburbs, or Italian areas of "diffuse urbanization."[25] A similar proliferation characterizes the service institutions of the third sector. Self-help and mutual-aid groups are a peculiarly contemporary development in that they are made possible by conditions of high standards of education and personal awareness.

The underlying concept of self-help groups is that only those experiencing the problem can really understand it. This understanding based on common experience, the group claims, produces the necessary bond of mutual interest and desire to do something about the problem; and the fundamental ingredient of this "doing something" is collective self-help.[26]

Alcoholics Anonymous is well known and long established, but there are thousands of newer groups, in health care particularly: patients with cancer, surgery patients, people with chronic diseases; or those with physical problems that otherwise find no support, such as smokers, overeaters, the deaf; or people who experience stress or grief and do not find adequate support in existing welfare institutions, such as parents of handicapped children, widows, relatives of disabled or seriously ill persons, and the like. Each group has a deep understanding of the nature of the needs expressed by its members, and of appropriate responses in terms of personal services. On the other hand, members of many of these groups, it has been remarked, do not feel they have much in common with the members of other groups.[27] This implies that what provides these groups with their specific identity, in addition to their actual transactions, is the process of assessing needs and experimenting with services in an area that has not been adequately defined and understood by existing welfare institutions. Research, discussion, and experimentation are basic ligaments among members and lead to a common understanding and very special bonds.

Voluntary organizations that are not based on the principle of mutual support among people sharing the same needs include traditional charities, the Red Cross, and what has been termed the "private philanthropy industry." Still, some sort of exchange takes place here as well, the giver receiving anything from affective gratification, through recognition, to exemption from taxes. In sum, whether within the cadre of the "new movements" or in the framework of voluntaristic associations, a broader range of satisfactions is aspired to than allowed for by earlier concepts of social security. Many of the movements are concerned with issues of physical and mental well-being; also, the actual practices within these groups have become increasingly sensitive to issues of interpersonal relationships and personal needs.[28]

Within this emerging fragmented pluralism, adult women play a special role: They make up a large share of the population involved in the service organizations. They form a majority of workers in service jobs and of clients in service agencies. They also do the servicing work in family, and in neighborhood networks, and make up a large share of those involved in third-sector agencies. Time-budget data and research findings on the organization of daily life as well as a growing literature on gender roles in several countries and across different social classes and generations confirm that women and men are located asymmetrically in the process of reproduction and service. In the previous social scenario, that of the welfare state, women came to be divided between two spheres: They were overburdened with double labor, but they were also given legitimacy outside of the family, in dealing with the tasks of reproduction. In today's "third scenario," women have just as strategic a role. They experience a full immersion in the network of service institutions, and this experience is unique to them. Women in earlier societies did not experience it, nor do men in contemporary society.

Coping with fragmented life-situations is something all women do. This has been cogently portrayed by Prokop[29] in terms of a "feminine social character." Women have some degree of command over plurality and fragmentation; perhaps their position might be viewed as leading, potentially at least, to a "service culture." This is not a subculture concerning a minority or one that is peripheral to the dominant value system, but a set of conditions and values concerning all. Their contemporary command over plurality and fragmentation must be understood not as a mere summary of life experiences, but as a structural process. Through their historical movement from the periphery to the center, women have been the major actors in the service society. This is not to argue that women have achieved adequate recognition for their participation, but merely that new conditions obtain for their special role. The trends toward pluralization create intermediate institutions, interstices, where women are typically located. Moreover, women appear to be particularly apt at dealing with the new fragmented situations, to be familiar with the experience of belonging to multiple life worlds and better equipped to face partial experiences and discontinuity.

Certainly a great number of people, women more than men, pay heavy costs in terms of fatigue, stress, and depression. Data on health and mental health, research on life-styles and quality of life, and the theoretical literature addressing issues of identity all convey these dramatic images. It has also been pointed out that the generation of women who are at present going through adulthood have to handle this experience at a time when previous models are inadequate. New rules are neither fully legitimated nor widely shared. Support networks are lacking. Still, in comparison with their previous condition, adult women today are very much in control of their lives. They have acquired control over reproduction, which is an enormous change subjectively and objectively, in that some time and space have become part of women's lives without their being constrained by others' dependence. Access to schooling has lifted millions out of illiteracy or utterly inadequate education to some degree of participation in intellectual activity.[30] Going out to work and entering professional careers have become a reality for far more women than in the past. Political and social participation, especially in the women's movements, provides yet another sphere for women to experience time and work of their own.

Thus, women appear to be crucial precisely because in a society of fragmentation and pluralism, their servicing work and needs-orientation are legitimated at a moment when happiness and rights and needs have come to be issues of major political significance. Issues of survival and well-being have come to occupy a central position in the political arena. Women can no longer be defined as marginal. This does not automatically imply that they are central or powerful, but they do have significant bargaining power under existing conditions. In a sense, women's role, and the role of the family, has not only changed under the impact of the public sphere but has helped break down the very separateness of the public sphere. Women, we have suggested, are strategically placed in the context of the post–welfare state fragmentation and pluralization of service agencies. Their own split lives have made them adept at playing a servicing role in fragmented organizations. The new agenda of meeting needs, rather than just seeking to fulfill rights and entitlements, made their culture essential.

But these very changes in the public agenda, in effect, were making it less public. Women moved powerfully into a public role as the very public–private dualism broke down. The scenario summarized by the search for *bonheur public* accompanied the search for state autonomy. Public welfare became the challenge for the autonomous bureaucracy and state apparatus: the assertion of the public domain precisely by its ministration to the minimum of private welfare. So, too, the scenario of the welfare state still postulated the classic public–private dualism. Now, however, that dualism rested on the concept of the private subject as public citizen. The basic well-being and dignity of the individual and the family could be fulfilled triumphantly only in the framework of a guarantee of public rights. Universal entitlements protected private needs but also reaffirmed the public sphere. The growth of the third sector, the perception of more complex needs, often psychological, the growth of intermediate organizations dedicated to servicing and quality of life, the proliferation of self-help, means recognizing far richer and more complex private needs. It involves a greater task for public involvement. But simultaneously it testifies to a reaction against the simple assertion of a purely public realm that would guarantee family welfare just as a civic right. Instead it recognizes an interchange between, on the one hand, private, often kinship, cadres for satisfying emotional, nurturing, basic custodial needs and, on the other hand, the role of public agencies. At the same time, it has relied on the particular roles that women have usually played in these areas, and in return has granted women more credentials and more public roles within a new public–private continuum. The changing boundary of the political in this case has become the dissolving boundary of the public–private distinction.

This suggests finally that whereas previous strategic minorities or targeted groups saw their enfranchisement march *pari passu* with the growing assertion of citizenship and the public realm, the emergence of women as politically entitled may have depended on the reaction to that two-century development, may have hinged more on the frank recognition of complexity in the providing of private needs. The emergence of women as citizens thus rests on a less restrictive dualistic concept of "citizen." Women's public role thus has waited for a concept of public welfare and happiness and institutional service that finally transcends the long search for public authority.

Conclusion

If we now relate these comments to those traits of contemporary society that have been discussed, namely, fragmentation, pluralism, differentiation, and the permanent necessity for "crisis management," women appear to be nonexpendable precisely because of their servicing work and needs-orientation within a system in which *bonheur* and rights and needs have come to be issues of major political significance. More than that: Issues of survival and well-being have come to occupy a central position in the political arena. Given the quantitative contributions they provide, but even more important the qualitative aspects in their activities, women no longer can be defined as marginal in our society. This does not automatically imply that they are "central" or that they are powerful, although they do have a significant bargaining power in the existing conditions. I should like to rephrase this statement in more general terms. Perhaps the relationships between state and citizens, state and collective actors, state and needs, should be reconsidered. Could it be possible that certain traits of the state today, as well as the position and action of certain groups in the society, are such that terms of relationship and negotiation between state and other subjects in the political system have changed?

These are not, evidently, "women's issues." But I do suggest that there may be conditions in contemporary society that affect women more directly, or more visibly or differently, than men – or than they did women in past societies. Possibly at present, because of structural conditions in the society as well as characteristics of political action, adult women occupy a particular position or have come to play a particular role. It is certainly not so because they are biologically or culturally to be singled out as "women." I take adult women in the society as a particularly significant group, but I also want to stress the relevance of such an analysis in more general terms. Other social groups might be viewed in the same perspective. Looking at women does not mean to investigate a given social situation in its specificity, rather, to assume that from this specific perspective, issues are addressed that are relevant for all.

Notes

1 J. H. G. von Justi, *Eléments généraux de police* [1768], cited in Jacques Donzelot, *La police des familles* (Paris: Editions de Minuit, 1977), p. 12.

2 Anthony Giddens, "Class division, class conflicts and citizenship rights," in G. Pasquino (ed.) *La società complessa* (Bologna: Il Mulino, 1983), p.19.

3 E. Wilson, *Women and the Welfare State* (London: Tavistock, 1978). See also M. McIntosh, "The State and the Oppression of Women," in A. Kuhn and A. Wolpe, eds., *Feminism and Materialism* (London: Routledge & Kegan Paul, 1978).

4 N. Luhmann, *Politische Theorie im Wohlfahrtsstaat* (Munich: Gunter Olzog Verlag, 1981).

5 Michelle Perrot, "Sur l'histoire des femmes en France," *Revue du Nord* 63 (1981); Zillah Eisenstein, "Developing a Theory of Capitalist Patriarchy," in Eisenstein, ed., *Capitalism, Patriarchy and the Case for Socialist Feminism* (New York: Monthly Review Press, 1979); Claudia Honneger and Bettina Heintz, eds., *Listen der Ohnmacht. Zur Sozialgeschichte weiblicher Widerstandsformen* (Cologne and Frankfurt am Main: Europäische Verlagsanstalt, 1981).

6 See Ulrike Prokop, *Weiblicher Lebenszuammenhang* (Frankfurt am Main: Aspekt Verlag, 1976), p. 67; and Prokop, "Production and the Context of Women's Daily Life," *New German Critique* 13 (1978):18–33.

7 J. Donzelot, *La police des familles*, p. 70.

8 Ibid., p. 42.

9 Philippe Meyer, *L'enfant et la raison d'état* (Paris: Seuil, 1977).

10 J. Donzelot, *La police des familles*, p. 80.

11 Louis–René Villermé, *Tableau de l'état physique et moral des ouvriers employés dans les manufactures de coton, laine et de soie*, col. 10/18 (Paris, 1971), p. 117. Cited in Gérard Leclerc, *L'observation de l'homme: une histoire des enquêtes sociales* (Paris: Seuil, 1979).

12 Cf. on this, D. Armogathe and M. Arbistur, *Histoire du feminisme français du moyen age à nos jours* (Paris: Editions des Femmes, 1977).

13 T. H. Marshall, *Citizenship and Social Class* (London: Heinemann, 1963), p. 19.

14 Hilary Rose, "Rereading Titmuss: The Sexual Division of Welfare," *Journal of Social Policy* 10, no. 4 (1981):488.

15 *Social Insurance and Allied Services* (the Beveridge Report) (London: HMSO, 1942); *Committee on Local Authority and Allied Personal Services* (the Seebohm Report) (London: HMSO, 1968).

16 H. Land, "Who Cares for the Family?," *Journal of Social Policy* 7, no. 3 (1978):275–84; and Land, "The Family Wage," *Feminist Review* 6 (1980):55–79.

17 See the cross-country study by Laura Balbo and R. Siebert Zahar, *Interferenze* (Milan: Feltrinelli, 1979), for this theme.

18 On these themes see the Finer Report, "Report on the Committee on One-Parent Families" (London: AMND 5629, 1974); also Dennis Marsden, *Mothers Alone* (London: Penguin, 1973); A. Hunt, *The Home Help Service in England and Wales* (London: HMSO, 1970); also Buxton and E. Craven, eds., *The Uncertain Future* (London: Centre for Studies in Social Policies, 1976), pp. 33–34.

19 Robert M. Moroney, *The Family and the State. Considerations for Social Policy* (New York: Longmans, 1976); also, Land, "Who Cares for the Family?," and J. Tizard, P. Moss, and J. Perry, *All Our Children: Pre-school Services in a Changing Society* (London: Temple Smith, 1976).

20 P. L. Berger, Brigitte Berger, and Heinrich Kellner, *The Homeless Mind* (Harmondworth: Penguin, 1974). L. Gallino, "Della governabilità," in G. Stateram, ed., *Consenso e conflitto nella società contemporanea* (Milan: Franco Angeli, 1982).

21 See N. Luhmann, *Politische Theorie in Wohlfahrtsstaat*.

22 On these tendencies, see V. Fuchs, *The Service Economy* (New York: Columbia University Press, 1968); Hirshorn, "Toward a Political Economy of the Service Society," Working Paper 229 (Berkeley: Institute of Urban and Regional Development, 1974); A. Gartner and F. Reissman, *The Service Society and the Consumers' Vanguard* (New York: Harper & Row, 1974).

23 P. Rosanvallon, *La crise de l'état-providence* (Paris: Seuil, 1981). See also R. E. Pahl and J. I. Gershuny, "Britain in the Decade of the Three Economies," *New Society* 34:7–9; M. Paci, "Onde lunghe nello sviluppo dei sistemi di welfare," *Stato e Mercato* 6 (1982).

24 Cf. E. Haavio Manilla, "Caregiving in the Welfare State," *Acta Sociologica* 26, no. 1:61–82.

25 For insightful descriptions on these tendencies, see A. Pitrou, "Le soutien familial dans la société urbaine," *Revue Française de Sociologie* 18:45–84; A. Leira, "Women's Work Strategies," in A. Leira, ed., *Work and Womanhood* (Olso: Institute for Social Research, Report No. 3, 1983); L. Balbo, "The Servicing Work of Women and the Capitalist State," in M. Zeitlin, ed., *Political Power and Social Theory*, 3 (Greenwich, Conn.: JAI Press, 1982).

26 M. Killilea, "Mutual Help Organizations: Interpretations in the Literature," in G. Caplan and M. Killilea, eds., *Support Systems and Mutual Help: Multidisciplinary Explorations* (New York: Grune & Stratton, 1976).

27 For a survey of research in Europe, see Stephen Hatch, "Voluntary Work: A Report of a Survey" (Berkham: The Volunteer Centre, 1978).

28 A classic analysis is C. Offe, "Advanced Capitalism and the Welfare State," *Politics and Society* 2 (1972):479–86. A more recent contribution is A. Melucci, *L'invenzione del presente. Movimenti, identità, bisogni individuali* (Bologna: Il Mulino), 1983.

29 Prokop, *Weiblicher Lebenszusammenhang*, p. 67; in English, see "Production and the Context of Women's Daily Life."

30 Cf. Laura Balbo, "The Servicing Work of Women and the Capitalist State," in Zeitlin, ed., *Political Power and Social Theory*.

7

Health care and the boundaries of politics

PAUL STARR AND ELLEN IMMERGUT

Politics has no clearly definable boundaries. Virtually any aspect of society is potentially an object of political interest, if only because of its possible symbolic uses. Terrorism, to take an extreme case, observes no boundaries to the political: Any person or object can become a target of exemplary violence through the complex transformations of the terrorist code. To the revolutionary terrorist, everything is political, and politics is everything. At some historical moments, even many petty details of ordinary life – items of clothing, phrases of speech – take on instantly understood political meaning. The sphere of the political expands particularly in periods of upheaval and change. Realities previously accepted as natural and objective facts become objects of political change. Matters formerly considered private and personal become political and public, and decisions once assumed to be technical matters for experts to resolve erupt into political controversy.

Yet this phenomenon – the "politicization" of elements of social life commonly believed to lie beyond politics – testifies that politics generally has an assumed sphere. The boundaries may be inexact and indistinct, but their location and the level of concern about respecting them are nonetheless a significant aspect of a political culture. Although the division of what is political from what is nonpolitical may be entirely conventional, it is a convention that helps to give order to a society by distinguishing how different domains of social life ought to be run. Boundaries to politics, if successfully defended, permit zones of autonomy from political power, but the boundaries also delineate where politics is to prevail. To push out the boundaries threatens to limit autonomy and private choice; to pull in the boundaries threatens to limit political contention and collective choice. "Politicization," as we understand the term, refers to a movement of political interest or control beyond previously accepted lines; "depoliticization," to the reverse process, the attempt to move some issue or activity out of political discussion or control. Each describes changes that may disturb established rights and powers. That may be why both terms are so often used with pejorative connotations.

The passage of elements of social life – decisions, activities, institutions – into and out of the sphere of politics needs to be distinguished from movements into and out of the sphere of government. For the boundaries of politics and government are not coterminous. At least in liberal societies, politics proceeds outside government, and not all that government includes is defined as political. Politics is a sphere that overlaps civil society and the state, a sphere where the relationship between the two is fought out.

From civil society, on the one hand, come (in the ideal liberal case) a variety of forces – interest groups, social movements, the media, individual citizens – that enter the sphere of politics seeking to shape the uses of governmental power. These groups vary in the extent to which they have become politicized. In the course of their development, they continually face choices about whether (or how openly) to pursue in the political arena the issues or problems that concern them as private individuals or in their nonpolitical associations. Decisions for or against politics are, of course, influenced not only by their beliefs and intentions, but also by the opportunities, incentives, and constraints of the political system itself; and in this sense, the structure of the state shapes the forms and levels of political activity that react upon and within it.

The various agencies of governments, like the forces of civil society, also vary in the extent to which convention, law, and interest allow or require them to enter into politics. In the interests of legitimacy and continuity, many states provide for offices, such as a monarchy, that are presumed to stand "above politics" and represent overriding traditions or principles. And, what is especially pertinent here, modern bureaucratic states typically distinguish a technical, professional, or administrative sphere in government, which they hold separate from politics. Indeed, the military, civil service, scientific agencies, and public health services are generally not only thought but legally required to be divorced from politics in the restricted but important sense of being nonpartisan and professional. This requirement is not merely imposed upon them; it permeates professional ideals and shows itself in what Karl Mannheim once described as the fundamental bureaucratic tendency "to turn all problems of politics into problems of administration."[1] The actual relationship between politics and administration is too complex to be thought of as a clean separation, but the received morality of professional and administrative abstention from partisanship constitutes a reality in its own right.

These distinctions – most significantly, between private and public, and between the technical and the political – are often ambiguous in their application and subject to revision and manipulation by diverse interests. However, the distinctions themselves are part of the permanent structure of the liberal state. They define the two boundaries of the political that are of primary importance in contemporary liberal societies: one, the boundary of the political with the domain of private decision; the other, the boundary of the political with the domain of technical decision. These two boundaries suggest at least two modes of politicization. An issue or an element of social life or government may become politicized by passing either from the private into the public sphere or from the technical domain (even if within government) into the realm of political contention or control.[2]

Correspondingly, the politicization of some set of problems may be resisted on the grounds that they are matters properly of private or technical choice: that they belong, in the former case, to the realm of private values and private economic exchange or, in the latter, to the realm of objective knowledge.

Similarly, depoliticization may also take two forms: the passage from the public to the private realm, or privatization; and the passage from the political to the technical, which may involve professionalization (turning political decisions over to self-regulating professionals), bureaucratization, or corporatization (in this context, the delegation of political decision-making to technical, quasi-governmental bodies with interest group representation).

These general relationships and processes may be usefully applied to understanding the relation of health care to politics. In certain respects, health and health care have been propelled from the private into the public sphere and from the technical into the political domain. But this process of politicization has been resisted precisely on the grounds that health and medicine are (1) private matters to be resolved individually and in the marketplace, or (2) technical matters to be resolved by professionals on the basis of scientific criteria or by interest groups in state-sponsored negotiations. The struggle over the proper definition of health and medical problems may be taken as a kind of case study in the battle over what ought to belong to the spheres of politics, technical knowledge, and private choice.

Whether an issue is defined as political, technical, or private is, as we have already indicated, a political – or, perhaps better said, "metapolitical" – question. Definitions have consequences, known or at least anticipated by different groups. To establish some matter as technical or professional is to confer power on those who have expertise. To insist that the same problem is political is to say that it ought to be open to lay judgment and either the control of political officials or the direct participation of the public. As science has risen to a privileged status in the hierarchy of persuasive belief, its institutionally validated interpreters – notably physicians, who are its emissaries in the most personal matters of physical and mental health – have developed stronger claims to authority, not only in scientific and clinical matters but also over the social and political relations surrounding them.[3] They are no longer, however, the only professional group with claims to relevant expertise. Health planners and administrators, too, claim scientific grounds for their policies and programs. In health care the varying forms of professional authority, whether of physicians or planners, easily spill over their core jurisdictions and become ways of advancing political ideals as well as economic interests under the definition of "medical need," a claim with such moral force that laymen are reluctant to contradict it. Writing about the British National Health Service (NHS), Rudolph Klein remarks that "it is tempting to argue that the real political battle in the health care arena is precisely a definitional one: whether or not specific problems or issues should be labelled as being essentially 'medical' in nature, and as such taboo for the nonexpert."[4]

If locating an issue on one side or the other of the political-technical boundary has significant consequences, so, too, does locating it with respect to the public-private boundary. In democratic states, to move something from the private to the public sphere is to subject it, however imperfectly, to open discussion and the will of majorities. And in social democratic and other welfare states, such a shift moves an issue into an arena where equality is a more significant aim or standard than it is in the private market. The public and private spheres afford different opportunities for collective and individual choice. Hence the battle over whether a set of problems is properly public or private typically calls forth a combination of material interests and ideological commitments.

Throughout the West, particularly since World War II, health and health care have become the objects of increased social investment, public and private. What once was of minor importance to the economy and the state is now of large consequence, but the extent and nature of political control is still hotly contested. The activities and decisions that make up health care straddle the political-technical as well as the public-private boundaries. How to draw the lines has been a subject of continual dispute, the outcome of which has varied among different societies and changed over time.

During the two decades after 1945, two tendencies pulled health care toward government and away from politics. On the one hand, the financing and organization of health care generally moved from the private toward the public sector. On the other hand, the increased authority of science and the medical profession kept health care defined as an arena of technical decision-making insulated from political contention and control. In both Europe and the United States, consequently, there was a depoliticized expansion of the public sector in health care. Beginning in the mid-1960s, however, with the emergence of new social demands, increased skepticism about technical authority, and growing economic constraints, health care became a more salient object of political concern. For our purposes, therefore, the politics of health care after World War II may be divided into two major phases: first, a period of state expansion achieved with a minimum of political conflict; and second, a period of increasing demands, retrenchment, and political contention. Finally, in at least some countries, there may be yet a third phase as a result of the conservative effort to limit public commitments for health and social services.

EXPANDING STATE, RESTRICTED POLITICS

The expansion of public commitments

Immediately after World War II, Western European countries embarked on unprecedented public commitments to health care. Prewar compulsory health insurance had been targeted almost exclusively at industrial workers and low-income earners; postwar reforms sought to provide adequate medical care for entire populations. Public funds on a large scale were devoted to hospital construction and medical research, and governments became increasingly involved in health care planning. With a few notable exceptions, debates about health policy became less public and political. The issues were discussed in highly technical terms, often in closed committees, and the organs of health insurance administration lost their partisan character as they were incorporated into state bureaucracies.

The expansion of governmental responsibility for health care is most dramatically illustrated by the cases of Great Britain and Sweden. In Britain, compulsory health insurance, providing medical benefits as well as compensation for lost income, had been introduced by the Liberal government of David Lloyd George in 1911, but the program applied only to low-wage workers. As late as 1945, it covered only 51 percent of the population, and a great variety of private as well as public institutions provided hospital care. After the war, Great Britain made health care a corollary of citizenship. Under the National Health Service Act of 1946, all of Britain's hospitals, except for private nursing homes, were nationalized and reorganized into a system to provide free medical treatment, financed by general tax revenues. The same year, a new national insurance act reforming sickness and disability pay broke with the principles of contributory insurance by setting both benefits and contributions at uniform rates for all citizens.[5]

After the war Sweden moved in the same direction as Britain, although not quite as far. In 1947 it converted its half-century-old system of voluntary, state-subsidized insurance, which then covered slightly less than two-thirds of the population, into a compulsory and universal national health program. Previous reforms had already consolidated a plethora of voluntary sickness funds into a network of territorially based organizations, but the 1947 law now turned them into official government agencies under the jurisdiction of the National Insurance Office. Sweden, however, stopped short of nationalizing its hospitals and putting its doctors on salary. The county councils, organs of local government, retained direct operating responsibility for hospitals under the supervision of the National Board of Health; and most doctors, including those employed by hospitals, continued to be paid on a private, fee-for-service basis for ambulatory care.[6]

Other nations took more modest steps. They expanded insurance coverage to new groups, but did not put hospitals under governmental administration. In 1945, France expanded health insurance coverage and benefits, but left private medicine and private hospitals intact. After further changes, the health insurance system covered 99 percent of the French population by 1967. Similarly, in West Germany successive increases in the income ceiling for compulsory insurance raised coverage of the population to 50 percent in 1955 and 89 percent in 1976. Norway introduced universal coverage in 1956. In Denmark, massive state subsidies, beginning as early as 1892, had increased membership in voluntary sickness funds to 60 percent of the population by 1920 and 90 percent by 1960, until in 1971 health insurance finally became universal and compulsory. Shortly before the war, national health insurance laws covering employees and their dependents had been passed in Austria, Italy, the Netherlands, and Belgium; after the war, they were extended to pensioners and the self-employed.[7] As a result of these and other measures, public expenditures for health care grew steadily in both absolute terms and as a proportion of national income throughout Western Europe.

Both long-run and proximate causes promoted this expansion of public commitments. The long-run causes are those responsible for the more general shift from individual to collective responsibility for the effects of social and economic distress – or, as T. H. Marshall saw it, the progressive redefinition of citizenship to include social as well as civil and political rights.[8] The modern welfare state may be seen as the outcome of the effort by bourgeois regimes attempting to preserve their control in the face of challenges by socialist and labor movements. This dynamic generated the initial measures introducing social insurance and the later efforts to extend it. However, the leadership of social reform changed. Before World War II the "bourgeois parties" dominated the formulation of social policy; in the postwar period socialists participated – and often led – in the development of new programs in welfare, education, housing, and health.[9]

World War II left a deep and lasting impression on health policy. The exigencies of wartime planning and, in the Allied nations, the need for cooperation with organized labor altered the balance of power among interest groups and reduced traditional sources of opposition to state intervention in health. Wartime sacrifice made it difficult for conservatives to reject an expanded conception of citizenship that included entitlements to health care, especially in countries such as France and West Germany where the Right suffered from its association with the Vichy and Nazi regimes. Moreover, at least in Britain, the strong role played by the state during the war provided a model for the total mobilization of resources advocated by planners, and the need to rebuild afforded a unique opportunity to reorganize health services along the lines that planners advocated.

Immediately after the war, large electoral victories by the Left helped to bring about the introduction of policies that had already been imagined and, in some cases, planned during the war. Labor's sweeping victory in Britain in 1945 enabled it to carry out the program William Beveridge had set forth in 1942. In Sweden, some of the same factors as in Britain prepared the way for health reform: a widespread commitment to social as well as political equality and a shift in power to the advantage of the Left. Holding an electoral majority, the Swedish Social Democrats also proceeded to carry out a program they had formulated during the war. In France as well, the Left played a vital role. De Gaulle's 1945 cabinet, which issued the new health insurance program, comprised socialists, communists, and members of the Catholic Left party, the Mouvement Républicain Populaire, which had been greatly influenced by the Resistance experience. In West Germany, Social Democrats returned to found new forms of social insurance administration, such as the Versicherungsanstalt Berlin, which consolidated a variety of public and private funds into a single scheme.

The entry of socialist parties into mainstream politics doubtless created pressure for public programs in health as in other areas of social policy. But although leftist parties were especially important in the movement for universal insurance, Christian parties and even occupying forces also took part in insurance expansion. As modern medicine and hospitals offered new possibilities for treatment, which simultaneously increased the financial risks of illness, middle-class patients became increasingly interested in health insurance. Political parties across the board turned to health insurance as an effective means to attract constituents. Consequently, health insurance reforms lost their association with earlier struggles for workers' rights.

The limits of political control

Though they succeeded in winning major initiatives in health policy, reformers did not get everything they wanted. Opposition came from business, the medical profession, and insurance carriers. State intervention per se was no longer the central point of dispute; the type of intervention and its limits occupied the public agenda. A fundamental question was whether governments would entirely replace the market, nationalizing hospitals and directly employing physicians, or – at the other extreme – only subsidize the purchase of medical care through insurance, leaving physicians as private practitioners and hospitals in whatever institutional forms they had previously taken. The basic conflict over the limits of political control was also expressed in countless disputes about the public–private boundary, such as the right of doctors in public hospitals to treat private patients, the extent of government regulation of sickness funds and private hospitals, and the role of government in developing local health centers or polyclinics that would compete with private office practice. Governments were usually forced to make concessions to the professional interest in maintaining a private sector in medicine, partly because conservative groups were able to marshal their political resources during the period between the initial legislation and the implementation of reforms.

Great Britain was the only country in Western Europe that immediately after the war established a national health service, but even British physicians succeeded in limiting political control of their professional work. During two years of negotiation between the passage of the NHS Act in 1946 and its implementation in 1948, the medical profession wrested concessions from the government on several points. Private beds in NHS hospitals and opportunities for part-time private practice by hospital specialists were preserved. General practitioners were to be paid by capitation (that is, per patient enrolled on their lists) rather than by salary, and they were guaranteed that they would never become state employees. Plans for health centers to be administered by local government authorities were thrown out. The doctors' opposition to the health centers resulted in an emphasis on hospital and private office practice that persisted until the early 1970s. Local authorities were also excluded from hospital administration. Instead, a special hospital service directly responsible to the Ministry of Health was established. The rights of physicians were clearly defined and specified, and professional interests were to be represented at all levels. So even though the British state increased its responsibility for the financing of health services, the medical profession was able to define the boundaries of political control. While the government controlled the allocation of resources to the NHS, physicians controlled the use of resources within it.

The limits to political reform were still more evident in Sweden. National health insurance passed easily. However, the medical profession and nonsocialist parties stood firmly opposed in 1948 when the socialist physician Axel Höjer, director of the National Board of Health, introduced proposals for more comprehensive government planning, including state provision of primary care and a salaried medical service. The controversy over the Höjer proposals may have contributed to the Social Democrats' large electoral setback in 1948. The plan was widely regarded as a total "socialization" of medicine and as a sign that the socialists were going "too far." The Swedish medical profession's fight for autonomy was aided by a general conservative backlash that marked the end of the Social Democrats' so-called harvest time. As in Britain, political struggles defined the limits of state expansion. After the failure of the Höjer plan, the government was careful to include more suitable representatives of the profession on its planning commissions. Health care politics during the 1950s and 1960s were characterized by uncontroversial, incremental reforms, always preceded by exhaustive Royal Commission reports notable for their careful presentation of data and neutral tone.

In France the strong leadership responsible for the Social Security Ordinance had begun to erode by the end of 1945. Under the First Constituent Assembly, which met for the first time only after the ordinance had been promulgated, opposition emerged to the administration's plan for a *caisse unique* (unitary organization of the insurance funds) and to labor's power in managing the funds. In addition, the medical profession regrouped and restored its prewar organization. As a result, proposals for physicians to practice as employees of organizations financed by social security were ruled out. Physicians' fees continued to be regulated by agreements between local medical societies and insurance funds, a practice that had long created financial difficulties for the funds. Although the state included hospital construction under its four-year plans, the independent development of private hospitals undermined the planning efforts.[10]

In West Germany an active antireform movement composed of doctors' associations, private insurance carriers, and the statutory sickness funds for salaried employees fought what they viewed as dangerously overcentralized models for consolidating insurance. This movement, in conjunction with conservative politicians and the Allied Military Control, was able to block major structural reforms. Soon after the Federal Republic was founded in 1949, the first Bundestag restored the health insurance system to its prewar organization.[11]

Health care issues occasionally drew general political attention and debate in the fifties and early sixties. For example, a proposal by Christian Democrats for increased cost-sharing led to widespread labor protests in West Germany in 1959–60; the plan was defeated. In Britain there were periodic pay disputes between the government and physicians.[12] But these instances of political contention do not contradict the main point. Their limited character illustrates the narrowing of political divisions that led Raymond Aron and Daniel Bell to talk about the "end of ideology." The positions of socialists and conservatives on issues like cost-sharing and doctors' pay reflected their deeper ideological differences, but in each country the prevailing direction of policy had been set and the issues in dispute were more administrative than political.

The depoliticization of insurance funds

The changing structure of insurance funds in postwar Europe illustrates the shift from political to technical decision-making in health care. Originally developed in connection with various kinds of voluntary associations, trade unions, parties, and religious groups, the sickness funds had long provided the insured with a voice, albeit a weak one, in health care administration. The opportunity for exercising influence was especially important to workers in the award of cash benefits (sick pay); for by virtue of their authority to approve sick pay, the funds had a role in workplace discipline and diminished the unilateral power of employers. Moreover, social insurance elections had helped to affirm the political identities of the insured and were an important resource in the mobilization of members for other ends, such as governmental elections and strikes.

Many of the new social insurance laws, however, did not provide for participation by the insured. The British NHS Act abolished local insurance committees in England and Wales. We have already observed that Swedish national health insurance turned the old voluntary funds into a system of government agencies. France, which introduced social security elections in 1946, eliminated them in 1967. The West German funds, once considered the "third pillar" of the labor movement, became increasingly depoliticized. In 1951 worker representation was cut from two-thirds to one-half. Moreover, as Heidenheimer notes, voting declined as the parties ceased to contest elections, and the public increasingly saw insurance institutions as "de facto parts of the state administration."[13]

Rather innocuous administrative changes, as well, transformed the political nature of the funds. In contrast to prewar insurance programs, which were restricted to specific social groups, the postwar programs had wider constituencies and were usually organized on a national basis. Efforts to reduce administrative costs resulted in a shift from funds based on occupation or party affiliation to territorially based funds, and, simultaneously, a conversion of these voluntary or private organizations into official (or de facto) government agencies. The number of German funds dropped from 22,000 in 1911 to 1,425 in 1976; and their status as "bodies of public law" was revived after the founding of the Federal Republic.[14] In the Netherlands, years of mergers "secularized" the funds. Only in Belgium, where sickness funds continued to be accused of being the "bankers" of the political parties, did the funds retain their partisan allegiances.[15]

The relation of unions and socialist parties to health insurance had changed. Earlier, the voluntary sickness funds had constituted a useful and protected political base for workers' organizations. Now able to work within the political sphere, the unions and leftist parties were no longer interested in maintaining a political subculture. Moreover, as the style of industrial relations changed, both unions and employers began to welcome the reliance on medical experts to determine questions of work incapacity or employment, whereas the old partisan funds had reflected and exacerbated conflict in the workplace.

Gradually, voluntary sickness funds were incorporated into state bureaucracies. New regulations, the existence of larger funds with more heterogeneous memberships, and a concern with illness as a scientific problem rather than an issue of workers' rights all contributed to the demise of the funds' political role. As collective responsibility for the consequences of disease increased, health financing became detached from politics.

Depoliticization and professional power

Throughout Western Europe, regardless of the socialization of health financing, political control of health care was limited by the power and authority of the medical profession. In part, the profession's power rested on the unwillingness of governments to confront a well-organized pressure group; but in a more fundamental sense, it also rested on the cultural authority of the profession – its ability to define issues as technical and scientific and therefore outside the purview of political decision-making. By placing representatives of the medical profession on policy committees and planning boards, governments officially recognized the position of the doctors. Moreover, regardless of representation, political leaders turned to professionals for judgments about the need and adequacy of services. Even in the one instance of nationalization, the British NHS, the objective of health policy, as Klein puts it, was "to create a world fit for experts to apply their skills to the entire population." Furthermore, the broad political consensus in the 1950s allowed "problems and issues to be defined within the health care arena through the perceptual lenses of the professionals."[16]

Although it evolved in a fundamentally different way, postwar health policy in the United States had some of the same characteristics as in Britain and the rest of Europe: expanded public expenditure, but restricted political contention and control. In the late 1940s, the U.S. Congress rejected any national health insurance plan, let alone a national health service, but it did inaugurate several major programs to augment medical resources. Two of these were programs of hospital construction: a greatly expanded system of veterans' hospitals and a major infusion of capital for community hospital construction. The federal government undertook significant responsibilities for the funding of medical research, establishing the National Institutes of Health (NIH); and it also became more involved in funding mental health services. But as one of us has written elsewhere:

All four of the major postwar programs – medical research, mental health, the VA [Veterans Administration], and community hospital construction – showed a common pattern in respecting the sovereignty of the medical professional and local medical institutions. While the functions of government were expanded, the sphere of political discretion was deliberately restricted. In NIH the mechanism for restricting political control was the required approval of [research] grants by panels of experts drawn from outside government. NIH, as Don Price has observed, was the only agency of the federal government whose full-time officers could not allocate money without the approval of part-time committees representing the beneficiaries! The mental health program was initially established under NIH and shared its orientation to research and training and its reliance on peer evaluation. Political control in the VA was restricted by granting the power to appoint physicians to the "dean's committees" of medical schools with which VA hospitals were affiliated. And in the Hill-Burton [community hospital] program a [statistical] formula for grant allocation and statutory prohibition of federal intervention in hospital policy limited political discretion. In effect, by earmarking money for specific purposes and then outlawing federal interference, Congress and the professions joined in restricting any tendency toward administrative rationalization.[17]

In 1965, when Congress enacted Medicare and Medicaid – the first, providing federal insurance coverage to the aged; the second, supporting state medical programs of varying scale for the poor – it was also reluctant to antagonize the medical profession and hospital industry. Once again, federal funds came with minimal political control. But within a few years, the failure to install effective cost controls became an impetus for expanding political intervention in an unprecedented way.

CONSTRAINED STATE, EXPANDED POLITICS

Equality and the public–private boundary

Beginning in the late 1960s, health care became a more politically contested arena. Initially, an intensified concern about equality led to efforts to change both the public–private boundary and the distribution of power between professionals and the lay public. The growing political contentiousness of health care in the 1970s also reflected a broader redefinition of technical questions as political and a wider skepticism about science and the professions. Increased health care expenditures and the economic difficulties of the advanced welfare states brought in new political interests. Under these changed circumstances, health care politics, like health care costs, could not easily be contained within older administrative frameworks.

In the early postwar period, while expanding public commitments to health care, Western European governments had all left a private sector more or less intact. The maintenance of a private sector in health care not only limits political control; it also preserves the opportunity of the economically stronger to seek more insurance coverage, greater freedom of choice, higher standards of care, shorter waiting times, and other possible advantages in the private marketplace. The appeal of private alternatives depends partly on the resources, organization, and standards of the public system as well as the tax treatment, subsidies, and regulation of private services. Therefore, even after governments expanded public responsibilities for health, a variety of public policies could influence the public–private mix and, thereby, the salience of class distinctions in health care.

The postwar governments had drawn the public–private boundary in different ways through health insurance, hospitals, and medical practice. Great Britain did away with the sickness funds and financed its health service out of general revenues; however, a small private insurance sector emerged to offer coverage of private care by consultants. Sweden retained an insurance system for health care finance, but put it under national control. The West German sickness funds were recognized as bodies of public law, but operated autonomously. For example, they negotiated independently with associations of insurance doctors; moreover, separate funds existed for blue-collar workers and white-collar employees. The French funds were legally considered "private bodies with a public law function" ("*organismes privés, chargés de la gestion d'un service public*"); and again, although much consolidation took place, separate funds persisted for different groups. However, the minimum benefits of both the German and French funds were set by government, and in that sense health insurance was politically controlled. The funds in the Netherlands were private associations and less governmentally regulated than the French ones.[18]

No Western European county put all its doctors entirely on public salary. Britain and Sweden placed their hospitals under governmental control, but most hospital-based doctors in both countries continued to have opportunities for private, fee-for-service practice. In France, private practice predominated, although the government sought to promote full-time, salaried practice in public hospitals. French hospitals were divided among three sectors – public, private nonprofit, and proprietary hospitals called *cliniques* – with public hospitals representing more than two-thirds of the bed capacity. A major priority of French policy in the 1950s and 1960s was the modernization of the public hospitals, many of which were old and venerable institutions with large open wards. In 1958 a series of decrees and ordinances – sometimes called the "Réforme Debré" after Professor Robert Debré, who headed a commission that prepared them – sought to coordinate the development and management of hospitals and to encourage doctors in public hospitals to shift from fee-for-service payment to salary. Fees from public patients, previously paid directly to the chief of staff, were to be collected by the hospital. As a transitional measure, full-time hospital physicians could continue to treat private patients during limited hours, but the revenues from such patients were government-regulated. In the private hospitals, however, physicians continued to collect unregulated private fees. This difference, of course, was an incentive for physicians to prefer to use the private hospitals, particularly for more affluent patients. The *cliniques* could also bill patients for more than the regular daily rate that social security paid to both public and private hospitals. During the 1960s, the growth of the *cliniques* outpaced expansion in the public sector, and the new *cliniques* typically had more attractive facilities. The public hospitals, although often dilapidated, continued to be the center of the most technologically complex, capital-intensive medical care, while the *cliniques* specialized in profitable routine obstetric and surgical services. The 1970 Hospital Law was intended to reduce this wasteful competition and to ensure that resources were allocated according to the needs of the population. Hospital construction, as well as expansion of facilities and equipment, were subjected to more stringent review by the Ministry of Health. Nonetheless, even though 15,000 new public hospital posts were created for full-time salaried hospital physicians, the importance of the private sector continued to grow, increasing its proportion of total bed capacity from 26.4 percent in 1963 to 34.3 percent in 1978.[19]

In health care, the relationship between public and private is exceptionally complex because the two are often not strictly separated – as they generally are, for example, in education. A child generally goes to a public or a private school, not both; a teacher generally works in one or the other. Not so in health care. In a nation where the two sectors coexist, patients may use public hospitals or doctors for one complaint and see a private physician in a private clinic for a second. Indeed, they may even consult the same physician first under the public or social insurance system and then as a private patient.[20] A physician's time and income may be divided in varying proportions between public and private services. Similarly, public hospitals may have private beds, and private hospitals may be subject to public planning and regulation. Thus the public–private boundary runs not only between hospitals and doctors in different sectors, but also inside hospitals and through the daily schedules of physicians. Indeed, it was precisely these mixed arrangements – private beds in public hospitals; doctors on public salary with private practice income; independent sickness funds with public functions – that gave rise to some intensely controversial political disputes and decisions, as new challenges emerged in the 1960s and 1970s to the compromises made in the early postwar era in the drawing of the public–private boundary.

Once again, Sweden and Great Britain, as two countries with the

most advanced public sectors and strongest commitments to equal
entitlement to health care, provide varying examples of the general
pattern. Until 1970, the 90 percent of Swedish physicians who were
employed by government – that is, by the county councils, which ran
the hospitals – continued to be paid on a fee-for-service basis by their
patients for outpatient care. The patients would then apply to the
insurance fund for a three-quarters reimbursement. In the late 1960s,
when health care costs were already rising significantly, the high level
of physician incomes became a political issue; doctors were also fea-
tured in some highly publicized cases of tax evasion. Moreover, the
different medical specialties varied widely in income depending on
opportunities for profitable outpatient fees; and these disparities obstructed efforts to strengthen services in the less remunerative fields,
such as primary and geriatric care, whose expansion was a political
and planning priority.

In 1968, campaigning on a platform of "increased equality," the
Swedish Social Democrats won a larger than expected victory in national elections. Soon after, they launched a major reform of the financing of medical services. One element was to establish a flat fee
of seven crowns, not quite $1.50 at the time, for all ambulatory visits.
(It was from this provision that the legislation, implemented in 1970,
took its name, the Seven Crowns Reform.) But the fee of seven crowns
went from the insurance fund to the county councils, not from patient
to doctor. For the reform also put all government physicians on
straight salary; fee-for-service practice was barred, except for the 10
percent of Swedish doctors who remained in private office practice.
In addition, for all government doctors, salaries across medical specialties were equalized; some specialties saw gains, but many doctors
experienced real losses. These measures were aimed at achieving
several objectives simultaneously: controlling health care costs, reducing physicians' incomes relative to other occupations, reducing
tax evasion, achieving greater income equality among physicians and
public employees in general, and encouraging a redistribution of physicians among specialties.

Several aspects of the Seven Crowns Reform are worth emphasizing. By all accounts, the moving forces behind it were political, not
administrative. No Royal Commission preceded the reform; the initiative came from the Federation of County Councils and the Social
Democratic leadership. The changes in medical financing emerged
from a broader political program of greater equality, not from a technical effort to solve problems of health care management. The medical
profession was not consulted at any point. The changes had support

from younger doctors, but the reform demonstrated how little power the Swedish medical profession exercised.[21]

Although Great Britain had no comparable reform, a comparable dispute erupted in the mid-seventies over the same fundamental issue: equality and the public–private boundary. Like the Swedish hospital-based doctors, the British consultants had preserved a profitable source of fee-for-service income, but from private NHS beds, not ambulatory care. These beds became the subject of what Klein calls "the most bitter political struggle [in health care] since the inception of the NHS."[22] The beds represented only one percent of the NHS total; nonetheless, they led to charges of a double standard of treatment and had a symbolic importance as a continuing source of class distinctions. There is little doubt that they were used by wealthier patients to jump queues, and that the concentration of opportunities for private practice in the wealthier regions obstructed efforts to equalize access to health care in the NHS. However, Labour had originally accepted private beds, as well as part-time contracts with NHS consultants, on the grounds that highly qualified consultants would be more likely to take NHS posts if they could conveniently supplement their incomes. In 1966, however, a Labour minister had cut the private beds from 5 to 1 percent of NHS capacity because of underuse; in recompense, he had also removed limits on consultants' fees for private patients. Thereafter, the pay beds were not the source of major controversy until the early seventies, when left-wing activists began to make them an issue. When Labour again assumed office in 1974, the new Secretary of State for the Social Services, Barbara Castle, announced that the government would seek to eliminate private beds from the health service. In addition, Labour also wanted incentives for full-time commitments written into the NHS contract with consultants.

"The attack on private beds," writes Klein, "was essentially ideological: an attack on visible symbols of privilege."[23] From the consultants' standpoint, private beds and private patients provided material advantages – an average supplement of about 20 percent of their salaries that was particularly important to them at the time since their real incomes had dropped significantly over the preceding decade. The consultants saw Labour's position as a repudiation of the basic agreements on which the NHS was established. In the ensuing uproar, the Labour government was forced to compromise. A government commission called, in principle, for phasing out the private beds, but accepted the right of consultants to a private practice. One thousand private beds were eliminated immediately; the fate of the rest was left to a board that included medical representatives. No deadline was set, and when the board was shut down by the Conservatives in 1980, it had reduced private beds by only about 40 percent. Ironically, the Labour effort to rid the NHS of private beds helped to stimulate the development of private hospitals.[24]

The same issue later arose in France under Mitterrand. In October 1982 the National Assembly, despite protests from the Senate, decided to withdraw private beds from public hospitals by December 31, 1983, and eliminate private consultations by January 1986 (deadlines extended later that year to March 31, 1984 and January 1987).[25] And, in Spain, analogous issues have been of political concern. Under Spain's extensive social security health care system, introduced by Franco, many physicians divide their time between public *ambulatorios* and private office practices. According to numerous complaints, many doctors neglect their public duties. Opinion polls before the 1982 elections showed that health care was a leading domestic concern, and one of the first actions of the new Socialist government was to take action against physicians who were failing to fulfill their public obligations – in some cases, holding posts with conflicting schedules.[26]

These various disputes and reforms – the French Réforme Debré, the Swedish Seven Crowns Reform, British Labour's effort to reduce pay beds in NHS hospitals, the Spanish Socialists' effort to enforce doctors' social security obligations – all emerged from the perception that earlier compromises mixing public and private in the same hospital or doctors' schedules were leading to the neglect of public responsibilities and, therefore, to class distinctions in health care. In a variety of ways, private practice interests of doctors were also obstructing efforts to achieve equal distribution of physicians by region and specialty. Insofar as the commitment to equality predominated in public policy, it led to an effort to expand public control and restrict private practice. In itself, this shift of the public–private boundary meant an enlargement of political control. But because such efforts were controversial – indeed, they had explicitly ideological origins – they also involved health care in renewed political contention.

The politicization of technical judgment

The revived interest in equality in the 1960s and 1970s also led to a reconsideration of the boundary between technical and political authority. Throughout the West, professional authority had become an increasingly significant basis of power and social privilege. Health care had become a more significant public concern, and much of the public was now unwilling to leave medical decision-making entirely in the hands of physicians. At the national level, public expenditures for health care began to threaten the solvency of the welfare state. In some countries, higher taxes were provoking tax revolts; everywhere, political leaders began to search for effective means of health care cost containment. The new political interest in health care was expressed in various forms: New consumer organizations and mass media reports articulated demands for better health care, or better consumer information, or more consumer representation in policy formulation; and, at the national level, political leaders intervened more directly in policy questions previously left to civil servants, medical administrators, or doctors. The judgments of physicians and administrators were seen not necessarily as scientific, but often as self-interested, prejudiced, and political. This was a theme of contemporary feminists in their criticism of medical practice. A rather extreme form was Ivan Illich's widely translated and much read jeremiad against the "medicalization of life" in *Medical Nemesis*.[27] In this respect, radical skepticism about the medical profession reflected the broader current of doubt evident in the ecology and antinuclear movements. But these views also enjoyed support from more conventional sources. For example, in a series of BBC lectures published as *The Unmasking of Medicine* in 1981, Ian Kennedy, a lawyer and director of the Centre of Law, Medicine, and Ethics at Kings College, London, severely criticized physicians' control of decisions in health care that affect the public's welfare, arguing that the rhetoric of science has served as a mask for power and that consumers are capable of exercising responsible choice.[28]

The American case is perhaps the best example of what one of us has called the "waning of professional sovereignty" because the turnabout was so dramatic. The medical profession had long enjoyed a relatively secure mandate to run its own affairs; public policy was premised on the assumption that private practice and professional prerogatives were not to be challenged. Then, beginning in the late 1960s, popular concern about access to health care, combined with increased concern in government and business about health expenditures, began to erode the deference to professional judgment. Out of the civil rights and consumer movements came a variety of efforts to establish health care rights, such as rights to informed consent, which challenged the physicians' monopoly in medical decision-making.[29] After a long hands-off policy, the federal and state governments began to pass a series of new regulatory and reform measures to improve access to services and control health care costs. In some respects, these new forms of regulation – such as reviews of physicians' treatment decisions for patients under government programs – were far more intrusive than the regulation of medical decision-making in Great Britain, where ostensibly a national health service meant that government control of health care was more advanced. But the British government could control health expenditures simply by appropriating less money to the NHS; it left clinical practice to the doctors. On the other hand, precisely because the United States did not have a national health service, it found little way to control health care costs except by setting up mechanisms to regulate the treatment and investment decisions of private practitioners and private institutions. In the early 1970s, even many American conservatives accepted the need for stronger political direction. One undersecretary in the Nixon administration made the point explicitly at a press conference in 1971: "In the past, decisions on health care delivery were largely professional ones. Now the decisions will be largely political."[30] Within the federal government, decisions previously left to civil servants were now more likely to be politically directed, as Hugh Heclo pointed out in a 1975 article on "increasing political control" of the Office of Management and Budget: "Increasingly interventionist policies – with civil servants dealing in questions of birth control, consumerism, medical care, environment, energy, transportation, civil rights, and so on – provide a legitimate justification for a much greater political interest in civil service decisions."[31] In the terms we used at the outset of this essay, there was an expansion of the boundaries of political interest and control into both the private sphere and the technical (even within government).

Even before these developments, the distinction between politics and administration may have been less observed in the United States than in Europe. "By institutional necessity, and also because of the historic absence of socialization as an administrative elite, American bureaucrats are more oriented toward traditionally political roles than bureaucrats in Europe," write Joel Aberbach, Robert Putnam, and Bert Rockman in a comparative study of bureaucrats and politicians.[32] But as they and other observers note, in Europe, too, "classical bureaucrats" disdainful of politics have increasingly given way to "political bureaucrats" more willing to accept and acknowledge policy-making, political roles. The expanded scope of government inexorably widens the social and economic functions of its administrators and professionals and makes them the object of greater political attention and new political demands.[33]

The same politicization of health care policy and management as happened in the United States took place in Great Britain in the early 1970s, a period when, as Klein writes, "technical questions increasingly became redefined as political issues."[34] A 1974 reorganization of the NHS gave more of a role to consumer representatives and local authorities than they originally had. Previously, the experts alone were organized; now, so were the consumers. A 1979 Directory of Organizations for Patients and Disabled People listed 230 separate groups. Furthermore, the NHS's own employees were becoming more vocal in their protests about wages and working conditions. These pressures converged on the NHS at a time when Britain's economic stagnation meant that even a Labour government could not easily make more money available to assuage the disaffected.

For decades, Labour and the Conservatives had moved closer together; now they moved farther apart, as each party went back to first principles. If political consensus in the 1950s allowed many problems in health policy to be left to the experts, ideological polarization in the 1970s meant that the policy issues were more subject to political contention. As Klein notes, neither party had much confidence in expertise – "the Right . . . because of its individualism, the Left . . . because of its commitment to wider participation in decision-making." The medical profession's capacity to dominate discussion was also undermined by the bigger stakes at issue. In *Pressure Group Politics*, a case study of the British Medical Association in the 1950s, Harry Eckstein argued that the BMA exerted more influence over decisions the less attention the decisions attracted beyond the Ministry of Health. Klein makes the same point:

The power of the medical profession is in an inverse relationship to the size of the stage on which a specific health care issue is fought out. When the stage widens to bring on actors who normally play no part in the health care arena strictly defined – when the Treasury and the Cabinet become involved – then the ability of the medical profession to get its own way diminishes.[35]

In the mid-1970s, the stage widened when the overriding problems became those of the national economy. No government could afford to ignore the increasing share of national income absorbed by public expenditures. In this way, economic constraint expanded the boundaries of political contention and control into the sphere of technical judgment.

The demand for cost control also brought in larger forces in other Western European countries. In West Germany, health care costs became a major concern in the mid-1970s. Although physicians attempted voluntarily to hold down costs, the West German government in 1977 enacted cost-containment legislation aimed at limiting total expenditures by sickness funds. Procedures were introduced to set prospective limits on medical services and drugs, and the rate of expenditure growth was tied to broader economic indicators, including the wage base of the funds and the cost of medical practice. The reforms also centralized negotiations between the doctors and sickness funds. Now total health expenditures would be set by a national commission, the Concerted Action in Health Affairs, whose sixty members were to represent the various interest groups, including doctors, hospitals, sickness funds, drug companies as well as state and federal governments.[36] The model here was the similarly conceived Concerted Action that brought together German labor and business for economic policy discussions.

Corporatization both restricts and expands the sphere of the political. As Offe has argued, corporatist devices for conflict resolution are a form of depoliticization: They take issues out of the broader political arena and turn them over to interest group representatives for confidential negotiations.[37] But while limiting political contention, corporatist regulation expands political control. In the new system of health expenditure regulation, as Fritz Beske writes, "the global sum of expenditures is determined by central decisions."[38] The West German system approaches the kind of global budgeting that exists in Britain, where the overall decisions on health expenditures are made politically even though the specific clinical choices remain in the hands of doctors.

The British solution is political control at the center, technical autonomy at the periphery – and there is little question that it works as a means of limiting public expenditures. "In Britain," Gordon Forsyth writes, "central control over resource allocation . . . allows political decisions to be made so that public expenditures on the NHS can be related to the state of the economy and . . . other perceived needs."[39] The other European countries do not have similarly strong political control over health costs. However, as the German case illustrates, by the late 1970s they were moving in that direction. Throughout Europe, capital investment in hospitals was being placed under political control. Previously, the charges for hospital care had included depreciation and capital development, but as Forsyth describes it:

in every country they have been taken out of insurance and are paid for by public authorities . . . with increasing government financial involvement has grown increased control. Every Western European country now has a regional plan for hospitals and all hospitals, public and private, must conform to it. If a hospital wishes to develop or extend a service then permission must be sought; and if new equipment is involved then an authorization certificate must be obtained from the regional office of the relevant Ministry.[40]

This kind of development would seem to epitomize the expansion in the boundaries of the political: Hospital planning is one of the new issues projected into the national political arena. But it is also one where political authority has proved exceedingly difficult to use. The countries with insurance systems that have sought to develop health planning have generally been unable to unite planning with finance (partly because of effective lobbying by health sector interests), and as a result rising health care costs have continued to seem an intractable problem.

CAN POLITICS CONTRACT?

Privatization in Britain and the United States

The questioning of science as a basis of rational authority eroded faith not only in the medical profession but also in rational planning by government. The New Left of the 1960s and 1970s took the limitations of expertise as an argument for democratic participation, decentralization, and cooperatively organized institutions. The newly revitalized conservatives and neoconservatives of the 1970s and 1980s took the same limitations as an argument for relying on the market and "mediating structures" such as the family and voluntary associations.[41] The same skepticism that encouraged a redefinition of technical questions as political encouraged conservatives to seek to redefine public questions as private.

The limitations of medicine could be interpreted in dramatically different ways – by the Left as requiring political remedies and by the Right as requiring private ones. In the view of the Left, the ineffectiveness of medicine in reducing sickness and mortality, when compared with public health measures, clearly indicated the wisdom of more emphasis on environmental control, occupational safety, and broader changes in capitalist civilization. The conservatives took the same data and saw a greater need for individual responsibility and changes in behavior: prevention with a conservative face.[42] One neoconservative even interpreted the correlation between income and health as proving that environmental and safety regulation damages public health because it allegedly slows economic growth.[43]

These trends in political sentiment, particularly the skepticism about the value of public expenditures and government regulation, became especially important with shifts in political power. The tax revolts and welfare backlash of the 1970s culminated in 1980 in the election of more radically conservative governments in Great Britain and the United States than either country had seen in half a century. With a revived enthusiasm for the free market, both Margaret Thatcher and Ronald Reagan sought to reprivatize a variety of responsibilities and services that governments had undertaken since World War II. Health care was not exempt from this shift in policy. However, because the two countries had established drastically different public sector activities in health care, the implications for each were different. Moreover, in Britain the NHS enjoyed overwhelming public approval, and similarly, in the United States Medicare had powerful constituencies of support that no conservative president, however popular, could easily ignore.

Although some right-wingers called for scaling back the NHS or replacing it with an insurance system, the Thatcher government embarked on no such policy. It ended Labour's campaign against private beds in the NHS, and it welcomed the development of private, for-profit hospitals. It also made employer's contributions to private health insurance exempt from income taxes for employees earning less than 8,500 pounds a year. As part of an administrative reorganization of the NHS, it allowed NHS hospitals to seek voluntary contributions to supplement public funds – a measure that Labour argued would favor wealthier districts – and it slightly increased the proportion of NHS income derived from charges to patients. But perhaps the greatest incentive it offered for resort to the private sector in health was holding down NHS expenditures.

Actually, housing and education bore the brunt of Thatcher's cutbacks in public spending. The NHS was allowed to grow, albeit ever so slightly. Between 1951 and 1975, NHS expenditures grew annually (in real terms) between 3 percent and 3.5 percent. Under Labour during the last half of the 1970s, the growth rate had already been cut to 1.5 percent. In 1982, the Conservatives announced that they intended to hold it to just 0.5 percent. Since the aging of the British population and technological development are believed to require a significantly higher rate of growth, it is likely that the quality of NHS services will erode and that this decline will further spur enrollment in private insurance.[44]

Even before the Conservatives' victory, private health insurance subscriptions were rising sharply, up 70 percent between 1977 and 1980. By that point, the private plans covered 3.6 million people, primarily from families of above-average income and education (although some expansion has come from newly added trade-union members).[45] However, this development can easily be misunderstood as signifying that such people had deserted the NHS. On the contrary, 96 percent of those covered by insurance were also enrolled with an NHS general practitioner.[46] British private health insurance is quite limited in its function. It is meant neither for primary care, nor for emergency care, nor for chronic care, but almost entirely for non-emergency hospitalization. According to Alan Maynard, the bulk of private insurance is used to cover about thirty surgical procedures. So even though by 1980, 6 percent of the population was covered by private insurance, the total expenditures of the insurance funds amounted to only one percent of the NHS budget.[47] The private insurance sector provides benefits that primarily allow a choice of consultant and hospital and, perhaps most important, jumping queues in the NHS. As Michael Lee puts it, "The private patient pays to avoid waiting; the NHS patient waits to avoid paying."[48]

The recent development of the private health sector in Britain is rich with irony. Labour helped to stimulate its growth in the late seventies. Labour's restriction of private beds in the NHS stimulated the construction of private hospitals outside the NHS. Labour's attempt to shift NHS priorities toward the care of the elderly and the chronically and mentally ill reduced the share of resources available for the kind of surgical repair required by the relatively healthy, employed population that has turned to private insurance and hospitals. And, finally, Labour's Incomes Policy controlling wages did not apply to employee benefits such as private health insurance.

On the other hand, the Conservatives, while sympathetic to the private sector, have in some ways actually made things harder for it. By once again accepting private beds in the NHS, the government, according to one report, "has made it more difficult for private hospitals to maintain their patient censuses, because everything else being equal, a consultant would prefer to limit his or her patients to one hospital" – and virtually all consultants are employed by the NHS.[49] While proprietary hospitals have increased in number, their charges have risen sharply. When the largest private insurer, the British United Provident Association (BUPA), reported an operating loss of 1.9 million pounds in 1982, it blamed it on the charges of the proprietary (in some cases, American-owned) hospitals.[50] As a result, it has begun to offer incentives for subscribers to use BUPA's own hospitals; in effect, it is becoming what in the U.S. is called a "preferred provider organization." BUPA is also moving toward closer scrutiny of claims, bolstering the view of some analysts that the growth of the private insurance sector in Britain will inevitably lead to an increase in health care regulation![51]

One of the more curious ironies is that the conservative economists who denounce the NHS argue that the relatively low share of Gross Domestic Product in Britain spent on health care – about 6 percent, compared with 11 percent in the United States and 8 percent to 10 percent in most of Western Europe – is evidence of *underspending*. They suggest that if there were a free market, consumers might well be spending more and deriving greater satisfaction.[52] However, several considerations are likely to give pause to any government inclined to accept these views. First, increased spending for private health insurance would have to come from somewhere; if from private employers, it would mean higher labor costs. The low cost of health care in Britain – and the high level of health in the population – has plainly been a comparative advantage for British industry (which does not have many). Second, the relatively higher levels of expenditure elsewhere have prompted government regulation precisely because of doubt that a private market in health care, backed by insurance, works efficiently. The record in other countries with private insurance scarcely invites imitation. Third, the organization of the NHS serves underappreciated political functions. The traditions of professional autonomy in the NHS relieve political leaders of onerous responsibilities. For example, the British have not provided renal dialysis at the same rate as other European countries or the United States. Some patients, particularly older patients, are being denied a form of treatment that could clearly prolong their lives. Remarkably, the protest has been limited and the government has not been pressed to changed its policies. For it is doctors, not cabinet ministers, who make the decisions about what patients are appropriate for treatment. As Henry Aaron and William Schwartz have shown in a study of health care rationing, British general practitioners have adapted to the resource constraints and developed clinical standards that rule out patients who in other countries would be considered acceptable candidates for dialysis.[53] To quote Rudolph Klein once again:

The definition of certain areas of decision-making as being medical – and the consequent diffusion of responsibility for the consequences – thus prevents overload at the centre. The fact that no patient under the NHS system has a legal *right* to any specific kind of treatment – that it is the clinician who determines what the patient "needs" – means that it is possible to fragment and dissolve national policy issues into a series of local clinical decisions. *Political problems are in effect, converted into clinical problems* (emphasis added).[54]

Finally, public approval of the NHS makes the political cost of any radical change simply too great for even an ideologically devoted Conservative government to undertake. "The government should understand," said Neil Kinnock in the House of Commons soon after assuming leadership of the Labour Party in 1983, "that the British people's affection for the NHS does not arise out of sentimentality. The public's affection is born of its usefulness and dependability. That is why they will fight to save it. The NHS cannot be dismembered or dismantled by British prime ministers or foreign economists, because it is not theirs to dispose of." If returned to power, Labour has said it will end all private practice in the NHS, nationalize any private hospitals useful to the NHS, and disband the private insurance plans.[55] This is testimony to the continued ideological polarization of British health politics: Not only have the Conservatives failed to re-privatize the NHS, but they have certainly failed to depoliticize it. However, just as Thatcher has been unable to put Conservative ide-ology into practice in health care, so may Labour find it difficult to prohibit a private sector. As already mentioned, some union members now have private insurance coverage, and private provision of sur-gical care frees NHS resources for primary and chronic care. The NHS may enjoy as much support as it does because there exists a small private sector to serve as an escape valve for the dissatisfied.

In the United States, as in Britain, conservative proposals for market reform in health care have met frustration and been limited in effect. Before assuming office, prominent members of the Reagan admin-istration had supported broad plans for greater "health care compe-tition." Some of these ideas had enjoyed the backing of the previous Democratic administration. Beginning in the mid-1970s, the Federal Trade Commission questioned professional codes restricting medical advertising and various rules restricting competition from nonphy-sician practitioners. Congress enacted laws promoting the develop-ment of health maintenance organizations and other alternative forms of health service. Yet, for most of the seventies, the main hope for cost containment, among Democrats and Republicans alike, was reg-ulation of hospital investment and clinical decisions. Toward the end of the decade, the Democrats sought to regulate hospital revenues directly; the defeat of this measure in 1979 presaged the emergence of a conservative movement to seek deregulation of health care. In the bolder schemes, some conservatives, such as David Stockman, Reagan's director of the Office of Management and Budget, envi-sioned fundamental changes in private insurance and public pro-grams that would encourage stiffer price competition and cost control in the medical market.[56] These plans, however, generally involved tampering with the private insurance market, and therefore caused anxiety among insurance companies and physicians – groups with influence in the Republican Party. In addition, the proposals involved additional expenditures to provide minimal coverage to the tenth of the U.S. population – roughly 28 million people – still without any kind of health coverage, public or private. As the priority of the Reagan administration became budgetary control, these comprehen-sive plans were ruled out. Only fragments were submitted to the Congress. Of those, only a few have passed, and the regulatory pro-grams, although weakened, managed to survive.[57] A stalemate in policy at the national level has meant a devolution of initiative to individual states, some of which, particularly in the West, have embarked on policies emphasizing greater competition. There has also been a significant growth of for-profit companies in the U.S. health care industry.[58] But the general program of competition and privatization has not succeeded; further expansion of the role of the public sector has stopped, but it has not been rolled back. However, as in Britain, excited talk of a rollback ensures that health care will remain ideologically contentious.

Health care, politics and the liberal state

In modern societies, contacts between national states and their citizens have expanded immensely in number and complexity. National governments used to be removed at a distance from the daily affairs of most of their people; now they are present in more direct ways. With the growth of public health agencies, government aid to medical research and education, and compulsory sickness insurance and national health services, health care has become one area where contacts between states and citizens have grown and where risks have consequently emerged of political control of private life, the professions, and the development of scientific knowledge.

Concerns about individual autonomy, or the autonomy of science, do not arise in societies that put no barriers on political decisions – where the rulers, for example, have an ideological program to make private conduct (indeed, the human personality) and human understanding conform to their ideals. Concerns about the proper limits of political control do arise, however, in liberal societies. For if liberalism means anything at all, it signifies the attempt to put boundaries on politics: to limit political control of (and contention about) religious and moral life and the private economy, and to maintain a distinction between facts and values and hence between technical and political judgment. The reasons for this commitment are complex. The boundaries do not arise exclusively out of an interest in protecting individual economic interests, as antiliberals so often contend. Nor is their inspiration simply to be understood as a bias against politics, although liberals do believe (with good reason) that political control would be stifling to private moral judgment, economic initiative, and the progress of science. Equally important is the conviction that the vitality of politics depends on keeping private moral and religious conflicts from disrupting politics. The public–private boundary preserves not just private liberty but the possibility of democratic public life. The same is true of the political–technical boundary. A government could not be democratically run if its administrative branches persistently injected themselves into the political choices that are supposed to be made by the people's elected representatives.

However, as we emphasized at the outset, the boundaries between public and private, political and technical, are ambiguous and become the basis on which various groups in society pursue their interests. Although the boundaries help to preserve spheres of autonomy from political power, they also allow spheres of power to develop apart from politics. That is their manifest aim, but it is also the source of the difficulties in observing them. Private economic power, technical and administrative authority, the professions – these, too, may threaten liberty and other legitimate social interests and prompt political interventions.

When Western governments became more involved in the provision of health care in the postwar era, they imposed limits on the boundaries of political control and contention. Partly, they were forced to compromise with entrenched interests, but this was not the only reason. Broader political forces endorsed such limits because of their commitments to the autonomy of science, the professions, and private life. Setting aside medical care and medical science as a domain of technical judgment serves to insulate them from potentially damaging politicization. The line of political authority does not go directly to the sick in their beds. Between them stands independent professional authority. Similarly, the private sector serves as a relatively independent counterweight, and in some cases as an alternative to public medical services. One has only to look at the use of medicine and psychiatry in the Soviet Union for an example of the consequences of failing to observe these boundaries: Medicine functions there as an arm of political supervision.

Yet the postwar solution in the West had difficulties. Under insurance systems, professional authority easily became the basis of professional aggrandizement, and obstructed the more rational coordination and management of services and broader public participation in decision making in both clinical and policy questions. The preservation of a private sector in health created problems of cost control and obstructed equal access to health care. In the context of a new political climate in the 1960s and 1970s, the postwar compromises broke down, and both the technical and the private spheres were increasingly subordinated to the political. The political character of technical decisions had to be more openly confronted; the private sector more directly controlled – until, of course, in the 1980s that movement was arrested. However, as we have seen, the effort to privatize is restricted primarily to Britain and the United States, and in those countries quite limited and hesitant in health care.

So although the boundaries have changed – health care has become more subject to political control and more politically contentious – they have not been erased. The distinctions between the public and private and the political and technical are still the terms in which we think and fight over the rules that shape how health care will be governed. The boundaries remain active fault lines along which political tremors will repeatedly occur.

The struggle over what is political is part of the struggle for political power – and for a free society. Those with private power or technical authority no doubt often benefit when their activities are put beyond the reach of political intervention. However, the boundaries of the political are more than convenient fictions for the protection of privilege. Politics without boundaries verges on oppression, even if conducted in the name of liberation and equality. Just as we need political freedom, so we also need freedom from the political. To observe boundaries to politics is to allow the possibility of action and thought independent of those who rule or seek to rule.

Notes

1 Karl Mannheim, *Ideology and Utopia* (New York: Harcourt Brace & World, 1946) p. 105.

2 The alert reader will have already observed that when referring to the boundaries of the political, we tend to use two sets of terms: those referring to the boundaries of "political contention" (or conflict, discussion, or interest) and those referring to the boundaries of "political control" (or intervention). The two sets are not equivalent. In an authoritarian regime, political control may be pervasive while the scope of political contention is severely restricted, whereas contention may be pervasive in an open society where political control is limited. Furthermore, political contention may accompany a transition across the public–private boundary; but once the transition is concluded, political contention may diminish even as political control increases. There are moments of political contention in processes that have prepolitical beginnings (in private complaints) and postpolitical endings (in professional administration). And there are moments of political control in matters ordinarily left to technical experts or private agents. These complexities need to be noted particularly because a spatial metaphor like "boundary" suggests an exaggerated fixity in these distinctions, which are ambiguous, multiple, and overlapping as well as being politically and intellectually contested.

3 On the growth of medical authority, see Paul Starr, *The Social Transformation of American Medicine* (New York: Basic, 1982).

4 Rudolph Klein, *The Politics of the National Health Service* (New York: Longman, 1983), p. 57. Perhaps more than any other work on recent developments in health care in Europe, Klein's addresses the problems of the changing public–private and political–technical boundaries in health care. We shall have frequent occasion to cite it.

5 On the origins of the British NHS, see Arthur J. Willcocks, *The Creation of the National Health Service* (London: Routledge & Kegan Paul, 1967); Harry Eckstein, *The English Health Service: Its Origins, Structure, and Achievements* (Cambridge, Mass.: Harvard University Press, 1958); and John E. Pater, *The Making of the National Health Service* (London: King Edward's Hospital Fund for London, 1981).

6 On Sweden, see Arnold J. Heidenheimer and Nils Elvander, eds., *The Shaping of the Swedish Health System* (London: Croom Helm, 1980).

7 Jan Blanpain, with Luc Delesie and Herman Nys, *National Health Insurance and Health Resources: The European Experience* (Cambridge, Mass.: Harvard University Press, 1978); William A. Glaser, *Health Insurance Bargaining: Foreign Lessons for Americans* (New York: Gardner, 1978); James Hogarth, *The Payment of the Physician: Some European Comparisons* (New York: Pergamon, 1963).

8 T. H. Marshall, *Class, Citizenship, and Social Development* (New York: Doubleday, Anchor, 1965).

9 Gösta Esping-Andersen and Walter Korpi, "Social Policy as Class Politics in Post-War Capitalism: Scandinavia, Austria, and Germany," in John H. Goldthorpe, ed., *Order and Conflict in Contemporary Capitalism: Studies in the Political Economy of Western European Nations* (New York: Clarendon Press, Oxford University Press, 1984), pp. 179–208; Peter Flora and Arnold Heidenheimer, eds., *The Development of Welfare States in Europe and America* (New Brunswick, N.J.: Transaction Books, 1981). On the early developments, see Gaston V. Rimlinger, *Welfare Policy and Industrialization in Europe, America and Russia* (New York: Wiley, 1971).

10 Henry C. Galant, *Histoire Politique de la Sécurité Sociale Française: 1945–1952* (Paris: Librairie Armand Colin, 1955); Henri Hatzfeld, *Le Grand Tournant de la Médecine Libérale* (Paris: Editions Ouvrières, 1963).

11 Florian Tennstedt, "Sozialgeschichte der Sozialversicherung," in M. Blohmke et al., *Handbuch der Sozialmedizin* (Stuttgart: Ferdinand Enke Verlag, 1977), vol. 3, pp. 385–492.

12 William Safran, *Veto-Group Politics: The Case of Health-Insurance Reform in West Germany* (San Francisco: Chandler, 1967); Harry Eckstein, *Pressure Group Politics: The Case of the British Medical Association* (Stanford, Calif.: Stanford University Press, 1960).

13 Arnold J. Heidenheimer, "Unions and Welfare State Development in Britain and Germany: An Interpretation of Metamorphoses in the Period 1910–1950" (Berlin: International Institute for Comparative Social Research–SPII, 1980), IIVG/dp/80–209.

14 Deborah Stone, *The Limits of Professional Power: National Health Care in the Federal Republic of Germany* (Chicago: University of Chicago Press, 1980), p. 79.

15 Glaser, *Health Insurance Bargaining*, p. 58.

16 Klein, *Politics of the NHS*, p. 47.

17 Starr, *The Social Transformation of American Medicine*, p. 351.

18 Jozef van Langendonck, "Private Diligence Versus Public Inertia? The Use of Private Sick Funds for Manpower Policy Under National Health Programs in Western Europe," in Christa Altenstetter, ed., *Changing National-Subnational Relations in Health: Opportunities and Constraints* (Washington, D.C.: U.S. Department of Health, Education, and Welfare, 1978). Victor Rodwin writes that the French funds are really "quasi-public" because they are under ministerial supervision and "parafiscal" because they are financed by employer and employee payroll deductions, not government revenues. Victor G. Rodwin, "The Marriage of National Health Insurance and *La Médecine Libérale* in France: A Costly Union," *Milbank Memorial Fund Quarterly/Health and Society* 59 (1981):19.

19 Jean de Kervasdoué, "La Politique de l'Etat en Matière d'Hospitalisation Privée, 1962–1978," *Annales Economiques* 16 (1980):23–57; J.F. Lacronique, "The French Health

Care System," in Gordon McLachlan and Alan Maynard, eds., *The Public/Private Mix for Health* (London: Nuffield Provincial Hospitals Trust), pp. 267–88; Victor G. Rodwin, "Health Planning in International Perspective," in Henrik L. Blum, *Planning for Health* (New York: Human Sciences Press, 1981), pp. 403–7; Albert Salon, "Les Centres Hospitaliers et Universitaires," *Notes et Etudes Documentaires*, No. 3373, March 15, 1967.

20 Rudolph Klein, "Private Practice and Public Policy: Regulating the Frontiers," in McLachlan and Maynard, eds., *The Public/Private Mix for Health*, pp. 102–3.

21 Budd Shenkin, "Politics and Medical Care in Sweden: The Seven Crowns Reform," *New England Journal of Medicine* 288 (1973):551–59; Arnold J. Heidenheimer, "Conflict and Compromises Between Professional and Bureaucratic Health Interests, 1947–72," in Heidenheimer and Elvander, eds., *The Shaping of the Swedish Health System*, pp. 119–42; and in the same volume, Mark Carder and Bendix Klingeberg, "Toward a Salaried Medical Profession: How 'Swedish' was the Seven Crowns Reform?" pp. 143–72; and Gösta Esping-Andersen, *Politics Against Markets: The Social Democratic Road to Power* (Princeton, N.J.: Princeton University Press, 1985), chap. 3. A representative of the Swedish Medical Association, Bo Hjern, speaking directly about the issue of politicization, distinguishes between two senses that correspond to our terms "contention" and "control":

> "The politicisation of the Swedish health system seemed to remain modest," Heidenheimer says. This is quite true if you mean that there have been no major fights between the different political parties concerning the questions of medical care. On the contrary all the so-called medical reforms during the postwar era have been supported by all the political parties. But if by politicisation you mean that the politicians have increased their influence on medical care, then there has been a politicisation.

Hjern then goes on to argue that within the county councils power shifted from "unpolitical civil servants" to politically elected commissioners. See "Commentary on Part Three," Heidenheimer and Elvander, eds., *The Shaping of the Swedish Health System*, p. 177.

22 Klein, *Politics of the NHS*, p. 117.

23 Ibid, p. 120.

24 Ibid, pp. 117–24; Alan Maynard, "The Private Health Care Sector in Britain," in McLachlan and Maynard, eds., *The Public/Private Mix for Health*, pp. 150–54.

25 *Le Monde*, January 15, 1983, and December 14, 1983; André Demichel, "La réforme hospitalière: éléments pour une problématique," *Revue Française de Finances Publiques*, no. 2 (1983):107–115.

26 Víctor Pérez-Díaz, "Médicos, administradores y enfermos: la calidad de la asistencia sanitaria," *Papeles de economía española*, no. 12/13 (1982):231–51; *El País*, December 10, 1982.

27 Ivan Illich, *Medical Nemesis: The Expropriation of Health* (New York: Pantheon, 1976). The book was given wide attention in Europe as well as America; see, for example, Michel Bosquet [Andre Gorz], "Quand la médecine rend malade," *Nouvel Observateur*, October 28, 1974. Illich himself was an indefatigable and extraordinarily clever propagandist for his own ideas. One of us saw him give a press conference in Switzerland in March 1975, answering about fifty reporters in their various languages: German, French, Spanish, and Italian as well as English.

28 Ian Kennedy, *The Unmasking of Medicine* (London: Allen & Unwin, 1981).

29 These developments are discussed in greater detail in Starr, *Social Transformation of American Medicine*, pp. 379–93.

30 The official was John G. Veneman, quoted in John K. Iglehart, "Prepaid Group

Medical Practice Emerges as Likely Federal Approach to Health Care," *National Journal* 3 (July 10, 1971):1444.

31 Hugh Heclo, "OMB and the Presidency – the problem of 'neutral competence,' " *The Public Interest*, no. 38 (1975):88.

32 Joel D. Aberbach, Robert D. Putnam, and Bert A. Rockman, *Bureaucrats and Politicians in Western Democracies* (Cambridge, Mass.: Harvard University Press, 1981), p. 96.

33 See, in addition to Aberbach et al., the essays in Mattei Dogan, ed., *The Mandarins of Western Europe: The Political Role of Top Civil Servants* (New York: Sage, 1975).

34 Klein, *Politics of the NHS*, p. 105.

35 Eckstein, *Pressure Group Politics:* Klein, *Politics of the NHS*, p. 56.

36 Stone, *The Limits of Professional Power*, pp. 151–59. See also J. Matthias Graf Schulenburg, "Report from Germany: Current Conditions and Controversies in the Health Care System," *Journal of Health Policy, Politics, and Law* 8 (Summer 1983):320–51.

37 Offe suggests there are several distinct mechanisms in "tripartism" that "can be expected to reduce the likelihood and intensity of conflict over public policy, and thus to depoliticize public life." See Claus Offe, "The Attribution of Public Status to Interest Groups: Observations on the West German Case," in Suzanne D. Berger, ed., *Organizing Interests in Western Europe: Pluralism, Corporatism, and the Transformation of Politics* (Cambridge: Cambridge University Press, 1981), pp. 144–45.

38 Fritz Beske, "Expenditures and Attempts of Cost Containment in the Statutory Health Insurance System of the Federal Republic of Germany," in McLachlan and Maynard, eds., *The Public/Private Mix For Health*, p. 256.

39 Gordon Forsyth, "The Semantics of Health Care Policy and the Inevitability of regulation," in McLachlan and Maynard, eds., *The Public/Private Mix for Health*, p. 73.

40 Ibid, p. 76.

41 On the coincidence of Left and Right in opposing centralization and professional expertise, see Nathan Glazer, "Towards a Self-Service Society?" *The Public Interest*, (no. 70, Winter 1983): 66–75: "Perhaps nothing so clearly indicates the possible future shape of the welfare society than the surprising convergence, in at least one respect, of the proposals of two such disparate regimes as the Socialist government of France and the right-wing Republican government of the United States: Both have committed themselves to a surprising degree of decentralization or devolution of central governmental powers."

42 Rosemary C. R. Taylor, "State Intervention in Postwar European Health Care: The Case of Prevention in Britain and Italy," in Stephen Bornstein et al., eds., *The State in Capitalist Europe* (London: Allen & Unwin, 1984), pp. 91–111.

43 Aaron Wildavsky, "Richer Is Safer," *The Public Interest*, no. 60 (Summer 1980): 23–39. Wildavsky, however, cites no evidence that environmental regulation actually reduces national income, or that this alleged loss of income produces a measurable effect on health. See Paul Starr, "Jonathan Swift Award," *Working Papers for a New Society* 8 (March-April 1981):4 (awarding Wildavsky the magazine's "Jonathan Swift award for specious reasoning on behalf of privilege").

44 Rudolph Klein, "The Politics of Ideology vs. the Reality of Politics: The Case of Britain's National Health Service in the 1980s," *Milbank Memorial Fund Quarterly/Health and Society* 62 (Winter 1984):82–109.

45 Forsyth, "The Semantics of Health Care Policy," pp. 61–62.

46 Ibid, p. 71.

47 Alan Maynard, "The Private Health Care Sector in Britain," in McLachlan and Maynard, eds., *The Public/Private Mix for Health*, pp. 132, 141.

48 Quoted in Henry J. Aaron and William B. Schwartz, *The Painful Prescription: Rationing Hospital Care* (Washington, D.C.: The Brookings Institution, 1984), p. 23.

49 John K. Iglehart, "The British NHS Under the Conservatives – Part II," *New England Journal of Medicine* 310 (January 5, 1984):66.

50 John Lister, "The British Medical Scene Since 1980," *New England Journal of Medicine* 308 (March 3, 1983):532–35.

51 Iglehart, "The British NHS under the Conservatives – Part II," p. 67; Forsyth, "The Semantics of Health Care Policy"; Maynard, "The Private Health Care Sector in Britain."

52 John Vaizey, *National Health* (Oxford: Martin Robertson, 1984).

53 Aaron and Schwartz, *The Painful Prescription*.

54 Klein, *Politics of the NHS*, p. 86.

55 Kinnock quoted in Iglehart, "The British NHS under the Conservatives – Part II," p. 67; Lister, "The British Medical Scene Since 1980," p. 532.

56 See, for example, David A. Stockman, "Premises for a Medical Market Place: A Neoconservative's Vision of How to Transform the Health System," *Health Affairs* 1 (Winter 1981).

57 On the political failure of the conservative design for health policy, see Paul Starr, "The Laissez-Faire Elixir," *The New Republic* (April 18, 1983).

58 Starr, *The Social Transformation of American Medicine*, pp. 420–49.

8

The politics of *Wissenschaftspolitik* in Weimar Germany: a prelude to the dilemmas of twentieth-century science policy

GERALD D. FELDMAN

Science policy in crisis

It is difficult to think of a realm in which the boundaries of the political have been more ambiguous and changing in recent times than that of science and scholarship in the advanced industrial societies of the West. On the face of it, this is rather surprising. The search for truth is constitutionally protected in such societies, and the legitimacy of the quest for knowledge for its own sake, insofar as it is the subject of much thought, is seldom questioned. Formally, science and scholarship have been viewed as realms of private enterprise and activity in the sense that the choice of subjects for investigation has been left to the investigators and the problems of personnel selection and accountability have been left to internal regulation through the mechanisms of co-optation and peer review, both presumably informed by accepted and reasonably rigorous codes of methodology and evidence. Indeed, as Sir Alan Bullock has pointed out, "the core of the enterprise is a methodology and the commitment to it. The real scientists are those who add to knowledge, not their auxiliaries. This is what brought them into the business and this is what still seems to them the sacred duty."[1] Herein rests the claim for the autonomy of science, its self-legitimation and self-sanctification.

In practical terms, of course, there have been very material constraints on science and scholarship which have necessarily affected

The support of the Volkswagen Foundation made much of the research for this chapter possible. I wish to thank Dr. Dietrich Schmidt-Ott for his generous assistance in connection with his father's papers. I wish to express my appreciation for the helpful suggestions made by my colleagues on the committee and my gratitude to Dr. Norma von Ragenfeld for her valuable advice and assistance. I also wish to thank Mr. Ed Todd and Dr. Bernhard vom Brocke for their critical and helpful reading of the manuscript, as well as Professor Thomas Parke Hughes and his seminar for their useful suggestions.

their autonomy, just as there is a long and often ghastly record of religious and ideological barriers to the unrestrained pursuit of knowledge. Yet the memory of those generations now at the height of their careers in science and scholarship must necessarily be colored by the fact that until fairly recently, both private agencies and governments have supported theoretical work with no immediate practical application and have permitted those working in the various fields to define their own research agendas. This has been true even of some industrial laboratories, such as the Bell Laboratories in the United States, which have lured leading scientists and economists with the opportunity to pursue their research interests free of all distractions. In the United States the massive infusion of public monies to support research in every field of knowledge, however much inspired by the cold war and especially by Sputnik, had few strings attached and was complemented by block grants from private foundations. The Ford Foundation grants in the social sciences, for example, were symptomatic of a general confidence that, properly supported, researchers and scholars would freely produce optimal results from the standpoint of science and scholarship and that society could best benefit if they left the setting of agendas to the experts. There was little questioning of the equation between the interests of science and scholarship on the one hand, and society on the other.[2]

Viewed from the perspective of those few years, there has been a great change since the late 1960s. Inflation, stagflation, recession, and threatening depression have undermined the material bases for the support of science and scholarship, while public enthusiasm for the works of science has been tempered by international dangers, ecological fears, and pressing social and economic problems. The most immediate result has been a growing desire for applied science and scholarship directed at specific problems and issues. The termination of block grants and the formulation of agendas geared to short-term problem-oriented research are symptomatic of the change in the environment of scholarship and science, and more than one scholar has expressed fear that research agendas will be determined by funding agencies to the detriment of scientific and scholarly autonomy and integrity. The danger is seen in the form not only of a triumph of the pedestrian and the "trendy," but also of interference with research by special interests in the name of particular causes. Atomic research, chemical research, and gene splicing do raise issues of public policy, while certain types of research – as, for example, into racial endowment – understandably have provoked sharp responses from potentially affected groups. The growing demand that science and scholarship be "relevant" and useful is thus further complicated by the insistence that its findings be palatable and benevolent. The rules of the game between science and scholarship, on the one hand, and their financial supporters, on the other, are in danger of changing because the goals of these enterprises are no longer seen largely from the perspective of personal or professional group choices but rather as objects of public policy, that is, of politics.

This change appears abrupt and sharp in the Anglo-American context, where there is a liberal tradition based on a fairly rigid dichotomy between the public and the private and an ideology that seeks to keep public involvement in the private sphere to a minimum. Actually, it is less dramatic than one would think, because the relatively slow development of federal support for science in the United States has been accompanied by a subdued but portentous struggle between proponents of federal support without government interference and those raising political demands that the nation's elected officials have a voice in how public monies are to be spent.[3] In Great Britain, where public support of science was particularly slow to develop, scholars and scientists themselves warned against a "weakening of private enterprise and philanthropy" through increased state support of research, and spoke contemptuously of the "paid scientific servant of the State, who for hire is working out the answer."[4]

Of necessity, Anglo-American scholars have changed their tune in the course of this century, but as Bullock has pointed out, they have often sailed the seas of public financial support under false colors:

Their dilemma is that to justify this activity and particularly the demands it makes for money and resources, scientists have had to act from a very early stage as propagandists for science.They suggested to people who were not scientists that the great justification for science was its usefulness, although in their heart of hearts this was not the justification they gave themselves. It is not merely the scientists who have fallen into this trap. In the university world most people, and not only scientists, are doing what they want to do, they like doing it – it interests them. But they know they have to justify the rather pleasant lives they lead, the degree of autonomy they have, and all the rest of it. So they say: "Higher education leads to economic growth," which is a very doubtful proposition. They don't really believe it much themselves. It is what might be called a second-order form of truth. What they may believe but hesitate to say is that the pursuit of knowledge is intrinsically important for its own sake.[5]

What has really come to grief is that "happy coincidence of interests"[6] which made it possible for the public to accept the claims of scientists and scholars without worrying about what they were getting for their money, as well as the state of affairs in which scientists themselves were uniformly certain of their own cause. Much of the criticism of the autonomy of science, after all, has come from scientists themselves in response to the threats to life, health, and privacy arising from recent developments in science.

In any case, at a time when both the United States and Great Britain are graced with governments committed to the systematic rollback of governmental expenditure and interference, it is not surprising to find them reducing their support for science and scholarship and demanding increasing accountability from the recipients of funds. Ironically, however, the free-enterprise ideologies of these regimes threaten to increase rather than decrease the impact of government on science and scholarship, since their dependence upon government has become so great, and the costs so high, that any reduction of support will invariably involve public decisions about what the priorities of science and scholarship should be. In short, there is reason to believe that the old ideology now supposedly being revived will have radically different consequences than it would imply because the world in which it is supposed to operate has changed so greatly. The traditional Anglo-American dichotomy between the public and the private is probably not capable of restoration.

This dichotomy has never been so rigid in other political cultures, however, and a much higher degree of fluidity between the public and private and ambiguity about their relationship has been accepted from the outset. This certainly is the case in the German liberal tradition, where corporate self-government and self-administration have often been comprehended in terms of the devolution of public functions upon private persons or bodies and where the legitimation of the liberties granted to civil society have derived not from natural law, but from a record of historical precedent strongly influenced by traditions of state responsibility for a broadly conceived realm of public welfare and the direction of a highly developed bureaucracy. The realm of the private has been those areas either where the state has had no immediate interest or where it was most functional and efficient for the state to permit the relative free play of persons and groups. This "German idea of freedom" has had some deplorable consequences; but in the context of the contemporary industrial world and the interventionist state, it has proven increasingly relevant to the formulation of public policy and the practice of social and economic management. Thus, here, as in other areas, the German experience may shed some light on problems confronted elsewhere.[7]

This is certainly the case with respect not only to "science policy," in which Germany has been a pioneer since the early nineteenth century, but also to the management of science policy in economic crisis and the problems of scholarly accountability in a democracy.

These last issues assumed particular importance in the Weimar Republic, and did so in a manner especially relevant to our concerns here as well as to the recent debates concerning science policy in the Federal Republic. In the remainder of this chapter, therefore, I will offer a short sketch of the historical background of science policy in Germany, then a consideration of science policy in the Weimar Republic, and finally a brief account of the Weimar experience's significance for science policy in Germany and elsewhere after 1945.

The origins of *Wissenschaftspolitik* in Germany

Science policy in Weimar, however, cannot be understood without some brief consideration of its historic context.[8] To begin with, the English term "science policy" is much more restrictive than the German term *Wissenschaftspolitik*; the former usually refers to the natural sciences alone, whereas the latter encompasses policy toward all branches of scholarly investigation. This distinction has very old philosophical roots, and it also has had and continues to have important practical implications. The foundations for modern organized science and scholarship in Germany were laid at the beginning of the nineteenth century by Wilhelm von Humboldt as part of the Prussian reform movement, which responded to Napoleon's defeat of Prussia by seeking to mobilize the material, intellectual, and spiritual resources of the people in order to liberate Prussia and Germany from Napoleonic domination. Humboldt and his fellow reformers deliberately rejected French "specialization" in the various Ecoles and promoted instead a concept of general cultivation (*Bildung*) grounded in the unity of all forms of knowledge, which would find concrete expression in the primacy of the philosophical faculty of the university. The University of Berlin, founded in 1809, was meant to serve as a prototype of a reformed university system based upon the autonomy and self-government of the faculties, privileges justified by their single-minded pursuit of *Wissenschaft*. Precisely for this reason they had to have "freedom to teach" (*Lehrfreiheit*) and "freedom to learn" (*Lernfreiheit*).

The Prussian and German university system, which was to have such strong influence throughout the Western world, especially in the United States, thus had built into it from the outset much of the ambiguity and ambivalence that has characterized *Wissenschaftspolitik* in modern times. It was created, in part, as a *Machtersatz*, a substitute for the military and political power that had been destroyed at Jena. Thus, *Wissenschaft* in Germany had an explicit relationship to state power that was to be more implicit elsewhere. The universities them-

selves were state institutions, dependent upon state support and subject ultimately to the will of the ministry in the crucial areas of finance
and appointments. Yet the faculty was made "autonomous" and supposedly placed beyond politics in the disinterested service of a *Wissenschaft* meant to be free of humdrum concerns about practical
application. Furthermore, the philosophical and intellectual bases of
the German concept of *Wissenschaft*, which were heavily influenced
by the *Naturphilosophie* of the period, favored philosophical and humanistic over empirical and applied studies and rested upon the unity
of teaching and research. That is, there was a built-in prejudice in
favor of the humanities, and academic respectability came to those
who identified themselves with the idea of *Wissenschaft*. Thus was
born what has appropriately been called the "mandarin" university.

The realities of the German university system, as they evolved over
the nineteenth century, were, of course, often in conflict with its ideals
and ideology. During the periodic episodes of political repression,
especially in the first half of the century, the state interfered with
both *Lehr-* and *Lernfreiheit*, and it persistently intervened in matters
of appointments. As late as the end of the century, Jews, Social Democrats, and Catholics found it very difficult or impossible to secure
university positions. At the same time, the philosophical foundations
of the idea of *Wissenschaft* were brutally undermined by the triumph
of empirical natural science and positivism as well as by the increasing
specialization of all branches of knowledge in the course of the nineteenth century, which was encouraged by the ministerial appointment
policies.[9] Tributes to *Wissenschaft* in the yearly addresses of university
rectors notwithstanding, as practiced in the universities it bore less
and less resemblance to the "Great Whole" it was supposed to be.
Furthermore, the industrialization of Germany and the demands for
practical knowledge created significant fissures between the industrial
middle class and the educated elite: The elite clung to the primacy of
the classical *Gymnasium* and the classical-historical portions of the
university philosophical faculty; the middle class demanded greater
recognition of and prestige for the *Realgymnasium*, with its emphasis
on modern languages and science, and the growing number of technical universities. By the late nineteenth century the evolution of
Germany as an industrial society, the growing enrollment in the universities, and the requirements and costs of scientific research were
straining a university system rooted in preindustrial institutions and
values. No less important, the progress of German science and scholarship were identified with the requirements of Germany as a great
world power and therefore seemed to demand direct state interference

of a more vigorous sort than the old spirit of university self-government would allow.

This interference was cheerfully and energetically provided by Friedrich Althoff, the *Ministerialdirektor* of the Prussian Ministry of Culture and Religion, who was charged with the direction of higher education from 1882 to 1907. Althoff has received mixed reviews from contemporaries and historians. While certainly guilty of treating inadequate faculty recommendations and especially nepotism with contempt and disregard, of humiliating professors with long hours of waiting in his anteroom for an audience, and, in his last years, of cynically playing upon the petty jealousies and vanities so abundant in academic communities in order to attain his goals, he must also be credited with greatly increasing material support for higher education and research. Althoff rationalized the university structure and bureaucratized its administration along more modern lines, accrediting the *Realgymnasium* and permitting the technical universities at long last to grant degrees, and even relaxing the barriers to the promotion of Catholics and Jews into the professoriat. Many of these modernizing reforms were undertaken against the entrenched academic establishment and thus seemed to bear out the argument of one of his latest biographers that thus "was once again confirmed a fact which has not been proven wrong to this very day, namely, that apparently reforms of higher education through academic self-government alone are impossible."[10]

One of Althoff's greatest achievements was his role in breaking down the university monopoly in scientific research; establishing a series of research institutes in medicine, applied physics, and the humanities; and laying the groundwork for the creation of the Kaiser-Wilhelm-Society for the Promotion of the Sciences, founded in 1911 shortly after Althoff's death, and the host of Kaiser-Wilhelm-Institutes which followed. The creation of such institutes, which ruptured the tradition of the "unity of teaching and research," was deemed necessary because of the inability of the universities to accommodate to the development of "big science," which required collaborative research and large-scale facilities, as well as the resistance of the humanistically dominated faculties to the necessary expansion of the natural sciences.[11]

The creation of these various institutes marks the beginning of a modern science policy in Germany; and it is significant that it received a particularly powerful impulse from the example and potential competition of the United States, where the expansion of scientific research in universities and private institutes was noted with interest and some alarm. The founding of the Rockefeller Institute and the Carnegie Endowment in 1902 made a particularly strong impression but the American model had impressed Althoff even earlier. He had energetically promoted what one East German historian has called "the copulation of industry and science,"[12] and his mobilization of industrial money through his friend the chemical industrialist Theodore Böttinger to fund the Göttingen Society for Applied Physics and Mathematics had saved Professor Felix Klein from accepting a chair in the United States and provided a harbinger of what was to come. The Kaiser-Wilhelm-Institutes followed a similar model, the state providing land, buildings, and a measure of financial support while private industrial and banking sources supplied the bulk of the money by buying membership in the society and its various divisions.

Although the societies became world-famous for their work in a wide variety of fields – they were the forerunners of the present Max Planck Institutes in West Germany – the relationship they established between scholarship and business was by no means universally regarded as licit. Socialists were not the only ones to argue that "the effort to Americanize our *Wissenschaft* in this manner is a stain upon German culture."[13] Traditional academics were no less concerned about the "Americanization" of German life and the potential subordination of *Wissenschaft* to material and special interests. That is, if the institutes represented a qualitative change in the socialization of academe and industry toward maintaining a steady interest in the support of both theoretical and applied research in the humanities and natural sciences, it was not only the industrialists who had to be persuaded. Obviously, they expected that the promotion of science would bring profit, and many German academics found this more than a little uncomfortable. Indeed, even the state's interest in the support of the humanities was not untainted, since the promotion of an Oriental academy and similar institutions was strongly motivated by the imperialist strivings of the period. Such motives, however, undoubtedly disturbed the patriotic German professoriat much less.

The claims of pure scholarship like those of scientific internationalism, therefore, often veiled very complex phenomena. Scholarly entrepreneurs and organizers such as the theologian Adolf von Harnack and the chemist Emil Fischer, both of whom played key roles in the events leading up to the founding of the Kaiser-Wilhelm-Society, were well aware that they had to sell the new organizations to their scholarly colleagues on one basis and to the business community on another.[14] Similarly, in spite of the scientific internationalism of the immediate prewar period and the lively interest in scholarly exchanges with the United States and other countries, there is ample evidence that scientists often paid close attention to what was going on in other countries from a competitive point of view. World War I and its aftermath were to demonstrate this frailty of scientific internationalism in full measure.[15]

In the halcyon days before the war, however, when economic prosperity seemed to promise unbounded progress in science and scholarship, it was easy enough to accommodate ambiguity and chart new paths within the framework of old values and ideologies. Harnack and Gustav Krupp von Bohlen und Halbach could be yoked together as, respectively, president and vice-president of the Kaiser-Wilhelm-Gesellschaft, and prominent professors from the universities and academies could serve in its senate alongside great industrialists such as Wilhelm von Siemens, Carl Duisberg (chemical industry), and Albert Vögler (heavy industry). The professors could be lured to the new institutes with the assurance that they would be free of both bureaucratic interference from the state and the demands of industrialist utilitarianism and would be self-governing bodies devoted to pure science. At the same time, bankers and industrialists could be assured that their patience and investment would be rewarded in the long run. Furthermore, there is no question that industrialists like Siemens and Duisberg firmly believed in basic scientific research, while the concerns of a more practical type like Vögler could be laid to rest with the founding of a Kaiser-Wilhelm-Institute for Coal Research. Thus, accommodation to the ideology of *Wissenschaft* and academic self-government was easy because it was affordable and patriotic, and those who profited from German clinical or physical research could also take pride in German Sanskrit scholarship and archaeological finds in the Near East.

Science policy in the Weimar Republic

World War I and its aftermath cemented the relationship between science and industry, exaggerated the nationalist component in the German scientific and scholarly community, profoundly undermined the material foundations upon which German research had rested, and significantly transformed the political environment in which science and scholarship operated.

The most famous illustration of wartime collaboration between science and industry was that of the nitrogen-fixation process discovered and put into production by Fritz Haber and Carl Bosch, but one should also add the work done on poison gases and food and textile substitutes. While it cannot be said that scientists and scholars of any country were particularly successful in transcending wartime hatreds and propaganda, pronouncements on the German side from these quarters, with their emphasis on the superiority of German *Kultur*, were particularly noxious. They were amply and often unfairly requited after the war, however, by Allied efforts to boycott and ostracize their German colleagues.[16]

While it would be interesting to explore the role these events and developments played in heightening the intellectual and emotional insecurity and instability in the German scholarly and scientific community – and thereby increasing and making respectable the nationalist and racist rubbish that not only blighted the social sciences and humanities but also produced such wonders as "German physics" – these issues would require both much more research and an extended and complicated discussion that would be out of place here. In any case, anxieties and problems enough for German science and scholarship were provided by the economic and political consequences of the war, which not only terminated budgetary increases in support of science and scholarship but, even more important, entailed a real reduction in their support because of inflation as well as a reduction in real incomes and a significant decline in the living standards and life-styles of most of those engaged in the various types of research. The replacement of the monarchy by a democratic, parliamentary republic under conditions of defeat and inflation could not be welcomed by these groups, especially since a solicitous bureaucracy had kept them fairly well insulated from involvement with parliaments and politicians under the old regime.

One possibility was to turn for help directly to private sources, namely, industry and banking, and here the prewar "socialization" of the leading academic scientists to procure support from the private sector as well as that sector's socialization into the support of science proved very useful. Furthermore, since the scientific and industrial communities both had long traditions of self-regulation and self-government and both felt vindicated in their sense of superiority by the war effort as well as hostile to government interference, there was a certain ideological and historical foundation for their collaboration.

Nevertheless, there were also certain limitations to dependence on private philanthropy as well as some threats to the autonomy of scientific research from these quarters. First of all, those best positioned to make such appeals for private funding were the scientists themselves and, as was so often the case, the chemists were the ones to take the lead. The scientific training of the leading entrepreneurs and managers of the German chemical industry, such as Carl Duisberg and Carl Bosch, made them particularly sensitive to basic research and its potential application. Their collaboration with such eminent scientists as Emil Fischer and Fritz Haber had paid off handsomely. In the last years of the war, both Duisberg and Fischer were aware that industry would have to spring into the breach cut by war and inflation into the resources available for training and research. Throughout the revolutionary period, they exerted steady pressure upon businessmen to support the Society for the Promotion of Chemical Instruction with large sums of money, Fischer using his connections with the authorities in Berlin to give assurances that such contributions would be tax deductible. Thanks to their support for coal research, Fischer and Duisberg were also able to secure considerable support from heavy industry. As a result, the society – renamed the Emil Fischer Society after Fischer's death in 1919 – could pour large sums into the Kaiser-Wilhelm-Society for Chemistry and the Adolf Baeyer Society to support chemical literature.[17]

Even with the support of the chemists and farsighted industrialists like Duisberg, however, it proved much harder to get heavy industry to support similar organizations for physics. The combined efforts of the chemical and electrotechnical industrialists were required to mobilize heavy industry to expend war profits for the Helmholtz Society, founded in October 1920. Like its chemical counterpart, the Helmholtz Society was to have an administrative council of industrialists and scientists to pass upon the recommendations of scientific experts. In this way, peer review would be combined with a mechanism for bringing industrialists and scientists into contact. Furthermore, Duisberg, whose initiatives were essential in the creation of the Helmholtz Society, was sensitive to the more practical, empirical, and anti-Berlin orientation of the Ruhr industrialists and helped procure a South German experimental physicist, Wilhelm Wien, to serve as vice-president under the steel industrialist Albert Vögler.

In the last analysis, however, the physicists themselves created more problems than the industrialists, since they were divided between a theoretical group in Berlin around Einstein and a more experimentally oriented group represented by Wien but also connected with two anti-Semitic Nobel Prize winners, Philipp Lenard and Johannes Stark, who did battle for "German physics" against "Jewish physics." The pragmatic Ruhr industrialists were unable to make heads or tails of this distinction, and the fact was that the interconnection between physics and heavy industry was not like the connection between chemistry and the chemical industry. Engineering, which interested the heavy industrialists immensely, was not simply applied physics, as the great physicists ingeniously claimed in their quest for heavy industrial money. If the bulk of Helmholtz Society funds went to the experimentalists, it was because a more empirical and anti-Berlin posture in all things was most congenial to the heavy industrialists. Vögler, for example, understood the conflict to be a battle between the universities and the technical universities, which is to say that he misunderstood it, and he ultimately found himself in the midst of an intrascientific brawl whose practical payoff was anything but clear. With the end of inflation in 1923–24 and the coming problems of stabilization and rationalization facing heavy industry, there is good evidence that the patience of Vögler and his colleagues had worn thin. Thus, in 1924, much to the horror of the chemical industrialists and their unshaken belief in theory, the heavy industrialists complained loudly about the character of the grant applications the Helmholtz Society was receiving in spectral analysis, spectroscopy, and radiation and wondered "whether German science ought not also to take greater account of the situation in which the unfortunate conclusion of the war has placed Germany and turn more toward such questions as lie in the direction of applied physics."[18]

Fortunately, however, the chief support for physics, as well as for science and scholarship in general during the Weimar Republic did not fall to the Helmholtz Society or to German heavy industry but rather to the Notgemeinschaft der deutschen Wissenschaft (NGW), the Emergency Society for German Science and Scholarship, also founded in late 1920, which was the forerunner of the present-day Deutsche Forschungsgemeinschaft.[19] In contrast to the postwar efforts concerned solely with natural science, the NGW had its origins in a concern with the condition of every branch of research affected by the problems arising from war and inflation. The first steps toward its founding were taken by the leading academies, who empowered Harnack to appeal on their behalf to the National Assembly for funds to restore subscriptions to scholarly journals, to support the publication of scholarly work, and to finance some major projects. This initial and unsuccessful effort was superseded by a more systematic approach initiated by Fritz Haber and Friedrich Schmidt-Ott, who had served as one of Althoff's chief collaborators, then as the ministerial official most involved with the Kaiser-Wilhelm-Society, and finally as the Prussian minister of culture during the war. They developed the idea of creating an emergency society encompassing all scientific and scholarly institutions to serve as "the center of coordination and interest representation for Wissenschaft in organizing and propagating the support of research through the state and the business community."[20]

An experienced and shrewd albeit somewhat authoritarian administrator, Schmidt-Ott was well versed in the art of selling Wissenschaft to businessmen and bureaucrats as well as at home in the world of

Wissenschaft and its ideology of self-government. Unquestionably uncomfortable in the Weimar Republic, as were many academics, Schmidt-Ott intended to insulate science and scholarship from outside interference by making the NGW a "self-governing body of German *Wissenschaft* with an all-powerful initiative"[21] while procuring the desperately needed funds from the state and the business world for scholarly and scientific enterprise. He, Haber, Harnack, Max Planck, and other associates were reasonably skillful both in advocating their cause and in creating an institution that conformed to their goals.

In a lengthy memorandum for the Reich Ministry of the Interior (which was charged with cultural affairs on the national level) on the "emergency of German *Wissenschaft*,"[22] Schmidt-Ott began by playing upon a theme which updated the role of *Wissenschaft* as a substitute for military power first enunciated in the days of Humboldt and arguing that German *Wissenschaft* "is today perhaps the only thing left for which the world still envies Germany." While certainly not neglecting the moral and spiritual benefits of scholarship and science, the document embedded these concerns in a sustained argument for practical utility so well demonstrated by the contributions of German science to the nation's economic development and its wartime effort as well as to be expected from its necessary role in the coming reconstruction. Yet, it argued, budgetary stagnation in the face of mounting inflation threatened to destroy German science because the institutes and laboratories could no longer afford to heat their buildings, buy equipment, or even feed experimental animals. The upkeep of the animals by this time matched or exceeded the salaries of research assistants. The low exchange-rate of the mark made it impossible to buy foreign journals or books, while price increases at home made it increasingly difficult for scholarly works to be published within Germany as well as for individuals and libraries to purchase them. It particularly emphasized the danger of Germany's failing to produce a new generation of scholars, since the difficulties of making a living during inflation combined with the lack of funds for travel and equipment would necessarily discourage young people from entering the various scholarly fields or encourage them to emigrate.

The authors of the memorandum estimated that a minimum of 56 million marks would be needed to maintain research at its present levels and called on the Reich to provide 20 million marks to prevent an immediate collapse of German scholarship. The founders of the NGW were successful in procuring this money from the Reich, but the rationale for the Finance Ministry's decision demonstrates that the utilitarian emphasis in the memorandum had its analogue in the negotiations themselves and was by no means misplaced. As Haber reported to Schmidt-Ott, the finance minister's "willingness to provide 20 million in the budget to be passed in September is exclusively thanks to his faith in the future success of chemistry. I avoided mentioning philology and everything connected with it."[23] While this may have been deception in a noble cause, it demonstrated that the difficulty of selling nonutilitarian *Wissenschaft* was not limited to the businessmen but also extended to the government and, as we shall see later, to the Reichstag.

The NGW, which was formally constituted on October 30, 1920, after months of preparation, was structured to insulate the distribution of money from the control of those from whom the money had been solicited. Membership was limited to corporate bodies, especially the academies, the universities, and the Kaiser-Wilhelm-Society. The principal organs of the NGW were the Presidium, composed of Schmidt-Ott and his three deputies, Haber, Harnack, and the Munich mathematician von Dyck; the Executive Committee (*Hauptausschuss*), which was charged with distributing resources among the various fields and activities; the membership meeting; and the special committees for the various fields. Schmidt-Ott held infrequent meetings of the Executive Committee, in which he defined the agenda and orchestrated the decisions, while the membership meeting was largely a public affairs event. Ultimately, therefore, it was the president and his staff who did most of the routine work but who also passed on the recommendations of the special committees.

The self-government within the NGW, such as it was, was embodied in the special committees and the practice of peer review. Especially important was the fact that the NGW gave its money to projects rather than in block grants to institutions. This approach not only reflected the fact that the shortage of funds required a more individualized granting of monies, but also ensured that the federal and state governments had no excuse to cut back their regular support for the infrastructure of scientific and scholarly institutions. In short, the entire conception of the NGW was to provide an autonomous organizational form that would make certain that science and scholarly policy would be determined in freedom from outside influences and on the basis of the principle of peer review and recommendation.[24]

This is not to say that the NGW was oblivious to the outside world, a practical impossibility given its dependence for funds. The first time it made its presence felt publicly took the form of a "parliamentary evening," which had the obvious purpose of winning over the support of Reichstag deputies, and Schmidt-Ott and his colleagues assiduously cultivated their Reichstag supporters, especially the Catholic Center Party spokesman on cultural matters, Prelate Georg

Schreiber. He, as we shall see, was to prove an ardent advocate of the NGW as well as its most impressive defender against critics. At the same time, Schmidt-Ott and his colleagues had great hopes of procuring substantial support from the German business community. They took up an old idea of Harnack's and organized themselves into the Associated Foundation of the NGW (*Stifterverband*) on December 14, 1920. Until 1934 this body was chaired by Carl Friedrich von Siemens, and Carl Duisberg and Albert Vögler played very active roles in it.

The difficulty was that the NGW was not the only organization with claims on the *Stifterverband*, since the Helmholtz Society was totally dependent upon industrial money. Consequently, a complicated formula had to be worked out for the giving of business funds to the two organizations, and although the amounts provided by industry to the NGW were disappointingly small – especially because it was only allowed to use the interest on investments, which evaporated in the inflation – the prominent role played by Siemens and Duisberg at least ensured that the theoretical physics practiced in Berlin would get its due. From a practical standpoint, however, the amounts given by the private sector to the NGW were pathetically small, amounting to 1.3 million marks between 1924 and 1933, as compared with 59.2 million provided by the Reich. The Americans (the Rockefeller Foundation) also provided significant help, but ultimately it was the Reich upon which the NGW depended.[25]

The potential difficulties and tensions between the NGW and the government were veiled to a considerable extent during the early years of its existence because the organization's name bespoke the reality of emergency, especially during the hyperinflation of 1922–23, and the inflation did create a real crisis for German science and scholarship. It is important to note that this was a social and not simply an institutional phenomenon. As a social group, German academics and scholars were often the second- and third-generation descendants of industrial or commercial families who had become economically dependent on annuities derived from investments, pensions, and other forms of fixed income based on liquid capital. Their entire style of life was linked to such investments, and the inflation not only forced them into a very ungenteel poverty but also affected the fate of their children, whose higher education was to be paid for by such investments. University students were forced to take jobs in order to complete their studies, something unheard of before the war, and were often compelled quite simply to terminate their education early or leave school. Indeed, the malnutrition of German students attracted international attention and charity, and the incentive to pursue studies to the point where one might try one's hand at original research had become very small indeed. Those already in academic positions found themselves living from hand to mouth. Germany, it was argued, was threatened with reduction to the cultural level of Poland or Romania, while its intellectual class, which should have been preserved at all costs, was receiving less remuneration than street cleaners.

The inflation did indeed challenge the elitist self-image of the scholarly community, an image widely shared and supported in the German middle class. The result was social resentment, and Schreiber was quite correct in warning that this could lead to political radicalization. As the *Kölnische Zeitung* remarked in December 1922: "Where lies the social understanding of the bureaucracy which, at a time when the Hamburg dock workers receive 2400 marks a day, grants only 45,000 marks a year to the economically weakest among the instructors in schools of higher education?"[26] What was at stake in German science and scholarship policy, therefore, was not simply the perpetuation of research and teaching, but the existence and status of a traditional social group which carried on the tradition of *Bildung*. The short-term privations of institutions in the German inflation were, to be sure, horrendous, and in December 1923 the poverty imposed by stabilization threatened to shut down even the Kaiser-Wilhelm-Institutes for Physical Chemistry, Electrochemistry, Biology, and Experimental Therapy.[27] The longer-term social legacy was far more serious: It raised the question of what kind of policy the NGW would pursue in dealing with the financial decimation of the bearers of Germany's humanistic tradition in the context of the constraints imposed by Germany's postinflationary situation. That is, what were its priorities going to be, and, no less important, how would the government and Reichstag, which provided the money, respond to those priorities?

The tactics pursued by Schmidt-Ott and his colleagues in the NGW, insofar as one can form a coherent picture of them, were a peculiar mixture of aggressively seeking to satisfy utilitarian demands in the natural sciences; supporting certain projects conducive to Germany's international prestige in the advancement of knowledge (for instance, expeditions); and remaining highly traditional in dealings with the humanities and social sciences as well as in the social recruitment of the intellectual elite. This pattern is best illustrated by the NGW policies in 1925, that is, when the stabilization had taken hold sufficiently for the leadership, especially Schmidt-Ott and Haber, to contemplate new initiatives. This was an important decision because, in a formal sense, the NGW had been created to deal with the crisis of German *Wissenschaft* rather than to expand its activities. How can one justify the perpetuation of an organization created to deal with an emergency? Schmidt-Ott had a broader interpretation of the emergency, however, and he argued that if the NGW was to fulfill its purposes, "it could not limit itself to granting or refusing such proposals as accidentally came its way. In order to bring about what can be called scientific reconstruction, it is necessary to work through and solve more than before specific, especially important research tasks."[28]

The object was not to create new institutions but rather to identify special areas where collaboration among researchers and new research would be singled out for encouragement and special funding, so-called *Gemeinschaftsaufgaben* (areas of common concern), the counterpart of today's *Schwerpunktprogramme* (priority programs). After consultation with various persons from industry, professional organizations, and the Kaiser-Wilhelm-Societies, the NGW leadership had identified certain areas in the national economy, public health, and general welfare which should be encouraged through the earmarking of funds: namely, the special qualities of metals, utilization of mineral resources and heat technology, aviation and aerodynamics, nutrition and workplace performance, body chemistry, and entomology. In undertaking this program, Schmidt-Ott made specific reference to similar approaches in the United States through the National Research Council and in England, but he rejected the idea of following tendencies he and his colleagues perceived in those countries, namely "a mechanization discouraging to individual research initiative."[29] Rather, the goal was to provide the financial incentive necessary to encourage researchers from various disciplines to work together in those areas as well as for individuals to undertake new projects in them, in sum, to encourage collaboration where it was appropriate, but more generally to produce a critical mass of research.

As noted earlier, this energetic program and the support of major scientific expeditions were attractive advertising for the NGW from the standpoint both of its utility and its promotion of the nation's prestige. Thus it was quite shrewd of Schmidt-Ott and Haber to couple the new program with a special plea for a substantial increase in individual research fellowships in all fields with the object of renewing, as far as possible, the body of scholars and researchers lost in the inflation. The public appeal to parliament for this goal was given to Haber, whose eloquent plea reflected that peculiar combination of nationalism, traditional social values, and imaginative utilitarianism that characterized NGW propaganda but was also a genuine reflection of Haber's character. Germany, according to Haber, was wasting the natural advantages it had over other nations: "Our educational system is better than that of the French; we are ahead of England in the close connection between our higher schools and the industrial network; we are ahead of the Americans in having the patience and reflectiveness which finds ultimate expression in long term enterprises."[30] Yet, when one compared Germany with the United States or "the awakened land of the Far East," Japan, which had responded to its great earthquake with the same will to reconstruction that, according to Haber, characterized the Prussia of Frederick the Great after the Seven Years War, then it seemed that Germany was failing to realize the need to pour money into its most valuable, human resources.

Haber, echoing the analysis of Schreiber, blamed the insufficiency of human resources devoted to research on the fact

that a certain middle stratum of the population, from whom the needed capacities have predominantly come, is impoverished and no longer has the means, which it had earlier, to have its sons train themselves in the most thorough way.... Where are those people now? The fathers strain themselves while the parental house skimps and saves so that the young people can at least make it through their basic years of study, and then they write their fingers to the bone and take a modest position in order not to burden their parents anymore. The competition for the few available assistantships is almost as severe as in a sports stadium, and when colleagues meet, then their favorite theme is how regrettable it is that this person and that person and a large number of the best young people cannot be allowed to have rigorous [research] training because there is no money and it cannot be procured.[31]

Haber's pleas were not without their effect, and the NGW was able to increase substantially its research fellowship support in the second half of the 1920s.

The stabilization after 1924 and these new initiatives, therefore, did not abate but actually increased the need of the NGW to lobby the government and the parliament for support. A parliamentary *Bierabend* thanking the Reichstag and the government for its support of the new NGW programs was also an opportunity to remind them that cooperative work and team research were not suitable to the humanities and that was why it was also important to have the new research fellowship program.[32] Special attention also had to be paid to the federal states (*Länder*), which had always been responsible for higher education and culture in Germany but which, under the Weimar Republic, had become financially dependent on the Reich. With the creation of orderly financial conditions, there was some feeling that Reich support of the NGW was depriving the states of resources and, in South Germany, that an inordinate portion of the NGW funds benefited the largest state, Prussia.

Schmidt-Ott poured a good deal of effort, and money, into defusing such claims and was particularly careful to cultivate the most powerful of the South German states, Bavaria. Hence, in his regular campaigns to keep the conservative Bavarians friendly to the NGW, he was able to enlist the support of the famed surgeon Ferdinand Sauerbruch, who felt impelled to declare that "we in Munich have always enjoyed the support of the *Notgemeinschaft* in the greatest degree, in the technical university, in the physical laboratories, and in the medical institutes." He praised the NGW for the unbureaucratic and speedy manner in which it supplied funds once a decision had been made, in contrast to the "dragging of oneself from one authority to the other, inquiries and required responses; quarrels over competence and the like" which had made things so difficult in the past. Consequently, Sauerbruch declared that "it is self-understood that the *Notgemeinschaft* should be maintained with at least the means which it happily has at present, and here not as some kind of postwar form of assistance but rather in the fundamental sense of a tried, purposeful, officially supported institution that is universally recognized as such."[33]

While Schmidt-Ott employed Sauerbruch to keep the Bavarian government friendly despite grumblings in some ministerial circles, Haber propagated the faith in Baden, where he pointed out that only the Reich could supply what was necessary to maintain German research:

Where are the parents, who can make possible the development of their children to scientific maturity out of their own means? Where are the foundations from which fellowships flowed before in order to complement parental help? What university in our country is able, like Harvard University, to distribute a million marks from endowment interest to superior young people? Where do we have contributors, like Carnegie and Rockefeller, who as individuals regularly contribute yearly endowments to *Wissenschaft* which are capable of funding institutions which match the performance of a large German state?[34]

Thus, in the mid-1920s, the leadership of the NGW had come to the conclusion that the NGW had to become a permanent institution and could only do so with federal government support rather than with the mixture of public and private sources on which it had based its initial hopes.

It was precisely this successful effort, however, which exposed it both to increasing governmental scrutiny and to public criticism. The fact was that the NGW enjoyed extraordinary freedom in both its decisions and its internal management. Although a Reich higher-education conference in December 1921 had passed a resolution calling upon the Reich minister of the interior to consult regularly with a committee of three or four state delegates about the NGW, attend all its Executive Committee meetings, and be informed about all expenditures made by the NGW, nothing was done to implement this resolution.[35] The states, formally charged with the tasks of higher education, were thus kept in the dark about the research policies and actual distribution of resources undertaken by the most important research organization in the country.

As noted earlier, the NGW itself was not exactly filled with consultation and discussion, for, once peer review took place, the ultimate decisions tended to be taken by Schmidt-Ott and the Executive Committee tended to be a rubber stamp. The membership meetings were expensive propaganda festivals at which the professorial membership had the opportunity to stay in good hotels and eat good meals. The management of the NGW, in fact, worried Haber, who was very supportive of Schmidt-Ott but felt that the administration was insufficiently collegial. Haber also feared the potential repercussions of Schmidt-Ott's insensitivity to public opinion. He noted, for example, that the Fifth NGW Report of 1926 contained figures for some categories of expenditure and not for others, thereby creating the impression that "the presidium had the intention of laying certain things open and hiding others."[36] At a time of industrial rationalization, he worried about the subsidization of books and journals to the point where it might be argued that the NGW was serving the special interests of the firms represented on the Publication Committee. Haber also felt that the report created a false and potentially harmful impression by revealing that 63.2 percent of the individual research grants had gone to the humanities while 36.8 percent had gone to the natural sciences, medicine, and related disciplines without explaining that the total NGW expenditures for the latter group exceeded the former significantly when the *Gemeinschaftsaufgaben* were taken into account. Because Haber made frequent public appearances for the NGW at the behest of Schmidt-Ott, he was concerned about such impressions and expressed willingness to participate in writing the reports.

The Prussian minister of education from 1925 to 1930, C. H. Becker, and his influential aide, W. Richter, however, were deeply concerned by the de facto absence of external accountability by the NGW as well as by the oddities of its internal functioning. They were fully convinced that a governmental policy of support for science and scholarship meant that the government had to have some voice in the way money was spent and could not simply yield to the views of the scientists and scholars or to Schmidt-Ott and his colleagues.[37] While by no means hostile to reasonable self-government and self-regulation, Becker recognized that these concepts were being implemented with a specific political thrust that was ultimately dangerous to the authority of the democratic state. He perceptively argued that

many forces are at work to push the dissolution of the state into self-governing bodies, so that the state is only of significance to various interests as a money distributing agency. I repeat myself: if that is what one wants to do and takes responsibility for it, then it should be done consciously and openly. But one should not do it out of carelessness and let it become a reality to one's own surprise if it is not what is desired. In my opinion, the leadership must be returned to the state authorities, also in the support of *Wissenschaft*, and really above all to the Reich.[38]

As cultural minister of the largest German state, which during the Weimar Republic was the state most consistently ruled by the parties supporting democracy, Becker felt it incumbent upon him to prod the other states into paying more attention to the NGW's activities and to mobilize the Reich Ministry of the Interior into an active policy that would enable the authorities in Berlin, that is, his own ministry and the Reich Ministry of the Interior, to exercise reasonable surveillance over the NGW. The period after May 1928 seemed particularly promising in this respect because the May 1928 elections had brought the Weimar Coalition into power in the Reich and the new minister of the interior, Carl Severing, was a Social Democrat. This political change had not been lost on Schmidt-Ott, who intensified his cultivation of Prelate Schreiber and the South Germans through his appointments to his staff. He also seems to have had strong allies on Severing's staff of career civil servants, since Severing initially celebrated Schmidt-Ott and the work of the NGW by presenting the group with a bust of the NGW leader and expressing the conviction that the NGW had to become a permanent institution whose governmental allocation should be raised from 8 to 10 million marks.[39]

These developments apparently mobilized Becker and Richter, who at the end of November 1928 invited the unofficial treasurer of the NGW, the banker Salomonsohn, to pay the Cultural Ministry a visit to discuss the NGW.[40] Becker accused Schmidt-Ott of being a "well taught student of Althoff," an "autocrat" who "understands how to set everything up so that no one knows what is going on" and who has surrounded himself in the Executive Committee with "a clique of old gentlemen who have an average age of 68 ½ years ... [and] who jealously watch that no young people make it through." Becker accused Schmidt-Ott of catering to Schreiber and south German interests inordinately and went on to charge that the NGW had been serving the special interests of the publishers to the point where no scholarly book was being published without a subsidy. Becker also felt that the launching of expensive archaeological expeditions when

Germany was engaged in complicated reparations negotiations was a great mistake. Becker stressed that he had no desire whatever to become involved in deciding who should receive grants and who should not, but he felt that he had a right to know the principles according to which these decisions were being made as well as to receive some accounting of the results of the money so invested. Becker went on to demonstrate that Haber's concerns of the previous year had been very much to the point. He declared that the major source of government information about the NGW was the published reports and that he, when trying to decide, for example, how much to give to pharmaceutical research, had no way of taking into account funds that might have been supplied by the NGW for the same purpose.

While Salomonsohn, obviously shocked by the criticisms, sought to defend Schmidt-Ott and warned that government interference would damage the reputation of the NGW at home and abroad and scare away important foreign contributors, Becker and Richter insisted that the government had to have a role in setting policy guidelines for the NGW as well as precise information about the allocation of funds. They also insisted that there be some turnover of personnel on the Executive Committee and some modification of the domination exercised by the elderly establishment. In December 1928, in collaboration with Severing, Becker and Richter sought to achieve these goals at a meeting of the Reich and state higher-education officials in Dresden, but they were only able to secure an agreement that there would be discussions every two or three months between the Executive Committee and the representatives of the Reich and states pertaining to the NGW programs and general guidelines. Apparently, the South German representatives wished no more surveillance than that, and they also had it explicitly stated that there was to be "no supervisory instance, no bureaucratization, only regular discussions."[41] Schmidt-Ott's South German connections had thus served him well.

Yet he and his colleagues had been put on the defensive, and this was to continue and produce a sense of crisis for the NGW throughout 1929. Becker had largely concerned himself with the procedures of the NGW and had been fairly restrained in making substantive criticisms of actual NGW decisions. The NGW, however, made some egregious political mistakes. For example, it had awarded a grant, which it was compelled to withdraw at the end of 1928, to the Greifswald mathematician and later high-ranking Nazi official Theodor Vahlen, who had been dismissed for insulting the republican flag. A similar case erupted in late 1929, when the Gobineau scholar and alleged cultural anthropologist Ludwig Schemann had to be informed of the withdrawal of his grant by Schmidt-Ott because of the blatant anti-Semitic material in his work.[42] These, however, were rectifiable "mistakes," for which one could apologize.

Far more damaging to the image of the NGW were the attacks on the "ossified scholarship" and reports concerning the "maze of German scholarly erudition" which appeared in the liberal and Socialist press in the spring of 1929 spearheaded by the Socialist deputy specializing in cultural affairs, Dr. Julius Moses. The press made particularly merry with theological topics such as the "Holy Fish in ancient religions and Christianity," and the "Holy Craftsman as presented in the Acta Sanctorum," but they also found projects such as the translation of Plotinus, the "theological ethics of Richard Rothe and its dependence upon Schleiermacher and Hegel," and the "policy of the Count of Barcelona in the 11th and 12th centuries and the elector Johann Wilhelm of the Palatinate" to be questionable expenditures of taxpayer money. Press commentaries and critics in the Reichstag during the three days of debate on the Interior Ministry budget in early June 1929 were especially critical of the travel funds provided by the NGW for trips to Paris and London to investigate the history of the viola, but also attacked journeys to Egypt to investigate the massive increase of insects and to the United States to study statistical methods in American laboratories.[43] At the same time, the critics, especially in the press, regarded much of this as a "political subvention" to the enemies of the Republic, pointing out that "Germany's academic youth slanders the state, insults those bearing political responsibility in the state. The Reich government, however, does very little to see to it that those involved are taught that taking money and insulting those who give it do not harmonize with one another."[44] They did not spare the "reactionary" Bavarian professors supported by the NGW either; they strongly suggested that the heavy dose of Catholic theology in the NGW grant was a payoff to Prelate Schreiber and, obviously well informed by Becker and Richter, attacked the "dictatorship" of Schmidt-Ott, the privileged status given to age in the NGW, the lack of NGW accountability, and the intransparency of its procedures.

As might be expected, the defense of NGW support for the aforementioned projects came from the professorial group in the Reichstag – indeed, the professors from the various parties formed a veritable party of their own for the occasion – and from the political Right. They warned against interference in the freedom of *Wissenschaft*, stressed the importance of not preempting the judgment of experts in the field, and emphasized the ignorance demonstrated by some of the criticisms, for instance, the failure to recognize the central importance of the fish symbol in early Christianity and the fact that it was as well known then as AGFA was in Weimar Germany, and the incapacity to understand the legitimacy of wanting to observe laboratory statistical methods on the spot. While stressing the very valuable work supported by the NGW that was of immediate use and application, its supporters warned that the study of history, theology, and other humanities was also essential for the maintenance of culture and civilization – a perspective, there were strong hints, not fully available to a Marxist with the name Moses. Significantly, very little effort was made to respond to one of Moses' chief criticisms, that the NGW had done very little to encourage or support work in the social sciences, especially in sociology, areas notoriously neglected by the conservative academic establishment in Weimar for their "Marxist" character.[45]

The Reichstag debates of 1929 cost the NGW a million marks, although whether the reduction from 8 to 7 million marks allotted to it was inevitable in the budget cutting then being undertaken or whether it might have been avoided if the NGW had not left itself so open to criticism is difficult to determine. It is interesting to note, however, that the business manager of the Kaiser-Wilhelm-Society, Friedrich Glum, when faced with a request from Schreiber to Harnack that the society come out strongly in support of Schreiber's efforts to defend the NGW, hastened to point out to Harnack that Deputy Moses, whom Glum had spent two days cultivating in Hamburg, was quite enthused about the work of the Kaiser-Wilhelm-Society and did not even mind that it was so heavily supported by industrialists. Glum feared that too many articles in the press on behalf of the NGW would only invite further attacks and concluded that "the attitude of Herr Moses and the Social Democrats toward the *Notgemeinschaft* is still extremely unfriendly, while it is very friendly to us. I would not think it right to change the good attitude toward us among these groups to the disfavor of the Kaiser-Wilhelm-Society by coming out too strongly for the *Notgemeinschaft*."[46] So much for solidarity! Such questions aside, however, Glum's attitude certainly reflects the NGW's loss of prestige and weakened position as well as the inevitability of some reform.

At the end of 1929 some limited but significant reforms were undertaken. The name of the NGW was changed to the Deutsche Forschungsgemeinschaft, although Schmidt-Ott stubbornly persisted in using the old name, and it must be said that the funding provided the NGW during the Great Depression of 1930-1933 certainly entitled him to speak once again of *Not*. More important, a written set of procedures and guidelines finally was devised for the NGW, and the Interior Ministry was given the power to appoint five of the persons to serve on the Executive Committee, which was expanded to fifteen members. Also, the minister, through his commissar, was to have full access to information and the right to a voice in the disposition of funds. In practical terms, these reforms, which included the election of two Social Democrats, Dr. Moses and Professor Radbruch, to the Executive Committee, did not seriously modify the subsequent operation of the NGW. As noted, the major problem after 1929 was money, and Schmidt-Ott, Schreiber, and the others associated with the NGW fought desperately to save what could be salvaged of their budget and the shattered German scholarly community. The ultimate blows, of course, came after January 30, 1933. The NGW was "coordinated," and Schmidt-Ott was replaced by the obnoxious Nazi physicist Johannes Stark. Here, as in all other branches of society and economy, the Nazis put an end to self-government in even the old conservative sense. The fate of free scholarship and science under that regime needs no elaboration here.[47]

Politicization through "finalization"? The contemporary debate

It is not very surprising that the politicization and instrumentalization of science and scholarship in the Third Reich as well as in the totalitarian phases of the communist regimes did much to strengthen support for the autonomy of science, its claims to self-regulation, and its traditional institutions. That the revolutionary impulses in National Socialism were directed, among other things, against the academic establishment helped promote the resurrection of many old institutions, ideals, and ideas after 1945. This tendency was strengthened by the extraordinary problems of reconstructing German science and scholarship after twelve years of Nazi rule. What could be more natural, after all, than taking as one's point of departure the ways and means that had provided such glory and fame in the past? The Kiel philosopher Kurt Hübner expressed all this quite well in a passionate defense of Germany's academic and research establishment in 1976 against proposals that would subject its activities to external direction:

The steering of *Wissenschaft*, where it is unavoidable, should be entrusted to a broad spectrum of decision makers. Among these belong the individual researchers, who must have the opportunity of deciding for themselves what they want to work on; among these belong the scientific institutes, be they public or private, the universities, the scholarly societies, the foundations, industrial management, the ministries and so on. None of these instances ought to be exclusively giving orders to the others; each is to be given a high degree of freedom; but all should work with one another.

How is that to be accomplished? The answer is: basically, just as it is still largely done in our country even if it is uncontestable that there is much that can be improved. . . . The existing scientific organizational forms were created neither by some shadowy professors, nor by any lust for power on the part of the bourgeoise, but they developed necessarily and logically from the nature of *Wissenschaft* itself. There is no cause to change them in any basic way and be seduced by fashionable slogans. This was an extraordinary achievement of a past age . . . . Through it German science achieved a leading position in many areas and high regard throughout the world. Not the failure of this system but only the interference of the National Socialists with *Wissenschaft* brought it down. Much lost terrain was won back after the war. Do we want to lose it again?[48]

One may or may not accept this position, but the preceding discussion of Weimar should make it very difficult to accept the historical analysis in which it is embedded. The challenge to the system was not initially raised by the Nazis but rather by representatives of the forces trying to save German democracy from the active and passive resistance of conservative elites to the reform of institutions which served as barriers to the democratization and modernization of German society. The Weimar experience is discomforting to the liberal academic who believes in the autonomy of science, among whose number this author would place himself. From the perspective of Anglo-American liberalism, it seems easy enough to reject Senator William Proxmire's assaults on the silliness of various academic research projects funded by the government as yahooism, to point out that the old predictions of the British Marxist J. D. Bernal about the triumph of basic research under socialism have proven hopelessly wrong, and that the demands of J. R. Ravetz of the University of Leeds that science be made instrumental and moral will destroy the enterprise whatever its short-term benefits.[49]

At the same time, however, most liberal academics would find it difficult not to come down on the side of Becker and Moses in their struggle against the NGW policies because of the political context of Weimar. Can one agree with Moses, however, when he argued that *Wissenschaft* is a "social construct," which could only be supported with public funds insofar as it had a "social nucleus" and that the "scholastic games" being played by those who received NGW support were nothing more than private entertainment, no more worthy of support than the "literary overproduction" reflected in the "mass production of worthless scholarly works"?[50] In truth, it was no accident that Moses was not upset by industrialist involvement in the Kaiser-Wilhelm-Society, since the attitude of the Social Democrats toward what should be funded was not terribly far from that of the less imaginative industrialists. Yet, while it may be argued that Moses was extremely insensitive to the values of some of the humanistic projects he derided, just as it may be argued that the pressing problems of German society were such that they could not be afforded, it must also be said that he correctly understood that there was a decided preference to support humanistic work of a certain kind rather than to nurture a critical social science. Support for the humanities was and still can be a conservative weapon against the development of critical social science.[51]

In contemporary Germany, as elsewhere in the Western industrialized world, the tensions surrounding science policy have become open and, in some respects, have taken forms which may be of future significance elsewhere. The crisis in the "external relations"[52] of science is familiar enough. It revolves around money and the "payoff" of public investments along with questions about the adequacy of institutional arrangements and "relevance." It is a traditional and probably endless conflict: Some argue that science and its institutions require outside interference and reform from external sources because they have traditionally proven incapable of reforming themselves; others, the defenders of the traditional establishment, insist upon the dangers of short-run determinations of relevance and warn that the encouragement of theory and creativity is the only effective antidote to a stifling bureaucratization.[53]

Less familiar and of indeterminate seriousness at the present juncture are the demands of a small group of social scientists, philosophers, and natural scientists for the "finalization" (*Finalisierung*) of science, that is, the external determination of the scientific enterprise for social and political ends. Strongly influenced by the Frankfurt School and Critical Theory, the advocates of finalization launch their arguments from an internalist perspective. Relying heavily on Kuhn's *Structure of Scientific Revolutions*, they argue that sciences reach a posttheoretical stage in which their claims to autonomy lose all legitimacy and in which they can and should be subjected to external determination for political and social ends rather than be permitted to develop along lines determined by self-interested members of the scientific establishment in the interest of the ruling economic and political establishment.[54]

That the debate over finalization in the early 1970s, which paralleled the university reform movement and involved experiments such as restricting mathematics at the University of Bremen to its applied branches, aroused considerable hostility and debate should hardly be surprising. That it consisted of an impassioned but very traditional defense of academic freedom, traditional structures, and traditional organizations much in the style of that of Hübner as cited earlier should be no less surprising.[55] It is a different disagreement from that in Weimar in many respects, and it certainly takes place in a very different political environment, arguments to the contrary by the Left notwithstanding. Nevertheless, there are obvious parallels in the broader issues and probably, unhappily, a parallel in the outcome of the debate, namely, that the extreme nature of the arguments serves to ensure that real problems and possibilities of reform get lost in the process.[56]

In any case, those involved in the debate would do well to pay some attention to the fact that it has a history. Insofar as history has any value in such a discussion, it certainly is not providing one-to-one relationships and simpleminded analogies but rather by creating a consciousness of the various components that define the problems involved in the support of science and scholarship, and that make it more and more a political issue. From this perspective, the Weimar experience is a particularly rich one, with many analogies to our own recent experiences: the negative impact of war and inflation on available resources; the increasing dependence on government resources for the funding of science and scholarship; the problems of defining priorities between basic and applied research, as well as among the natural sciences, social sciences, and humanities; issues of public accountability and the question of the relationship between those who give and those who receive money for research; the entrenched interests and values of those who engage in research, their demands for autonomy and self-determination, and their relationship to the public welfare and the cultural values entertained by society; and the social position and recruitment of those engaged in research and scholarship.

In the best of all possible worlds, that is, a world with reasonably sufficient resources from a variety of public and private sources – a world that was known on occasion before World War I and after World War II – the political aspects of the support of science and scholarship have been in the background or have been dormant. Economic crises and heavy dependence upon public funding, however, inevitably create some measure of adversary relationship between those who give and those who receive. This forces the scientific and scholarly establishments to behave more and more like interest groups – idealism and claims to objectivity notwithstanding – and the guardians of the public purse to engage increasingly in oscillation between intervention in the public interest and withdrawal in appreciation of the efficiency of expert peer review and self-government. In the last analysis, however, as the Weimar experience illustrates and as we are constantly learning, the issues are political and therefore legitimately subject to the public debate and discussion that we are likely to experience increasingly in the future.

Notes

1 *Civilization and Science in Conflict or Collaboration*, Ciba Foundation Symposium 1, (Amsterdam: Associated Scientific Publishers, 1973), p. 64.

2 On the role of Sputnik, see Walter A. McDougall, "Technocracy and Statecraft in the Space Age – Toward the History of a Saltation," *American Historical Review* 87,4 (October 1982):1010–1040. Some of the author's observations here are based on his experience as a member of the Advisory Council and Executive Committee of the Institute of International Studies at the University of California at Berkeley and his participation in the work of The Joint ACLS-SSRC Committee on Western Europe.

3 Daniel J. Kevles, *The Physicists: The History of a Scientific Community in Modern America* (New York: Knopf, 1977), pp. 45–51, 140, 343ff.

4 Michael Foster, "The State and Scientific Research," *The Nineteenth Century and After* 55 (1904): 742–743. More generally, see Peter Alter, *Wissenschaft, Staat, Mäzene: Anfänge moderner Wissenschaftspolitik in Grossbritannien 1850–1920* (Stuttgart: Klett, 1982).

5 *Civilization and Science*, p. 65.

6 Edward Shils in ibid., p. 41.

7 Leonard Krieger, *The German Idea of Freedom: History of a Political Tradition* (Boston: Beacon, 1957). On the contemporary relevance of the German experience, see Gerald D. Feldman, "German Interest Group Alliances in War and Inflation, 1914–1923," in Suzanne D. Berger, ed., *Organizing Interests in Western Europe*, Cambridge Studies in Modern Political Economies (Cambridge: Cambridge University Press, 1981), pp. 159–184.

8 The actual term *Wissenschaftspolitik* was first employed by the theologian and founder of the Kaiser-Wilhelm-Society Adolf von Harnack in 1900 and used in his history of the Prussian Academy of Sciences with reference to Prussian promotion of scholarship and science since the time of Leibniz. For general background see Charles E. McClelland, *State, Society and University in Germany, 1700–1914* (Cambridge: Cambridge University Press, 1980); F. K. Ringer, *The Decline of the German Mandarins: The German Academic Community, 1890–1933* (Cambridge, Mass.: Harvard University Press, 1969).

9 R. Steven Turner, "The Growth of Professorial Research in Prussia, 1818–1848: Causes and Context," *Historical Studies in the Physical Sciences* 3 (1971): 137–182.

10 Bernhard vom Brocke, "Hochschul- und Wissenschaftspolitik in Preussen und im Deutschen Kaiserreich, 1882–1907: das 'System Althoff,' " in Peter Baumgart, ed., *Bildungspolitik in Preussen zur Zeit des Kaiserreichs* (Stuttgart: Klett, 1980), pp. 9–118, citation on p. 63.

11 Ibid., pp. 53ff. On the Kaiser-Wilhelm-Society, see also Lothar Burchardt, *Wissenschaftspolitik im Wilhelminischen Deutschland: Vorgeschichte, Gründung und Aufbau der Kaiser-Wilhelm-Gesellschaft zur Förderung der Wissenschaften* (Göttingen: Vandenhoeck & Ruprecht, 1975); and Günter Wendel's important *Die Kaiser-Wilhelm-Gesellschaft, 1911–1914: Zur Anatomie einer imperialistischen Forschungsgesellschaft* (East Berlin: Akademie-Verlag, 1975).

12 Wendel, *Kaiser-Wilhelm-Gesellschaft*, p. 113.

13 Ibid., p. 324.

14 Gerald D. Feldman, "A German Scientist Between Illusion and Reality: Emil Fischer, 1909–1919," in Imanuel Geiss and Bernd Jürgen Wendt, eds., *Deutschland in der Weltpolitik des 19. und 20. Jahrhunderts* (Düsseldorf: Bertelsmann Universitätsverlag, 1973), pp. 341–362.

15 Brigitte Schroeder-Gudehus, *Les Scientifiques et la Paix: La Communauté Scientifique Internationale au cours de Anneés 20* (Montreâl: Montreâl University Press, 1978).

16 Ibid., and Feldman, "A German Scientist," p. 361.

17 Ibid., pp. 359–362.

18 The discussion here is based on Paul Forman's "The Helmholtz Gesellschaft: Support of Academic Physical Research by German Industry After the First World War," which he kindly placed at my disposal. The quotation is from pp. 207–208 of the manuscript. Some of his more important findings are published in his article "The Financial Support and Political Alignment of Physicists in Weimar Germany," *Minerva* 12, 1 (January 1974): 39–66. See also his "Weimar Culture, Causality and Quantum Theory, 1918–1927: Adaptation by German Physicists and Mathematicians to a Hostile Environment," *Historical Studies in the Physical Sciences* 3 (1971):1–115.

19 The basic work on the Notgemeinschaft is Kurt Zierold, *Forschungsförderung in drei Epochen: Deutsche Forschungsgemeinschaft—Geschichte, Arbeitsweise, Kommentar* (Wiesbaden: Franz Steiner, 1968). For a brief but excellent survey, see Thomas Nipperdey and Ludwig Schmugge, *50 Jahre Forschungsförderung in Deutschland, 1920–1970: Ein Abriss der Geschichte der deutschen Forschungsgemeinschaft* (Berlin: Deutsche Forschungsgemeinschaft, 1970). For a basic interpretative discussion, see Brigitte Schroeder-Gudehus, "The Argument for the Self-Government and Public Support of Science in Weimar Germany," *Minerva* 10, 4 (October 1972):537–570.

20 Nipperdey and Schmugge, *50 Jahre*, p. 14.

21 Haber to Schmidt-Ott, 14 September 1926, Bundesarchiv Koblenz (hereafter BA), R 73, Nr. 46.

22 Reprinted in Zierold, *Forschungsförderung*, pp. 561–573.

23 Haber to Schmidt-Ott, 2 August 1920, BA, R 73, Nr. 37.

24 Zierold, *Forschungsförderung*, pp. 40ff.

25 Ibid., pp. 29ff.

26 Quoted in Georg Schreiber, *Die Not der deutschen Wissenschaft und der geistigen Arbeiter: Geschehnisse und Gedanken zur Kulturpolitik des deutschen Reiches* (Leipzig: Quelle & Meyer, 1923), p. 43.

27 "Bericht über Finanzlage, 3. Dez. 1923," Bibliothek und Archiv zur Geschichte der Maz-Planck-Gesellschaft, Berlin, Nr. 345.

28 Hauptausschuss Sitzung, 9 January 1925, BA, R 73, Nr. 89.

29 Ibid. See the "Denkschrift über die Forschungsarbeiten der Deutschen Wissenschaft im Bereich der nationalen Wirtschaft, der Volksgesundheit und des Volkswohles, 25. Mai 1925," in Zierold, *Forschungsförderung*, pp. 576–822.

30 Quoted in ibid., pp. 583–584.

31 Ibid.

32 "Notiz über Bierabend am 10.2.26," BA, R 73, Nr. 15.

33 Sauerbruch to Duisberg, 9 December 1926, BA, R 73, Nr. 8.

34 Fritz Haber, "Über Staat und Wissenschaft," Karlsruhe, 20 January 1927, BA, R 73, Nr. 91.

35 "Vermerk über die Sitzung am 1.12.28," BA, R 73, Nr. 17.

36 Haber to Schmidt-Ott, 9 March 1927, BA, R 73, Nr. 17.

37 Schroeder-Gudehus, "Argument for the Self-Government and Public Support of Science," pp. 560–561.

38 Kurt Düwell, "Staat und Wissenschaft in der Weimarer Epoche," in *Historische Zeitschrift*, supp. 1 (Munich, 1971), pp. 31–65, citation on pp. 55–56.

39 Richter to Becker, 28 July 1928, Nachlass C. H. Becker, 3404, Preussisches Geheimes Staatsarchiv Berlin-Dahlem.

40 The discussion that follows is based on Salomonsohn's notes in the Nachlass Schmidt-Ott, Nr. 5, Preussisches Geheimes Staatsarchiv Berlin-Dahlem.

41 "Notiz. Besprechung in Dresden 1.12.28," ibid. For the Bavarian position on these matters, see Bayerisches Hauptstaatsarchiv, MA, Nr. 100 134.

42 Zierold, *Forschungsförderung*, pp. 120, 131.

43 *Berliner Tageblatt*, 9 April 1929 in BA, R 73, Nr. 17. For the debate in the Reichstag from 8 to 10 June 1929, see *Verhandlungen des Reichstages*, 79th–84th sessions, Vol. 425 (1929).

44 *Karlsruhe Volksfreund*, 3 February 1929, BA, R 73, Nr. 17.

45 See note 43.

46 Glum to Harnack, 12 September 1929, Bibliothek und Archiv zur Geschichte der Max-Planck-Gesellschaft, Berlin, Nr. 352.

47 Zierold, *Forschungsförderung*, pp. 173ff.

48 Kurt Hübner, "Die Finalisierung der Wissenschaft als allgemeine Parole und was sich dahinter verbirgt," in Kurt Hübner, et al., eds., *Die politische Herausforderung der Wissenschaft* (Hamburg: Hoffmann & Campe, 1976), pp. 95–96.

49 J. R. Ravetz, "Criticisms of Science," in Ina Spiegel-Rösing and Derek de Solla Price, eds., *Science, Technology and Society: A Cross-Disciplinary Perspective* (Beverly Hills, Calif.: Sage, 1977), pp. 71–89. The classic Western Marxist argument for the "socialization of science" was presented by J. D. Bernal, *The Social Function of Science* (London, 1939).

50 Julius Moses in *Sozialistische Bildung* 8 (August 1929) in BA, R 73, Nr. 17.

51 It is interesting to observe the development of the National Endowment for the Humanities under the Reagan administration from this perspective.

52 The term is that of Edward Shils in *Civilization and Science*, p. 39.

53 H.-G. Gadamer, "Die Unverständlichkeit der Wissenschaft und das Verständnis der Öffentlichkeit," in Rudolf Schmitz, ed., *Wissenschaft und Gesellschaft: Herausforderungen und Wechselwirkungen in Ihrer Zeit* (Stuttgart: Wissenschaftliche Verlagsgesellschaft, 1978), pp. 25–36.

54 The basic statement of this position is G. Böhme, W. v.d. Daele, and W. Krohn, "Die Finalisierung der Wissenschaft," *Zeitschrift für Soziologie* 2 (1973):128–144; for further theoretical discussion and illustrations of "finalization" at work, see G. Böhme et al., *Die gesellschaftliche Orientierung des wissenschaftlichen Fortschritts*, (Frankfurt am Main: Suhrkamp, 1978); for a discussion in English, see G. Böhme, "Models for the Development of Science," in Spiegel-Rösing and de Solla Price, eds., *Science, Technology, and Society*, pp. 319–351.

55 See the essays by many distinguished German academics in Hübner et. al., *Politische Herausforderung*.

56 Some of these problems arose from the very reconstruction of the institutions of science and scholarship in Germany after the war. For a valuable discussion, see Thomas Stamm, *Zwischen Staat und Selbstverwaltung: Die deutsche Forschung im Wiederaufbau, 1945–1965* (Cologne: Verlag Wissenschaft und Politik, 1981), esp. pp. 273ff.

9

The survival of the state in European international relations

MILES KAHLER

Europe, originator of the modern state system, has since 1945 been the principal experiment and hope for those who see a means for transforming the old state-centered model of international relations in the receding boundaries of a circumscribed and beleaguered state. In one respect – demotion of the high politics of military competition – those hopes seemed to be fulfilled through the demotion of Europe itself within the international system. The security-dependent civilian states that resulted, however, have recently faced renewed concern from their populations in an environment of deteriorating superpower relations.

In a second and equally important domain, the competition between state and international market, early predictions by the heralds of interdependence and the disciples of European integration can now be seen as overdrawn. Later cries of alarm concerning a mercantilist onslaught were equally exaggerated: The prevailing liberal organization of the international and European political economies persists, even though the activism of the state has grown in meeting the new conditions of international openness. A new and perhaps stable balance may have been struck between the postwar politics of domestic economic stabilization and the demands of international economic interdependence. At the same time, the new boundaries of the political are being subjected to strains by a perceived increase in international insecurity (and concomitant return of the concerns of traditional high politics), by shifts in the international division of labor, and by the growing inefficacy of domestic economic management in conditions of high economic openness.

The decline of high politics

International politics was once far more important for the societies of Western Europe. The birth of a state system during the age of ab-

287

solutism shaped the process of state formation itself, pushing dynastic regimes toward economic rationalization and construction of civil and military bureaucracies. The relative intensity of the security dilemma faced by the European states had long-lasting effects on the political paths they would follow.[1] The early modern state could claim the lives and property of the inhabitants within its boundaries but was not concerned with claiming their positive and active allegiance. Only the emergence of mass nationalism in the nineteenth century forged the crucial links among international environment, state, and citizenry. Nationalism and the external projects it fostered gave each state far greater resources of participation and legitimacy than it had previously possessed, granting elites their most powerful means (together with religion) for ensuring loyalty in an age of democracy.

The nation-state's resilience was demonstrated in the cauldron of total war from 1939 to 1945 and was confirmed by the relatively weak effects that the war and its aftermath had on political and social arrangements in Western Europe (with the exception of Germany).[2] The war did produce revulsion against domination of social life by the demands of foreign policy, however, and more generally against traditional high politics and nationalist political programs. Definition of and defense against external enemies (one description of the substance of high politics) seemed to be rendered obsolete by a resolution of the European security dilemma in a radically new form: High politics became the prerogative of those dominant in international politics, and Europe was no longer at the pinnacle of the international diplomatic and military hierarchy. Dwarfed by the United States and the Soviet Union, the European states system was, for the first time since the seventeenth century, firmly embedded in an international order dominated by others. In addition, Europe, formerly predominant in military technology, now lagged behind the United States and the Soviet Union in the new coinage of international power, nuclear weaponry.

Changes in Europe's status were accompanied by simplification in defining security requirements. Although there were disputes over strategy toward the Soviet Union, the dominant domestic coalitions in Western Europe agreed in their definition of the external foe; other rivalries (such as that between France and Germany) faded in significance. Not only was the national adversary neatly defined, the security threat was a strictly *European* and *military* one. Despite the lingering global engagement of France and Britain, strategy was set by Europe's senior American partner and the role awarded Europeans was gradually limited to their continent. Anxieties over economic security faded as an American military presence (and American multinational corporations) assumed the role of guaranteeing secure supplies of petroleum and other raw materials essential to the burgeoning European economies. In these new conditions, relieved of much of the ceaseless diplomatic and military competition that had brought Europe conflict, demotion of the European state system seemed to promise *greater* security rather than less.

The dwarfing of Europe also resulted in domestic devaluation of traditional international relations, reinforcing the repudiation of mass nationalism that characterized the postwar internal settlement. The European state itself, born of international threat and internal mobilization, had finally become a *civilian* state, providing confirmation for Schumpeter's pacific image of the bourgeois political order. The long-standing link between a remnant of the landed aristocracy, their military ethos, and the external role of the state was finally broken; those reduced military bureaucracies that remained played a distinctly subordinate political role. The new nuclear technology also had a curious deadening effect on internal political debate and the demands that governments placed on their citizens: High politics ceased to be politics. The social dimension of warfare had grown increasingly important during the twentieth century, and it remained central in the succession of colonial conflicts fought by European countries after 1945. Within Europe, however, that dimension was gradually set aside in considering conflicts that were likely to erupt.[3] Instead, strategic policy was sterilized politically and insulated bureaucratically. Ironically, that triumph of technocracy sought by many in the construction of a united Europe could be discovered instead in the reduced sphere of high politics. The severing of high politics from political discourse was reinforced because the "new science" of nuclear strategy and the entire field of international relations was dominated by the United States, reflecting ideologically the configuration of international power. As in the case of military technology, Western Europe lacked for the most part an infrastructure of foundations, research institutes, and universities (supply side) and governments with global international strategies (demand side) that would have encouraged the development of a field linked to the domestic political debate.[4]

These new international and domestic circumstances did not wholly prevent what Hoffmann has called the "tyranny of the external" from impinging on the politics of these societies. Transition to new patterns of international relations could be politically treacherous. Demotion from global to medium-power status occasioned intense domestic political conflict and nationalist reaction (Suez in Britain, Algeria in France). The new bipolar configuration of international power that subordinated the European state system also permeated the political life of those societies with large Communist parties, intensifying the link between international alignment and internal politics that had already appeared in the 1930s. Domestic concern with questions of war and peace also broke through the surface of political life at those times when the superpowers' predominance seemed to add to European insecurity rather than to reduce it – during the Korean War, again briefly in the early 1960s with the Campaign for Nuclear Disarmament. As the constraints of their international position pervaded the political process, however, most Europeans accepted that the only political options were membership in one of the blocs or a risky attempt to opt out of the competition altogether (neutralism). More grandiose possibilities could only be imagined by the few who saw the unification of Europe as the route not to the final abolition of high politics, but to the construction of a supranational great power.

While applauded by many who had witnessed the carnage of two European wars in this century, the strategic dependence of Western Europe and the gradual fading of high politics as a political issue posed a threat to political legitimacy in two respects. Most serious was the inability of the state in the new era to keep its primordial bargain with its citizens – to protect them against external threats. The final demise of the impermeable territorial state and its boundaries (in the military sphere), the possibility that the life of the society itself could be placed at risk, imposed the political strategy described above: removing high politics and the social dimensions of military policy from domestic political debate. The Left accommodated itself to the new international strictures, failing to advance any alternative that would take account of Europe's reduced position and seek to transform it: Neutralism or a change in bloc membership remained the only effective prescriptions from this quarter. Only temporary surges in perceived insecurity threatened the success of the strategy of depoliticization.

The devaluation of high politics also meant the loss of long-standing outward-directed political appeals and strategies that served to consolidate political support and meet the internationalist arguments of the Left. Nationalism as a political program was replaced (Gaullism excepted) by the new international demands of anticommunism and, more significantly, by the promise of economic prosperity. In the links between that goal and the boundaries between state and international economy, there were other surprising developments after 1945.

State and market: the mercantilist alternative

Europe's military dwarfing and the new domestic limits that it imposed on high politics meant that the boundaries of the political in international economic relations were elevated in importance. Historically, tension between nation-state and international market had been nearly as great as that among the warring states of the European system. Baechler has described the origins of capitalist expansion in the political disintegration of early modern Europe; that political source of capitalist development also raised the possibility of state intervention, which threatened to constrain (in the interests of its own autonomy and power) the engine of economic growth.[5]

Repeated state efforts to harness the benefits of incipient capitalism have given their name to a more general category of state actions that interfere with or distort the international market: mercantilism, which, in the absence of a powerful socialist alternative, has remained the principal challenger to liberalism as a model for organizing the international political economy. Because of the wide and often vague usage given to the term (as in contemporary "neomercantilism"), the sets of policies represented must be defined precisely. The appearance and reappearance of mercantilist options within Europe has been a significant marker of the shifting boundaries between market and state.

Mercantilism is not, as some have argued, *any* state intervention in international economic transactions. It is a *strategy* of such intervention, a bundle of policies based on certain presuppositions about the international economy, pointed toward regulation and at least partial closure to attain certain ends. The different goals represented in contemporary neomercantilism were first seen in successive historical waves of mercantilist strategies:

Classical mercantilism attempted to use the state to ensure that economic transactions, domestic and international, would serve the end of power and status, the goals of high politics. The degree of conflict or harmony that was perceived between the goals of wealth and power is a matter of debate, but the international economy within which these goals were pursued was viewed as static and marked by zero-sum conflict. The state's external policies emphasized reducing imports and the promotion of exports, winning the largest possible share of international services (such as shipping) for one's citizens, and securing supplies of raw materials vital to national security. Underlying the classical mercantilist strategy was a bullionist view of national wealth and the underpinnings of military power.[6]

Developmental mercantilism appeared during the industrialization in the nineteenth century; its array of policies was adopted by late-industrializing states to further their autonomous economic development: Tariffs and other devices to protect local manufacturing, exchange controls, and controls on foreign investment.[7] Such measures have also been applied in other regions concerned about their place in the international division of labor: Eastern Europe in the 1920s and 1930s, Japan since 1867, and Latin America and other developing areas since World War I. These state-led strategies may aim at the expansion of the state's power (as in classical mercantilism), but only through the medium of economic growth: In contrast to the classical mercantilist view, the international economy is seen as dynamic, but still laden with conflict.

Countercyclical mercantilism came to characterize the international economic policies of most industrial countries in response to the Great Depression of the 1930s. In the absence of domestic recovery programs, governments under pressure tried to reduce the apparent external sources of economic disruption. The measures included quantitative and tariff restrictions on trade, depreciation of currencies, exchange controls, and systems of commercial discrimination.[8]

These three variants of mercantilism can be viewed as the *external* instruments used by the modern state to guard against market outcomes that are politically unacceptable: military weakness, economic dependency, and debilitating fluctuations in economic activity. From 1919 to 1945, Europe witnessed an unusual conflation of these three strands of mercantilism in its organization of international economic relations. World War I had produced widened state control of the European economies, even in liberal Britain. Relaxation of these wartime controls was delayed in the 1920s by continuing political disorder and military insecurity. Postwar fragmentation of Eastern Europe and the nationalist aims of new European states to industrialize rapidly added an important element of developmental mercantilism. The Great Depression then brought a turn to widespread countercyclical mercantilism. By the mid-1930s, when progress toward lowering the level of state controls and stabilizing the major industrial economies seemed feasible, resurgent military insecurity reinforced mercantilist policies of the classical sort. The adoption of autarchic policies by Germany and Italy in support of their rearmament stimulated similar responses from other European states.[9]

Any possibility that the international economic order in Europe after the war would be less state-directed than the prewar model seemed slight for two reasons: War had once again expanded both state intervention externally to meet the demands of security and state activism domestically to win the support of the working class for the war effort.[10] International conflict had produced a great leap forward in expectations that the state would manage the economy and in confidence that the state could undertake such management: "The legacy of the war was a consciousness that the economy could be directed in the desired channels, some knowledge of how to direct it, and the acquisition of a great store of facts about the economy. To this was added some degree of political and economic agreement about the aims of the economy in peacetime."[11]

The birth of Keynesian economic stabilization and the welfare state might well have pointed toward closure, particularly in the context of disrupted trading relations and a dollar shortage.[12] Instead, wartime controls were gradually stripped away; by the late 1950s the international economy and the Western European economy resembled the liberal model more closely than any mercantilist image. As described above, the embedding of a divided Europe in a superpower-dominated international system reduced security concerns. Classical mercantilist alternatives, appealing to national security and power, were defeated: Britain, despite rhetorical commitment, turned from attachment to imperial commercial and financial arrangements; France, despite a painful decolonization, chose Europe and relative openness over a discredited colonial mercantilism.

Developmental mercantilism also seemed irrelevant. The European economies narrowed the technological gap with the United States, but other competitors lagged far behind. Externally, the place of Europe at or near the top of the international division of labor seemed assured; internally, microefficiency appeared to depend on effective macroeconomic policies, not on government intervention. Only the French planning mechanism was a partial exception to Keynesian and liberal logic.

The remnants of countercyclical mercantilism – exchange controls and trade barriers – took some time to strip away, but through the International Monetary Fund and the General Agreement on Tariffs and Trade (GATT), European states mutually bound one another not to use these instruments except under very narrowly defined conditions. Economic stabilization under the guarantees of a regime of fixed exchange rates would depend on fiscal and monetary policy; even the limited exchange-rate flexibility permitted under the Bretton Woods regime soon disappeared. As the European economy entered its longest period of sustained expansion in this century, it was buoyed by an even greater expansion in international trade and investment. The frontiers of the state seemed to have been permanently rolled back.

Sovereignty and then interdependence at bay

By the late 1960s, postwar growth in economic interdependence within Europe and between Europe and the United States had become an accepted feature of international relations. Produced by declining tariff barriers, removal of foreign-exchange controls, creation of the Eurodollar market, lower transportation costs, direct investment by multinational corporations, and (within Europe) increased labor mobility, national economies had become increasingly sensitive to developments outside their formal boundaries.[13]

As Richard Cooper carefully documents, the principal drawback of increased economic interdependence had been the constraints it imposed on the conduct of national macroeconomic policies. Postwar policies of economic management had been based on a now eroded separation of markets; national monetary policies in particular had become increasingly ineffectual under a regime of fixed exchange rates with free capital movements. For liberal economists, who viewed the national state and its boundaries as economically inefficient and even obsolete, these inconveniences hardly outweighed the advantages of the economic trend; and

the efficiency gains from market integration are maximized by ignoring the boundaries of the nation-state; for private transactions in goods and factors of production, the optimum size of the integrated area is the world. By implication, the economic justification for the nation-state must lie in the existence of public or collective goods – including stabilization targets, the distribution of income, and the regulatory climate – and of differences in national consumption preferences for such goods.[14]

Rather than fear for loss of national autonomy, most economists were concerned that floundering governments, in the fashion of the 1930s, might try to reestablish control over the domestic economy by adopting defensive measures against disturbances from the outside, thereby reducing the gains made in the postwar period.

In the hands of noneconomists, the concept of international economic interdependence was expanded to describe a more elemental transformation of international relations. Not only were governments incapable of managing their domestic economies and controlling the behavior of multinational corporations, but these new constraints, when combined with a devaluation of traditional concern with status and power, could produce more cooperative behavior on the part of states. Keohane and Nye summarize this challenge to the realist view of international politics in the image of complex interdependence, one which seemed to fit closely the new pattern of European international relations: proliferation of channels between societies that were not controlled by the state, displacement of security issues from the top of the international agenda, and abstention from the use of military force.[15]

This view, characteristic of the "first wave" of those analyzing international interdependence and deeply influenced by the postwar experience of Western Europe, reached its apogee in the scholarly and public minds during the late 1960s and early 1970s. Governments were seen as hemmed in by the workings of the international market; an element of their traditional sovereignty was at risk. Choice among strategies remained: As Cooper emphasizes, nations could attempt to reduce their levels of openness, to exploit the new relationships to their national advantage, to bob passively like a cork on an economic sea that they could not influence, or (the preferred choice) to cooperate with other states in regaining a measure of control.[16] The possibility of closure was admitted, but the mercantilist past had receded so far that most first-wave interdependence theorists assumed national elites would find it politically difficult to impose the costs of closure on their economies and populations. Thus, the growth of economic interdependence (and openness more generally) was often regarded as a historical trend that was desirable and probably irreversible.[17]

Abrupt changes in the early 1970s – the collapse of the Bretton Woods system, dramatic increases in oil prices in 1973–74, deep economic recession that signaled the end of the last postwar boom – led to a darker and more political view of interdependence, one more measured in assessing its costs, its inevitability, and, above all, its political prerequisites. The concept itself was marked by the turmoil of the 1970s: In Keohane and Nye's account the costs of sensitivity are emphasized, and to the notion of sensitivity is added the more political dimension of vulnerability ("an actor's liability to suffer costs imposed by external events even after policies have been altered").[18]

A second revision followed from renewed awareness of the growing political contention that surrounded international economic relations as the boundaries between domestic and foreign policies blurred. Steady growth of openness and interdependence could point not to an equally steady growth in cooperative solutions, but also to greater economic conflict between nations and within them, as international issues impinged on domestic debates over distribution of burdens and benefits. Rather than the benign vision of the first wave – troublesome states increasingly hemmed in by the growing demands of a harmonious international economic environment – the second wave of interdependence scholarship recognized a state hemmed in by domestic political demands, and hence a state often willing to seek the resolution of its dilemmas by externalizing them.[19] Growing economic openness could create a dialectic that pointed to a reversal of interdependence, or at least an upper limit.

A third dimension of the reconsideration of interdependence in light of economic disorder during the 1970s was the reintroduction of high politics in a realm from which it had once been banished. Second wave theorists, having witnessed the fraying of the postwar economic order, began to search for the basis of growing openness and interdependence not in historical processes, but in a particular *structure of power* in the international system. American political and military hegemony or American economic leadership, it was argued, had been crucial in maintaining the open international economy that characterized the years after 1945. The corollary, seldom stated, was that the diminution of Europe in the sphere of high politics, described earlier in this chapter, also contributed to the persistence of the open postwar economic order.[20]

Two lines of structuralist argument have used the distribution of international power – and the predominance of the United States after 1945 – to explain the particular characteristics of the international economy that seemed threatened after 1970, whether openness, stability, or the regimes that provided those qualities. The first, put subtly and persuasively by Robert Gilpin, emphasized political and military preponderance: American military hegemony, the American dollar, and the expansion of American multinational corporations reinforced one another, supporting the American position in the international system and sustaining the liberal order constructed after World War II. The United States made economic concessions to Western Europe and Japan to further their reconstruction; Europe and Japan acquiesced in American predominance, accepting American direct investment (in the case of Europe) and an international monetary system based on the dollar. The strategy was self-liquidating, however, as the American competitive edge and eventually its economic and political edge were eroded by its chosen instrument, the multinational corporation. This relative decline of the United States and "the closing of the technology gap in commercial (though not military) technology among the industrial and certain industrializing countries" endangered the stability of existing international economic rules and produced a world "on the brink of an intense mercantilistic struggle."[21]

A second set of arguments, produced by Charles Kindleberger, were even more insistent on the necessity of a single dominant power for international economic stability.[22] The leader enforced those rules necessary for the provision of the "public good of stability." It also, historically, performed certain specific functions, serving as a linchpin of the international economic system: Britain in the nineteenth century, according to Kindleberger, provided a market for distressed goods in its open market and flow of capital to offset economic fluctuations, coordinated domestic economic policies and exchange rates through the gold standard, and served as a lender of last resort in financial crisis.[23] Kindleberger draws from the 1930s lessons that he applies to the 1970s: "For the world economy to stabilize, there has to be a stabilizer, one stabilizer."[24]

Both structural hypotheses, developed by American scholars, emphasize the changing role of the United States in the world economy; both variants, implicitly, are hostile to the notion that the existing liberal framework could be sustained *jointly* by the United States and Western Europe. Despite the appealing parsimony of these explanations, however, they display serious shortcomings theoretically and in their reading of the recent history of relations between the United States and Western Europe. The emphasis on a direct relationship between power capabilities and international economic outcomes tends to ignore mediation that necessarily takes place within a particular structure of bargaining, mediation that may obscure the underlying causal relationship. Measuring power capabilities, even if they are disaggregated by issue area, is controversial: Some European scholars, for example, challenge the assumption that American power has declined over the last two decades.[25]

Another puzzle concerns the role of the hegemonic power in relation to others in the international economic order. The hegemonic variant fails to make clear how the United States could bring its military predominance to bear in the economic sphere. The implication of the term "hegemony" is that the leader employs "coercive threats," at least occasionally, to maintain the rules of the system. Evidence for such behavior in American postwar policy toward Europe is slight, despite the security dependence of Europe on the United States. Hirsch and Doyle use the examples of Suez, in which economic issues were not at stake, and German agreement not to undermine the Bretton Woods regime in exchange for America's continued security guarantee. Counterexamples abound, particularly in the sphere of East – West trade. Even at the peak of the cold war in the early 1950s the United States was unable to impose its preferences in favor of a more complete trade embargo on its European partners, who were eager to reestablish their historic markets in the East.

Leaving aside the question of whether exchanging security guarantees for economic acquiescence is a genuine indicator of hegemony, very few episodes demonstrate the usefulness of American military or political leverage in its economic bargaining with Europe. More convincing is the argument of Richard Cooper: that the postwar economic system was characterized by the *separation* of high and low politics, that trade was not contaminated by questions of military advantage or diplomatic maneuvering.[26] One could argue, of course, that the security relationship was a constant backdrop to economic relations: Through the logic of "anticipated reaction," the Europeans conceded more than they would have otherwise. Even so, American ability to force desired change in the 1960s should have been greater. Prevailing American impotence within the existing rules of the game could be explained by a decline in perceived security threats to Europe; the years of economic disarray were also the years of detente. Although such a shift in the international environment may have contributed to changes in the early 1970s, the fact that cooperative solutions are more likely in the face of a common threat is not evidence that hegemony or hegemonic leadership is necessary for system stability.

If the United States seemed incapable (or unwilling) to utilize its power resources in the military sphere to make economic gains – as predicted by one type of structuralist argument – perhaps it employed incentives, side payments, or bribes to induce compliance. Structuralist accounts describe inducements offered by the United States to ensure cooperation by its reluctant economic partners – the lopsided trade concessions initially made by the United States to Japan or the European Community, for example. But if the leader must make endless side payments in order to win consent, why should the leader wish to lead? Presumably the collective good represented by the existing order is worth its disproportionate contribution. Nevertheless, arguments from the innate economic preferences of large states are not convincing; one could just as easily argue that a large, relatively closed economy, like the United States, would have benefited most from bilateral economic relations with smaller, weaker states rather than participation in the multilateral postwar system. Three possible explanations present themselves: The costs to the leader were disguised (many becoming apparent only with the passage of time); noneconomic justifications were found for economic concessions on the part of the dominant power (the cold war produced an "exploited hegemon"); or the side payments necessary (and the leadership that they represented) were insignificant because there was underlying elite agreement on the parameters of the international economic order.

If structuralist arguments provide a less than complete explanation for United States behavior or the response of the Western European states in the postwar period, such arguments also fall short in explaining the pattern of international economic outcomes since 1945. The image of the Bretton Woods–GATT system presented in nostalgic accounts of the 1970s exaggerates its longevity and the degree of openness in that system. The Western European states did not accept convertibility of their currencies until 1958; only a few years later the first cracks in the monetary system had appeared and stopgap measures were instituted. Emphasis on the trade concessions made by the United States to ensure European and Japanese cooperation underlines the lingering of discriminatory trading arrangements during the 1950s, and the construction of new ones (such as those between the European Community and its former colonies) in the 1960s.[27] The postwar order was closer to a neoliberal than a neomercantilist model, but there was considerable differentiation in what John Ruggie has described as its "embedded liberalism." [28]

If the immediate postwar decades were not a liberal dream, the 1970s, despite the gloomier prognostications of the structuralists, was not a neomercantilist nightmare. Two predictions emerge from the structuralist emphasis on the distribution of international power. Either the European states should have mounted a coherent challenge to the leadership of the United States to match their growing economic weight (the dream of a European superpower), or, following the Kindleberger variant, the economic order should have collapsed and fragmented into regional blocs with the decline or disappearance of American leadership after 1970. The 1970s did not fulfill either set of predictions. The system that has persisted in Western Europe and among the industrial countries is one that retains high levels of economic openness, despite a certain politicization of economic relations; one in which the boundaries of the political have expanded without the appearance of wholesale mercantilism. If first wave interdependence theorists saw their hopes overturned by the 1970s, the more austere structural theories cannot explain the outcomes of the 1980s. Before we turn to alternative explanations for the new boundaries of the political, however, international economic relations within Europe must be examined. Here, as well, early predictions of the demise of the political were exaggerated.

The European Community: political sources of integration

First wave interdependence theorists postulated a weakening of high politics as a web of economic relationships was woven to restrain the state. Functionalist and neofunctionalist students and proponents of European integration (they were often the same) made similar assertions, with greater certitude, for the European states. For the functionalist, the enemy *was* high politics – source of Europe's bloody civil wars in this century – and the goal was political federation. The pattern of integration was clear: Incremental decision-making by technocrats (nonpoliticians) in areas that were less contentious (non-political) would spill over into other sectors, inspiring more cooperative behavior. Gradually, the hold of the nation-state would be undermined; the web woven here would be even tighter than that proposed by the theorists of economic interdependence.

Neofunctionalists, borrowing from the American pluralist model, accepted politics in the process of integration, arguing that the interest groups and bureaucrats involved in European institutions would demonstrate a transfer of loyalties in the course of bargaining in a new context according to a new "procedural code." But the politics here were of a particular sort as well, drained of ideological conflict, subject to brokerage of the best American kind:

The Europe of adaptative interest groups, bureaucracies, technocrats and other units with modest but pragmatic interests [resembles] the traditional nationalisms of *Grosspolitik* only very remotely.... In such a setting there is but little trace of a purely political dimension ... there is no longer a distinctly political function, separate from economics, welfare, or education, a function which finds its reason for being in the sublime heights of foreign policy, defense and constitution-making.[29]

Although Haas and other neofunctionalists were prepared to toss Gaullism and other nationalist ideologies into the dustbin of history, later expansion of the role awarded the Council of Ministers and Committee of Permanent Representatives (COREPER) within the European Community demonstrated that the European states have outlived de Gaulle. The realm of high politics, once labeled obsolete, seemed to be jealously preserved by the member states.[30]

The role of national states within the European Community extends beyond a simple contrast between high and low politics, however. Measured in terms of domestic political sensitivity, nearly any issue can be high politics for one or another state; questions traditionally categorized as low politics can be more contentious than those touching on defense and diplomacy:

The Community experience tends to show that welfare issues are those in which governments are heavily involved and to which they are obliged to commit political resources. Governments have come to be regarded as welfare agents in Western Europe; their widespread intervention in most aspects of the economy adds an inevitably political dimension to "functional" sectors such as coal and steel and the regulatory aspects of a common market.[31]

At recent meetings of the European Council, statements on foreign policy were often agreed, while issues such as fisheries were not, neatly illustrating this point: Traditional high politics in postwar Europe may represent *lower* domestic political stakes, be more easily insulated from politics, be more "technical" than economic and social questions.[32]

Thirty years of constructing European institutions has produced little erosion of national power along the lines of the neofunctionalist model. Not only has the shift in the hierarchy of issues failed to reduce conflict, little evidence can be found for a transfer of loyalties on the part of national groups or state managers. The "gatekeeping" role of the national states remains effective, although some transnational coalitions have been constructed. In implementing Community policy, national influence is even more significant, given the limited direct means of the Community itself. Whatever the progress in harmonization of national policies or in more positive measures of cooperation, the national governments remain very much in control, confirming Puchala's description of Community institutions as "instruments essentially used by national governments for purposes of domestic problem-solving."[33] Despite fears that currency instability would lead to renationalized agricultural policies, it was quickly discovered that "the Brussels forum offers to the national political leadership a convenient scapegoat and alibi mechanism when it becomes realistically impossible to meet excessive and specialized demands of farm interest groups."[34] Regional policy in the Community resembles the familiar American model of "pork-barrel politics" but does not transcend it; a full-fledged industrial policy hardly exists at the Community level, since governments seem more inclined to deal with such questions of adjustment at the national level or in more global international organizations.[35]

Uneven development in Community policies and institutions has been ideally suited to the *expansion* of state autonomy. Given real hindrances to management of a highly organized domestic political economy open to the international market, the ability of the national elites to choose *among* different forums (national, European, OECD) offers a means of resolving difficult economic dilemmas. The political choices permitted by Community institutions were apparent in the formation of the European Monetary System in 1978. Nothing in the genesis of the EMS fitted the old models of European integration. Although the president of the commission, Roy Jenkins, had floated the idea in late 1977, it was not until the German chancellor and the French president agreed on the initiative that it was undertaken (through the European Council, in contravention of the Treaty of Rome and supranational ideology).[36] The two national leaders sought to further their own economic and political projects through the new monetary arrangements. Chancellor Schmidt could hope to counter the effects of American monetary management on European currencies and, at the same time, assert Germany political leadership within a European context. President Giscard d'Estaing could employ the external levers in the new system to continue an economic strategy shaped by Raymond Barre.[37] Although the EMS could serve as a partial solution to national dilemmas, it was not a sufficient instrument: American monetary policy could still sink the new arrangements; failure to achieve a measure of economic convergence would also undermine the EMS. Economic interdependence and some of its undesirable consequences had encouraged formation of the EMS but did not demand it. National resistance, which quickly surfaced in France, delaying formation of the European Monetary Fund, could still threaten the new system. Politics and the national state were still in command; sovereignty was less at bay than were the forces that pointed toward integration.

Changing boundaries of the political: high politics and the new state activism

The apparent irrelevance of high politics in postwar Europe produced two opposed images of the boundaries of the political in European international relations. The beleaguered state of the early theorists of interdependence and European integration was called in question by renewed state activism in the economic circumstances of the 1970s, yet the malign mercantilist state of the structuralists was nowhere in evidence. State intervention had grown to meet the new conditions imposed by openness to the international market, but such activism has not meant a coherent strategy of partial closure.

The new boundaries of the political, which were not predicted by either the economic determinists or the structuralists, may be unstable, however. In the 1980s a deterioration in relations between the superpowers called into question the permanent demise of security concerns in European politics and produced new fears of politicization in international economic relations as well. The longest and deepest postwar recession, following a weak recovery from the downturn of 1974–75, also threatened the delicate balance between new state roles and the openness of the European economies. The temptations of mercantilist strategies were resisted, but voices advocating such courses received a wider hearing, as Europe groped for a new growth path and solutions to its problems of structural adjustment.

A new international environment: the revival of high politics?

Two mutually reinforcing features of the postwar environment had forced traditional concerns with international security and status from the center of European attention: internationally, the demotion of Europe to security dependence within an international system that offered an acceptable level of guarantee against external threat; domestically, a forswearing of any revival of mass nationalism coupled with the transformation of military strategy into harmless technics. In the 1980s, these familiar features of dependence and depoliticization were challenged more seriously than at any time since 1945.

The first underpinning of Europe's ability to turn from preoccupations of security – stability of the security environment – was weakened by a growing perception of insecurity, military and economic, during the 1970s. Dependence, coupled with growing economic weight (and vulnerability), generated no longer complacency but a galling sense of powerlessness. European dependence on imported petroleum and other raw materials produced in the Third World, sources vulnerable to supply disruptions, meant that concerns for economic security and extraregional stability became prominent once again.

Perceptions of insecurity caused by irresponsible superpowers were also shaped by a dramatic end to the politicization of security questions. While some had hailed the armed division of Europe as guarantee of an era of peace unknown since the nineteenth century, a large and active part of the European public now began to see Europe not as an island of calm, but as a potential battleground. Disarmament and peace movements, often linked to an ecological and antinuclear orientation, enjoyed a resurgence that was strongest in, but not limited to, northern Europe.

In the face of such a potential sea change in European perceptions of their security environment – an environment that had permitted thirty years of carefully sterilized concern with issues of war and peace – some argued for a rebirth of a *European* high politics, a revived military and diplomatic role for the collectivity of European states.[38] Despite the persistent appeal of such a devolution of responsibility within the existing alliance structure, obstacles remain formidable. Many in Europe and the United States do not see a clear divergence between Europe's perceptions of its security requirements and those of its superpower protector: The present set of conflicts can be placed in a postwar pattern of contradictory European fears of too little American commitment on the one hand, and too much confrontation with the Soviet Union on the other. Certain underlying differences, particularly in economic relations – for example, the greater European involvement in Eastern Europe – may tug Western Europe away from the United States; others, such as Europe's greater dependence on Middle Eastern oil reinforced European dependence.

Even perception of clearly divergent interests might not be sufficient to produce a renewed European activism in crafting its own security arrangements. An appropriate organization for European defense is required, and such a role would demand a domestic political base and greater economic resources. The response of the mobilized peace movement to a widened European defense role is unclear: That movement seeks the transformation of the existing defense arrangements in Europe, not their consolidation in a slightly new form. Domestic opposition would also be reinforced by additional costs that could be difficult for flagging European economies to bear. Even Germany, least affected by the reduced growth rates of the 1970s, has had to resist large increases in defense spending urged on it by the United States. While France has managed to extract a substantial real increase in defense spending from its citizens in recent years, the domestic competitors of the defense budget seem too powerful in most European societies to sustain a resurgent reliance on traditional military and diplomatic means for increasing security.

Renewed international economic insecurity might also have stimulated a turn toward external policies reminiscent of classical mercantilism. In the more congenial environment of the 1950s and 1960s, state interference with the market to further goals of international power or to ensure economic security were no more than a quiet counterpoint to the main themes of European economic relations. France in particular had long pursued policies that protected and encouraged sectors crucial to a militarily advanced state – the armaments and nuclear industries, aeronautics and space, and electronics.[39] Concerns over security of supply, heightened after repeated oil shocks and wildly fluctuating commodity prices, also pushed France – energy- and resource-poor – to undertake state-led strategies overseas to develop sources of petroleum, uranium, and other raw materials.[40] Despite a shift in control toward the developing countries, however, most European states, better endowed than France in either multinationals or resources, continued to rely on modified market policies. The classical mercantilist would have attempted to establish more direct political influence over the needed resources; a neoliberal policy of diversification of supply and stockpiling was chosen instead.

The difficulties the European states had in responding coherently (and collectively) to perceived increases in international insecurity suggested to their critics a failure of will, the beginnings of decadence.

The European predicament poses in its sharpest form a more general question, however: whether the "civilian states" that emerged during the stable conditions of the postwar period can re-create policies characteristic of the "security state" of traditional international relations theory. Indeed, at issue in the continuing debate between the inheritors of Gaullism, advocating traditional state roles and strategies, and the new peace movement is whether *any* state can offer its citizens the security against external threats that was formerly a principal claim to its legitimacy. The state may lower risks (through a portfolio approach to such questions as energy or raw materials supplies) and it can attempt to sterilize the issue of external security within the domestic political arena. But military and diplomatic activism in the manner of traditional high politics seems to offer less security of an often irrelevant kind, at a growing cost to the national society and economy.

The interventionist state and the changing international division of labor

If a devaluation of high politics and weakness of classical mercantilist policies had been based in a permissive security environment, European unwillingness to embrace a developmental variant of mercantilism sprang from two persistent features of the European political economy: attachment of the dominant elites to liberal economic ideology, and Europe's relatively secure place in the hierarchy of the international division of labor. Europe's dwarfing within the international power hierarchy had served to inoculate it against one mercantilism; its quick recovery of economic parity with the United States, despite the setbacks of wartime destruction and disrupted trading patterns, served to save it from the second.

Attachment of European capitalism to a generally liberal foreign economic orientation was based on a postwar political constellation that had defeated both the socialist Left and mercantilist or nationalist Right by the early 1950s. The Communists, espousing an autarchic model of socialist development, were shoved to one corner of political life; the dominant Christian Democrats, Social Democrats, and even Conservatives accepted the goal of external liberalization and a reduced role for the state in managing trade and capital flows. Movement toward European integration won its strongest support as well from the center of the political spectrum and from the core of the European economy – the productive belt from Amsterdam to Milan.

In the 1960s there were signs of renewed developmental mercantilism in the face of an "American challenge" across a new generation of industrial sectors. The fear that Europe, falling behind, would become a continent of "hewers of wood and drawers of water" was closely related to the quest for national autonomy described above. Such anxieties found political expression in efforts to restrict American domination of certain sectors, particularly computers, and in industrial policies designed to support a national presence in advanced sectors. More often than not, these strategies foundered on the requirements of the international market and the fragmentation of European industry.[41]

Concern deepened in the 1970s, when it became apparent that the European economies faced competition not only from the United States giant, but from the Japanese intruder as well. Japan was no longer a producer of simple, labor-intensive goods, but a competitor in the core industrial sectors on which European prosperity had been built: steel, automobiles, and shipbuilding. More worrying, the electronics industry, accepted as the pivot of industrial development for the remainder of the century, was increasingly dominated by the United States and Japan. Persisting national attitudes and structures in much of European industries, often encouraged by national industrial policies, prevented European firms from enjoying the same economies of scale and lavish research and development programs as their rivals. Joint European efforts were often unable to submerge the identities of national firms in a common strategy. Frequently, European companies and their government sponsors turned to American and then Japanese partners in search of technological gain.[42]

Fears of falling behind Japan and the United States in the next wave of industrial innovation has spurred state intervention in the form of industrial policy, often in the form of subsidies or disguised protection directed toward sectors regarded as key to the national economic future. Such policies have had an indirect effect on trade among the industrialized countries, leading the United States to push for a subsidies code and other mechanisms for dealing with nontariff distortions of trade in the Tokyo Round of trade negotiations. It has been a second threat to the European position, however, that has produced a "new protectionism" in the 1970s: shifts in comparative advantage toward the developing countries and Japan in a number of core industrial sectors.

Although trade disputes, particularly regarding "surplus capacity" sectors, have continued to flare between the two preponderant poles in the world economy – the United States and Europe – the principal cleavage in trade disputes over the last decade has been between those two on the one hand and Japan and the developing countries on the other. A steep climb in unit labor costs after the mid-1960s indicated that "for activities with a high labor content, the competitive position of the developed countries as a whole, and that of some of them in relation to others has deteriorated since 1968." By this measure, Europe's position has deteriorated more than that of the United States.[43] Pressure on a number of labor-intensive industries – textiles, footwear, consumer electronics – has grown, and so have protectionist measures, although the significance of those measures for developing country exports is a matter of dispute.[44] Most of the threat to prevailing commercial arrangements has come from piecemeal restrictions benefiting particular sectors and particular groups in the work force. In those sectors severely affected by surplus capacity during the 1974–75 recession and again in 1980–83 (textiles, steel, shipbuilding), government intervention and the role of quasi-corporatist interest groups rose. The solutions effected, however, resembled a model of organized trade with limited protection rather than the closure of domestic markets.[45]

The official view of Third World industrialization remained benign, emphasizing the benefits of North–South trade to European economies in aggregate terms and pointing out the much greater effect of technological change on employment. Even official prose, however, could not disguise the likelihood of substantial social costs in adjustment, particularly in individual sectors and among unskilled and semi-skilled workers; and governments bore some responsibility for accelerating the shfit in comparative advantage through policies of investment guarantees and export credits, policies which spurred the migration of industry to the south.[46]

Given the prospect of politically painful adjustment and a rhetorical and institutional attachment to free trade, governments turned to a combination of policies that would secure the benefits of economic openness, while cushioning its more uncomfortable aspects. In dealing with changes in the pattern of international competition, the new model of intervention in the 1970s was not a revival of the "strong state," blocking out international market signals to the detriment of future economic development, but the "smart state," accepting shifts, however reluctantly, in international comparative advantage or changes in the costs of imports (such as energy) and forcing its economy toward a structure better suited for international competition. Designing policies aimed at microeconomic change rather than simply macroeconomic stabilization, the smart state would ideally face structural change by using its array of policies to encourage positive adjustment rather than deploying state power to arrest change.

Use of industrial policy (defined as instruments to promote structural change in the economy) by such a state was not a self-evident boon in the eyes of laissez-faire critics of intervention. They questioned the ability of any state, however intelligent, to second-guess the market through its analysis and policy prescriptions. Such policies could easily become a form of disguised protectionism – less transparent than older forms and subject to less international scrutiny and no time limit.

Other criticisms have been political: the smart state must *also* be a strong state to carry out such a forecasting and steering role, and the existing European polities are simply not strong enough. States that aspire to such roles are also *penetrated* states, reflecting existing patterns of international competition and existing industrial structures. Undertaking a program of positive or even preemptive adjustment would require the political feat of state action oriented toward parts of the economy that were only beginning to develop and state neglect of those sectors, no matter how powerful, that were judged to lack a future in international competition.

Although industrial policies have been widely employed by European governments, the record of success is mixed at best: While macroeconomic policies could at least pretend to remain above the political fray, sectoral policies are by their nature intensely political. Each decision taken – for example, whether to close a plant or to subsidize investment in it – is filled with direct, easily perceived distributional consequences. Given the political balance, the result is, in many cases, protection of lame duck industries rather than the encouragement of "sunrise" (and therefore politically weak) sectors for the future.[47] Even less targeted programs to deal with shifts in international economic position, such as incentives to increase investment in plant and equipment, raises the question of investment by whom, for whose benefit. A consensus in Sweden on the need to respond to changes in the international division of labor (declining markets for Sweden's raw materials exports and a shift in favor of new industrial competitors) did not produce consensus on the Meidner Plan proposals to award labor unions greater control over companies in exchange for wage restraint. In such circumstances of social conflict, industrial policies may become not evidence of political intelligence in the face of international competition, but simply incoherent, piecemeal means of shifting the burdens of adjustment from one group to another.[48]

Throughout the debate over these ostensibly domestic policies runs the thread of protectionism. The question posed by Wyn Grant – "can one combine a selective intervention policy with an essentially nondiscriminatory trade policy?" – is a two-sided one. If opponents of such state intervention view industrial policies as eroding the liberal trading order, proponents wonder if they have any hope of success without at least temporary shielding from international competition.[49] Even though governments in the 1970s and 1980s clung to their liberal rhetoric and attempted in an ad hoc way to deal with the pain of adjustment, other observers took a much more alarmist view of Europe's position in the international economy: "Powerless to lift itself to the level of dominant industrial nations, closely followed by the developing countries, France is caught in a vise."[50] Confronted with the growing international economic instability of the 1970s and the apparent threat to Europe's position from the onrushing newly industrializing countries, more coherent and radical criticisms of the liberal nostrums in European external relations have been raised. Before the 1978 legislative elections in France, government spokesmen called for "a genuine organization of international trade" and "organized liberalism." Soon thereafter, Jean-Marcel Jeanneney, a prominent civil servant under de Gaulle, delivered a manifesto in favor of a "new protectionism," breaking with the "sudden unanimity" that developed after 1945 around free trade. Jeanneney employed many familiar arguments – protection of infant industries, avoidance of excessive dependence on the international market, lowering the social costs of adjustment – but made a clear break in declaring that control of commercial policy is a legitimate instrument of economic management.[51] His arguments for protectionism or "managed trade" at the European level were later echoed by André Grjebine and Wolfgang Hager.[52] None of these newest protectionists attacked liberalized trade among the European (or Atlantic) industrialized economies; indeed, Hager makes part of his argument for protectionism the threat that national responses to international competition may pose to the European Community and its internal market. Grjebine and Hager both award the newly industrializing countries (NICS) a primary role in the assault on Europe's previously dominant place in the international division of labor; for Hager in particular, the alternatives – positive adjustment, an assault on real wages in Europe, and increasing government subsidies – are all much less desirable than a turn toward protectionism. In any case, adjustment would be not to some posited world market but to the interventionist policies of other states, particularly those in the developing countries.

Although such ideological assaults on free trade may serve to erode its hold on European politics, the evidence of such erosion, apart from the piecemeal protectionism already described, is not yet perceptible. The threat of a genuine protectionist strategy has sprung not from the shifting international divisions of labor, but from the demands of macroeconomic management.

The state as stabilizer: external and internal demands

Countercyclical mercantilism, a policy born of desperation during the Great Depression, disappeared from Western Europe after the successful stabilization of capitalist economies through Keynesian demand management and the creation of the welfare state. In place of policies that could at best reduce insecurity while at the same time reducing potential growth, the European economies seemed to combine successfully a new domestic activism on the part of the government with gradual liberalization externally. (Agriculture was a major exception: It had heralded the slump of the 1930s and remained the object of protectionist stabilization policies after 1945.)

The experience of the open economies of Western Europe suggests, counter to certain economic orthodoxies, that state intervention has been linked to, and may have been necessary for, the receding of government control over external transactions. David Cameron has associated the size of the "public economy" in a number of European cases with the structural effects of openness.[53] Peter Katzenstein, in comparing the experiences of the smaller European states, ties domestic economic management and external liberalism more closely:

The experience of the small European states suggests instead that political intervention in the domestic economy in the interests of stabilization does not constrain international liberalization but is its necessary concomitant. In the 1970s conspicuous deviations from the principle of free trade occurred primarily where well-designed broad-ranging domestic stabilization policies were lacking.[54]

This happy marriage of domestic intervention and external openness may be less stable than Katzenstein suggests, however. International and domestic contradictions within the virtuous combination of the postwar consensus became evident in the 1970s. First, the efficacy of the instruments of stabilization was less certain in conditions of increased sensitivity to the international economic environment. While some hoped that a regime of floating exchange rates would solve the dilemma portrayed by Richard Cooper and restore policy autonomy to national governments, a decade of more flexible exchange arrangements has not provided a high degree of policy insulation. A recent summary of research on the effects of exchange rate flexibility concluded that

in a world of high international capital mobility and high substitutability between assets (including monies) in different countries, policy autonomy is a myth, regardless of exchange rate regime. . . . Since policy autonomy is not achievable anyway, all countries have an interest in policy coordination to ensure that their macroeconomic and exchange-rate policies do not work at cross purposes.[55]

To regain a measure of control in the management of their economies, then, national elites must give up some autonomy in the course of international bargaining over strategies of economic management. So far, that leap has not been taken successfully, within the confines of Western Europe or within the Atlantic area. Although the European Monetary System, more flexible than the preceding "snake," has survived a deep international recession and conflicts in the macroeconomic policy choices of its members (particularly France and Germany), the brinksmanship and hard bargaining that has surrounded successive exchange rate realignments suggests the domestic political stakes associated with such choices. In addition to persistent differences in the preferences of national elites and their electorates (unemployment and inflation trade-offs, for example), political business cycles are also often out of step. Differing national institutional structures have given most countries a bias toward one set of instruments, which may not match the demands of coordination. Even if coordination were being attempted by economies less interdependent, the lags between decision and effective implementation would often produce perverse results. Despite token efforts at economic summits, therefore, national elites have chosen the certainty of declining effectiveness over the perils of coordination with the same risk.[56]

Other potential conflicts have arisen between the existing cluster of stabilization policies and the imperative of economic openness. Conservative critics have argued with increasing force that the welfare state – used to cushion external shocks and render them politically palatable – may produce yet more distortions in the pattern of international trade.[57] In this view, the protective canopy of the welfare state might hinder adjustment to changing patterns of international competition or external shocks by increasing rigidities in the labor market. Thus, one of the pillars of the postwar political and economic consensus, already under attack for budgetary and ideological reasons (as discussed in this volume by Pen and Goldthorpe), is subjected to criticism as a disguised form of protection. Yet, if its cushion is removed, political reaction against high levels of economic openness might produce a political consensus for closure that is still absent in most European societies.

If conservative critics attack welfare state policies for their external implications, those on the Left see the contradiction between economic openness and macroeconomic policy in different terms. A strategic break with the postwar consensus has appeared in Britain, an economy that has scarcely benefited from European integration, a peripheral economy threatened, in the eyes of some, with deindustrialization. The intellectual inheritance for this protectionist argument is less the developmental mercantilism of List (as in the cases of Jeanneney or Hager) than of the protectionist Keynes of the Great Depression.[58] A group of Cambridge economists, led by Wynne Godley and Francis Cripps, have argued that British manufacturing is trapped in a disequilibrium position characterized by low investment, poor export performance, and high import penetration. This secular industrial decline cannot be halted by conventional means "at socially acceptable levels of output, employment and the exchange rate."[59] To break out of the existing disequilibrium and halt the decline of British industry, a higher level of growth and investment is required; that course is barred (or will be barred, after North Sea oil production declines) by Britain's high propensity to import manufactures and the resulting fragility of its balance-of-payments position. The New Cambridge solution: abandoning free trade in favor of a system of general, not selective, import controls.

The countercyclical bases of this neoprotectionist strategy is made clear by the New Cambridge emphasis on general import controls, in contrast to their counterparts elsewhere in Europe. The targets of protectionism are not the newly industrializing countries, but persistent surplus industrial countries, especially Germany and Japan.[60] Concentration on the threat from other industrial countries whose industrial base has grown more successfully in the recent past brings back all the dilemmas of coordinating macroeconomic management. Recent statements of the Cambridge Economic Policy Group have shifted from advocacy of British withdrawal from the European Community to concern with the need for concerted reflation of the European economies. But the need for macroeconomic coordination at the European level – already proven difficult to achieve – accords ill with the protectionist elements in the Cambridge strategy, with the ever-present threat of spiraling retaliation.

This and other variants of protectionism as a strategy for European states have found echoes in the politics of only two European states, Britain and France. Germany, more successful to this point in adjustment and more centered on Europe in its trading patterns, has continued to defend liberalized trade within the European Community and without. The absence of widespread protectionist themes in Italy may reflect an awareness of the requirements of economic interdependence across the political spectrum or simply the achievements of formal and informal Italian protectionism already in place.[61]

On the British Left, and particularly among the trade unions, the strategy of general import controls has been assimilated to the more familiar selective protectionism designed to protect ailing industrial sectors. It is in France, however, that the key debate over external strategy has taken place in the 1980s, and at its base has been not anxiety over France's place in the future international division of labor, but a conflict between the expansionist macroeconomic strategy pursued by the Mitterrand government in 1981–82 and the balance-of-payments constraint which that strategy encountered during a global recession.

Despite rhetoric of "reconquering the internal market" and echoes of Grjebine's strategy of "self-reliant development" (*développement autocentré*), the external economic policies of the Socialist government in France did not initially depart radically from those of the past. The government's hints at protectionism were balanced by a strong Europeanist and *tier-mondiste* orientation. As the government pursued its Keynesian expansionism in the face of resistance from its principal trading partners (particularly Germany), it was forced to undertake successive devaluations of the franc and to impose a wage freeze painful for its working-class supporters. This overt conflict between internal demands and external constraints led some within the Socialist coalition to propose a protectionist alternative. The key decision against such a strategy came in March 1983, when Mitterrand decided in favor of the program of his finance minister, Jacques Delors – a third devaluation and even more stringent fiscal measures to correct the external imbalance. The debate within the Socialist Party was far from over when the Right came back to face comparable alternatives. For both coalitions the division concerned not so much protectionism in itself, but rather whether France should attempt a clear-cut and general policy of import controls or continue with disguised and selective measures.

The Mitterrand government's choice of orthodox stabilization measures within the European community suggested both the power of the postwar ideological consensus on trade liberalization (even in the country where external liberalism is weakest) and the importance of international restraints on national economic policy after decades of growing economic openness in Western Europe. Nevertheless, the fact that a debate challenging those tenets could take place in a major European state indicates the erosion that could take place in the context of worsening economic conditions, an economic context produced in part by the inability of governments to coordinate their macroeconomic policies.

The external face of politics: state roles and political boundaries

Using received images of the state in its international context – such as mercantilism – may point to continuities, but reliance on those images in new circumstances may be misleading. The state of traditional high politics has played a minor role in European international relations since 1945, yet the concerns of high politics – war and peace, dealing with external threats – have not disappeared. The frustration sometimes displayed by the Europeans differs only in degree from the plight of other states whose traditional instruments for ensuring security seem to have less and less utility. Disputes between the United States and the Europeans over Middle Eastern policy are in certain respects an argument between those who still accept the traditional notions of military power and diplomacy directed toward a well-defined adversary and those who interpret threats to economic security as more diffuse and difficult to define, threats against which traditional instruments of diplomacy and force are likely to prove ineffective at best. An even deeper challenge to traditional notions of security has been mounted by the European peace movement, calling into question both the technocratic approach to security policy and those tenets of deterrence endorsed for more than three decades. Despite the success of the movement in political mobilization, a convincing security alternative for Western Europe – apart from modifications of the present strategy of flexible response – has yet to be presented.

In similar fashion, despite the pressure placed on existing economic and social policies by new conditions of economic openness and rapid evolution in the international economy, no new mix has emerged to replace the combination of domestic economic intervention and external liberalism in the way that present policies replaced the neomercantilism of the 1930s and 1940s. From one vantage point, the present boundaries of the political are both stable and beneficial. The foundations of Western Europe's liberal external orientation remain in place: continued separation of security and international economic policies (despite efforts by the United States to link the two); attachment to a liberal external strategy by most elements of both Left and Right; a reasonably secure place in the international division of labor, despite alarms and anxieties concerning Japan and the NICs. The state has replaced crude instruments in dealing with the international market with a more sophisticated approach that accepts its limitations in confronting the demands of economic openness.

A less optimistic view notes passive, "civilian" states incapable of devising collective or individual strategies to secure external security;

states too penetrated to serve the steering role necessary in difficult world economic conditions; states incapable of effectively carrying out the tasks of economic stabilization and unwilling to concede any part of that role to a cooperative arena where the chances of success might be greater. Existing political boundaries of the state in Western Europe can be viewed in either way. Despite the strains that have appeared after a decade of rising insecurity and economic shocks, however, a major shift in the international boundaries of the political seems unlikely.

Notes

1 This theme has been developed in the work of Otto Hintze and, more recently, in Theda Skocpol, *States and Social Revolutions* (Cambridge: Cambridge University Press, 1979), and Perry Anderson, *Lineages of the Absolutist State* (London: New Left Books, 1974).

2 Charles Maier, "The Politics of Productivity: Foundations of American International Economic Policy After World War II," in Peter Katzenstein, ed., *Between Power and Plenty: Foreign Economic Policies of Advanced Industrial States* (Madison: University of Wisconsin Press, 1978), p. 47.

3 Michael Howard, "The Forgotten Dimensions of Strategy," *Foreign Affairs* 57, 5 (Summer 1979): 982.

4 Stanley Hoffmann, "An American Social Science: International Relations," *Daedalus* 106, 3 (Summer 1977): 41–60.

5 Jean Baechler, *The Origins of Capitalism* (Oxford: Basil Blackwell, 1975), p. 77.

6 The classic statement is Eli Heckscher, *Mercantilism*, 2nd ed. (New York: Macmillan, 1955). Heckscher's emphasis on power as the sole goal of mercantilist policy was contested by Jacob Viner in "Power Versus Plenty Under Mercantilism," in D. C. Coleman, ed., *Revisions in Mercantilism* (London: Methuen, 1969), p. 71.

7 The original and most influential statement of developmental mercantilism is Friedrich List, *The National System of Political Economy* (New York: Longmans, Green, 1928).

8 W. Arthur Lewis, *Economic Survey, 1919–1939* (London:Allen & Unwin, 1949), chap. 12; League of Nations, *Commercial Policy in the Interwar Period: International Proposals and National Policies* (Geneva: League of Nations, 1942), chap. 4.

9 A good general account can be found in the League of Nations study cited in note 8.

10 For example, the sterling bloc, a fairly loose arrangement in the 1930s, was reinforced by the financial demands of war. J. D. B. Miller, *Survey of Commonwealth Affairs: Problems of Expansion and Attrition, 1953–1969* (Oxford: Oxford University Press, 1974), p. 441.

11 Alan S. Milward, *War, Economy and Society, 1939–1945* (London: Allen Lane, 1977), p. 130.

12 Ibid., pp. 352–355.

13 Richard Cooper, *The Economics of Interdependence* (New York: McGraw-Hill, 1968), p. 10.

14 Marina v. N. Whitman, *Sustaining the International Economic System*, Essays in International Finance no. 121, (Princeton, N.J.: Princeton University, International Finance Section, 1977) p. 3.

15 Robert O. Keohane and Joseph S. Nye, *Power and Interdependence* (Boston: Little, Brown, 1977), pp. 24–37. Edward Morse also described the "increased significance of low policies and the emergence of cooperative strategies in foreign policy" as a result of transnational relations and interdependence, but then swiftly noted that the degree of cooperative behavior should not be overestimated, in his *Modernization and the Transformation of International Relations* (New York: Free Press, 1976) pp. 92–93.

16 Richard Cooper, "Economic Interdependence and Foreign Policy in the Seventies," *World Politics* 24, 2 (January 1972): 168–171.

17 Although Nye and Keohane share some of the characteristics of the second wave of theorists (to be described below), they stated that complex interdependence "will increasingly characterize world politics," because of "long-term historical change with deep causes of its own." (*Power and Interdependence*, p. 227).

18 Ibid., p. 13.

19 Politicization was emphasized by Fred Hirsch and Michael Doyle in *Alternatives to Monetary Disorder* (New York: McGraw-Hill, 1977), pp. 12–14.

20 During the late 1970s, the structural point of view became a new conventional wisdom in the study of international political economy in both Europe and the United States. Variations include Hirsch and Doyle, *Alternatives to Monetary Disorder*; Robert G. Gilpin, *U.S. Power and the Multinational Corporation* (New York: Basic, 1975); Stephen D. Krasner, "State Power and the Structure of International Trade," *World Politics* 28, 3 (April 1976):317–347; and Robert Skidelsky, "The Decline of Keynesian Politics," in Colin J. Crouch, ed., *State and Economy in Contemporary Capitalism* (New York: St. Martin's, 1979), pp. 55–87. Keohane and Nye tested the structural hypothesis for regime change in *Power and Interdependence*.

For a closer look, see Robert O. Keohane, "The Theory of Hegemonic Stability and Changes in International Economic Regimes, 1967–1977," in Ole R. Holsti, Randolph Siverson, and Alexander George, eds., *Change in the International System* (Boulder, Colo.: Westview, 1980), pp. 131–162. Unfortunately, Keohane was attempting to test for regime change, whereas most of the structural theories are designed to explain stability or openness, not quite the same thing. More recently, some have taken a more critical look at the assumptions of structural theories in different historical contexts: David Laitin, "Capitalism and Hegemony: Yorubaland and the International Economy," *International Organization* 36, 4 (Autumn 1982): 687–714; Timothy J. McKeown, "Hegemonic Stability Theory and 19th Century Tariff Levels in Europe," *International Organization* 37, 1 (Winter 1983): 73–92; Peter F. Cowhey and Edward Long, "Testing Theories of Regime Change: Hegemonic Decline or Surplus Capacity?" *International Organization* 37, 2 (Spring 1983): 157–188.

21 Gilpin, *U.S. Power*, p. 260.

22 Kindleberger develops his argument in *The World in Depression, 1929–1939* (Berkeley and Los Angeles: University of California Press, 1973) and his "Systems of International Economic Organization," in David P. Calleo, ed., *Money and the Coming World Order* (New York: New York University Press, 1976), pp. 15–39.

23 Kindleberger, *World in Depression*, p. 292.

24 Ibid., p. 305.

25 For example, Susan Strange, "*Cave! hic dragones*: A Critique of Regime Analysis," *International Organization* 36, 2 (Spring 1982):481–483.

26 Richard N. Cooper, "Trade Policy Is Foreign Policy," in Richard N. Cooper, ed., *A Reordered World* (Washington, D.C.: Potomac Associates, 1973), pp. 46–61.

27 Gardner Patterson, *Discrimination in International Trade: The Policy Issues, 1945–1965* (Princeton, N.J.: Princeton University Press, 1966), describes the discriminatory commercial arrangements during the period.

28 John Gerard Ruggie, "International Regimes, Transactions, and Change: Embedded Liberalism in the Postwar Economic Order," *International Organization* 36, 2 (Spring 1982); 379–415.

29 Ernst Haas, "Technocracy, Pluralism and the New Europe," in Stephen R. Graubard, ed., *A New Europe?* (Boston: Beacon, 1964), pp. 67, 71.

30 Stanley Hoffmann, "Obstinate or Obsolete? France, European Integration, and the Fate of the Nation-State," in Stanley Hoffmann, ed., *Decline or Renewal?* (New York: Viking, 1974), pp. 363–402.

31 Carole Webb, "Introduction: Variations on a Theoretical Theme," in Helen Wallace, William Wallace, and Carole Webb, eds., *Policy-making in the European Communities* (New York: Wiley, 1977), pp. 10–11. I have drawn upon Webb's account of competing theories of European integration throughout this section.

32 William Wallace, "Walking Backwards Towards Unity," in ibid., pp. 309–310.

33 Donald J. Puchala, "Domestic Politics and Regional Harmonization in the European Communities," *World Politics* 28, 4 (July 1975):519.

34 Werner Feld, "Implementation of the European Community's Common Agricultural Policy: Expectations, Fears, Failures," *International Organization* 33, 3 (Summer 1979): 362.

35 Helen Wallace, "The Establishment of the Regional Development Fund: Common Policy or Pork Barrel?" in Wallace, Wallace, and Webb, *Policy-making*, p. 161; Michael Hodges, "Industrial Policy: A Directorate-General in Search of a Role," in *Policy-making*, p. 130; Loukas Tsoukalis and Antonio da Silva Ferreira, "Management of Industrial Surplus Capacity in the European Community," *International Organization* 34, 3 (Summer 1980): 355–376.

36 Tom de Vries, *On the Meaning and Future of the European Monetary System*, Essays in International Finance no. 138 (Princeton, N.J.: Princeton University, International Finance Section, 1980), pp. 8–9.

37 Ibid., pp. 10–11.

38 Recent statements of this perspective include Pieter Dankert, "Europe Together, America Apart," *Foreign Policy* 53 (Winter 1983–84): 18–33; and Hedley Bull, "European Self-Reliance and the Reform of NATO," *Foreign Affairs* 61, 4 (Spring 1983): 874–892.

39 The best account of Gaullist policies to stimulate technological and scientific development remains Robert G. Gilpin, *France in the Age of the Scientific State* (Princeton, N.J.: Princeton University Press, 1968).

40 Robert J. Lieber, "Energy Policies of the Fifth Republic: Autonomy Versus Constraint," in William G. Andrews and Stanley Hoffman, eds., *The Fifth Republic at Twenty* (Albany: SUNY Press, 1981), pp. 311–328.

41 As described in John Zysman, *Political Strategies for Industrial Order: State, Market, and Industry in France* (Berkeley and Los Angeles: University of California Press, 1977). French policy has taken the form of mergers, export support, and the creation of protected internal markets through public purchasing and controls over direct investment.

42 *Facing the Future*, Interfutures Report (Paris: OECD, 1979), pp. 336–346; Raymond Vernon, *Storm over the Multinationals* (Cambridge, Mass.: Harvard University Press, 1977), pp. 48–51.

43 *Facing the Future*, pp. 152–154.

44 *The Rise in Protectionism* (Washington, D.C.: International Monetary Fund Pamphlet no. 24, 1978). The literature on the newly industrializing countries grew nearly as fast as their exports in the 1970s. Some examples: *The Impact of the Newly Industrializing Countries on Production and Trade in Manufactures*, Report from the Secretary-General (Paris: OECD, 1979); "The Newly Industrializing Countries and the Adjustment Prob-

lem," Government Economic Service Working Paper no. 18 (London: Foreign and Commonwealth Office, 1979); Commissariat général du plan, *Le défi économique du tiers-monde* (Paris: Documentation française, 1978). For a less alarmist view of the new protectionism in Europe and its impact on the developing countries, see Helen Hughes and Jean Waelbroeck, "Foreign Trade and Structural Adjustment: Is There a Threat of New Protectionism?" in Hans-Gert Braun, Helmut Laumer, Willi Leibfritz, and Heidemarie C. Sherman, eds., *The European Economy in the 1980s* (Aldershot, England: Gower, 1983), pp. 1–29.

45   Susan Strange, "The Management of Surplus Capacity: Or How Does Theory Stand Up to Protectionism, 1970s Style?" *International Organization* 33, 3, (Summer 1979): 332.

46   *Facing the Future*, p. 159.

47   Suzanne Berger, "Lame Ducks and National Champions: Industrial Policy in the Fifth Republic," in William G. Andrews and Stanley Hoffman, eds., *The Impact of the Fifth Republic on France* (Albany: SUNY Press, 1981), pp. 160–178.

48   An excellent summary of the tortuous history of industrial policy in one European country – Britain – is given in Wyn Grant, *The Political Economy of Industrial Policy* (London: Butterworth, 1982).

49   Ibid., p. 128.

50   Christian Stoffaes, *La grande menace industrielle* (Paris: Calmann-Levy, 1978), p. 87.

51   Jean-Marcel Jeanneney, *Pour un nouveau protectionisme* (Paris: Seuil, 1978).

52   André Grjebine, *La nouvelle économie internationale*, 2nd ed. (Paris: Presses Universitaires de France, 1982). Hager's arguments, which have become more explicitly protectionist, may be found in the following: "The Strains on the International System," in Christopher Saunders, ed., *The Political Economy of New and Old Industrial Countries* (London: Butterworth, 1981); "Industrial Policy, Trade Policy, and European Social Democracy," in John Pinder, ed., *National Industrial Strategies and the World Economy* (Totowa, N.J.: Allanheld, Osmun, 1982), pp. 265–288; "Protectionism and Autonomy: How to Preserve Free Trade in Europe," *International Affairs* 58, 2 (Summer 1982):413–428.

53   David R. Cameron, "The Expansion of the Public Economy: A Comparative Analysis," *American Political Science Review* 72, 4 (December 1978): 1243–1261.

54   Peter J. Katzenstein, "Capitalism in One Country?: Switzerland in the International Economy," *International Organization* 34, 4 (Autumn 1980):533.

55   Morris Goldstein, "Have Flexible Exchange Rates Handicapped Macroeconomic Policy?", *Special Papers in International Economics* (Princeton, N.J.: Princeton University, International Finance Section, 1980) pp. 64–65.

56   Jacques Pelkmans, "Economic Cooperation Among Western Countries," in Robert J. Gordon and Jacques Pelkmans, eds., *Challenge to Interdependent Economies* (New York: McGraw-Hill, 1979), pp. 116–117.

57   For example, Melvyn B. Krauss, *The New Protectionism: The Welfare State and International Trade* (New York: New York University Press, 1978).

58   For Keynes's move toward protectionism during the Great Depression and his subsequent endorsement of liberalized trade, see R. F. Harrod, *The Life of John Maynard Keynes* (London: Macmillan, 1951), pp. 424–431, 446, 608–610.

59   Ajit Singh, "UK Industry and the World Economy: A Case of Deindustrialisation?" *Cambridge Journal of Economics* 1 (1977):128.

60   Francis Cripps, in a recent article, stated that the "most important issue of all is the Common Market for industrial products, since the main external sources of competition causing deindustrialisation in the UK are industries in other member

countries within the Community" ("Government Planning as a Means to Economic Recovery in the UK," *Cambridge Journal of Economics* 5 [1981]: 100).

61 One of the economists of the Italian Communist Party described Italy's position: "Some attribute the instability of the Italian economy to its high degree of foreign dependence, but every illusion, all wishful thinking about self-sufficiency should be rejected, [for] the increasingly marked interdependence of Italy with respect to the world market is determined by the peculiar, objective nature of our country." (Cited in Robert D. Putnam, "Interdependence and the Italian Communists," *International Organization* 32, 2 (Spring 1978): 315–316.

Part III

Uncertain boundaries for political economy

10

Expanding budgets in a stagnating economy: the experience of the 1970s

JAN PEN

The budget as mirror

The shifting boundaries between the political and the private are reflected in the ratio (hereafter rendered G/Y) of government expenditures to the national income. In this sense the budget can be seen, according to Kurt Heinig, as a mirror of the sociopolitical situation. If taken lightly, this image is illuminating. Upon reflection, it becomes dubious. One might say that the mirror is funny: Important types of government intervention (cruel prosecution under a dictatorship) can be introduced or abolished without government expenditures showing what is happening. Regulatory power in economic affairs is not necessarily proportional to the number of government employees. On the other hand, some substantial increases in public outlays reflect not so much increasing government operations as transfers between citizens, for instance, the prosperous expansion of the grants economy. Another shortcoming of G/Y as a measure of the balance between the activities of governments and governed is that budgets do not reveal the full size of activities on behalf of the authorities, which are often costly. For instance, the labor of the tax-filing, tax-paying citizen is nowhere registered.[1] As shifts between the public and the private domain are occurring in opposite directions it is not certain that their net impact is truly measured by the increase in G/Y. The recent retreat of some European governments on the issues of abortion, homosexuality, and pornography did not lead to a significant decrease in government outlays; but the substantial advance in education, housing, and welfare did lead to strong and sometimes explosive increases. One might hypothesize that governments have been retreating in the less expensive sectors, while the intensified public programs are costly. Education and the health industry are examples of very expensive operations.

323

However that may be, G/Y plays a crucial role in current political discussions. One obvious reason is that government outlays have to be financed. The ratio G/Y corresponds, more or less, to the tax "burden." Another reason is that G/Y has shown a steady upward trend. This is in accordance with Adolph Wagner's law; the assertion that the government's share in the economy will rise with rising income is about a hundred years old. This is one of the best-fulfilled predictions in economics. In particular, postwar Western Europe has shown a clear upward movement in the quotient of government expenditures over GNP. On average, this ratio rose from roughly 20 percent in 1950 to roughly 45 percent in 1980. This is the figure for the German Federal Republic, France, and the United Kingdom. In the Scandinavian countries and the Netherlands G/Y well exceeded 50 percent. In Italy the ratio was lower – about 40 percent in 1980. In Spain it was still below 30 percent. If the trend resumes, G/Y will, as an impressionistic Western European average, exceed the 50 percent mark.[2]

At the same time, many observers suspect that a continuing increase in the government's share cannot go on without harming the economic and political systems. Concern, and sometimes alarm, are inspired not so much by the public programs themselves, but by the amount of taxation necessary to finance them. It is said that private enterprise and the market economy cannot bear the high tax rates. The ratio of tax revenue, including social security premiums, to the GNP now exceeds 40 percent (this is lower than G/Y because of budgetary deficits). The ensuing market failure, unemployment, and loss of tax revenue will backfire into political life. Milton Friedman and his partisans are known to predict stagnation and eventual doom if the trend is not reversed. According to this school, there exists "a line we dare not cross,"[3] which seems to be located at 60 percent. Now these glum reflections lose some of their credibility, first, because in the 1960s high levels of G/Y proved compatible with very rapid economic growth, particularly in Sweden, the German Federal Republic, and the Low Countries; and, second, because the Friedman school are no friends of government intervention in general – their warnings are tailored to their ideological preferences. But in recent years the suspicion that budgets have come close to the limits of what the economy and the polity can bear has become more widespread. Critics of the increasing tax burden and of growing budgetary deficits are now to be found among those who are not politically adverse to the welfare state. Even some socialists feel uneasy about steeply rising tax rates and social security contributions. Their misgivings have been sharpened by the recession and stagnation of the late 1970s and early

1980s. Unemployment rates of almost 10 percent draw attention to the fact that the welfare state needs a sound private sector. It is basically a mixed economy – and there is much talk of increased tax burdens being incompatible with a satisfactory recovery of private investment and private employment and even with the long-term viability of the business sector.

These concerns are acquiring a new edge now that future growth rates of the GNP, which over the period 1968–78 were still about 3.5 percent, are likely to diminish, perhaps to zero. The European average for 1980 was one percent. Britain's GNP went down by 2.5 percent. The combination of a stagnant Y and an increasing G/Y is seen as particularly threatening. Sometimes governments are blamed for this combination – critics from various quarters say that they have been governing insufficiently. Problems like inflation, pollution, unemployment, and crime have been drifting. But in other fields the public sector has been too aggressive, in particular with respect to taxation and therefore to private investment, which has indeed suffered a setback. Controlling or redirecting public expenditures will become one of the most acute issues of the coming decades. This paper discusses the prospect of rising budgets in a typical welfare state combined with slow growth, unemployment, and continuous wage inflation.

The basic idea put forth in this chapter is that budgets are made not by abstract "forces" but by governments in a democratic environment – that is, by political and bureaucratic decision makers who have to reconcile many goals, some of them contradictory. My approach stresses that there is scope for options. But it cannot be denied that government expenditures are determined by many "automatic" processes. They originate from the fact that, given institutional and legal arrangements, citizens have acquired rights, which they may use. The extent to which these rights are called on is the result of social and economic developments, which governments cannot fully control. The right to unemployment compensation is a conspicuous case in point: Stagnation and "jobless growth" may lead to enormously increased public outlays. But there are many similar mechanisms, for example, swollen interest payments as public deficits grow. The problem of expanding budgets in a stagnating economy is therefore a peculiar mixture of freedom and necessity.

Transfer expenditures versus the genuine public sector

In one particular sense G/Y is an exaggerated indicator of the government sector: public expenditures partly consist of transfer payments to private persons or institutions. They are not "public" or "collective" in the usual sense of nonexclusivity or indivisibility. This point is well known, but its implications are often overlooked. Government activity is best measured by the government's command over real resources, G_R. These are outlays for labor (the civil service, teachers: such outlays equal public production) plus purchases from private firms (road building, military equipment, and so on). Unfortunately, G_R lacks a generally accepted label; perhaps "genuine public expenditures" is the least confusing term.[4]

Transfers, G_T, are made to private persons, foundations, and firms. They include social security benefits, subsidies to agriculture, grants to hospitals and orchestras. Their main purpose is income maintenance, although in some cases that goal consists of influencing and directing economic activity. This is the case with much-debated "merit goods," especially in housing, health, and the arts. These transfers certainly point to government responsibilities and political goals – indeed, they are an essential ingredient of the welfare state. But their rapid increase is a misleading measure for the shifting boundaries between the public and the private. Grants widen the spending power of the recipients, at the cost of the taxpayers, without increasing government production or government consumption. Transfers increase the power of the authorities in the sense that they decide who is eligible; they also increase the power to impose on the beneficiaries certain types of behavior (job search, the production of plays, industrial innovation). Yet this power is not measured by the total amount of the transfers. Social security outlays – combined with part of the direct expenditures on education, housing, and the medical sector – are a plausible measure for the welfare state, but not for the public command over resources or for the degree of public intervention.

The distinction between G_R and G_T is vital to our understanding of what has recently happened to the public sector.[5] The term G_R is an allocative measure for government activity; it is a crude indicator for the share of government in the economy. The term "G_T" is not an allocative figure but a distributive measure. In 1950 European budgets were still dominated by government spending on education, defense, road building, and the civil service. Transfer expenditures constituted the smaller part of G. They amounted to less than 10 percent of GNP. But since then the size of the two categories has been converging. As a European average, G_T is now over 20 percent of GNP. The major part of these grants consists of social security benefits; they amount to roughly 15 percent of GNP. The dramatic increase in G/Y, from 20 percent to 45 percent, resulted in particular from a sharp rise in social security payments. The cost of education also increased rapidly, to a level of roughly 5 percent of GNP in most countries, but some of the traditional budgetary items lagged behind: defense stood in 1950 still at 5 percent of GNP; in 1980 this percentage has almost been halved.

These facts can also be represented by the following figures. While direct public outlays multiplied, between 1950 and 1975, by a factor of 25, transfer outlays multiplied by a factor of 35. This indicates that Wagner's law has been more manifest in the transfer sector, which is basically a rather private affair, than in genuine public programs. Moreover, the contention that Wagner's law has been at work in G_R at all has been denied by some critics of traditional statistics. They assert that these increases, which are purely nominal, should be translated into real figures, which make the outcome look quite different. Government "consumption" – that is, the genuinely public sector – is said to lag behind the growth of GNP.

A relatively declining volume of the real public sector?

It is obvious that we should distinguish between nominal and real increases in G. From 1950 to 1975, money outlays of European governments have risen by a factor of 30, but in physical terms the increase was, of course, much more modest. We can avoid the whole issue by looking at G/Y and assuming that both G and Y are blown up by inflation to the same degree. This is the usual procedure, but it is criticized by a school of researchers, of whom Morris Beck is the most articulate.[6]

Beck looks at eleven European countries plus Canada and the United States from 1950 to 1975. He uses different deflators for G_T and G_R. As a deflator for G_T he takes the consumption price level. For G_R, and this is the rub, he takes the government's input price level, which corresponds roughly to an index of nominal wages. The argument for doing so is twofold: First, government services do not command a price in the market, so we have to look for a deflator other than the consumption price level. And, second, productivity in the government sector is supposed to be constant. The result is that the deflator for G_T rose by a factor of 4, and the deflator for G_R by a factor of 7.8. The outcomes for the real expansion are that the volume of G_R increased by a factor of 2.8 and the volume of G_T by no less than a factor of 7.4. In the same period GNP went up by a factor of 3. Beck's conclusion is therefore that the physical volume of G_R has been lagging to GNP. Also, Beck concludes that in a real sense G/Y was in 1975 smaller than the conventional estimate; instead of about 40 percent,[7] the "real size" of the public sector was, according to Beck, only 33.7 percent.

If we accept Beck's hypothesis, our view on the shift between the public and the private will be seriously influenced. Instead of maintaining that G/Y has been increasing because of the combined workings of G_R and G_T, we would have to conclude that the full responsibility for the operation of Wagner's law has been falling on the transfer budget. The genuine public sector – what Beck calls "government consumption" – has been relatively contracting. If we accept my argument that G_R indicates the degree of government intervention, this would suggest a shift in favor of the private sector. Moreover, if – as Friedman tells us – there is a line we dare not cross, we as sophisticated observers a la Beck might counter that the line we actually have been crossing is six percentage points lower than meets the eye.

However, Beck's calculations need not be accepted. His use of the specific deflator for G_R is arbitrary. It is true that a "natural" price index for the government's output does not exist, but that does not mean we have to take recourse to the input price index. Instead, shadow prices for government services might be constructed more or less in line with those of the business sector. And the hypothesis that productivity in government administration does not increase at all is even more vulnerable. It is indeed likely that there is a productivity lag between the public and private sectors; this implies that the government is running an increasingly costly operation. The phenomenon was described by William Baumol; it leads to an increasing tax burden, deteriorating public service, or both. This has been called "Baumol's disease." But zero productivity growth is an extreme variant of the disease, and a somewhat unlikely one, if only because the computer has been introduced into many branches of government. Beck's result, that the volume of G_R has increased less than the volume of Y, is therefore unwarranted.[8]

Moreover, Beck's figure of 33.7 percent for the "real share" of the government in GNP is misleading. There is nothing particularly "real" about this fraction. For one thing, it is sensitive to the choice of base year. If Beck had started his comparison in 1900 instead of in 1950, the real share would have been much lower. The significance of the figure is this: The difference from the traditional estimate of 40 percent is the amount that the citizens had to pay in increased taxes over the period 1950–1975. It is the price for their governments' having frozen productivity in their bureaucracies while remunerating their employees at the same level as employees in the private sector. Here, indeed, Beck has a point. His method reveals that citizens may have to pay such a price, although its exact size is uncertain. We should keep in mind that one reason among many for the operation of Wagner's law is that governments are slow in productivity growth and therefore expensive producers.

The political message of this observation is, however, not straight-forward. A right-wing commentator might conclude that the public sector should be curtailed because it apparently does not produce its money's worth. A left-wing observer might point out that the real public sector is smaller than it seems to be; therefore, it should be expanded. An efficiency-minded person or a politician facing reelection might stress the need for a productivity-oriented policy in the civil service. A fourth possible recipe is to cure Baumol's disease by lowering civil service salaries.

To sum up, the most realistic figure for G/Y for Western European countries in 1980 is about 45 percent. This is the percentage that has to be paid in taxes and social security contributions if governments want to avoid budgetary deficits. As such, the ratio is of prime importance. But it does not measure the genuine size of the public sector, because the value of the grants cannot be considered indicative of government activity. The size of the public sector is perhaps best indicated by G_R/Y, and this is about 25 percent. Even this figure includes activities by private firms: construction of government buildings, roads, military equipment. In these areas the decision to produce the goods is taken by political bodies and there is no "market" in the ordinary sense, but production would be called "private" by most observers. We might put this sector at 5 percent of GNP. This leaves us with a "private" sector of roughly 80 percent of the economy, while the "market" sector amounts to 75 percent.

A public sector fraction of 20 percent or 25 percent is not a guide to the degree of "interventionism." Education, for instance, is not a regulatory activity but government production. Government regulations are applied by agencies that are only a small part of total public activity. Murray Weidenbaum estimates that the imposition of requirements on business firms costs the U.S. government less than one percent of the federal budget, and similar small figures may well apply to Europe.[9] Political commentators have a certain freedom to pick their own figures; when discussing the tax "burden" they may refer to almost 50 percent, but it is misleading to suggest that the public sector now consists of almost half of the economy. The ratio between the public and the private sectors of Western European economies is difficult to quantify. I would stylize the foregoing figures by saying that it hovers around an average of 1:3. This is, by and large, an allocative measure.

Explanation for the increase in G/Y

Public expenditures increase because budget makers make decisions but also because basic social variables change. This nexus, although not the most conspicuous one, has been studied by economists. When Solomon Fabricant in the early 1950s tried to explain the differences in expenditures of American states and communities, he chose as explanatory variables family income, degree of urbanization, and population density. Fabricant's regression analysis took care of 70 percent of the variance in per capita G. Later research in the same vein added demographic structure: Children and aged people are costly citizens. This type of reasoning has a deterministic character, which is, from a scientific viewpoint, as it should be. The analysis explains the course of events by pointing to basic relationships. But, at the same time, it takes for granted a number of strategic relationships and the political decisions behind them: Elderly citizens are costly to the community because there are laws and institutional arrangements that make them so. Recent history shows an increase in these legal arrangements, and this development is not explained by the economist's multiple regression analysis.

That is one reason why we should look more closely at the decision-making process. But there is another reason. The deterministic approach, although intellectually satisfying, emanates from the notion that the fundamental relationships between G and a number of other variables cannot be changed. Thinking about Wagner's law itself has this impact. It suggests that there is hardly any political choice. The income elasticity of the demand for public goods exceeds unity – according to Beck it is 1.8; according to the 1979 OECD report *Public Expenditure Trends* it is about 1.25 (this estimate seems rather low) – and therefore G/Y grows. If Y goes on growing, so will G/Y. It looks as if there are no options left.

The alternative way of looking at Wagner's law is the public choice approach – its very name creates the impression that there are at least some margins for discretion by politicians. This approach stresses the different views of decision makers, their clashing interest, and the institutional procedures that determine the outcome of their debates.

Some of these models are starkly simplified. Anthony Downs's original contribution confronted a single-minded government with a mass of voters having given preferences and the choice between two or three political parties; he assumed that the government's policy aimed at vote maximization.[10] His followers (such as W. H. Riker and P. C. Ordeshook) looked into the type of behavior we could expect when competing platforms influence one another, but the main goal remains popularity. This train of thought was much improved by authors who recognized that governments consist of ministers with different viewpoints; the spending departments advocate increasing budgets, which are opposed by the minister of finance. That official is often depicted as being weak and having few friends.

Other models introduced the bureaucracy as a separate force. Bureaucrats want power and prestige; they also want to serve the public cause. This makes for expansion. Parts of the civil service act as levers for social interest groups (agriculture, education, road building). Also, the civil service has been compared to those private firms with monopoly positions that act under a profit constraint and are supposed (by Armen Alchian and Reuben Kessel) to spend their money on soft carpets, big cars, luxury furniture, pretty secretaries, and long lunch hours. In some countries the private interests of the authorities are supposed to be promoted to such a degree that at least one observer (Dick Wolfson) speaks of a kleptocracy. For most European countries a more realistic hypothesis says that the cost of government bureaucracies rises by the inclination of civil servants to do their jobs in such a manner that they are safeguarded from criticism: Decisions are well-considered and therefore slow. The public can wait. Still other observers (C. Northcote Parkinson) simply take it for granted that bureaucrats want more. In one mathematical model (by William Niskanen) bureaucrats are supposed to aim at maximizing their bureaus and to haggle with politicians over the money they get. An additional element has been highlighted by Gordon Tullock: Bureaucrats are voters themselves; an expansion of the government sector automatically increases the part of the electorate that has an interest in further expansion. The growth of the bureaucracy is thus self-generating. Most of these authors want to show that government is, in one sense or another, too big. (The opposite view is held by Anthony Downs and, of course, John Kenneth Galbraith.)

In the same vein, the impact of outside pressure groups and their professionalization is brought to the fore; the military complex and the welfare establishment, *bien étonnés*, are supposed to know the ropes within the polity (judging by outcomes the military has been less successful than its welfare colleagues). Another theorist (Mancur Olson) tells us that small interest groups, being more strongly motivated, have the advantage over larger ones. Some American theorists (such as Charles Lindblom) observe that these pluralistic ways of decision making will lead to "disjointed incrementalism," and, although the American budget system is certainly more disjointed than those of the European states, there can be little doubt that pluralism will exercise an upward pressure on spending. Only a few commentators (such as Roland McKean) believe that there is an "invisible hand in government" at work, a process of implicit exchange and bargaining among the thousands of participants that leads to acceptable, or perhaps optimal, results. Others reject the optimality of the bargaining process because some sectoral and local interests (for instance, agriculture) are overrepresented. Diffuse and future interests are underrepresented. Our grandchildren are not represented at all.

All these relationships can be modeled; solutions depend on the goals, coalitions, and strategies assumed.[11] For instance, conflict minimization leads to a different outcome than does vote maximization. These exercises may certainly increase our insight into the shifting balances of power. It is no doubt true that segmented interests are better organized now than immediately after the war. Spending departments spend more – either with an eye to their own interests or with an eye to the voters. If the minister of finance is seen as the guardian of the treasury, he or she has lost ground to cabinet colleagues. But it is also true that the formal models obviously lack two strategic aspects. First, they assume that budget makers are in control of budgets – that is, the models tend to overlook the expansive force of entitlement programs. Second, they do not consider the ideological element. They take preferences of ministers and voters more or less as given; in point of fact, these preferences have been shifting over the last decades. All the actors in the democratic game – whether politicians, bureaucrats, advocates of interest groups, or plain voters – are part of a political culture, which is subject to its own dynamics. If we want to understand Wagner's law and the development of the welfare state, we cannot avoid going into the changes in political values.

Shifts in political values

Shifts in political values are, as everything else in the social scene, complex. Only a few observers have succeeded in reducing the complexity to a simple picture. James Buchanan and Richard Wagner ascribe what they consider to be the unduly swollen government sector to the Keynesian revolution.[12] Permanent budget deficits, the creation of money, inflation, unemployment, misallocation of resources, and burdens on later generations – these are the dire consequences of the fact that politicians and voters alike have fallen victim to the Keynesian doctrine and in particular to the idea that the budget need not be balanced. This doctrine has unleashed the Leviathan.

Keynesianism eventually disrupts the economic system and constitutional democracy as well. This American diagnosis has been applied only to the United States. For Europe, and even for the United States, it does not fit the facts.[13] One might concede, however, that Keynesian ideas, or their abuse, may have been contributing to the lessening of budgetary discipline and that in this sense the increase in G/Y, even if not fully covered by new taxation, has been facilitated. Moreover, the increase in public debt itself has led to additional interest payments (from 1.5 percent of GNP in 1950 to almost 3 percent in 1980). But these are probably minor factors in the change of the intellectual climate. After all, Keynesian doctrine does not imply an ever-increasing G/Y but merely an adaptation of both G and taxation to the exigencies of full employment, without inflation. In times of overspending – the 1960s – a Keynesian policy requires lower G or higher taxes. It is certainly not true that the only Keynesian remedy for unemployment is more public spending; some Keynesians may prefer more private spending and, in particular, more private investment.

A much more important change in political values is the heightened sensitivity of politicians and voters to market failure. The qualification has a ring of objectivity, but the failure is in the eye of the beholder. The market mechanism may fail in various manners, and only a few of them have led traditionally to government intervention. Even in these fields (agriculture, housing) the increases in public outlays can be interpreted as being caused by new values and new insights. Take housing: Today politicians recognize the desire for independent households by young and old people. Because the purchasing power of these age-groups is below average, public spending seems in order. Also, the insight has taken root that the urban crisis is likely to become a self-perpetuating process; the vulnerable parts of old cities can be saved only by massive public investment.

Similar arguments are brought to bear upon the cultural sector. When the dynamics of cultural processes are taken into consideration, the unfettered workings of the market are under suspicion; they easily lead to the vicious circles of cultural deprivation. Consequently, the cultural sector shows, all over Europe, situations that are not left to the private calculus of profit and loss but are influenced by public spending. From zoos to soccer and from the preservation of ancient art to the promotion of the avant-garde, governments spend money where half a centruy ago private spending was considered sufficient. The realm of "merit goods" has expanded considerably, and not only because pressure groups have become stronger. In all these cases the ruling ideology has clearly been in favor of a new political responsibility. (A curious aspect of increased financial aid to the arts is that it aims at more freedom for the artist and the consuming public. The apparent paradox is worth discussing, but not here.)

The strongest ideological shift has, of course, taken place in transfers to individuals and families. Europe has witnessed since 1950 a deep change in attitudes toward minimum incomes. This has led to social security benefits of about 15 percent of GNP in 1980, which is twice as high as in 1950.[14] The motives behind this shift can partly be interpreted as selfish ("sickness, unemployment, and so on can happen to me"). Also, the insight has become commonplace that poverty is not automatically eliminated by economic growth under free competition. According to some observers, poverty is a "culture" that tends to perpetuate itself. But, on top of this, there can be little doubt that the social security system represents an aspect of a new moral order characterized by a higher degree of solidarity than before ("caring"). If we do not recognize this landslide in political values we are left with the puzzle (sometimes called "Musgrave's paradox")[15] that these grants increase rapidly in times of rapidly rising per capita income. The explanation is simply that Western Europe has acquired, since World War II, an increased interest in income distribution and that egalitarian attitudes have gotten the upper hand. In particular, the idea that nobody should fall below a certain minimum standard of living – in some countries equal to the minimum wage for adult workers – has been widely accepted. If this norm is taken seriously, Wagner's law can go ahead.

How things get out of hand

Most theories of budget making assume that budget makers make budgets. These persons are pushed and pulled by many forces and considerations; they have to keep an eye on pressure groups and voters, but eventually they do decide on public expenditure. The increase in G/Y is, therefore, intentional. This picture is not always unrealistic. Public outlays for education, for instance, have probably been growing in accordance with the intentions of budget makers. Politicians can proudly point to what they have deliberately achieved. But often the situation is different: The financial outcomes are at variance with the manifest preferences of budget makers. The voluntaristic story overlooks the fact that the same budget makers (ministers and members of parliament) also make laws that incapacitate their freedom to decide on public outlays. The resulting budgets may startle them out of their shoes. The issue is, in a somewhat milder form, known to budget reformers as *controllability* – defined as the possibility of reducing spending without affecting previous legislation. According to Robert Haveman, the controllable items of the U.S. federal budget shrank from 50 percent of total expenditures in 1969 to 24 percent in 1976, and a similar tendency can be seen in Europe.[16] This decrease may give rise to concern, although controllability itself is not necessarily a primary political goal. The difference from the more alarming phenomenon that I have in mind lies in the ex post acceptance of the result. Outlays can be perfectly uncontrollable in the technical sense but still in agreement with the political preferences of the government and the parliamentary majority. Things are out of hand when Wagner's law seems to descend upon politicians as an undesired fate.

A good, albeit small, example of unwanted or at least unpredicted increases in G is found in the West German constitution. It recognizes the right of asylum: political refugees may enter the country and stay there. The authorities have to decide who is a political refugee and who is just an immigrant. But the legal system knows many safeguards against arbitrary decisions; anybody can contest the authorities' decision by going to court. Because West German lawmakers have erected a solid system of legal guarantees against abuse of bureaucratic discretion, the procedures may easily last several years. The results of these arrangements are remarkable. Events occur in Ethiopia, Afghanistan, or Turkey and people pour into the German Federal Republic claiming to be political refugees. While their cases are studied they have to be housed and fed, partly at the cost of the West German treasury.

A similar example is the involuntary increase in Dutch public expenditures as a consequence of the independence of Surinam in 1974. In the agreement between the new state and the Netherlands, citizens of Surinam acquired free access to the Netherlands, at least until 1980. They have the right to stay there and receive social security benefits. From 1974 to 1980 a third of the Surinam population emigrated to "Holland." Public outlays – mainly G_T – increased. Budget makers had little choice but to accept the swollen welfare payments; they did so under frequent protests.

A more substantial case is public health expenditures. They are one of the most rapidly rising components of European budgets (from 2 percent of GNP in 1950 to well over 5 percent in 1980). The outlays are partly G_R and partly G_T – the actual mix is difficult, if not impossible, to ascertain. The legal, institutional, and financial arrangements differ from country to country, but their effects have been very similar: strong increases in physical volume and input prices – the latter so much that the term "hyperinflation" is not out of place. The basic forces determining the growth in public health budgets are the following: (1) advances in medical technology; (2) shifts from general practitioners to specialists; (3) increases in the number of patients because of demographic changes; (4) higher standards of health care, set by both doctors and patients; (5) sharply rising incomes for the medical profession, caused mainly by a short supply of specialists; (6) a shift between private and public spending – social insurance taking the place of private insurance. These six forces are interrelated and strengthen one another. The whole network – the medical-welfare complex – is run by highly professional people who are rather growth-minded. The system operates on the basis of laws and regulations; it therefore leaves budget makers little room for decisions. They often complain that they have lost control. The ceremonial occasions for such complaints are many (the opening of new hospitals, discussions in the literally thousands of committees that characterize the network). Continuous debates on thorny issues like user charges, control of medical fees, reduced consumption, eligibility, increased efficiency, prevention policies, and a partial return to private insurance schemes are interesting but have not resulted in a decreasing growth of outlays nor in the feeling that politicians are masters of their own fate. They are certainly not masters of their own budgets.

A complicated story is that of European agriculture. During the Depression of the 1930s farmers were hit by adverse market conditions that led to income maintenance programs. These programs were expected to be temporary. The strategic policy option was whether income maintenance would be achieved by price regulation or by subsidies. The former type of intervention is, from a budgetary point of view, inexpensive: The burden is laid on the consumers. Subsidies, on the other hand, lead to substantial public outlays. The policy mix differed from country to country and from product to product, but instead of financing short-term surpluses the income maintenance programs acquired a structural character. One reason for this unintended course of events is that agriculture is a relatively declining sector; in the 1930s about 20 percent of GNP originated from it; this has now shrunk to roughly 5 percent. Presently, the budget of the European Economic Community is dominated by subsidies on milk and dairy products. The curious thing is that in 1980 these appropriations were considered unacceptable by the European Parliament. They exceeded 10 billion ecu, which is two-thirds of the European Community budget. Yet the parliament is not capable of rolling them back. Even more curious is that the governments of West Germany, Belgium, and France refused to pay their statutory European Community contributions for agriculture (and the Social Fund). They went on a temporary tax strike.

The agricultural example is all the more relevant because its basic features are spilling over to manufacturing. The 1970s witnessed developments in a number of old European industries that can be labeled unfavorable, bad, or catastrophic, depending on the commentator's mood. There was also a general profit-squeeze going on, at least in countries like West Germany, the Benelux, and, in particular, the United Kingdom. The factors behind this adverse course of events were many and much debated; they will be discussed later. But it is certain that European governments have not succeeded in restoring profitability. Instead of stopping the profit squeeze, they subsidized particular industries in distress. Losses were compensated not because the goods produced possessed special merit, but to maintain employment and sometimes productive capacity in skills and machines. This type of emergency policy is likely to develop its own dynamics for at least three reasons.

The first is rule of law. Firms need to know whether they are entitled to a subsidy or not. This requires a system of criteria. Moreover, decisions can be delegated only to the lower tiers of the civil service if such a system is in existence, and parliaments need it to evaluate government policies. Criteria and rules tend to harden and start a life of their own. This is exactly how things get out of hand, especially when business conditions worsen.

The second element is the duration of subsidies. Rescue operations are usually conceived to be short-term. One of the criteria for rendering assistance is that the industry can prove its long-term viability. This requirement is intended to keep the government's commitments within limits. But nobody knows exactly what "long-term viability" means. Optimistic predictions have to be made – in bad times, a precarious exercise. They easily lead to financial involvements that are difficult to untangle. Management and trade unions get a common interest in the perpetuation of the grants, in particular in times of high unemployment. It will be argued that the real burden of the subsidies is smaller than it seems to be because unemployment compensation has to be deducted (which assumes that there will be no other jobs in the near future). Here again the system will develop dynamics of its own.

The third reason why subsidies will proliferate is that manufacturing may well share agriculture's fate of becoming a relatively declining part of the economy, with services taking over. Such a shift from primary to secondary to tertiary production has, of course, long been predicted by Jean Fourastié, Colin Clark, and many others, but governments, trade unions, and the business community do not look on this trend with equanimity. The factory is still considered to be especially "productive" by Marxists and industrialists alike. If the downward trend and political resistance to it both continue, financial aid to industry is bound to increase.

The foregoing cases show a good deal of similarity in the dynamics of government outlays (mainly transfers). They are merely intended as examples of how increased spending can be conditioned by circumstances that can hardly be controlled by politicians. There is more necessity and less freedom in the process than meet the eye. The examples are by no means complete. The next section enumerates twelve factors that will push up the G/Y fraction in the near future.

Will the European economies obey Wagner's Law in the coming decades?

The European economies will indeed obey Wagner's law in the future. The reason is not that trends always continue, but that the forces behind the increase in G/Y are far from spent. Whatever theory we hold about the nature of these forces, there are indictions that the balance will shift farther in the direction of the public sector. Transfer payments will also increase. Here are some predictions.

1. Beck's mechanism will persist: government operations will become more and more expensive relative to private production. This is particularly true in certain heavily subsidized sectors, for example, health.
2. There will be new demands for subsidized housing, particularly on behalf of young people and low-income groups. Also, the reconstruction of cities will require massive amounts of money. The arguments adduced to expand these programs will be those of the welfare state in combination with crime prevention. Riots in Berlin, Amsterdam, and London will act as a support for these demands.
3. The military sector will grow. The NATO commitment of a 3 percent increase in real budgets will in itself probably exceed real income growth. A decrease in military tensions does not seem likely.
4. Demographic shifts will continue: There will be fewer children and therefore fewer schools, but more aged people and therefore more pensions, more publicly financed homes for the elderly, more health expenditures. The net effect may well turn out to be positive.
5. Pressure groups will go on organizing themselves. They are likely to speak louder. Professionalization of lobbies will also continue. Their intertwinement with the bureaucracies will become more intense.
6. Governments will try harder than ever before to please the voters.

This is likely because their popularity will decrease under conditions of low growth. Political stability will be threatened for various reasons, the increase in unemployment being the most obvious. In general, an intensified struggle over scarce means can be expected. Budget making will more often lead to the fall of cabinets. This instability will make for higher expenditures to satisfy the demands of powerful groups.

7. Concern over income distribution will not diminish. The reasons for this will be discussed in the next section. In most European countries the welfare state is still full of gaps, and these will be resented in a stagnating economy.

8. Differences in the G/Y ratio between European countries will probably be leveled in an upward direction. There are many reasons why countries like Italy and Greece will move toward the present average ratio of 45 percent. And this average itself will rise.

9. A new factor will develop: The costs of protecting the natural environment will certainly rise. This is partly so because governments will try to prevent further pollution, which implies expensive shifts in production processes that cannot be fully financed by private industry. New funds, fed by special taxes, will proliferate to facilitate the required substitutions. The energy sector in particular will require heavy government spending. The second reason the public budget will be burdened by environmental expenditures lies in the recent past. In the 1960s and 1970s an enormous amount of dangerous waste was dumped, often stored in metal drums with a life expectancy of about twenty years. The effects of these time bombs are beginning to show up now. A few miles north of Amsterdam over 5,000 barrels containing poisonous materials (like dioxin) have been found buried under layers of domestic garbage. The removal of this material and its subsequent disposal will have to be financed by the government. The cost of this and similar operations (there are hundreds of poisonous dumps in the country) is estimated at almost one percent of the national income. Moreover, dwellings will have to be removed and their owners compensated. This type of cleaning up will become one of Europe's great growth industries.

10. Interest payments on the public debt will rise. The debt itself will increase because government expenditures will grow faster than tax revenue, which will be affected by the slower growth rate. To show a possible course of events: The present European ratio of government debt to national income is roughly 40 percent (Italy is at the top with 65 percent and France at the bottom with 14 percent). Suppose that the government runs a deficit of 7 percent of the national income (the present average) and suppose further that the rate of growth of the nominal national income is also 7 percent; then the ratio of debt to income will become 60 percent in 1990 and 75 percent in the year 2000. This increasing debt can probably only be financed at higher rates of interest than the present, which range from 12 percent to 20 percent. At the moment,

interest payments on the public debt are in an order of magnitude of 3 percent of the national income. (The United Kingdom is at the top with 6 percent and France at the bottom with less than 1 percent.) This percentage will definitely increase; in the foregoing example a doubling of the ratio in the coming decades can be predicted.

11. In a stagnating economy subsidies to industry will tend to increase. Moreover, unemployment compensation may rise. The total amount of unemployment compensation is presently about 4 percent of the national income – it corresponds to an unemployment level of about 10 percent. But these are only the most obvious examples of rising expenditures in a stagnating economy. Under welfare state conditions there are many more. For instance, public substitutes for private alimony to divorced women will increase. Health expenditures tend to increase when business conditions are bad, in particular when the compensation for sickness or disability exceeds the unemployment allowance.

12. In slump conditions the government will be under constant pressure to act as an employer of last resort (according to Richard Musgrave). The argument can be formulated in Keynesian terms. Of course, a Keynesian policy can also be pursued by lowering taxes, but here the growing budgetary deficits will act as a more obvious brake than when it comes to expanding the number of teachers, welfare workers, and civil servants. This political asymmetry between additional spending and tax cuts is enhanced because the employment effect of government spending is more direct and visible than the employment effect of tax reductions. There actually exist some hyper-Keynesian theories (Haavelmo's theorem) predicting that the impact of government spending on employment is much higher. Although these theories have been discredited by now with economists, it is not certain that they will be rejected by politicians.

13. Some countries have tried to combat the recession by deliberately increasing the public sector. This was the early intention of the Mitterand government of 1981. This experiment created an interesting alternative to the restrictive British policy of the Thatcher government. Other European countries followed a kind of middle course; they are trying to restore the health of the private sector without unduly harming public employment, but this course will almost certainly lead to a higher G/Y.

The thirteen expansionary forces listed above may be uncertain in their scope, but their direction is clear. The present European value of G/Y, being almost 50 percent, will probably increase to 60 percent in the coming decade. The tendency will be all the more marked because the growth in Y may easily slow to zero. It is difficult to think up counterbalancing forces of a gradual and incremental character. (Cost-benefit analysis, Program Planning and Budgeting Systems, zero budgeting, and sunset budgeting are recommended as devices to control and rationalize government spending, but until now their effect has been limited. One reason is that a quantification of benefits is hampered by the near impossibility of putting figures on essential values like health, security in the streets, and human life). It is much simpler to imagine some kind of a breakdown of the welfare state itself. Before probing this gloomy possibility, a brief discussion of some of the shortcomings of that system is in order.

Shortcomings of the welfare state

One might expect that a society characterized by increasing real incomes, increasing transfer payments, social security, and a good deal of leveling would show an appreciable degree of harmony and tranquillity. This was the serene belief of the 1950s and early 1960s. It now looks rather old-fashioned. The welfare state has come under severe criticism, and not only from right-wing commentators who believe that personal responsibility is jeopardized by guaranteed incomes and that people who rely on government programs will remain in a perpetual state of dependence. There is a widespread feeling that welfare in the welfare state is not what it should be. This disillusion is partly inspired by phenomena that are difficult to understand by simple economic reasoning: increased consumption of alcohol and other drugs, more criminal behavior, more violence in the streets, more terrorism. Some commentators perceive a cultural crisis of sorts, but the connection between that crisis and the welfare state is not easy to ascertain. It will be left aside in this chapter, which will consider some obvious economic deficiencies.

The first and foremost deficiency is that affluence for the great mass of the people has not yet been reached in the countries of Western Europe. Galbraith's "affluent society" probably did not exist in the minds of American workers of the 1950s. It certainly does not exist in the minds of British, French or Italian workers of the 1980s. A family of four living in Birmingham on average pay suffers from an unpleasant income constraint. Their situation is not aptly described by Fred Hirsch's term "commodity fetishism."[17] Average workers and their families feel the basic economic category of scarcity – that is, the gap between wants and their satisfaction – as a daily experience, even if their income is now almost twice as high as in 1950. Wants have increased with income, and part of the sense of well-being is lost in this "preference drift." Unsatisfied wants are, of course, even more pressing for family living on half the average income. Now the British welfare state increases the average income by a whole system of benefits – family allowance, child benefit, Family Income Supplement – and it deducts income tax, employees' national insurance contributions, and so on. The net result is that such a family, instead of receiving 50 percent of average weekly earnings, gets 61 percent. The increase in the family's relative position is clear but limited. Inequality is diminished but not abolished. If the family consisted of two parents and four children (aged three, eight, eleven, and sixteen) the initial income ratio of 50 percent would increase to 63 percent.[18] This, again, can hardly be labeled affluence.

The welfare state does not abolish feelings of poverty. Take again a British example. According to the findings of W. Beckermann, social security benefits eliminate 96 percent of the poverty gap.[19] But a single person or a family that has no earnings at all (for the well-known reasons of age, health, unemployment, or being the female head of a family) and lives on general assistance (what the British call the Supplementary Benefit) may perceive this income as low. It is, for a single person, about 40 percent of the average wage rate. People in this income bracket – in Britain about 20 percent of the population – may compare their position with that under a laissez-faire system and thank the welfare state for what it does provide; but they may also compare their position with that of their well-to-do contemporaries and blame society for being harsh.

Statisticians have similar options. Some compare the income share of the lower fifth of income recipients under welfare state conditions to that share in, say, the year 1900 and notice a decrease.[20] One may erroneously conclude that distribution is getting more and more unequal. Others believe that "there has been no steady trend towards greater equality in the distribution of family income."[21] For Europe this trend is a fact of life, and part of it is caused by transfer expenditures.[22] But what counts in subjective well-being is not what the statistics show or what is written in books. There can be little doubt that most non-aged income recipients in the lower 20 percent bracket consider their incomes quite inadequate.[23] The welfare state is, for the least favored of its citizens, an unsatisfactory affair, that is, in the United Kingdom, West Germany, and even Sweden. In Italy, Greece, and Spain poverty is still so intense and widespread that it catches the eye of the most superficial observer. In Naples a guaranteed minimum income does not seem to exist.

But the meagerness of the welfare state is not its only deficiency. A second reproach is that part of the transfers are going to the well-to-do. This may be rather obvious for cultural subsidies – the middle classes and the rich visit the concert halls and theaters that are subsidized by the average taxpayer. It is less obvious for education. In 1969, W. Lee Hansen and Burton A. Weisbrod launched a peculiar discussion on this subject when they drew attention to the fact that (in California, but the idea is well-substantiated for all Western nations) children of well-to-do families are heavy users of the state universities. Some concluded from this that subsidized higher education resembles Santa Claus, who favors the children of the rich. But other commentators pointed to the fact – also brought to the fore by the Hansen–Weisbrod study – that the children of low-income families who receive a university education get higher net benefits from it than those of rich or middle-class families, because the latter pay a greater share in taxes. Therefore, the educational system favors low-income groups, provided that they have the "right" type of children. Both views, although seemingly contradictory, are correct. The partisans of free or nearly free university education (that is, the traditional adherents of the welfare state) and the partisans of higher admission fees (that is, the traditional adherents of the market principle) can each bend the argument in their own way.

The issue led to some confusion but also to a new interest in possible transfers from lower- to higher-income groups. The case of subsidized higher education opened eyes to unintended distributive effects of the grants system. Much detailed work has been done since, by researchers such as Martin Pfaff and many others. It led, inter alia, to the suspicion that agricultural subsidies increase income inequalities between farmers and that certain governmental services favor property owners or big contractors. These are the more or less unavoidable side effects of large-scale government intervention. The general conclusion from this type of research is that part of the transfer payments is not channeled to the poor. But this need not surprise us, because the share of transfer payments in the national income – about 20 percent – is much higher than the income share of the lowest fifth of households: about 6 percent in the United Kingdom and Germany and 7 percent in Sweden.[24] In this sense the welfare state is not particularly effective. Of course, one has to remember that equity is not its only goal. Avoidance of the means test may be another. Also, increased provision of merit goods is a goal in its own right.

A third critique of the welfare state says that its provisions are abused not so much by the wealthy, but by workers who do not want to work and by adroit profiteers with unreported jobs. This type of critique is partly inspired by the fear that the supply of labor will diminish or that the incentive to get ahead in life will falter – this is the supply-siders' worry. Voluntary unemployment and faked poor health will take the place of regular, gainful jobs. This alarming story contains, however, at least one attractive element: The welfare state creates additional options for those who dislike work in the factory or the office. Economists have always been sensitive to the argument that the preferences of subjects should be respected. The widening options for not working can be seen as a form of progress. But the "improper use" of facilities raises moral, political, and financial problems. Bitter comments on the practice are of a populist nature. They are fed by the experience of those who happen to know a neighbor, cousin, or acquaintance from the cafe who is boasting of the advantages he or she extracts from the authorities. Voluntary unemployment, whatever its impact on the economy as a whole, may incite a populist right-wing resistance to guaranteed minimum incomes. It robs the system of a part of its legitimacy and makes its political stability less sure.

A fourth deficiency of the welfare state is that it incites tax evasion and tax fraud but cannot effectively deal with these types of criminal activity. The size of the unobserved nontaxpaying sector is estimated in various manners (by tax experts, statisticians, and adherents to the indirect method, which uses monetary multipliers) and with various quantitative results (between 5 percent for Britain and roughly 25 percent – probably not too high — for southern countries). It is obvious that this constitutes a serious threat to public finances. If all taxes could be collected and economic activity would not decrease under such a strict regime, the present budget deficits that terrorize European politicians would practically disappear. But other observers tell us that the strict regime would lead to economic collapse – that the unobserved economy is the pillar that supports economic activity. Real income is presently higher than it seems, unemployment is lower, the recession is less bad than is recorded by official statistics.[25] So much is certain, the distribution of benefits is very skewed. According to Dutch research, the top 2 percent of tax criminals get two-thirds of the total unreported income – on average they manage to withhold a per annum income of five times the average wage income in the Netherlands. This poses, of course, a severe moral question. It undermines the legitimacy of the system.

Yet all this does not necessarily wreck the welfare state. The general disappointment may provoke a political swing to the Right in the sense that citizens no longer support those political parties of the center and the Left that wish to sustain the full employment policy and social provisions. But such a victory of laissez-faire – e.g., the Thatcher experiment – is not a predictable consequence of the shortcomings just sketched. They may well lead to the desire to improve and strengthen the welfare state – as in France. The really dangerous threat to that arrangement lies in the possibility of a deep and prolonged economic recession. The crisis of the welfare state arises when it cannot cope with the depression.

The crisis of the welfare state

The truly alarming possibility is a continuous decline in real income combined with high-level unemployment. In itself, the present unemployment figure of about 10 percent is already contrary to the tenets of the welfare state – it points to blatant policy failure. Moreover, declining real income will lead to substantial losses everywhere – in business firms, in households that cannot pay their bills – and these losses will be shifted to the state. These transmission mechanisms are characteristic for the welfare state. The most conspicuous is a declining tax revenue. Increased unemployment compensation and other welfare payments work in the same direction. The danger is that the welfare state will break down just when it is most urgently needed.

There are three stories about this possibility. One tells us that such a crisis is inherent in the capitalist system. It is the result of international instability – instability in profit rates, instability in capital investment, instability in international capital markets. The welfare state is basically a capitalist economy, and its meager provisions are not responsible for the breakdown. On the contrary, the welfare state will become the victim of the crisis – the ruling class will use the argument of bad times to dismantle the social provisions. This attack should be resisted. Governments should follow an expansionary course; that is, they should leave the social security system intact and expand government expenditures for housing, health, education, and so on. Finance for such programs can be found, provided the political will to do so is sufficiently strong – there is always money to be extracted from multinational corporations, banks, and insurance companies.

The second story lays the blame at the door of the welfare state itself. If told well, it is full of doom. It is about the dark forces being unleashed – greedy, vulgar, stupid people taking over the state and all other political bodies. Hedonism blocks a long-term perspective, so consumption increases and investment decreases. Swollen government expenditures are directed toward immediate satisfaction to please the masses. Income leveling and high taxation combine in paralyzing not merely economic incentives, but faith itself. People want more and more, but their ambitions cannot be satisfied by the welfare state. They become frustrated and rebellious. There is blood in the streets. The collapse is basically a moral and cultural crisis, the *Untergang des Abendlandes*.

Fortunately, there is a third story. It does not deny certain difficulties but asserts that difficulties are ubiquitous. This is not the first time that the *Untergang* has been held up before us. The relativistic story leans heavily on the real national income as the main criterion for economic welfare. It looks at the trend of this variable and ascertains almost uninterrupted growth. Perhaps slow growth, and temporary stagnation, but the prospects are that the trend will more or less continue. That means that real income may well double in a period of, say, thirty years. Unemployment is caused by a divergence between the growth rates of two macrovariables: the real national income and labor productivity has increased steadily. Production has increased by leaps and bounds but by and large much slower than productivity: The difference consists in the shortening of working time, which has roughly been halved over a century. Presently, productivity is increasing somewhat faster than production without working time being shortened. This leads to unemployment, but the methods for reducing the number of working hours per annum are now more varied than ever: a shorter day, fewer days a week, fewer weeks a year, fewer years per lifetime, flextime, permanent education. So the unemployment problem can be solved, provided that labor is sufficiently mobile and long-term growth of production can be sustained.

The relativistic view looks at the problems of the welfare state with concern but without alarm. It is the view officially held by most Western governments and by international organizations like the OECD. Their question is not whether the European economies will return to the trend, but when — this year or next. This chapter proceeds on the assumption that this view is basically correct. But that begs the question of whether the welfare state is compatible with such a prospect. It brings up the crucial issue of the economic burden of the public sector and the carrying capacity of the economic system.

The burden of the public sector

Contrary to common prejudice, the public sector does not put a burden on the economy. That is, if everything is in order. Real income does not decline if government expenditure increases, and real income is our criterion when we look for burdens. Of course, additional real expenditure implies opportunity costs (the government uses factors of production and the citizens do the same to comply with the regulations); in this sense the private sector "bears the burden" of the public sector. But the opposite is also true: The public sector "bears the burden" of private consumption and private investment; we all "bear the burden" of the food and textile industries.

Although real income is not directly affected by a shift in the proportion between the public sector and the private sector, satisfaction of wants may either increase or decrease. Government spending that does not satisfy the wants of citizens is obviously a waste. Here we skate on thin empirical ice; little is known about the degree of satisfaction brought about in the minds of citizens by the police, regional planning, free museums. Moreover, one citizen's satisfaction is the next one's disgust. Sweeping generalizations about human happiness being increased or diminished by governments have always been *en vogue* – Adam Müller believed that all true productivity and spiritual values stem from the state – but in this field we can discover as many positive and negative burdens as we please.

There is no easy way out of this dilemma. We may assume, on purely formal grounds, that a democratic decision leading to a particular increase in government spending will increase general well-being, but that kind of "revealed preference" view is a rather meaningless tautology. Even in a well-behaved democracy, government intervention may in special cases well lead to a decrease in welfare. Heavy bureaucracies, unforeseen circumstances, downright stupidity – may all contribute to waste in government. In those cases the governed are worse off. We all know examples. Another possibility: Government regulations may well slow innovation of products and production methods and therefore hurt the growth of GNP. Some audacious economists have tried to estimate these "dynamic" costs of specific types of government intervention, but the methodological difficulties of these calculations are tremendous.[26] It is easy to show that restrictions on the production of dangerous chemical products may work out in a lower GNP, but these restrictions are good for human welfare. The inhabitants of the Italian village Soveso, which was poisoned by dioxin, might wish that the GNP had been a bit lower. We cannot exclude the possibility that intervention is clumsy, restrictive, and a brake on progress, but we should not forget that the absence of intervention may be disastrous to a number of people. A comprehensive view of these failures of the visible hand is difficult to obtain. Research programs estimating the loss in psychic welfare caused by mistaken policy measures have not yet been started. In this field ideology takes the place of knowledge. The ideology of most liberals and social democrats implies that the net effect of total government activity is beneficiary, if only because education, road building, and other substantial chunks of policy are to be evaluated positively. In this sense there is no obvious burden – on the contrary.

The tax "burden" is not a macroburden either. Abolish all taxes and society's real income does not increase. That is, if in the original situation all productive factors were used and productivity was unaffected by progressive rates. Without taxation, the opportunity costs of government spending would be distributed over individuals by inflation, queuing, or even more brutish methods. But, of course, the individual citizen feels her or his individual tax as a burden; and, indeed, his or her spendable income is decreased by it. At the microlevel the comparison between the situation with the tax and without the tax is not made. It could not be made, because to the individual the no-tax situation is impossible to imagine. Omniscience would be necessary to show the distribution of the tax burden in the sense of the difference, per individual, between the situation with tax and without. This exercise would lead to a multitude of positive and negative burdens, with sum zero. But all this is true only if taxation is not, in some sense, too high, a possibility that will be discussed later.

The image of the public sector as a burden is closely associated with another image: that of the private sector's carrying capacity. Every variety of economic fundamentalism used to have its own special notion of a basic activity "carrying" other activities: Agriculture is basic in the physiocratic view, trade and shipping in the mercantilistic view, manufacturing in the classical view, the steel industry in the view of old-fashioned development planners, the private sector in neoclassicism. The public sector is, according to most commentators, the least "basic" of all, although there are exceptions to this rule (Adam Müller, Othmar Spann). There is much mysticism in these ideas, but it is, of course, true that the various sectors may well possess different economic characteristics. For instance, the product of the public sector cannot be exported and this puts limits on the expansion of public employment in countries suffering from a balance of payments deficit. And, of course, public production is financed by taxation; this constrains its expansion as far as there are limits to tax capacity. Indeed, these limits are crucial in the context of this chapter.

This is so because taxes are not a burden provided that they are not excessive. Overtaxing decreases the use and efficiency of productive factors. It harms the growth of GNP. In particular, if the growth rate is already endangered, taxation may add to stagnation. The unintended loss of real product constitutes a genuine burden on citizens.[27] The channels along which taxation may hurt production are well known. High and progressive tax rates will diminish the supply of labor, the supply of savings, and the rate of business investment. The supply of labor will be affected because some suppliers – in particular those who are in a position to determine their own working time or retirement age – prefer leisure over income-after-tax because young people have less incentive to be schooled, and because schooled workers may emigrate. Diminshed investment is a matter not only of slackened incentives but also of a reduction of available funds. But the quantitative impact of high tax rates on individuals' decisions to be schooled, to work overtime, or to invest is unknown; moreover, the impact of these decisions on real income is unknown. The point where real income is seriously hurt by overtaxing is a matter of speculation. Every commentator has rather wide options to estimate the relevant parameters, and the outcomes of various conjectures are widely divergent. There have been overly confident guesses on tax ceilings. C. F. Bastable said in 1900 that 15 percent was a maximum tax rate; Colin Clark believed in 1945 that 25 percent could not be exceeded; and C. Northcote Parkinson told us in 1960 (tongue in cheek) that 36 percent would mean "disaster, complete and final" (but he added, with a certain caution, "although not immediate").[28] But in the blooming 1960s the economies of Western Europe thrived on macrotax ratios of 40 percent. The Norwegian GNP grew in the 1970s at a yearly rate of more than 4 percent, while the tax ratio was approaching 40 percent. Ceilings are obviously elastic, and Milton Friedman's "line we dare not cross" was put at 60 percent.

The slippery nature of the maximum tax rates that can prevail without visibly harming GNP need not surprise us. Much depends on the tax structure and, in particular, how profits and investment are taxed. Most countries have special legislation for capital investment in buildings and machinery. Also, marginal rates are more important for decision making than the general ratio of tax revenue to GNP. In many northern countries marginal income tax rates are about 70 percent; they have been at that level for decades without smothering growth.[29] It may seem strange that this can happen, but pure logic cannot solve quantitative empirical problems.

The most important reason why sweeping supply-side generalizations about the quantitative impact of taxation on GNP are inadmissible is that so much depends on other growth factors. Under conditions of high demand and strong technical change, an economy can stand a much higher tax ratio than under conditions of faltering demand and low investment. More specifically, when profits are sufficient to push the economy of the welfare state along a high-growth path, tax burdens, in the sense of negative influences on GNP, are likely to be small or nonexistent. But when profits and growth rates are already insufficient, there is a chance they will be depressed further by taxation. In that case the public sector becomes a burden. A somewhat closer look at this situation seems in order.

The profit squeeze: external shocks and the response of the welfare state

A continuous fall in European profits has taken place during the last decades, and in particular the 1970s. Both the share of profits in national income and the rate of return on capital have been declining. The exact figures differ among researchers, if only because there are various ways to define profits. Sometimes this income category is defined in such a manner that rents, interest, and even labor incomes of the self-employed are included. This leads to a kind of residual income; its order of magnitude is about 25 percent of the national income. This residual is less sensitive than profits because in the 1970s interest rates went up and there was a shift from corporate profits toward the cost of capital. We need a much narrower concept: profits in the true sense of revenue minus all costs (with the exception of interest on the firm's own capital). The share of profits proper in national income started to decline in most European countries in the 1960s, when growth rates and capacity utilization were still high; the decline accelerated in the 1970s, when the recession and the rise in oil prices joined the slower working forces that had been operative before. There can be little doubt that in the 1970s a genuine squeeze was going on.[30] Around 1980 profits in the manufacturing sector were, macroeconomically, roughly zero.

The consequences of the profit squeeze make themselves felt in investment and disinvestment in machines and buildings. The link via investment activity is well known and much discussed, but the exact quantitative relationship between the level of profits and the level of investment in an economy is a matter of speculation. The main reason for this uncertainty is that investment is also influenced by interest rates, the rate of change in demand (accelerator), and overwhelming psychological factors – which Keynes dubbed "animal spirits." Moreover, it is not so much actual profits as expected profits that count for the investment decision. For all these reasons the investment function is a slippery relationship in any model. Not withstanding these complications, the positive correlation between profits and investment is obvious. That means that positive relationships exist between profits and growth, between profits and real income, and between profits and employment. These are relationships that the welfare state cannot get away from.

Less attention has been paid to the link between profits and disinvestment, or, more exactly, between losses and accelerated scrapping of old vintages of the capital stock. Yet this channel between the profit squeeze and unemployment is probably of strategic importance. Empirical research in the Netherlands has made it plausible that the disappearance of quasi-rents on old machines and plants has led to a fast loss of jobs. The steep increase in unemployment during the 1970s was predicted in 1974 by a vintage model of the capital stock (labor productivity and employment being a function of the installment year of a vintage).[31] Later, the model was linked to a Keynesian expenditure sector and used by the Central Planning Bureau. Its predictions were glum.

The causes behind the decline in profits, although complex, can be summarized in two groups: deficiency of demand and cost increases that cannot be fully shifted into prices. The former is not typical for the 1960s: High growth rates usually create their own demand, and there was a general tendency toward overspending. The slow but persistent decline in profit *margins* was a matter of wage inflation (that is, the relative increase in money wages minus the relative increase in labor productivity), increased tax rates, and since the beginning of the 1970s, higher prices of imported raw materials. Shifting of higher costs was incomplete, and even a shifting elasticity of 0.8 (estimate for the EEC countries, 1970–1980) is sufficient to explain a profit squeeze, provided cost inflation is substantial and persistent.

Such persistence is characteristic for the welfare state. One of the main weaknesses of this sociopolitical arrangement is that money wages rise as a reaction not only to productivity increases but also to rising costs of living. Included in these costs are increased taxes and social security contributions. This means that the "burden" of the public sector is transformed into higher labor costs, on top of the wage inflation that follows from trade unions' strong market position. The weight of the welfare state came to rest on residual income and in particular on profits. In the 1960s and early 1970s the process was slow because the fast growth of demand and production acted as a buffer.[32]

The wage-tax-wage spiral was in operation in the 1970s with a vengeance when outside shocks hit Europe. The first shock was the breakdown of the Bretton Woods system of fixed exchange rates; it led to messy conditions in the currency markets, which are bad for trade. At the same time the prices of imported materials began to rise, and this movement gained dramatic momentum when, in 1973, the OPEC cartel started to increase oil prices. In seven years they had risen tenfold. This shock had several consequences. First, it created enormous deficits on the balance of payments of almost the whole world except OPEC; in 1980 the developed countries of the West were running deficits of roughly $75 billion, the developing countries showed similar gaps, and OPEC had surpluses of $150 billion. This monetary imbalance led to a contraction of international demand. In itself the slackening of demand sharpened the profit squeeze. Many industries incurred losses because of shrinking production and unused capacity. But an additional effect of the oil shock was that the worsening of the terms of trade was shifted through the system until it came to rest on the most vulnerable part of the national income: profits. In the middle of the 1970s, when the growth of GNP was zero, European wage inflation was about 20 percent. Not only wage earners but most recipients of social security payments as well were compensated under the *scala mobile* in its various forms. The government sought compensation by higher taxes. The Beck mechanism was accentuated. Unemployment rose. The vicious circle of the welfare state (unemployment leading to higher social security fees) came on top of all this; again, tax increases were shifted to business firms. The carrying capacity of the private sector came under severe stress.

Nor is this all. The violent wage–price spiral of the 1970s translated itself into higher (nominal) rates of interest. In the course of the 1970s interest rates doubled. And borrowing increased, too, because the business sector experienced an increased need for funds. Manufacturing firms had to pay more to banks, pension funds, insurance funds, and other lenders. Around 1980 the remaining profits of the private sector were mainly made in the financial sector and not in the production of goods. Increased taxation, insofar as it has contributed to the spiral, has probably sharpened this transfer from producers to financial intermediaries.

All these mechanisms tend to weaken the dynamic part of the private sector. We cannot but conclude that the welfare state may be suspected of harming real income growth and creating unemployment. This tragic development is inherent not so much in the growth of G itself but in the way the tax incidence is shifted throughout the economy. The quasi-burden of the public sector is turned into a real burden.[33]

The double choice

The foregoing argument suggests that society has to make two sets of interrelated choices. One set is about G/Y. By and large, these decisions are made in a political context. They require some kind of democratic consent, even if blind mechanisms operate in such a manner that things may easily get out of hand. An urgent task of the welfare state is to provide a sufficient political carrying capacity for the continuous shift between the private and the public.

The other set of choices concerns tax capacity and tax incidence. We surmise that tax capacity – which is mainly determined by national income – strategically depends on the distribution of the national income between profits and nonprofits. The share of profits in national income is the outcome of an economic process. The trouble with the welfare state is that it has hardly any grip on this process.

It is partly left to the decisions of the institutions dealing with wage bargaining. Employers' organizations and trade unions are outside the government's control. The other part of the profit-generating process is left to the market. Here a strategic role is played by the degree to which increased costs can be shifted forward to consumers. Moreover, the national income, and therefore tax capacity, is influenced by interactions between various spending categories – consumption, investment, exports – and the government's grip on these interactions is less effective than Keynesian optimism would have it. Therefore, the great challenge for the welfare state consists in handling the incidence of increasing taxation so that profits are spared. In times of a profit squeeze the challenge is even greater: The tide must be turned.

The urgent question is which policy methods, if any, are available to restore the share of profits to a level compatible with a reasonable growth rate and a satisfactory level of employment. Three methods are discernible.

The first is to operate directly on after-tax profits, either by specific tax measures or by subsidies to firms. Tax measures favoring profits are feasible, in particular when they aim at invested profits. Indeed, tax credits for investment abound in many countries, and they can be extended. It would also be helpful if the European tax authorities accepted inflation accounting – a measure long overdue. But tax reform of this type has little significance for restoring the general level of profits, if only because it does not apply to firms making losses. Subsidies are more effective, but they meet a host of practical and political questions. (Some of them were raised in the section "How Things Get Out of Hand.") A policy of compensating losses by government money will be criticized by the adherents of the free market, the adversaries of discretionary power for bureaucrats, the left-wing opponents of grants to private capitalists, firms that do not need the subsidies and complain that they are supporting their competitors, and firms that claim to be eligible but are turned down. Therefore, a regime of subsidies will become a heavy burden on any democratic government because it will be blamed for the misadventures of all the industries in trouble. Although the disadvantages are well known, European governments will almost certainly follow this dangerous road to preserving employment unless the profit squeeze itself is reversed. In fact, the restoration of sufficient profits seems imperative if only to avoid the complications of large-scale subventions to contracting industries.

The second way of restoring profitability, that of expanding demand, is at first sight much more promising. This is the Keynesian recipe. A higher level of demand translates itself into a higher national income, and it is particularly good for profits. Capacity utilization is presently very low – in many manufacturing sectors as low as 70 percent, and it remains low notwithstanding the scrapping of old machines, the shipbuilding, steel, and textile industries. Firms operating below capacity run into losses. A Keynesian policy of stimulating demand will be realized almost automatically insofar as the government expenditures increase, but the effect will be overruled if tax rates are simultaneously being increased. A convinced Keynesian will therefore favor tax cuts or at least constant tax rates. But this medicine is hard to swallow in the face of mounting budgetary deficits. Ministers of finance do not take these deficits lightly, and we must concede that their motives are not necessarily imaginary or mistaken. We saw in the section "Will the European Countries Obey Wagner's Law in the Coming Decades?" that interest, paid by governments, will certainly increase; and although this interest is not necessarily a real burden on the economy, it may well become a budgetary nuisance.

But budgetary deficits are not the only stumbling block on the Keynesian road. In the setting of the 1980s, European deficit on the balance of payments is worse. A policy of expanding domestic demand attracts imports without stimulating exports. Normally, this difficulty can be overcome when all countries boost their home markets together, but in recent circumstances the deficits on the balance of payments have been a general ailment of the western world. The complementary surplus has been concentrated outside Europe. This makes the hope for a coordinated policy between surplus and deficit countries slight. This is a major reason why a Keynesian policy can only be limited in scope.

That leaves us with the third option: the suppresion of domestic cost inflation. Part of it – caused by the increase in G/Y – can hardly be avoided. That makes a reduction of labor costs the only logical option. There is rather wide agreement that this is desirable, but opinions vary as to the policy instruments to be used. Some hard-boiled or defeatist monetarists seem to believe that wage inflation should be cured by high rates of interest or tight money. This means that stagnation and the profit squeeze are fought by more stagnation and a sharper profit squeeze. The result became visible in Britain in the late 1970s. The government followed a restrictive policy, reduced G/Y, tightened the money supply, and let the recession follow its own course. In 1981, the rate of interest stood at 20 percent. The unemployment rate rose to 10 percent. Notwithstanding the increase in the production of North Sea oil, GNP fell by 3 percent. Industrial production fell by more than 10 percent. The inflation rate was 15 percent. Wage claims were not exactly mitigated by the restrictive policy; in 1980 unit labor costs in manufacturing rose by no less than 20 percent. The failure of this approach meets the eye. The approach itself is destructive to the welfare state.

There can be little doubt that an incomes policy is a more civilized method to deal with the wage-tax-price-wage spiral. Since 1945 it has been advocated on several grounds – being a natural complement to a full-employment policy, equity between various types of incomes, and the fight against inflation – to which in the context of this chapter an extra argument can be added. Some kind of an incomes policy seems almost necessary to make a further increase in G/Y possible without catastrophic stagnation and unemployment. The combination of increasing tax rates, a wage-and-interest push, rising oil prices, weak demand, and desperate monetarism came close to being more than European business could stand. If such a combination resumes, the crisis of the system will descend on us in the form of a persistent decline in real income for both workers and recipients of transfer incomes and a further sharp increase in unemployment. The welfare state will condemn a growing number of citizens to welfare.

What it takes

If the economy can be prevented from sliding into depression and disaster, but cannot be prevented from low growth, the combination of increasing G/Y and restoring profits will have remarkable consequences on the required money and real wage levels. Reflection on these consequences will show the far-reaching nature of the policy problem.

Avoidance of further domestic cost inflation means that the level of money wages is allowed to rise in accordance with labor productivity – that is, at most 3 percent. ("Wages" include salaries of the middle and higher echelons of business and government officials, labor income of the self-employed, and the professions.) Probably the maximum is even less, because productivity increase will be less; but 1 percent, 2 percent, or 3 percent does not make much difference – all these nominal wage ceilings are well below actual figures. In 1980, European money wages rose by roughly 8 percent, with the United Kingdom at the top with 20 percent and Germany at the bottom with 6 percent.[34]

A money wage increase of 3 percent will imply a fall in real wages – at least in the short run. Price increases will initially exceed this percentage by at least 5 percent. This is so for three reasons. First, profit margins should be restored. Second, a backlog of old cost increases will have to find its way into the price level. Third, import prices may be expected to rise further, and this deterioration of the terms of trade cannot be compensated in the *scala mobile* without further harming profits. And these three reasons do not yet take into account a further increase in G/Y. It comes on top of the wage restraint necessary for suppressing the spiral.

Now, it is obvious that a deliberate decrease in real wage income of, say, 5 percent cannot be accepted. Not only is this politically impossible, but such a policy would affect purchasing power and further destabilize the economy in a downward direction. In a stagnating economy with zero growth, the increase in real wages should not be forced far below zero – not farther than the increase in G/Y and the restoration of profits dictate. That means that governments will have to compromise. The spiral cannot be abolished right away; and tax rates cannot be increased immediately in conformity with rising budgets. Indeed, tax cuts can be offered as a quid pro quo for wage restraint.

A package deal combining wage restraint and tax cuts seems, therefore, a possible type of compromise. The quantitative impact of such a policy has been studied by the Netherlands Central Planning Bureau. The outcome of their calculations is roughly as follows. Suppose that G/Y is constant and that the government wants to compensate workers for a money wage reduction of one percent. The tax ratio should be reduced by somewhat more than 0.5 percent. The tax cut and the wage restraint are supposed to stimulate production and employment in such a manner that the initial increase in the budgetary deficit will disappear in a few years. The consequent increase in production is estimated at one percent, and the increase in employment at 0.5 percent. The policy will have to be continued for at least ten years.

These figures are not intended to be reliable predictions of what will happen if an incomes policy is combined with tax reductions, but an exercise in consistent possibilities. They illustrate the nature of the present malady. They may also be used as a political device to influence the public debate on the strategic issues – a form of econometric *Seelenmassage*. The calculations can easily be criticized because they depend on a rather vulnerable model and apply to an open economy, but critics should be aware of their obligation to furnish both better calculations and better policy combinations.

To understand the gloomy nature of this exercise, it should be remembered that its starting point is a constant G/Y ratio. In the more realistic case of an expanding budget, every increase in G/Y should be reflected in a decrease in real wage rate. Here the figures are the following: a one percent point increase in G/Y should lead to an additional decrease in the real wage level in the order of magnitude of 0.33 percent. This is the price the average worker has to pay for the shift between the private sector and the public sector. It can be easily born in an expanding economy – whether it will be accepted in a stagnating economy remains a matter of conjecture.

Conclusion

This chapter focuses not so much on the level of government expenditures or its share in the national income, but on the gradient of these magnitudes. That is, on the *shift* in the balance between the political and the private. The impact of G/Y – whether it is 20 percent or 45 percent – on society is difficult to evaluate because it depends on so many factors: the character of government activities, the character of the tax system, and unpredictable citizen reactions to expenditure programs and to various types of taxation. Limits to G/Y – 50 percent? 60 percent? – are utterly impossible to indicate. It is simply not true that the higher the level of G/Y, the more vulnerable a country is to inflation or to stagnation. The opposite may be true, provided that public programs are expansionary. The idea that government outlays are a burden on the economy is generally false.

But a fast and continuous *increase* in G/Y and, in particular, the consequent increase in the tax ratio may be suspected of imposing strains on the workings of the economic system. The European growth rate of G/Y has been about 3 percent per year since 1950. In the period 1977–80 it was slightly higher. The impact on GNP was probably negative. This is mainly so because taxes ultimately tend to fall on a strategic part of the economy: enterpreneurial activity. Tax increases are shifted until they come to rest on firms already coping with a profit squeeze caused by cost inflation and weak demand. An economy that is already stagnating may be further paralyzed if the increase in G/Y is substantial. The danger of tax increases is greater when the country suffers from a strong wage push. This is exactly the threat to the European welfare state of the 1980s: the fast rise in taxes (and in money wages) may well translate itself into a real burden in the sense of losses in real income. It also makes for unemployment, low investment, and eventually, the impossibility of maintaining social security.

The danger can be mitigated if techniques are found to put the incidence of increased taxation on wages and salaries (labor income of the professions included) by means of incomes policy. However, this requires changes in attitudes and institutions to make the policy effective. This condition is not yet fulfilled.

For those who like very broad conclusions, the shift between the public and the private, as mirrored by the expanding budget, constitutes a form of social change, and it is a well-known hypothesis that there are limits to the degree of change that society, and in particular, a society with a stagnating GNP, can take. The dilemma should be recognized by the adherents of the welfare state. They should accept the need to spare the dynamic section of the economy, or the welfare state itself will be seriously endangered.

Notes

1 The cost of complying with government regulations has been estimated for the United States at 5 percent. See Tibor Scitovsky, "Can Capitalism Survive? An Old Question in a New Setting," *American Economic Review* 2 (1980):3. This figure does not reveal the dynamic cost of these regulations, that is, the growth of GNP sacrificed by the government's policy. This issue will be discussed later.

2 The value G includes social security benefits. The public business sector (railways, postal services, telephone), is excluded, but subsidies to public utilities are included. The Y term is interpreted as gross national product. My main source is *Public Expenditure Trends* (Paris: OECD, 1979), which indicates 43 percent for the period, 1975–1978. I have updated these figures by using OECD economic surveys. The OECD figures do not include the budget of the European Community, which is financed by tax revenues from member countries. I have included these expenditures (about 1% of the GNP of the Community), which brings the G/Y ratio for Western Europe to 45% in 1980. The figure for the U.S. is lower, 35%. If Y is interpreted as net national product (or national income), G/Y approached 50% in 1980. The Swedish figure was 65%. The increase has not been steady in all countries; in 1976 G/Y declined in West Germany and in Britain there was even a decline between 1975 and 1980, from 50% to 45%.

3 The title of a 1976 article in *Encounter*.

4 Pigou's expression "exhaustive expenditure" has not caught on and has an undertone of physical fatigue. The expression "government consumption" (used by Beck, see note 6) is misleading, because G_R has a nominal aspect and a real or volume aspect – a point I will discuss later. "Government production" is smaller than G_R insofar as the government's purchases from private firms are part of G_R but not part of government production, which equals the public outlays for manpower.

5 The distinction, although vital, is not at all unambiguous. A grant to a private institution may have practically the same effect on the use of productive factors as a direct government expenditure; subsidies to museums and orchestras are examples. The health sector abounds with arrangements that can technically be classified as transfer expenditures to hospitals or patients but are economically similar to a partial public health service. In some cases, government activities are deliberately organized in foundations so the strict regulations (concerning promotions and salaries) of the civil service can be evaded. In most countries this shady area between G_R and G_T may be on the order of 10% of national income.

6 Morris Beck, "Public Sector Growth: A Real Perspective," *Public Finance* 3 (1979):313.

7 This fraction is lower than the 45 percent mentioned in the opening because Beck includes the United States with a relatively low G/Y. Moreover, his final year is 1975, while mine is 1980.

8 The doubtful validity of Beck's hypothesis is also brought to the fore when we look at the share of public employment in total employment. For the United Kingdom – a case in which Beck concludes that the "real share" has diminished between 1950 and 1975 – the share of public employment (services only) was 15 percent in 1970 and 20 percent in 1978. This increase of one-third may have been compensated by the divergent development of public and private productivity, but the plausibility of this compensation is a matter of belief.

9 Murray Weidenbaum, *Challenge* (November-December 1979).

10 Anthony Downs, *An Economic Theory of Democracy* (New York: Harper & Row, 1957).

11 An interesting synthesis between economic and "politometric" modeling is that of Bruno Frey and Friedrich Schneider, "An Econometric Model with an Endogenous Government Sector," *Public Choice* 34 (1979), which follows the idea of the "political cycle" introduced by Michael Kalecki. Voters are supposed to evaluate the government's economic performance by looking at the growth in real disposable income, inflation, and unemployment: This evaluation is expressed by a popularity function. The policy function specifies the impact of various instruments (it includes G_R, G_T, and the rate of taxation) on economic performance. In this way the budget variables are endogenized. Frey and Schneider estimate their popularity and policy functions for West Germany over the period 1958–72. Public expenditures and public wage levels are raised when an election the government fears it will lose approaches. This analysis is a great step forward compared with the politico-economic view of Kalecki, who believed that capitalists remain politically averse to full employment. The most sophisticated model is probably that by F.A.A.M. van Winden, *On the Interaction Between State and Private Sector* (Amsterdam: North Holland, 1981). It contains production functions for the state and the firms, a maximum tax rate, and separate parameters for the preferences of politicians and bureaucrats, and for their relative strength.

12 James M. Buchanan and Richard E. Wagner, *Democracy in Deficit: The Political Legacy of Lord Keynes* (New York: Academic Press, 1977).

13 See the rather devastating comments of Stein, Meckling, Campbell, and Olson in James M. Buchanan and Richard E. Wagner, *Fiscal Responsibility in Constitutional Democracy* (Leyden–Boston: Martinus Nijhoff, 1978).

14 The total of G_T is higher; I put the European figure at 20 percent of GNP. The difference of 5 percent between G_T and social security benefits of GNP is explained by interest payments and subsidies to firms and foundations. Of course, total grants within Western Europe are much higher than 20 percent of GNP; they include private grants from business firms to foundations (a small amount), from families to families, and, in particular, within families. These last transfers are difficult to estimate, but their amount is certainly very substantial. It was estimated (for the United States in 1970) at one-third of GNP (James N. Morgan and Nancy A. Baerwaldt, "Trends in Inter-Family Transfers" (paper delivered to a joint session of the Association for the Study of the Grants Economy and the American Economic Association, New Orleans, 1971).

15 Richard A. Musgrave, *Fiscal Systems* (New Haven: Yale University Press, 1969), pp. 80–81.

16 Robert H. Haveman, *The Economics of the Public Sector* (New York: Wiley, 1976), p. 95.

17 Fred Hirsch, *The Social Limits to Growth* (London: Martin Robertson, 1977).

18 Figures for 1977 from the Royal Commission on the Distribution of Income and Wealth, *Report No. 6 on Lower Incomes* (London: HMS, 1978), p. 321.

19 Ibid., pp. 100–101.

20 This is what Gabriel Kolko does in *Wealth and Power in America: An Analysis of Social Class and Income Distribution* (New York: Praeger, 1962).

21 The quotation is from S. M. Miller and Martin Rein, "Can Income Redistribution Work," *Social Policy* 6 (May 1975):3. It concerns the United States and is based on the comparison of the income share of the lower deciles over time. These authors, and many others, overlook the fact that before 1950 these deciles were populated by workers; now they contain the elderly, the disabled, and the unemployed, who had almost no income before 1950. This is the paradox of the welfare state: The introduction of social security and social assistance may well lower the income share of the lower fifth of the population.

22 See, for instance, Jan Tinbergen and Jan Pen, *Naar een rechtvaardiger inkomensverdeling* (Amsterdam and Brussels: Elsevier, 1977). According to these authors, Dutch income inequality has been halved between 1938 and 1975. About 50 percent of this equalization can be explained by the combined affects of taxes and transfers.

23 Some observers defend the view that a person's subjective perception of his or her own absolute welfare level is determined by that person's place in the frequency distribution of income. See in particular B. M. S. van Praag and A. Kapteyn, "Individual Welfare Functions and Social Reference Spaces," *Economic Letters* 1 (1978). If this is a correct description of reality, economic growth is not conducive to human happiness – the "preference drift" keeps our well-being at the same level. The view is interesting but hardly convincing in the face of the historical reduction in bitter poverty that has been taking place.

24 Royal Commission on the Distribution of Income and Wealth, Report No. 6 on Lower Incomes, p. 213.

25 This position is taken by E. L. Feige, who derives the size of the irregular economy by the monetary multiplier. See E. L. Feige, "The United Kingdom's Unobserved Economy: A Preliminary Assessment," *Journal of Economic Affairs* (July 1981).

26 E. F. Denison, "Effects of Selected Changes in the Institutional and Human Environment upon Output per Unit of Input," *Survey of Current Business* (January 1978).

27 There is another, more subtle, definition of overtaxing, which takes into account that maximum growth of GNP need not be government's only target. Then, taxation is excessive if it hampers achievement of the policymakers' goals. If they set their growth goal at zero (for Club of Rome reasons) and this is achieved, one cannot say that a tax burden exists. Also, full employment can be distinguished as one of the goals of tax policy; in that case, taxation is excessive when general unemployment exists. I would, however, prefer my own definition of the tax burden: the unintended loss in GNP.

28 C. Northcote Parkinson, *The Law and the Profits* (London: John Murray, 1960), p. 79.

29 Marginal rates may well exceed 100 percent if we are prepared to consider loss of subsidies as well. Under welfare state conditions grants for housing and schooling are linked to income. In the Netherlands a family living in a subsidized home with children at the university may experience a marginal tax rate of 120 percent at rather moderate income levels. If income is higher – say, twice the average – the rate drops again, because at that level eligibility for the grants has disappeared. These kinks in the tax-cum-subsidy curve are, however, restricted to rather special cases of family structure.

30 Among the first authors to substantiate the decline for the United States were A. M. Okum and G. L. Perry: "Notes and Numbers on the Profit Squeeze," *Brookings Papers on Economic Activity* 3 (1970). An international comparison (and an explanation) is found in S. B. Brown, "Cyclical Fluctuations in the Share of Corporate Profits in National Income," *Kyklos* (1978). See also T. P. Hill, *Profits and Rates of Return* (Paris: OECD, 1970). This last publication shows a clear decline, between 1965 and 1976, in the share of profits in manufacturing for Sweden (from 23 percent to 17 percent), the United Kingdom (25 percent to 7 percent), and Germany (29 percent to 17 percent). In other countries, such as Netherlands, the OECD estimates point the other way: an increase from 30 percent to 33 percent. But these are figures about residual income; no correction is made for labor costs of the self-employed, interest, or rent. The residual is insensitive to accelerated depreciation caused, for instance, by wage inflation; if whole chunks of the capital stock become obsolete, these losses are not reflected in the residual. The OECD outcome for the Netherlands – 33 percent in 1978 – is at variance with business reality. Net profits in the manufacturing sector as a whole were in that year close to zero. The profit squeeze is manifest in the behavior of share prices; they lag behind inflation and in many countries actually fell between the mid-1960s and 1980. See Martin Feldstein, "Inflation and the Stock Market," *American Economic Review* (December 1980):839.

31 H. den Hartog and H. S. Tjan, *Investeringen, lonen, prijzen en arbeidsplaatsen* (The Hague, 1974). See also their "Investment, Wages, Prices and the Demand for Labour (A Clay-Clay Model for the Netherlands)," *De Economist* (1976):32ff.

32 This tendency was documented by T. Huppes in *Inkomensverdeling en institutionele structuur* (Leiden, 1977). He shows that the sum of residual income (profits, interest, rents) and transfer income G_T constitutes an almost constant fraction of national income in Belgium, Denmark, West Germany, Italy, the Netherlands, the United Kingdom, and Sweden. The fraction differs among countries, but it is virtually constant over time.

33 This, then, is the central hypothesis of this chapter. It needs (1) more proof than can be given here; and (2) quantification, which is not even tried. More proof means that I should substantiate the proposition that the shifting elasticity of prices with respect to tax-induced cost increases is below unity. This I tried to do in "Wages, Prices, and Employment," in *Pioneering Economics: International Essays in Honor of Giovanni Demaria* (Padua: Cedam, 1978), but the result is hardly convincing. Quantification of the increased taxation requires a comparison of potential but not realized growth rates under conditions of constant tax rates and realized growth rates. The growth rates that would have occurred without tax increases are accurately depicted in what Anatole France termed the *archives-si* the voluminous files of might-have-beens preserved in a part of heaven to which we have no current access. This precarious comparison is comparable to the estimation of the loss in GNP caused by cyclically adjusted fiscal policies, which is made by the OECD secretariat. This calculation, which includes the impact of the fiscal drag, leads to a figure of minus 2 percent per annum for the period 1978–81 (*Economic Outlook* [Paris: OECD, December 1980]). My guess would be that the burden of the public sector is in the same order of magnitude: a loss of few percent of GNP per annum.

34 *Economic Outlook* (Paris: OECD, December 1980).

11

Problems of political economy after the postwar period

JOHN H. GOLDTHORPE

Introduction

The postwar period of the economic history of the capitalist societies of the West is at an end. In the course of the 1970s, it became apparent that the standards of economic performance achieved by these societies over the previous twenty-five years were no longer being maintained and, furthermore, that there was no assurance – and indeed little prospect – of any rapid return to these standards. An observer of Western economies around 1965 might well have concluded that steady and sustained growth, at a high level of capacity utilization and with no more than modest inflation, had in effect become institutionalized. The progressive acceptance of Keynesian economic theory and associated techniques of economic management, together with the growing control exercised by public authorities over the functioning of the economic system, seemed to have inaugurated a new era of capitalism in which stability and dynamism were reconciled and guaranteed. However, ten years later these same economies were for the most part characterized by greatly reduced growth rates and moreover, by a tendency for unemployment and general price levels to rise simultaneously. In other words, it emerged not only that the business cycle was not after all obsolete; but further, and much more disturbing, that recession and inflation could now be *complementary* rather than alternative expressions of economic disorder. A "discomfort index," created by summing the rate of unemployment and the rate of inflation in seven major Organization for Economic Cooperation and Development (OECD) countries, rose from around 5.5 percentage points for the decade 1959–69 to 17 percentage points for 1974–75.[1]

In these circumstances it was scarcely surprising that economic policymakers should reveal a rather sudden waning of confidence in

363

the theory, techniques, and instruments of control on which they had previously relied. Basically, the dilemma they faced was the following: The need was more apparent than at any time since World War II to revive economic activity by the classic Keynesian means of expanding demand. Yet to pursue such a course threatened to increase inflation to a still more dangerous level. Thus, insofar as a commitment to the essentials of Keynesianism was retained, only one thing could be attempted: to seek some critical level up to which demand might be expanded, sufficient to encourage a recovery in business confidence and investment but not so high as to raise inflationary expectations to a yet greater pitch. However, whether any such level actually existed was unknown, and it came to appear increasingly doubtful.[2]

A situation of such evident difficulty created ample opportunity not only for various ad hoc attempts at modifying and supplementing the standard policies of the postwar years (most notably by price and pay controls), but also for more radical responses: that is, for proclamations of the death of Keynesianism and the development of alternative conceptions of economic policy, entailing far-reaching reassessments of the proper *ends* of such policy as well as of its means. What for present purposes is of major interest is that these new developments reveal departures from the postwar consensus which go in quite different, indeed contrary, directions in the role that they would accord to government – and hence to politics – within the economic sphere.

To understand the full significance of this divergence, it is first of all necessary to recognize that the establishment of Keynesianism within the Western democracies, from the 1930s to the 1960s, represented more than simply the acceptance of a new body of economic theory and techniques.[3] Also involved was a major political development: in effect, a historical compromise between contending ideologies and opposing class interests. In one important sense the establishment of Keynesianism did indeed mark the end of laissez-faire: that is, government not only extended its control over the functioning of the economy as a whole but, more important, took upon itself responsibility for ensuring the "success" of the economy, as defined by the twin criteria of full employment and growth.

But, in historical perspective, the triumph of Keynesianism must at the same time be seen as representing the defeat of an alternative approach to controlling the economy: that proposing extensive public ownership and centralized planning, and thus the effective abolition of the free-market capitalist system.[4] In contrast with this approach, Keynesian interventionism was characterized first by its strictly limited extent; and second by its considerable reliance on the market itself as an instrument of control. Under Keynesianism, the focus of governmental concern is on the level of total output, the crucial objective being to secure (in the words of the general theory itself) "an aggregate volume of output corresponding to full employment."[5] This is to be achieved via *indirect* means: that is, governmental action – primarily in the form of monetary and fiscal policies – designed to influence the pattern of choices made in the market by businesspeople, consumers, and others rather than via controls on economic behavior of a *direct*, administrative kind. The allocation of resources and the distribution of rewards within the economy remain processes beyond the normal range of governmental intervention, at least for so long as the free play of market forces is not excessively harsh and disruptive in its consequences or the distortion of the market by organized interests does not become too gross.[6]

Thus, the paramount attraction of the Keynesian "middle way" was that it afforded the possibility – and indeed for some time the reality – of a degree of consensus over issues of political economy which had been amply revealed as capable of generating serious social unrest and instability. On the one hand, labor was assured of protection against the material and psychological ravages of large-scale and long-term unemployment and was offered the prospect of sharing in the benefits of sustained economic progress. But, on the other hand, the economy remained essentially capitalist, and no grave threats were posed to the key institutions of capitalist society nor thus to the associated structures of power and advantage.

Nonetheless, as the Keynesian formula has steadily declined in its effectiveness, the ideological and political compromise that it made possible has become increasingly strained and in turn exposed to a dual challenge: on the one side, from those who would wish to reconstitute the economic and social order of free-market capitalism; and, on the other, from those who seek to move beyond present-day "managed" capitalism to some new order in which the degree of political control over the functioning of the economy will be considerably enlarged. In what follows the nature of these challenges to the Keynesian middle way will be examined and an attempt made to show how each represents a response to current economic problems in the face of which Keynesianism is apparently inadequate. However, it will further be argued that, at least as so far formulated and reflected in policy proposals or – to a lesser extent – in actual applications, these challenges are themselves seriously underdeveloped, especially in their political viability or, more generally, the political conditions and consequences of their success. Thus, unless and until these questions are engaged with and resolved – ultimately as a major political accomplishment which will entail significant changes in the structure of power and advantage in society – neither what one may term the "new laissez-faire" nor the "new interventionism" is likely to be effectively implemented. The Keynesian compromise may have broken down, but what might be described as the Keynesian impasse – with an attendant high level of economic discomfort – could well persist.

The new laissez-faire

It is the basic claim of those who wish to move back from Keynesianism to the restoration of a more laissez-faire political economy that a solution of present-day economic problems can be found only in an acceptance, by all parties concerned, of the disciplines and incentives provided by the free working of market forces. Exponents of the new laissez-faire have achieved greatest prominence and actual influence through the proposals they have advanced for countering inflation. These entail policies aimed at the strict regulation of the money supply, which would represent the principled refusal of government to provide any further monetary accommodation for inflationary wage settlements and price increases. Only in this way, it is contended, can the inflationary expectations which keep up the momentum of the inflationary process be reduced and eventually eliminated from the economy.

However, what is of major significance here is the fundamental redefinition of the proper objectives and concern of government within the economic sphere that lies behind such a "monetarist" approach to the defeat of inflation. In effect, the policies in question require that, in direct repudiation of Keynesianism, government should disavow – and explicitly so – any responsibility for the overall level of economic activity, and hence for the achievement or maintenance of a state of full employment. To overcome inflation via monetarist policies requires, as monetarists themselves acknowledge, a "stabilization crisis," in which unemployment unavoidably rises – to an extent and for a period that cannot be accurately predicted. And, furthermore, it is seen as essential to long-term price stability, and, indeed, to the possibility of any return to full employment, that government should provide *no guarantee* of full employment. For, paradoxically, only when government refuses to try to boost the level of employment via the standard policies of Keynesian demand management can it avoid regenerating the inflationary expectations and, in turn, the inflation-inducing behavior, that in the end lead to higher unemployment than would otherwise have occurred.

It is, then, this position that chiefly justifies one in speaking of a return to a laissez-faire outlook. While recognizing certain fundamental changes from the nineteenth century which cannot be *entirely* reversible – in, for example, the state provision of social welfare services and the scale of the public sector of the economy – exponents of the new laissez-faire nonetheless share with their nineteenth-century predecessors a basic conception of the capitalist market economy as a quasi-natural system. This system possesses powerful self-regulating properties, yet at the same time may be easily disequilibrated by external interference, even when the objective is to promote its more efficient operation. From such a conception, a distinctive view of economic policy derives. Governments should be concerned primarily with sustaining *an institutional context* within which the economy may freely operate according to its own inherent logic and should modify their claims to be "in control" or even "in charge" of the economy itself. Indeed, they should seek to emphasize the strict limits on their ability to ensure economic success, or to stave off crisis, independently of the courses of action followed by those who play the key roles within the economic system as investors, employers, union leaders, and so on.[7]

Furthermore, it may be observed that the new laissez-faire is obviously akin to the old in seeing specifically *political* costs and dangers in the governmental regulation of economic life. In fact, its exponents have introduced into the political argument a major new development. In the nineteenth century the chief political objection to interventionism was that it threatened individual liberty by increasing the coercive power of the state. But what is now added is the contention that, as practiced in the context of a modern democracy, interventionism also threatens the governmental system itself by subjecting it to serious "overload." The assumption by government of responsibility for the satisfactory operation of the economy forces it into ever-widening efforts to control or influence economic outcomes – in regard to not only employment but to pay, prices, profits, investment, and so on. Thus, the determination of these outcomes, instead of following automatically from the working of market forces, must in each case constitute a political issue: The "domain" of politics becomes, in other words, progressively enlarged. However, so does the extent of the conflict generated among different social groupings and their representative organizations as they press their often incompatible claims and interests on government – up to a point at which the institutional containment of such conflict becomes problematic. In sum, interventionism is inevitably socially divisive and potentially socially disruptive. A modern democracy can function effectively only if the domain of politics, and hence the degreee of conflictual political activity, is subject to some delimitation, and reliance wherever possible on "the judgment of the market" in place of governmental decision offers an important means of achieving this.[8]

The new laissez-faire constitutes, then, a relatively coherent body of doctrine, and one from which indications for policy follow rather directly. But the crucial question that must be raised here is whether the restoration of a free-market capitalist economy to the extent envisaged is a feasible political objective; or, better, what are the conditions necessary for it to become so and, in turn, the wider implications of such an objective being realized. The difficulties likely to be faced by a government seeking to disengage itself from the political economy of Keynesianism by embarking on a more laissez-faire course may be usefully considered under the two following, obviously related, heads: first, distributional dissent – the problems of securing the acceptability of market outcomes, especially on the part of members of those social groups and classes with the least advantaged market situations; and, second, organized labor – the problems posed by the practice of trade unionism and the existence of labor movements, representing in effect the attempt by those least advantaged in the market to compensate for their weakness in this respect through organization and collective action.

Distributional dissent

In seeking to explain the decline in standards of economic performance in the capitalist world, exponents of the new laissez-faire give major importance to misguided governmental policy. Inflation is seen as the result primarily of governments' failure to control money supply in relation to the potential growth of output. Typically, this failure results from attempts to maintain a commitment to full employment via demand management, which are, however, themselves destined to fail and, indeed, through their inflationary effect, to be counterproductive. Thus, in the end the least desirable outcome, stagflation, is arrived at. Correspondingly, then, and as already noted, the key to a solution is seen in a strict monetary policy – with its laissez-faire implications – that would dispel from the economy the inflationary expectations created by previous monetary laxity, and in turn steadily run down the inflationary process: Expecting inflation to fall, economic decision makers will no longer to the same extent act in an "inflationary" fashion. The concomitant of such a policy would be a period of contraction in economic activity and rising unemployment; but this would need to be accepted as the unavoidable cost of returning the economy to a state from which healthy and sustained growth could begin again.

The foregoing analysis, it should be noted, is crucially dependent on the laissez-faire assumption that free-market capitalism is a fundamentally stable and efficient system, if only left to regulate itself. Thus, inflation is in no way seen as being generated endogenously: Its source is exogenous governmental action, to which actors within the system merely respond. Once, therefore, government ceases to create inflationary pressure, such pressure will disappear.

It is revealing to compare this understanding of inflation with the alternative one, in which inflation in modern Western societies is represented as primarily the monetary expression of distributional dissent: or, to be more precise, of a heightening of such dissent, which can be seen as the result in part of the delegitimation of existing social inequalities and in part of a shift in power differentials in favor of organized labor. In this view, it is the conflict among different groups and classes over their relative shares in the national product which forces governments into monetary laxity – as in effect some kind of solution, or at least resolution, of the problems of dissent that the functioning of the market economy directly generates.[9] What is pointed up by this comparison is that within the laissez-faire analysis a further important assumption is in fact implicit: that actors within a free-market system will in general be prepared to accept market outcomes, in the sense that, whether they find them pleasing or not, they will recognize that they represent the best that can properly be hoped for and will not attempt to change them through nonmarket means. However, this is to assume precisely what must be in question; and, indeed, the assumption covers up the most serious area of weakness and disarray, both theoretical and practical, in the entire laissez-faire position.

Au fond, supporters of the free-market system face a dilemma over whether the basis of the acceptability of market outcomes should be seen, and presented politically, in moral or instrumental terms. Those who have provided the most philosophically coherent defenses of the system – such as F. A. Hayek and Frank Knight[10] – have maintained that it is inappropriate to judge the distribution of rewards and deprivations resulting from the operation of the market in moral terms: for example, by criteria of "fairness" or "social justice." This is so because the market can in no sense be regarded as a moral agent: on the contrary, it operates in an entirely impersonal and automatic way, producing outcomes for which no particular participants can be assigned responsibility.

Moreover, the logic of the market does not provide for any direct relationship between the inputs of ability, effort, and so on, by individuals in producing goods and services and what they get in return: In the end, all that counts is the (marginal) value of these goods and services to others in the market. Distributional outcomes may appear as rewards or deprivations from the point of view of individual participants; but within the market system the function of these outcomes is not so much to recompense actors for their *past* performances as to serve as indicators and incentives which will influence the course of their *future* behavior. It follows, therefore, that while it is an error to condemn the inequalities generated by the market as morally wrong – as egalitarian critics seek to do – it is also misguided to try to legitimate market outcomes as being just in terms of "merit" or "desert." For as market conditions fluctuate, in ways that no individual can predict or control, rewards and deprivations will reflect, over and above differences in individual ability and effort, a range of other factors that can only be subsumed under the headings of circumstance or chance.

From this point of view, then, rather than the acceptability of market outcomes being given a moral basis, the free market must be argued for in instrumental terms: that is, on the basis of the unique value of the market as a social institution. It is the only means as yet discovered through which information about wants and the possibilities of supplying them – information which in modern societies is widely dispersed among vast numbers of individuals – can be efficiently utilized for the benefit of all. The logic of the market makes for a size and composition of total output which ensures that the shares assigned to each individual – whether via merit, chance, or whatever – are, simultaneously, as large as they can be. Furthermore, through its incentives and disciplines, the operation of the free-market system also maximizes the possibility of economic growth, from which again all can benefit; and the least advantaged will stand to do so to a far greater extent than they could from even the most radical program of redistribution. Thus, in the context of a dynamic economy, the preoccupation of egalitarians with relative rather than absolute standards is revealed as essentially irrational: It can only be understood, whatever their claims to idealism, as the expression of an underlying ressentiment or envy.

This argument pretends to a high intellectual level, and a critical response, it might seem, should be offered on a similar plane. However, what for present purposes is chiefly relevant is not how well the argument itself stands up to philosophical or social scientific scrutiny, but rather how effective it is likely to be as a legitimation of market outcomes in sense of actually conditioning perceptions and actions in society at large. And, judged from this standpoint, the chances of its success would seem small. Its basic weakness is that the attempted veto on judging market outcomes in moral terms – whatever its philosophical merits – goes directly counter to popular tendencies. A variety of evidence indicates that in society at large, differences in incomes and other rewards are indeed very frequently and readily assessed in terms of their "fairness" – in relation to ability and effort, and also to other criteria such as individual or family need, or the inherent deprivations or the "social value" of different occupations. To be sure, because of this diversity of criteria and for other reasons, such judgments are to a large extent confused or inconsistent. Nonetheless, their pervasiveness leaves little doubt that inequalities generated by the market are widely *felt* to require moral legitimation on some basis.[11]

It is indeed significant that among publicists for free-market capitalism who operate somewhat closer to the political battlefront than do its more philosophically oriented supporters, the rejection by the latter of any direct moral defense of inequality has always been a cause of considerable disquiet. For it has been clearly seen that, as one writer has put it (in direct reproach of Hayek), "men cannot accept the historical accidents of the market place – seen merely as accidents – as the basis for an enduring and legitimate entitlement to power, privilege and property," and moreover "cannot for long accept a society in which power, privilege and property are not distributed according to some morally meaningful criteria."[12]

However, while this objection carries sociological force, it in turn raises the difficulty of what moral grounds for the acceptability of market outcomes can in fact be provided. The approach chiefly favored by those arguing the need for such grounds has been a "meritocratic" legitimation of inequality. But this runs into formidable objections of the kind raised by Hayek and Knight and also by critics from other, quite different, sociopolitical standpoints.[13] Again, of major relevance for present purposes is that meritocratic arguments seem in various important respects unlikely to be persuasive among the population in general. For example, the processes through which a range of life chances are influenced by social origins, quite independently of individual merit, may not always be of the highest social visibility; but they are still sufficiently apparent for fairly realistic popular ideas to form about the actual limits to "equality of opportunity" – on which principle, of course, a meritocratic legitimation of inequalities of condition must depend.[14] Again, and yet more damaging, in a context of rising unemployment notions of merit – or demerit – become rather obviously inept in accounting for what befalls individuals, in view, first, of the marked class bias in the incidence of unemployment and, second, of the way men and women often become unemployed not as individuals but rather collectively, in consequence of their association with particular enterprises, regions, or industries.

One might then reasonably infer that attempts to meet the need for a morally based legitimation of market inequalities will quickly lead to a renewed appreciation of the advantages of the instrumental case. But, in fact, to underline the difficulty faced here by exponents of the free-market system, one must finally note the doubts that have of late also arisen in regard to one of the strongest features of this case: the claim that the possibility of growth removes any rational argument for redistribution.

The origin of such doubts may be traced to an observation widely made during the social and political unrest of the late 1960s and early 1970s: namely, that a quarter of a century of unprecedented economic growth had in fact done little to reduce concern over questions of inequalities and "relativities" in incomes and living standards. If such a concern must be adjudged irrational, then irrationality was widespread, and the actual achievement of growth had made it no less so. However, various analysts have subsequently sought to provide more satisfactory explanations for persisting distributional dissent than ones leading merely to a crude psychologism and invocations of ressentiment, envy, and so on. And in so doing they have in fact exposed further major – and politically consequential – weaknesses in the intellectual basis of the free-market system.

Of greatest relevance here is perhaps Fred Hirsch's account, derived from his distinction between the "material" and "positional" economies.[15] This distinction becomes important, Hirsch argues, as with economic advance a growing proportion of consumption takes on a social as well as an individual aspect: that is to say, the amount of satisfaction or "utility" an individual gains from the consumption of a good or service becomes dependent on the social context in which the consumption occurs – which will include the consumption of the same good or services by others. Greater utility may be obtained through more exclusive consumption, as, for example, with cars or with houses or holidays in "select" areas; or utility may depend not only, or even primarily, on the individual's absolute level of consumption but indeed essentially on his or her level *relative to* that of others – most obviously with recognized "status symbols" but also, for example, with education and training when considered as investment goods.[16] Thus, alongside the familiar material economy, grounded in physical scarcity, one must recognize the positional economy, grounded in social scarcity.

Moreover, the further, crucial difference is that while the material economy can be expanded, so that all can become better off at the same time, the positional economy is by nature "no-growth." Social scarcity cannot be reduced, and in the struggle for positional advantage what one wins another must lose. The idea of growth as an alternative to redistribution can thus never apply to the positional economy – and at the same time *the very existence of the positional economy undermines the validity of this idea in regard to the material economy.* For, because income and other material resources are the individual's main means of pursuing positional goods and holding his or her place in the positional economy, relativities in incomes and other conditions become charged with great significance; and a concern with such relativities, even where absolute standards are generally rising, must therefore be reckoned as entirely rational.

In sum, then, the assumption, implicit in the analyses and policy proposals of the new laissez-faire, that market outcomes will in general prove acceptable must be reckoned extremely doubtful. Neither instrumental nor moral considerations would seem capable of providing such outcomes with any very effective popular legitimation. Rather, a free-market economy must be regarded as one that is at all events charged with a large *potential* for generating distributional dissent, which will not be dissipated by either the prospect or the achievement of general material advance.

In fact, analyses such as Hirsch's give further plausibility to the argument earlier referred to that distributional dissent is the chief source of inflationary pressure in modern societies, and that inflation itself – in the sense of a general rise in the price level – is a means of accommodating the associated conflict which has indeed some attraction from a governmental standpoint: that is, in avoiding direct sociopolitical confrontations and at the same time making it difficult to tell exactly who are the winners and the losers, or to what extent they are winning or losing.[17]

In turn, if this view is taken, the laissez-faire approach to the control of inflation must be seen as likely to give such conflict a sharper definition. For, if a government imposes a strict monetary policy and disavows the objective of maintaining a high level of employment, this must, of course, entail more than providing a salutary check to inflationary expectations. It implies the underwriting by government of the actual structure of market power and advantage producing the outcomes whose acceptability is in question. Thus, even if such an approach is successful in achieving greater price stability, not only will the potential for distributional conflict remain but, further, government will become more obviously involved in this conflict in that it will be seen, at least by the relatively disadvantaged, to be acting in a clearly ex parte manner.[18] In other words, and somewhat paradoxically, the role of government gains greater social visibility when it invokes the new laissez-faire strategy of "squeezing inflation out of the economy" than when inflation is in effect tolerated as containing the more basic, distributional problem. And, in turn, the laissez-faire approach is also more likely to provoke adverse reaction.

One form this reaction may take is direct resistance by employee groups to the consequences of government policy. For example, workers may in some instances be prepared to engage in "trials of strength" with employers who, under the pressure of a tight monetary regime, offer wage increases that are inadequate to maintain real living standards. Strikes, or perhaps sit-ins or plant take-overs, may occur in opposition to impending redundancies or closures, the frequency of which will increase as part of the stabilization crisis. In short, one may expect a heightening of industrial conflict of a clear political significance: for as well as in some cases involving government directly, as the employer in the public sector, such conflict will in any event be seen as stemming ultimately from the constraints that government's economic strategy imposes.[19]

If widespread, and thus a source of major disruption in the economy, such conflict could itself undermine the political viability of a laissez-faire program. However, a more serious threat is that likely to be posed by an adverse electoral reaction, in particular to the return of large-scale and long-term unemployment. With such a development, the full implications of the breach of the Keynesian compromise will become apparent. Moreover, mass unemployment is, of all aspects of market operation, the least amenable to moral glossing, and the electoral record of liberal democracies over the postwar years has suggested a tendency for voters to regard it as an unattractive exchange for lower inflation. For example, when the "liberal experiment" conducted in France by Giscard and Premier Barre was terminated by the election of 1981, it was accepted that the administration's greatest failure lay in its record on unemployment. Barre's strategy required acceptance of rising unemployment "in the short term" as the cost of checking inflation and restoring profits; but as the longer-term horizon for the turnaround steadily receded and the numbers of those out of work reached a new postwar level, public confidence in the strategy rapidly ebbed away.[20] It is not, therefore, surprising that a frequently voiced anxiety of supporters of the new laissez-faire should be that a government espousing its policies might not be able to survive electorally for long enough to allow their effective implementation, or for their long-run benefits to be realized.

In the face of such difficulties, the best strategy available to government would appear to be that of presenting its policies in such a way as to encourage an essentially fatalistic acceptance of them: that is, as policies in fact dictated by the exigencies of the new and much harsher economic world. Thus, in the Thatcher administrations in the United Kingdom – which may be taken as the most consistent and politically successful exponents of the new laissez-faire to date – the basic justification of their policies is simply that there is no alternative. High rates of unemployment – and low rates of growth – must not be seen as the consequence of government policies, but rather as resulting entirely from exogenous factors beyond government's control (usually subsumed under the label "the world recession").

However, it is doubtful that the British Conservatives' election victory of 1983 and their second term can be seen as an indication of the general viability of this kind of strategy. While the evidence of the interwar years shows clearly enough that fatalism and apathy can indeed be the response to mass unemployment, this is now less easily represented than before the Keynesian period as some kind of quasi-natural misfortune – at least where such an interpretation is contested by an effective political opposition, which is also capable of rebutting the claim that no policy alternatives exist. After the Conservatives came to power in Britain in 1979, their popularity rather quickly declined as the nature of their economic policies became evident, indeed, to such an extent that there were repeated demands from among the government's supporters for a "change of course."[21] This situation was significantly altered only with the success of the military adventure in the Falklands in 1982; and then, in the subsequent period of electioneering, the Conservatives were able to preserve their advantage chiefly on account of a divided opposition and the chaotic state of the Labour Party.

The campaign itself, it should be noted, provided little support for the idea that public concern over high rates of unemployment is tending to diminish: On the contrary, poll data consistently revealed unemployment to be the leading issue. What, rather, saved the Conservatives in this respect was that the "Alternative Economic Strategy" offered by Labour was ill-prepared and widely found unconvincing. Even so, the Conservatives' share of the total vote in 1983 *fell* (to 42.4 percent, equal to only a 30.8 percent support rate among the electorate as a whole), and their increased number of seats was entirely the result of the vagaries of the electoral system. There remains, then, a serious point to the question raised by new laissez-faire theorists of whether parliamentary democracy may not ultimately need to be qualified – by constitutional restraints on the powers of "temporary" majorities – to allow continuity for those policies which, in their view, are essential to a free-market system and hence to upholding the "higher" value of personal liberty.[22]

Organized labor

In the early decades of the twentieth century, it was often held – and from contrasting sociopolitical positions – that trade unions and free-market capitalism were antithetical. On the one hand, supporters of capitalism represented unions as a threat to the efficiency and in the end to the viability of the capitalist economy, at root because unionism was inimical to the individualistic values on which the capitalist social order was founded. On the other hand, among those morally and politically opposed to capitalism, the trade-union movement was seen as the main basis of resistance to the ethos and practices of the capitalist system, and further as crucial to the development of working-class consciousness to the stage at which a total rejection of, and revolt against, this system would occur. But, as the actual coexistence of unions and capitalism continued, alternative interpretations of their relationship were naturally encouraged; and, indeed, in the postwar period, when unionism and capitalism appeared typically to *flourish* together, their affinities rather than their incompatibilities came to be emphasized.

For example, in American "political" liberalism – as distinct from the older European "economic" liberalism – trade unions were no longer viewed as alien and threatening to the prevailing social order, but rather as integral to it and with a large part to play in preserving its stability. In the context of a "managed" capitalist economy, the interference with the working of market forces that resulted from union activities could not be regarded as of major consequence. Far more significant than this, and of any curtailment of economic freedom, was the fact that unions actualized the principle of freedom of association and, in providing their members with an organized representation of their interests, both industrially and politically, could make a reality of their participation within a genuinely "plural" society. Thus, instead of being seen as the agencies of working-class opposition to capitalism and the development of a radical class consciousness, trade unions were seen as key agencies of what was termed the "civic reintegration" of the working class.[23] Correspondingly, then, basic reappraisals of the historic role of the unions in the struggle for socialism were made on the Left. And to many it appeared that, at least in the absence of the political stimulus and direction of a revolutionary party, unions were likely to become largely supportive of the capitalist order, as the liberals argued. Encouraging their members to define their interests within the context of this order and permitting some measure of success in the pursuit of these interests, the unions could scarcely serve as the "schools of socialism" that Marx had envisaged; they were destined rather to become an effective means of the "accommodation" and control of the working class.[24]

Today, however, with the postwar period at an end, it may well be argued that the wheel has come full circle; that once again the compatibility of trade unions and free-market capitalism is crucially in question, at all events in the sense that the unions now stand as a major barrier to the successful realization of a new laissez-faire program. Explicit acknowledgment of this opposition is indeed often made, and not least by exponents of the new laissez-faire themselves in their recurrent attacks on what they refer to as union "monopoly power" and restrictiveness. But what for present purposes is important is to go beyond the rhetoric of these attacks and bring out exactly why and how unions should pose so strong a threat to the viability of a laissez-faire approach to current economic difficulties.

The understanding of trade unionism found in the postwar political liberalism just alluded to was essentially correct in two important respects: first, in the significance attached to unionism as the organized representation of the interests of members of the working class – broadly, those who live by selling their labor power in return for wages; and, second, in the recognition given to the close relationship between the growth of trade unionism and the extension to the working class of citizenship rights, betokening full membership in the national community. However, liberal writers were in one respect in serious error: that is, in supposing that the integration of labor movements into the pluralist institutional structure of Western democracies – and any associated decline in working-class consciousness and the appeal of socialist ideology – were necessarily developments favoring greater social harmony and cohesion. On the contrary, one could better claim that it is indeed *as* unions have separated themselves from nineteenth-century revolutionary traditions, concentrated on building up a stable membership and sound organization, and established themselves institutionally within the capitalist system that their compatibility with this system has become especially problematic.[25]

This point is, in fact, to some extent recognized in the laissez-faire analysis of the present problems of capitalism. Although it is not believed that union activity in the labor market can in itself have an inflationary effect (in the way suggested by cost-push theorists), it is emphasized that, where the power of unions in collective bargaining is complemented by political influence, they do typically play a quite crucial part in the inflationary – and stagflationary – process: that is, by forcing up the general level of wages faster than productivity increases, and by then exerting pressure on government to expand the money supply unduly in an effort – which must ultimately fail – to stave off the unemployment that their wage demands threaten to produce.

The strategy of the new laissez-faire would be characterized, as already noted, by a refusal to yield to such pressure. The aim would rather be to allow the discipline of the market to operate freely and thus to bring home to the unions and the public at large the full consequences of "excessive" pay settlements. An open rejection of any attempt to mitigate the adverse effects of such settlements is indeed essential to demonstrating government's determination not to provide inflationary pressures with any monetary accommodation, and hence to achieving the crucial goal of a reduction in inflationary expectations. However, again as was earlier remarked, a basic weakness in this analysis lies in the assumption that market outcomes can command general acceptance – rather than being themselves a source of dissent and conflict, which in turn creates inflationary pressure. And what must here be added is that to the extent to which unions have become institutionally established, the practical difficulties stemming from this analytical weakness are enormously amplified. Trade unionism, as it has developed within the working classes of Western democracies, may be regarded as, in effect, the organized expression of the unacceptability of free-market outcomes on the part of those who are likely to be most disadvantaged by them; or, in other words, an attempt by those who, as individuals, have little power *in* the market to compensate for this precisely through organization and collective action directed *against* the market. Indeed, it is from this point of view that the laissez-faire theorists' attacks on unionism must be understood – although, of course, they are unable to acknowledge that the unions' "monopoly power" is simply a countervailing force to the market advantages that derive from the ownership of productive property or the possession of credentials to technical knowledge and expertise.[26]

There is, then, little reason to suppose that unions will respond to the economic policies of the new laissez-faire in the way that supporters of these policies would wish. Rather, in the context of what unions will define as an economic "free-for-all," they may be expected to use their bargaining power – both organizational and strategic – in an unrestrained fashion to obtain the best possible results for their members. For example, there would seem little reason why government's predictions of the *future* rate of inflation should exert any moderating influence on unions' wage claims where the actually prevailing rate is higher. Moreover, in the face of such a union reaction, it will avail government little to press the argument that militancy makes unemployment worse than it need be. The deterrent effect of this argument is limited in that there is no necessity, nor in many cases even a high probability, that the workers who secure "excessive" pay increases will be those subsequently most exposed to unemployment.

Thus, if under a regime of monetary strictness wage claims *are* reduced – as they may well be – this will be most realistically understood as resulting not from a downward shift in inflationary expectations or from the unions' acceptance of the logic of governmental macroeconomics, but simply from their recognition that a new balance of power exists in the context of a depressed labor market. As Tibor Scitovsky has argued, given that inflation does to an important extent derive from changing power relations in intergroup and interclass distributional conflicts, it will be possible for it to be "cured" through unemployment – provided that this is sufficiently severe and prolonged to constitute a threat to the long-term security of workers' incomes and living standards.[27] However, if this interpretation of the linkage between monetary restraint and a decline in the rate of inflation is accepted, what must then follow is that far from the root causes of inflation having been eliminated – by virtue of dispelling inflationary expectations – they have rather been merely suppressed; and thus the "cure" that has been achieved has to be reckoned a highly conditional one.

It may therefore be said that the presence of trade unions and their predictable patterns of response to the new laissez-faire carry two major implications. First, the stabilization crisis that a laissez-faire strategy in any event entails will be made longer and more severe; and, second, no assurance can be provided that its costs will not be in vain. It is a rather well-known weakness of the monetarist approach to the control of inflation that the underlying theory is unable to specify over what period the main effects of "bringing the money supply under control" will be felt on the level of economic activity rather than on the level of prices; and it is indeed usually accepted that in this respect institutional factors will be of crucial importance. Thus, following this argument, trade unions, which play an integral part in national systems of wage determination and of industrial relations generally, may be regarded as forming a particularly serious barrier to any rapid and positive adjustment of the economy by means of imposition of a monetarist regime.[28] Furthermore, as this adjust-ment is eventually made, and the level of economic activity increases, there would seem to be nothing to prevent union activity in tighter labor markets from once more generating inflationary pressure and thus again confronting government with the choice of either accom-modating this pressure or turning back to restrictive policies.

In these ways, then, further serious strain may come to be placed on the political viability of the new laissez-faire. For apart from the likelihood of union action aggravating the problem of unemployment, a protracted crisis which still does not appear likely to banish the specter of inflation – and thus create the conditions thought necessary for sustainable growth – threatens a yet more politically damaging consequence: that is, to create doubts and fears over government policies, and in the end perhaps open opposition to these policies, within the business community itself. Thus, to return to the British case, the first Thatcher administration was almost from the start sub-ject to pressure from large and small employers alike to take more account of the effects of its economic strategy on business prospects, and to adopt a "less rigid" position on matters such as interest rates and even incomes policy. During 1982 this pressure eased, and as an election drew near employers' organizations rallied to the Conserva-tives and lent support to their claim that an economic upsurge was under way. However, because it is now becoming apparent that under Conservative rule the British economy has in fact experienced not only the most severe contraction but also probably the weakest re-covery within the industrial world, the future of relations between the new administration and business must be reckoned doubtful. In any such instance of a government committed to free-market capi-talism becoming estranged from what would seem its natural con-stituency, the ultimate danger must, of course, be that business interests to some extent actually redirect their political support – as, say, in the British case, to the Social Democratic Party.

Because, then, for a government pursuing the policies of the new laissez-faire, the power "against the market" of institutionally en-trenched unions so evidently increases both the economic and political risks entailed, an attempt to cut back union power must be seen as an essential part of its overall strategy – in discharge, one could say, of its "disciplinary" function of ensuring that an institutional context appropriate to the operation of free-market capitalism is created and preserved. Theorists of the free-market system have indeed made it clear that, ideally, such a context would be one in which collective bargaining over wages and conditions of employment would have no place, so that the chief raison d'être of trade unionism would cease to exist.[29] However, not only can the abolition of collective bargaining be set clearly beyond the limits of the politically possible in Western democracies, but, in fact, major political difficulties can be expected to attend any serious attack on the bases of union power. It is in this regard that the full importance appears of the connection between the growth of trade unionism and the development of citizenship rights. The expansion of union power in the course of the twentieth century may be seen as founded upon, and at the same time the most forceful expression of, the emergent status of the worker as citizen: that is, as a member of a national community who possesses a range of rights – civil, political, social, and, increasingly, industrial – in virtue of this membership, and independently of his or her market position. Thus, it is scarcely possible for any attempt by government to reduce union power decisively to avoid appearing as – and indeed to avoid being – an attempt also to abridge already established citizenship rights.

To turn once more to the British case, it may be noted that no less an authority than F. A. Hayek has several times declared that the monetarist policies being applied cannot achieve their intended effects unless they are accompanied by radical "union reform": specifically, by the rescinding of "all special privileges" granted to the unions by law – or, in other words, by effectively undermining the right to strike.[30] However, while the logic of Hayek's argument is apparent, what is significant is the difference between what he would propose and the approach to the problem that has actually been followed by the Thatcher administrations. This has, in fact, been distinctively cautious, and the "antiunion" measures taken thus far at least – through the Employment Acts of 1980 and 1982 – have been aptly described as "politically cosmetic rather than fundamentally damaging to trade union interests."[31] Further legislation is planned, but despite the government's parliamentary supremacy and the mandate for union reform that it could claim from the 1983 election, it is still very questionable if this legislation will extend to more consequential action, such as outlawing the closed shop or unofficial strikes, or requiring that collectively negotiated contracts be legally binding. Although there can be little doubt that the government would in principle wish to move toward more radical measures of this kind, it will be actually ready to do so, one may suggest, only if unusually favorable political circumstances were to arise – as might be occasioned, say, by serious disunity within the union movement or events creating widespread and extreme antiunion sentiment.

Thus, the problems of the political viability of the new laissez-faire may be summarized as follows:

1. The distributional outcomes generated by the free-market system lack any widely persuasive legitimation, and their acceptability among the population at large is highly problematic. Because of these facts, a government which, through its economic policies, in effect underwrites such outcomes will not be generally viewed as acting in merely a technical, instrumentally rational fashion, as laissez-faire theorists would wish. Rather, it is likely to be seen by members of the groups and classes least advantaged in the market to be intervening against their interests in issues of distributional dissent and conflict.

2. The most direct political threat to a government following a laissez-faire strategy, and thus refusing to accept responsibility for maintaining any given level of economic activity, will come because for a sizable number of the labor force the significant market outcome will be unemployment. Although the attempt may be made to present such a situation as one that is beyond government's control, and thus to induce a fatalistic response, high levels of unemployment must still be reckoned as in general rendering governments electorally vulnerable.

3. The unacceptability of distributional outcomes determined purely by power in the market to those who have little such power finds its organized expression in trade unionism. With their increasing involvement in the processes of wage determination and work regulation generally, unions have come to represent a major source of power against the market, and hence a major barrier to both easy implementation and lasting effectiveness of laissez-faire policies. Thus, the political viability of these policies may be further threatened in that their heavy costs and uncertain outcome reduce their attractiveness even to business interests.

4. Attempts by government to reduce union power will themselves be likely to raise serious difficulties, in that the growth of this power is closely bound up with the growth of the idea of national citizenship and with the expansion of citizenship rights – rights, in fact, often designed explicitly to offset market power.

The new interventionism

The new laissez-faire constitutes a relatively coherent body of doctrine pointing rather clearly toward a set of policy objectives, albeit ones that give rise to major political problems. As will now be argued, comparable problems attend the programs of those who seek a significant enlargement in the degree of governmental control over economic processes. However, in this case it must be added that further problems result from some frequent division or uncertainty of purpose. The crucial issue here is whether the ultimate aim of wider-ranging and more powerful governmental intervention is essentially to *preserve* capitalism by extending the management and organization of the economy in what might be termed a progressively "corporatist" direction, or whether the aim is in the end to *replace* capitalism by some form of socialist economy and society.

This argument may best be developed by reference to incomes policy. If for proponents of the new laissez-faire the key to the solution of present day economic problems lies in control of the money supply, then correspondingly for proponents of the new interventionism, in whatever version, it is control over the rate of increase in money wages and salaries that is crucial – even though this may in some instances be concealed for ideological or tactical reasons.[32] Moreover, just as the major difficulties facing the new laissez-faire arise from the requirements and consequences of imposing monetary strictness, so for the interventionists it is the various implications of achieving the desired regulation of incomes that pose the serious questions of political viability. However, depending on the ultimate purpose for which, and the context within which, incomes policy is pursued, these questions take on a clearly different form.

The attempts widely made during the postwar years to bring about "restraints" in pay settlements were generally seen by their authors as a natural extension of Keynesian political economy in a period in which the primary goal of full employment had been largely achieved. After all, Keynes himself had envisaged that collective bargaining under full employment would be likely to generate inflationary pressure, and that this would have to be contained chiefly through political contrivance.[33] But while, from one point of view, the logic of incomes policy as a complement to the Keynesian strategy for the maintenance of full employment is evident enough, from another, any attempt to intervene in the determination of incomes must appear as a significant departure from Keynesianism, and indeed one with considerable disruptive potential.

As was earlier argued, the acceptance of Keynesianism may be seen as representing a "historical compromise" within the Western democracies on crucial issues of political economy. Keynesianism, it appeared, allowed governments to assume responsibility for full employment and economic expansion, while removing the need for them to become involved in forms of intervention that would seriously change the character of prevailing processes of allocation and distribution. Intervention could for the most part be limited to the macro level and operate through – rather than in opposition to – the capitalist market system. In this perspective, then, it becomes at once apparent how a resort to incomes policy, even if perhaps providing short-term support for Keynesianism, must in the longer term threaten to undermine its entire rationale. For incomes policy, if it is to be at all effective, does, of course, entail intervention that is of a generally more detailed kind than that required by the standard Keynesian techniques of economic management and, more important, intervention which cannot be undertaken simply by the manipulation of market variables.

A successful incomes policy must, rather, require the imposition of pressures or constraints on economic actors sufficiently forceful to make them act in ways *other than* they would have if influenced by market forces alone. Moreover, the problems that are in this way created for Keynesian political economy are only a beginning: Incomes policy opens up a veritable Pandora's box. For if incomes are to be controlled on any effective and long-term basis, then at the very least demands can be expected from wage and salary earners that prices and profits should be subject to some corresponding regulation. And, in turn, as will subsequently be shown, further arguments easily can, and in all probability will, be developed which require that incomes policy be associated with far more radical forms of political intervention: that is to say, ones that, in clear contrast to Keynesianism, must eventually imply some direct challenge to capitalist institutions and related aspects of social structure. If established on the political agenda, therefore, such arguments would seem destined to become a source of severe and rather fundamental social conflict.

In sum, as a recent author has argued, to the extent that Keynesianism seeks to incorporate incomes policy, it faces the danger of losing its major political advantage, that of providing grounds for consensus. With incomes policy, "the basic conflict which post-war Keynesian politics seemed to have transcended returns again as planning and freedom stand once more opposed."[34] However, as earlier observed, the political problems that arise for those who seek to go beyond Keynesianism will differ significantly according to whether the aim is to sustain further or to transform capitalism. In the former case, the key problem is that of denying, obscuring, or otherwise limiting the radical implications that may be drawn from the need for, and the practice of, incomes policy. In the latter, the key problem is precisely that of being able to exploit these implications – in the face of the political difficulties and opposition that efforts in this direction will surely encounter.

As with the new laissez-faire, further discussion of these problems of political viability can most usefully proceed under the headings of distributional dissent and organized labor. On the one hand, the difficulty faced by the new laissez-faire in securing the acceptance of market outcomes is matched by that faced by the new interventionism of securing the acceptance of the distributional implications of incomes policy; on the other hand, the difficulty of the new laissez-faire in overcoming union opposition and its disruptive effects is transposed, for the new interventionism, into that of finding some coherent and effective basis for union cooperation.

Distributional dissent

It was previously argued that if inflation is seen not merely as the result of governmental failure to control the money supply, but rather as the monetary expression of intensified distributional dissent and associated social conflict, then a weakness is at once apparent in the counterinflationary strategy of the new laissez-faire: namely, the assumption that the distributional outcomes generated by the capitalist market system have widespread acceptance among the population at large. Similarly, to view inflation as being thus socially grounded also reveals a major weakness in interventionist approaches. As already observed, the crucial (if sometimes hidden) requirement of interventionist strategies is that of securing some degree of control over the rate of growth of money wages and salaries. But if distributional dissent is the main source of inflationary pressure, then, it may be supposed, this dissent will in itself constitute a serious obstacle to any solution via incomes policy.

When in the postwar years governments resorted to incomes policy, their initial attempt was usually to present this as essentially a technical measure: that is, an additional instrument of economic management which was needed in a situation of full employment and buoyant demand to prevent different groups of wage and salary earners from engaging in a futile, but nationally damaging, chase after "confetti" money. However, such a view could never carry much conviction, and its credibility was rather rapidly undermined as the actual experience of incomes policy became more extensive. In the context of a money economy, the regulation of money incomes implies the regulation of real incomes; and it follows that incomes policy can never be *simply* an antiinflationary device. It must always at the same time represent a political intervention in the distributive process. And this is no less the case where governments maintain that incomes policy is designed to be "distributionally neutral" – as, for example, where a percentage norm for pay increases is established. For to take the means of influencing the distributive process and then use them in such a way as not to disturb the status quo is, of course, no less a form of intervention than one with explicit redistributive intent.[35]

Furthermore, the idea of an incomes policy which is "distributionally neutral" even in the previous, rather misleading, sense is itself highly questionable. For it would seem inescapable that incomes policy, even where it is designed to "treat everyone with same," must in fact be particularly directed against, or in all events bear particularly on, various specific groups within the work force: that is, those who – as a result of market shifts, organization, greater awareness of their strategic advantages, or whatever – have strengthened their bargaining positions, and who might thus be expected, in the absence of incomes policy, to push toward an improvement in their relative income levels. Indeed, there can be little doubt that incomes policy has been most frequently regarded by Western governments as a means of countering the capacity of certain sections of the organized working class to generate inflationary pressure: that is, their capacity to engage in "leapfrogging" pay settlements or to establish pay targets for workers in general that are insufficiently related to advances in productivity. In other words, it could be said that the major objective of incomes policy has been to control the growth of wages of industrial labor in a period when its market and organizational power has tended to increase.

Correspondingly, it is in no way surprising to find that incomes policy has been viewed by organized labor as imposing a serious limitation on its freedom of action, and has therefore been either opposed, or accepted only under conditions which represent, whether tacitly or openly, some form of quid pro quo. In the course of the postwar period it became evident that in fact incomes policy could not operate unless the cooperation of the trade unions was secured; and, further, that for this cooperation to be extended the unions must be assured that government would, at the very least, protect the living standards of their members from any adverse effects. The historical record reveals that those national incomes policies which "succeeded" in the 1950s and 1960s, in the minimal sense of achieving relatively long-term political acceptability (whatever their economic results), were generally complemented by attempts at price control and dividend limitation and formed part of an overall economic strategy aimed at full employment and expansion.[36]

However, it should at the same time be recognized that incomes policy has as yet become established on what could be reckoned a permanent basis in few Western societies, and also, of course, that its actual effectiveness in regulating the growth of wages and salaries, other than in the short term, remains much in question. Moreover, what for present purposes is of greatest relevance is the argument that over time the problems involved in maintaining incomes policy will become progressively more difficult. It is evident enough that the economic circumstances that have signaled the end of the postwar period are not conducive to union cooperation with government, and particularly not in cases where reduced levels of economic activity and consequent rising unemployment can be rather directly attributed to government policy. But it is not only, or even primarily, to the course of historical change that this argument refers. The essential claim is, rather, that as experience of incomes policy grows, in whatever historical context, those subject to it display a "learning curve" which leads to greater awareness of the nature and implications of the policy, and then, in turn, especially on the part of organized labor, to heightened resistance to it or a significant enlargement of the conditions for its acceptance.

As already implied, it cannot be expected, in a context of distributional dissent, that trade unions will exercise restraint in pay bargaining as in effect, an act of simple altruism toward the rest of the community[37] – or, in other words, that working-class groups will simply cede the increased power and advantage they have built up. Rather, as several commentators have by now remarked, the typical union strategy that develops vis-à-vis governments seeking to implement incomes policy is pursuing a new form of bargaining: that is, one in which restraint within the labor market is offered in exchange for greater influence, exerted in one way or another, within the political sphere.[38] It has then further to be recognized that it is characteristic of this, as of other bargaining processes, that the parties to it will be ready, where it appears appropriate, to redefine their bargaining positions. And, as governmental attempts at incomes policy have continued, it would seem clear that the tendency has been for unions steadily to increase what they believe they can – and in their members' interests must – demand in return for their cooperation.[39] Thus, while price control and dividend limitation, plus growth, appear to have served for the most part as an adequate quid pro quo up to the late 1960s, the deals with unions that governments have needed to work out subsequently have been generally wider-ranging. In exchange for their efforts at wage restraint, unions have often sought gains in return through new labor regulation – in regard to both working conditions and employee and union rights; through fiscal and pensions policy; and, most important perhaps, since the mid-1970s through active labor market and job-creation policies aimed at holding unemployment in check.

However, there is little reason to suppose that deals of the kind in question might represent some kind of equilibrium state. On the contrary, it would seem to be virtually inherent in the dynamics of bargaining over incomes policy that two further, rather fundamental, issues must sooner or later be encountered if governmental efforts to regulate incomes persist. These are first investment and second the range and determinants of income inequalities.

It has often been seen as a virtue of incomes policies that they help prevent profits from being "squeezed" in a way that would be detrimental to investment. At the same time, if controls are to be imposed on the growth of wages and salaries, it is politically difficult for them not to be extended to profit. In this respect, Keynesian advocates of incomes policy have typically stressed the distinction between profits that are paid out to owners of capital as income and profits that are retained by firms to finance investment. It has then been supposed that incomes policy need concern itself only with the former, as, say, through providing for dividend limitation in some form. However, so far at least as wage and salary earners are concerned, it is doubtful if this distinction can for long remain decisive. If through their restraint in using their bargaining power employees are contributing to an increase in *total* profits, then they are in a position to claim not only that control should extend to distributed profits, but further that they should acquire some legitimate interest in the way the profits that are retained are actually used – or, in other words, in the amount and type of investment that is undertaken.[40]

Thus, one version of this claim would be that investment should be adequate to maintain high levels of employment and that, if necessary, this should be ensured by direct governmental intervention, whatever institutional entrenchment on the capitalist order this might entail. But it could also, and still more radically, be argued that since the investment of retained profits is to the long-term advantage of the holders of equity, then to the extent that such investment depends on restraint in pay settlements, employees are entitled to some share in the equity of their firms – otherwise, the income that their unions refrain from extracting is applied simply to increase the wealth and power of others. It is, for example, essentially an argument on these lines that underlies the Meidner Plan advanced in the mid-1970s by the Swedish trade unions as an appropriate complement to their "solidaristic" wages policy and accepted, in its main principles, by the Social Democratic government returned to power in 1982. While recognizing the need for increased investment to safeguard the competitiveness of Swedish industry, and hence the danger of using their labor-market power to squeeze profits unduly, the unions have in effect raised the issue of the distributive terms on which this new investment is to be brought about. What is proposed is a partial collectivization of profits via a system of "wage-earner funds" which would, as the proportion of total equity capital in such funds steadily built up, lead to the effective demise of private-property institutions as the basis of large-scale economic activity and to a corresponding shift in power to the agencies controlling the funds.[41]

Issues of incomes inequality deriving from attempts at incomes policy have thus far been discussed chiefly from the standpoint of the difficulties governments face in arriving at appropriate criteria for "relativities," especially between different occupational groups in the industrial workforce. Difficulties of this kind may indeed be acute, and in particular in the context of securing union cooperation in incomes policy – as will subsequently be argued. But the point that must here be emphasized is that the practice of incomes policy further has the potential to open up the question of the much broader inter-class inequalities that prevail in pay and in work rewards generally: most notably, the inequalities apparent (especially if a lifetime perspective is taken) between the rewards of the mass of manual and routine nonmanual exmployees on the one hand and those of professional, administrative, and managerial personnel on the other. If the determination of pay and conditions of employment can no longer be left to the interplay of market forces, and if unions are to restrain their organized bargaining power, then the whole of the existing range of differences in work rewards must in principle become open to reconsideration and, indeed, to politicization. In particular, the unions are given a basis for challenging how the position of more advantaged classes is dependent on the operation of a variety of influences which could be described, in economic terms, as imposing severe restrictions on the supply side of the labor market; or, alternatively, as generating class-based inequalities of opportunity – for example, in the form of differences in family and community resources, bias in the functioning of educational and training systems, limitations on occupational access via "credentialism," and so on. From such a challenge it is then an obvious step to seek to link incomes policy to the development and strengthening of a range of social policies aimed specifically at creating a greater equality of life chances; or, in other words, to the launching of a forceful attack on salient features of the prevailing class structure.[42]

Such implications of incomes policy have then evidently the potential to become major sources of sociopolitical controversy and division. For attempts to follow them through could scarcely avoid inciting opposition from among the most powerful and privileged sections of society – opposition which need not be confined to the electoral process. If it is accepted that the inflation which creates the need for incomes policy is at root the expression of heightened distributional dissent, then it cannot be supposed that incomes policy is capable of providing some purely technical means of overcoming the problem. On the contrary, the argument must be that incomes policy – in much the same way, in fact, as a policy of monetary strictness – can be effective if at all only through bringing dissent and conflict into the open, and thus making it evident that any decisive solution to the economic problem will have to be a sociopolitical, rather than simply a technical, one and one out of which clear winners and losers will emerge.

For those whose aim is to preserve an essentially capitalist form of economy and society, it will be important to try to suppress the radical implications of incomes policy: that is, to try to operate such a policy as far as possible as one of wage restraint *tout court*.[43] And, to the extent that concessions have to be made to obtain union cooperation, it will then, from this point of view, be preferable to make them to union *leaders* – by giving them a greater voice in general economic policy making and also perhaps greater powers vis-à-vis their memberships – rather than to make them through policy initiatives that could be threatening to the basic social structures and processes of capitalism. In other words, the strategy must be one which aims to bring organized labor under control through involving its leaders in the management of capitalism as part of a technocratic elite. However, what must be questioned is whether such a strategy can in fact succeed in containing trade-union pressure as exerted at the rank-and-file level; or, at all events, whether it can do so without the fateful development of what has been termed "bargained corporatism" into a corporatism of an imposed and authoritarian kind.

On the other hand, for those who seek a mode of transition from capitalism to socialism, the need for and radical potential of incomes policy present an evident opportunity. From this point of view, it is essential that the range of possibilities for political bargaining and exchange be fully appreciated by unions, and that they make a progressive attempt to translate their industrial power into political influence and, in conjunction with allied parties, into wide-ranging programs of a socialist character. But, in this case again, the actual nature of union response must be reckoned problematic. In particular, it remains uncertain how far union leaders will be converted – and can in turn convert their members – to the view that the members' interests will be better served through a decisive incursion of the unions into the political arena – and a decisive commitment to socialist objectives – rather than through the continuation of traditional methods based on "free" collective bargaining and "independent" pressure-group action.

Both conservative and radical strategies in regard to incomes policy, then, must be expected to meet with serious problems of implementation. But before any final assessment of their viability can be made, it is evident that more specific consideration is required of the difficulties for the new interventionism, in whatever form, that stem from the very presence of organized labor.

Organized labor

Previously, trade-union opposition to the new laissez-faire was seen as deriving crucially from two characteristics of unionism as it has evolved in Western democracies: first, that it represents the organized expression of the unacceptability of free-market outcomes to those with little individual power in the market; and, second, that it is founded on, and at the same time gives real force to, the emergent status of the worker as national citizen. In the present context, these same characteristics are again of central relevance, although with somewhat different emphases. In the perspective earlier adopted, unionism was readily revealed as a major obstacle to the proper functioning of free-market capitalism, and hence to the successful realization of the new laissez-faire; but in this same perspective it is also apparent that unionism is essentially *a product of* liberal capitalism and, as it presently exists, is dependent upon this form of capitalism for its very raison d'être. As was earlier noted, more sophisticated analysts on the Left have for some time now recognized how trade unions "are dialectically both an opposition to capitalism and a component of it"; and further "the power and durability of the notion of 'the two sides of industry' as the immutable framework of trade union action."[44] It follows, then, that attempts at radical change in prevailing economic and industrial relations institutions, in any direction, must be directed against institutions in which organized labor has an important stake.

Thus, for those who have advocated incomes policy as a necessary technical adjunct to Keynesianism, the commitment of unions to collective bargaining has represented no less an obstacle than for proponents of the new laissez-faire. And, indeed, the former may be scarcely distinguishable from the latter in the vehemence of their attacks on union power and the ignorance of union leaders, or in their conviction that current economic problems would be opened to rational solution *if only* collective bargaining could be somehow suspended and union leaders find some alternative way of using their time.[45] Where governments have gained unions' acceptance of incomes policy by affording them greater opportunities for exercising political influence – in other words, enabling them to replace labor-market by political bargaining – it is, of course, an important feature of such "deals" that some alternative function for union leaders *is* created. But the crucial question in turn arises of whether trade unions, as they have developed in Western capitalism, are or can become capable of operating effectively in the new mode required of them.

In this respect, most commentators have so far concentrated their attention on the formal structures of national labor movements. It has been widely observed that those movements which, in the postwar period, have become most integrated into processes of policy formation have tended to be unified and centralized. Where such a structure exists, governments are able to treat with an uncontested and well-defined union leadership; and, in turn, once a political bargain has been made, such a leadership would seem to have the best possibility of "delivering" its members – that is, of ensuring their compliance with the terms of the bargain, crucially, of course, in regard to pay.[46] A related factor which has also been emphasized is the extent to which labor movements have achieved success within the political system itself. A bargained form of corporatism would indeed appear to have advanced farthest in societies in which working-class parties either have held lengthy periods of office, as in Sweden and Norway, or have formed part of the "elite cartel" of a "consociational" democracy, as, for example, in Austria. Under these circumstances, as one author has expressed it, "an essential compensation for the peculiar strains to which trade unions expose themselves by co-operating in incomes policy" is found in their "privileged access to governmental and administrative centres of decision."[47]

However, it may still be reckoned as uncertain whether the strains in question can be sufficiently eased, even in societies such as those mentioned, for union involvement in political bargaining to provide in itself an effective basis *either* for a stabilized capitalism *or* for a progressive transition to socialism. In one aspect, the problem is that already considered of the adequacy of the quid pro quo offered to unions for restraint in their labor-market activities; but this problem is in fact seriously complicated by the organizational dynamics of unions and labor movements, whatever their formal structure.

To begin with, the rewards obtained from political bargaining need not be the same for all levels in the union organization. For example, the rank and file may gain less in the material ways that are chiefly of interest to them than leaders gain in influence and prestige; and national leaders are likely to gain more in these respects than regional or local leaders.[48] Again, even where union leaders are able to influence economic or social policies to the undoubted advantage of their members, there remains the difficulty of what has been called the "interpretation gap."[49] The gains from political bargaining, unlike those from collective bargaining in the labor market, are usually not direct and immediate, but rather indirect and long-term. Thus, it is far less easy for the rank and file to evaluate the deal that the leadership has made on their behalf; and the danger is clear that, for the rank and file, any loss of immediate advantage resulting from pay restraint will have greater subjective salience than the prospect of benefits to come, at some indeterminate time, via government action.

Also relevant here is the rather neglected issue of how exactly the "constituency" of the unions is to be defined. It is evident that the exchange of labor market power for influence in national policy making has to be conducted not only in a long-term perspective but also with reference to rather broad, indeed essentially *class-based*, interests. Thus, for the results of such bargaining to be fully appreciated among the union rank and file, it would seem necessary – though in fact far from certain – that they share with the leadership a conception of the unions' constituency as extending beyond current membership rolls: for example, as comprising not only former union members who may have become unemployed or retired, but, further, the dependents and semidependents – children, aged parents, and so on – of trade unionists considered *in general*.

In this regard, moreover, difficulties may be expected to derive from the vertical as well as the horizontal lines of divisions in union organization – or, in other words, from what is usually referred to as sectionalism. Workers in different enterprises, occupations, industries, and sectors will, of course, at any one time face labor-market situations with different potentials for collective bargaining over wages and conditions. Thus, in giving up their freedom of action in such bargaining and accepting a policy of restraint, some groups of employees will inevitably forgo greater advantage than will others. But what political bargaining can then obtain in return, via economic and social policy, will typically be of benefit to a wide range of workers and is unlikely to give any specific compensation to those who sacrificed most in terms of labor-market power.[50] Again, then, rank and file approval and acceptance of political bargaining would seem to depend to an important extent on the existence of a level of class awareness, ideology, and solidarity that is capable of transcending sectional identities and interests.[51]

Finally, the problems that sectionalist tendencies create for a strategy of political bargaining are likely to be exacerbated in that such a strategy compels union leaderships to take up a position on pay relativities across the range of employments in which their members are concentrated. As already argued, the cooperation of unions in incomes policy gives opportunity for their leaders to question the bases of broad interclass inequalities in work opportunities and rewards. But at the same time, as "partners" of government in operating incomes policy, union leaders can scarcely avoid sharing responsibility for its intentions and effects in regard to differences in pay and conditions *within* the ranks of organized labor. Most often, unions have favored, in the name of solidarity, a policy of gradually reducing such differences, but this has predictably aroused discontent among those groups of workers who see their former advantages eroded; and what is then significant is that this discontent is directed not so much against employers as against the prevailing policy and, in turn, the union leaders who have underwritten it and seek to impose it.

In sum, it becomes apparent that while opportunity to exercise political influence may well be seen as "an essential compensation for the peculiar strains to which trade unions expose themselves by co-operating in incomes policy," this opportunity is still unlikely to *remove* the strains in question to any significant degree. And, indeed, evidence of their persistence is readily discernible in the historical record of almost all societies in which the attempt has been made to substitute political for labor-market bargaining, not excluding those in which the experience of this process is most extensive and in which most may be claimed for it. Most typically, employee dissatisfaction with incomes policy has been expressed either through attempts to evade its restrictions by informal or perhaps illicit bargaining at the local level, as revealed in the phenomenon of "wage drift"; or, more overtly, through various forms of protest against union involvement in pay restraint, culminating often in unofficial strike action.[52]

For present purposes, then, two points of major significance emerge. First, it is clear that even where the new interventionism has developed, with the cooperation of union leaderships, into a form of bargained corporatism, the presence of organized labor still remains as a potentially serious destabilizing influence and, moreover, one which would tend to be exerted not in the direction of socialism but, rather, toward a return to the practices of collective bargaining as they have evolved under capitalism. It is indeed here that one may identify probably the gravest threat of all to the political economy of the new interventionism: that is, a rebellion by large sections of organized labor against any acceptance of incomes policy, no matter what inducements are offered in the way of union involvement in policy formation. A rebellion of this kind has, of course, been frequently urged by left-wing minorities within those union movements that have engaged in political bargaining. But it would, in fact, seem most likely to be promoted, under present economic circumstances, by general working-class disillusionment with the benefits that appear possible through action in the political sphere and, further, by certain groups of workers with above-average labor-market power and some assurance against unemployment coming to believe that they at least would be better off under a regime which allowed free collective bargaining – and which perhaps was at the same time committed to paring back social welfare provisions and collective consumption as a whole to reduce taxation.[53]

In this case, then, sections of the working class would become politically aligned with other class elements hostile to governmental deals with unions and interventionist strategies in general. And such a rebellion could, therefore, be regarded analogous to that earlier envisaged by the business community against the new laissez-faire: that is, as one resulting in the formation of a cross-class opposition to prevailing policy, which would, electorally and otherwise, be extremely difficult to resist.

Second, though, the foregoing analyses also indicate what would be required for an interventionist political economy to have the best possibility of retaining the support of organized labor. Rather paradoxically, from some points of view, this possibility would be maximized not through the labor movement being persuaded into greater "moderation" – as this term is usually understood – but rather through a particular kind of radicalization. To overcome the problems posed by the "interpretation gap" and by sectionalism, it would seem necessary for union leaderships to seek to encourage their rank and file to view trade unionism and its objectives in a "class" perspective: that is, to view unionism as being concerned not only with protecting and improving the pay and conditions of men and women in particular employments but also – and increasingly – with advancing the interests in society at large of all members of a broadly defined working class. Because of the essentially long-term and rather generalized character of the benefits that political bargaining can provide, it is only within this perspective that the advantages of a permanent (as opposed to merely an occasional and opportunistic) union involvement in such bargaining can fully appear, and at the same time its strains be reduced.

What this means, then, is that to seek simply to sustain a system of bargained corporatism as the institutional basis of macroeconomic management can scarcely be a realistic objective for union leaderships; for this would leave the threat of rank and file rebellion unaverted. Rather, union development in political bargaining must have as its concomitant a major effort at political mobilization and creativity, aimed at fostering working-class awareness and solidarity and at basic changes in existing social institutions and structures in directions favoring working-class interests. Thus, the key concern of union leaderships must be actually taking the lead in the escalation of the terms of cooperation in incomes policy, the logic of which was previously outlined, and in turn engaging in the wide-ranging controversy and conflict these terms will inevitably arouse.[54]

One may then best indicate the magnitude of the obstacle which organized labor presents to the new interventionism by saying that it will only be diminished to the extent that the union movement can succeed in transforming itself into something other than essentially a creature of capitalism. The strategy of political bargaining may be reckoned crucial to this process – enabling unions to function as more than defensive or reactive organizations within capitalism. But, for its own success, such a strategy would seem to demand a significantly different ideological context from that of conventional collective bargaining, one, it must be recognized, which few national labor movements are as yet even within sight of achieving and one which, moreover, for many union leaders would in fact appear as more dangerous than desirable.

In summary, the problems of the political viability of the new interventionism may be stated as follows:

1. Control over money incomes, in some form or other, is a crucial component of the new interventionism. But such control cannot be exercised as simply an extension of Keynesian techniques of economic management. Incomes policy necessarily involves government in distributional issues, dissent over which is a key source of the inflationary pressure such policy is intended to contain. In other words, incomes policy can never be purely technical, but is rather inherently contentious, and through its introduction the "Keynesian compromise" in political economy is jeopardized.

2. Incomes policy must take as its major objective the control of the money wages of organized labor: that is, it must entail restraint in collective bargaining. Any long-term policy at least will thus require the cooperation of trade unions. However, unions will expect some quid pro quo. Typically, they will be prepared to withhold the full use of their power in the labor market only in return for influence over government economic and social policy: They will seek to substitute political bargaining for more conventional collective bargaining. Moreover, as experience of incomes policy grows and its implications come to be more fully appreciated, the demands made by unions as the price for their cooperation may be expected to widen and, in fact, to threaten rather basic institutional and structural features of capitalist society. In this way, then, the conflictual character of incomes policy will be heightened and its pursuit will meet with

considerable opposition from the groups and strata whose superior power and advantage within the status quo is placed in question.

3. At the same time, though, the long-term involvement of unions in incomes policy, as under forms of bargained corporatism, requires them to function in ways significantly different from those that have shaped their evolution within capitalism and places severe strain on their capacity to "deliver" their memberships. Rank and file and sectional pressures for a reversion to unrestricted wage bargaining seem almost invariably to emerge and threaten to bring about either a loss of effective control over wages, and hence the discrediting of incomes policy, or, indeed, open rebellion against such policy and the entire political economy of which it is part.

4. Unions can only develop in such a way that they will be better able to carry their memberships with them, as partners of government willing to engage in political bargaining, through a widening of their objectives so that they become more than the defenders of particular interests within the working class. They must, rather, encourage among their members a general class awareness and solidarity in the context of which the appeals of political bargaining will be strengthened and become in effect agencies of the political mobilization of the working class as a whole. But whether within the union movement of any of the Western nations the political will and resources exist to achieve such a development – and to face the severe conflict that it would entail – must at present remain in doubt.

Conclusion

It was claimed in the introduction that, as so far formulated and actually implemented, both the new laissez-faire and the new interventionism are seriously underdeveloped in regard to questions of their political viability. The major concern of the two central sections of the chapter, then, has been to substantiate that claim. In effect, the purpose of the argument has been to show that while, following the demise of Keynesianism, these alternative conceptions of political economy may well hold attractions for governments, it still remains far from clear that either is capable of establishing itself sufficiently securely to have an adequate opportunity of realizing the full program it proposes or implies. Changing the boundaries of the political, in relation to the economy, at least, is far more easily envisaged in theory than achieved in practice, even when standards of economic performance are in manifest decline. In this final section of the chapter, it would seem apt to consider in a more general sense why this should be so, and, further, what would be entailed if either the new laissez-faire or the new interventionism were to succeed more decisively.

It will have become apparent that the understanding of current economic problems of Western capitalism that underlies the arguments of this chapter sees these problems as being to a major degree *endogenously* produced. Although "external shocks" – such as the Vietnam War and its financing, harvest failures, oil price rises, and so on – have certainly played a part, they are largely regarded as having exacerbated more basic difficulties which stem from the long-term development of Western capitalist societies. More specifically, the position adopted is that the increase in inflationary pressure – which is what chiefly undermined Keynesian policies – must fundamentally be related to processes of secular change that have brought about distributional dissent and conflict of both a more intense and a more equally matched kind than hitherto: that is, by in certain aspects weakening the legitimacy of prevailing social inequalities and, in others, reducing the extent of such inequalities. In this last respect, major emphasis has been given to the increase in power and advantage in the struggle for "relative shares" that large sections of the working class have gained, primarily through the extension of citizenship rights and the growth of union organization, but also through the generally high levels of employment that the Keynesian compromise afforded.

From this standpoint it follows that current economic problems cannot be viewed either as ones which could have been avoided if governments had not lapsed into policy errors, or as ones which could now be solved by essentially technical measures – if only there could be found economists clever enough to devise these, and governments wise enough to put them into effect. Rather, it must be maintained that, in attempting a "solution," any government will be engaged – in addition, of course, to contending with technical matters – in specifically political action and, moreover, in action that will inevitably be of an ex parte kind in that it will bring government itself into the center of the distributional conflicts in which the economic problems are grounded. Thus, as observed, the new laissez-faire involves government in underwriting the distributional outcomes generated by the free-market capitalist economy, in withdrawing responsibility for preserving high levels of employment, and, so far as it dares, in directly aiming at curtailing trade-union rights and immunities. On the other hand, the new interventionism implies that government will seek directly to control the distributional process in order to obtain outcomes different from those that would have resulted from the interplay of market forces alone and, further, that government will need to bargain with, and make concessions to, trade unions and their constituencies across a widening range of economic and social issues in return for their cooperation in wage restraint.

In this perspective, therefore, it becomes evident enough why a commitment by government to either of these approaches, in the face of its economic difficulties, is likely to meet with opposition sufficiently widespread and forceful to raise serious questions of political viability. For in each case alike, the attempt to change the boundaries of the political in relation to the economy must be seen as an attempt to shift the actual balance of power and advantage in society; and the achievement of such a shift would be as integral to the success of the policies pursued as the movement of economic variables in the direction desired. Thus, what would be entailed in the success of the new laissez-faire would be a reduction in the power of organized labor and a general enlargement of social inequalities as part of the process through which the disciplines and incentives of the market were permitted to operate more freely. The success of the new interventionism would involve a transfer of the power of organized labor from the industrial into the political sphere, accompanied by the legal and institutional consolidation of this power and by economic and social policies aimed at further advancing working-class interests.

The primary source of the problems of political viability that both approaches can be expected to face may then be reckoned as that of class-based opposition. However, it may well be that a wider opposition will also develop, arising in part out of the very conflict generated. This may perhaps result from a rather diffuse shift in opinion among a population becoming tired of sociopolitical confrontation and the attendant disturbance to the tenor of its everyday life; but more specific and yet more damaging adverse reactions may also come about. Business interests may turn against strict monetarist policies on account of the costs they impose and their doubtful chances of extirpating inflation in the presence of a powerful union movement; or sizable sections of organized labor may rebel against incomes policy because, in the face of the opposition of other classes, political bargaining between unions and government cannot provide what workers would regard as an adequate recompense for wage restraint. In sum, and in the terminology favored by political scientists, one may say that governments may be attracted to new conceptions of political economy on account of their growing problems of *effectiveness* in relation to economic performance – but, in pursuing the policies involved, they are likely to encounter no less serious problems of *consent*; and, further, problems of effectiveness and consent threaten to interact in a highly negative fashion.

The concern of this chapter, it should be made clear, has not been political prophecy. In particular, its intention has not been to claim that either the new laissez-faire or the new interventionism must be doomed to failure whenever and wherever the effort may be made to implement them. For one thing, the possibility must, of course, be recognized that especially favorable conditions for one or the other strategy could result from historical contingencies and conjunctures that are in principle beyond any prediction – such as, for example, the disintegration of the Labour Party or, still more striking, the "Falklands factor" in recent British politics. Furthermore, though, it is also evident that economic, social structural, and cultural conditions directly relevant to the chances of viability display considerable cross-national variation: for example, patterns of involvement in international trade, the formation of classes and class alliances, the organization and ideologies of labor movements, conceptions of "the state," and so on. Thus, it is certainly easier to envisage the secure establishment of the policies of the new laissez-faire in Britain than, for example, in the Scandinavian countries. It would likewise seem far more probable that Sweden, Norway, or Austria might develop further a political economy based on the new corporatism than that Britain – or, say, the United States – would move even as far in this direction as the former countries have already done.

Nonetheless, what *is* implied by the arguments advanced here is that nowhere in the Western capitalist world will the broadly defined "postwar" political economy be readily transformed. Simply because in its economic consequences the Keynesian compromise appears far less attractive now than during the 1950s and 1960s, this does not mean that its political logic has lost its force. Rather, one may anticipate that while in their economic strategies different Western societies will seek to move in different directions and degrees away from their versions of the postwar model, thus creating much greater diversity than hitherto, the strong political pull of Keynesian policies –and their economic effects for good or ill – will still be widely displayed. Thus, for example, the economic strategy of the Socialist regime inaugurated in France in 1981 was in fact largely premised on the achievement of higher levels of economic activity and increased growth through the classic Keynesian methods of directly stimulating consumption and investment; and the aftermath in the form of inflationary and balance-of-payments problems, leading in turn to the imposition of "austerity measures" is, from a British standpoint, remarkably reminiscent of the experience of the Wilson administration between 1964 and 1967. Again – "Reaganomics" notwithstanding – renewed growth in the United States was assisted by high budget deficits and a notable monetary relaxation, to the accompaniment of dire forecasts from Friedman and others that this expansion would simply generate higher inflation, which would then have to be followed, after the next presidential election, by a return to restrictive policies and further recession.

In sum, the survival, or at least the twilight life, of Keynesianism after the postwar period may come to be seen as the way in which within the field of political economy decisions, even if only implicit, to give priority to the avoidance of serious conflict find their most typical expression. If, as has been argued here, the viability of radical alternatives is rendered problematic by the balance of class power and advantage, then most Western nations may forgo the possibility of pursuing these alternatives as the price to be paid for social peace.

Notes

1 See *Towards Full Employment and Price Stability* (the McCracken Report) (Paris: OECD, 1977), p. 42. This report provides a convenient documentation, but a basically unsatisfactory analysis, of the declining performance of Western economies. For an excellent critique, see Robert O. Keohane, "Economics, Inflation, and the Role of the State: Political Implications of the McCracken Report," *World Politics* 31 (1978).

2 McCracken and his colleagues speak in this respect of "the narrow path" back to stable growth. See *Towards Full Employment and Price Stability*, chap. 6. It should be noted, though, that in the next chapter, they urge supplementing better demand management policy with a policy of "nonaccommodation" of inflationary pressure. This would in turn entail a crucial deviation from Keynesianism in that government could no longer accept responsibility for maintaining a high level of employment. This will be discussed later.

3 The first applications of Keynesianism, as understood in this chapter, in fact occurred *avant la lettre* in Sweden under the guidance of Wigforss after the Social Democratic access to power in 1932, and also in Hitler's Germany. In the postwar period the German Federal Republic could be regarded as the last major Western society to adopt a Keynesian approach – following the "social market economy" policies of Eucken and Erhard – with the entry of the Social Democrats into the Grand Coalition in 1966.

4 Robert Skidelsky, "The Decline of Keynesian Politics," in Colin J. Crouch, (ed.), *State and Economy in Contemporary Capitalism* (London: Croom Helm, 1979).

5 J. M. Keynes, *The General Theory of Employment, Interest and Money* (London: Macmillan, 1973), p. 378.

6 Keynes himself was always clear that his policy proposals were, as he expressed it in his essay "The End of Laissez-Faire," "directed toward possible improvements in the technique of modern capitalism by the agency of collective action." And he added that "there is nothing in them which is seriously incompatible with what seems to me to be the essential characteristic of capitalism, namely the dependence upon an intense appeal to the money-making and money-loving instincts of individuals as the main motive force of the economic machine." *Essays in Persuasion* (London: Macmillan, 1972), pp. 292–293.

It could, of course, be said that Western societies have differed rather widely in the extent to which they have resorted to "economic planning" over the postwar years (see, for example, the detailed comparative accounts given in Andrew Shonfield, *Modern Capitalism* (London: Oxford University Press, 1965). But even where the cameralist tradition has most prevailed, as, for example, in France, such planning has been essentially "indicative" and could itself be very readily subsumed under the formula of action "directed towards possible improvements in the technique of modern capitalism."

7 The major intellectual sources of the new laissez-faire would be generally regarded as the works of F. A. Hayek and Milton Friedman (although there are interesting divergencies in their views). See, for example, F. A. Hayek, *The Constitution of Liberty* (London: Routledge, 1960), and *Law, Legislation and Liberty* 3 vols. (London: Routledge, 1973–79); and Milton Friedman, *Capitalism and Freedom* (Chicago: University of Chicago Press, 1962), and (with Rose Friedman) *Free to Choose* (London: Secker & Warburg, 1980). However, less extreme and in some respects more sophisticated exponents should also be noted: for example, in Britain, Samuel Brittan, *Capitalism and the Permissive Society* (London: Macmillan, 1973), *The Economic Consequences of Democracy* (London: Temple Smith, 1977), and *How to End the "Monetarist" Controversy*, 2d ed. (London: Institute of Economic Affairs, 1982).

8 For rehearsals of the "overload" thesis, see Michel J. Crozier, Samuel P. Huntington, and Joji Watanuki, *The Crisis of Democracy: Report on the Governability of Democracies to the Trilateral Commission* (New York: New York University Press, 1975). On the dangers of the steady expansion of the boundaries of the political see Brittan, *Capitalism and the Permissive Society*, esp. pp. 109–117.

9 Several different versions have been offered toward an understanding of present-day inflation along the lines in question. See, for example, in the idiom of economics, Tibor Scitovsky, "Market Power and Inflation," *Economica* 45 (1978); and, from a sociological standpoint, John H. Goldthorpe, "The Current Inflation: Towards a Sociological Account," in Fred Hirsch and John H. Goldthorpe, eds., *The Political Economy of Inflation* (London: Martin Robertson, 1978). An analysis of the increased relative power of organized labor and its implications for social conflict similar to that in Goldthorpe but developed independently and to a more generalized level is Walter Korpi, *The Working Class in Welfare Capitalism* (London: Routledge, 1978). See also Korpi, "Conflict and the Balance of Power," *Acta Sociologica* 17 (1974); and, more recently, Gösta Esping-Andersen, "Class Alliances in the Making of West European Economies," *Political Power and Social Theory* 3 (1982).

10 See Hayek, *Constitution of Liberty*, chap. 6, and *Law, Legislation and Liberty*, esp. vol. 2; and Frank H. Knight, *The Ethics of Competition* (New York: Harper, 1935).

11 For a valuable review of the evidence and issues, see Richard Hyman and Ian Brough, *Social Values and Industrial Relations: A study of Fairness and Inequality* (Oxford: Blackwell, 1975).

12 Irving Kristol, " 'When Virtue Loses All Her Loveliness' – Some Reflections on Capitalism and 'the Free Society,' " *Public Interest* 21 (1970).

13 See, for example, Claus Offe, *Leistungsprinzip und industrielle Arbeit* (Frankfurt Main: Europäische Verlaganstalt, 1970).

14 For example, evidence has recently shown the rather remarkable degree of accuracy with which opportunities for social mobility are assessed among the British population. See Martin Harrop, "Popular Conceptions of Mobility," *Sociology* 14 (1980).

15 Fred Hirsch, *Social Limits to Growth* (Cambridge, Mass.: Harvard University Press, 1976).

16 See in this connection Raymond Boudon, *L'inégalité des chances: la mobilité sociale dans les sociétés industrielles* (Paris: Colin, 1973); and Lester Thurow, *Generating Inequality* (New York: Basic, 1975).

17 On inflation as a means of accommodating distributional dissent and conflict, see W. B. Reddaway, "Rising Prices for Ever?," *Lloyds Bank Review*, July 1966; and James

Tobin, "Inflation and Unemployment," *American Economic Review* 62 (1972); and on the difficulties of determining the distributional effects of inflation, see David Piachaud, "Inflation and Income Distribution," in Hirsch and Goldthorpe, eds., *Political Economy of Inflation*.

18 This view is, moreover, likely to be strengthened in that the new laissez-faire approach can scarcely avoid creating, initially at least, an evident *widening* of social inequalities. Tax cuts, benefiting higher income groups in particular, are part of the prescription for the revival of market incentives; on the other hand, the combination of tax cuts, monetary strictness, and a concern not to "crowd out" private investment by high levels of government borrowing must make for severe downward pressure on levels of public expenditure, and, in turn, on the standard of social welfare services. In principle, the new laissez-faire is not incompatible with high standards of social welfare – at least if provided on a "selective" basis – as exponents of the idea of a "social market economy" have argued. (See Brittan, *Economic Consequences of Democracy*, esp. chap. 14.) But in practice, and in present economic circumstances, it is difficult to see how a deterioration in standards could be avoided, even if this were regarded as a matter of much concern.

19 See Keith Bradley and Alan Gelb, "The Radical Potential of Cash Nexus Breaks," *British Journal of Sociology* 31 (1980).

20 See Janice McCormick, "The Limits of Liberalism: The Defeat of the French Experiment," (Paper delivered at the Convention of the American Political Science Association, September 1981). For a general review of electoral responses to unemployment and inflation, see Bruno Frey, *Modern Political Economy* (Oxford: Martin Robertson, 1978), esp. chap. 11.

21 Indeed, it could be argued that in some respects changes *were* made: for example, in the imposition of a de facto incomes policy in the public sector or, more seriously, in the failure to pursue systematically the policy of allowing "lame duck" companies to collapse.

22 See Samuel Brittan, "The Economic Contradictions of Democracy," *British Journal of Political Science* 5 (1975), and "The Wenceslas Myth: Economic Illusions About Government and Other Self-Deceptions," *Encounter* (May 1981); Hayek, *Law, Legislation and Liberty*, esp. vol. 3.

23 See, for example, Clark Kerr, John T. Dunlop, Frederick H. Harbison, and Charles A. Myers, *Industrialism and Industrial Man* (Cambridge, Mass.: Harvard University Press, 1960); Arthur M. Ross and Paul T. Hartman, *Changing Patterns of Industrial Conflict* (New York: Wiley, 1960); and Reinhard Bendix, *Nation-Building and Citizenship* (New York: Wiley, 1964).

24 See, for example, the papers collected in Tom Clarke and Laurie Clements, eds., *Trade Unions under Capitalism* (London: Fontana, 1977), esp. pt. 5.

25 One of the earliest – and still most incisive – arguments to this effect is in fact in the work of an American liberal of somewhat earlier vintage than those previously referred to (and remarkably disregarded by them). See Charles Lindblom, *Unions and Capitalism* (New Haven, Conn.: Yale University Press, 1949). Perhaps the best illustration of the converse of the argument is provided by the French trade union movement. See the discussion in Duncan Gallie, *In Search of the New Working Class* (Cambridge: Cambridge University Press, 1978), esp. pt. 4; and Martin A. Schain, "Corporatism and Industrial Relations in France," in Philip G. Cerny and Martin A. Schain, eds., *French Politics and Public Policy* (London: Frances Pinter, 1980). See also, on the Italian CGIL, Marino Regini, "Changing Relationships Between Labour and the State in Italy: Towards a Neo-Corporatist System?," in Gerhard Lehmbruch and Philippe C. Schmitter, eds., *Patterns of Corporatist Policy-Making* (Beverly Hills, Calif.: Sage, 1982).

26 For apt comment on the one-eyed nature of condemnations of unions' "monopoly power", see Hirsch, *Social Limits to Growth*, pp. 155–156.

27 See Scitovsky, "Market Power and Inflation," pp. 228–229.

28 It is, in fact, now becoming recognized, even among supporters of the monetarist counterrevolution against Keynesianism, that monetarist analyses have tended to be seriously overoptimistic in the extent to which they have supposed that a strict control of the money supply would have an impact on prices rather than activity *even in the absence* of strong trade unions. See, for instance, Brittan, *How to End the "Monetarist" Controversy*, pp. 20–33.

29 See, for example, Brittan, *Capitalism and the Permissive Society*, esp. pt. 1.

30 See for example, Hayek's letter published in the *London Times*, June 13, 1980.

31 David Soskice, "The UK Economy and Industrial Relations, 1979–1983: Government Strategies and Business and Union Responses,"(paper delivered to the MIT–Turin Conference on Strategies of Adjustment, July 1983).

32 See Leo Panitch, "The Development of Corporatism in Liberal Democracies," and Gerhard Lehmbruch, "Liberal Corporatism and Party Government," both in Philippe C. Schmitter and Gerhard Lehmbruch, eds., *Trends Towards Corporatist Intermediation* (Beverly Hills, Calif.: Sage, 1979). Incomes policy, it should be stressed, is here interpreted in a broad sense, to include cases based on largely informal understandings and arrangements.

It is chiefly in left-wing socialist circles that a reluctance exists to acknowledge the centrality of incomes policy to any attempt to impose greater control over the functioning of a modern economy. See, for example, Tony Benn, *Arguments for Socialism* (London: Cape, 1979), in which the author's evasiveness on the question of incomes policy must be regarded as at best disingenuous. Compare, in the British context, William McCarthy: "a continuous and enthusiastic commitment to incomes policy should now be accepted as the distinguishing characteristic of the serious socialist," "Socialism and Incomes Policy," in David Lipsey and Dick Leonard, eds., *The Socialist Agenda: Crossland's Legacy* (London: Cape, 1981), p. 110.

33 See, for instance, Keynes's comments published in *Activities 1941–1946: Shaping the Post-War World; Bretton Woods and Reparations* (London: Macmillan, 1980), p. 38. It may be noted that, for a time, the "discovery" of the Phillips curve appeared to some Keynesians to make it possible to endogenize the determination of money wages to the economic system and thus to rely on demand management policy alone to achieve an acceptable trade-off between inflation and unemployment. Such a possibility – attractive both politically and from the standpoint of the intellectual imperialism of economics – was, however, destroyed, together with the stability of the Phillips curve, from the late 1960s on. See M. J. Artis, "Incomes Policies: Some Rationales," in J. L. Fallick and R. F. Elliott, eds., *Incomes Policies, Inflation and Relative Pay* (London: Allen & Unwin, 1981).

34 Skidelsky, "Decline of Keynesian Politics," p. 71. See also Lehmbruch, "Liberal Corporatism and Party Government," p. 154.

35 An analogous point can be made regarding proposals advanced by those economists – who might perhaps be thought of as "inverted Keynesians" – who believe that more effective control over modern economies would be achieved if demand management (monetary, fiscal, and exchange-rate) policies were used to maintain a steady rate of growth in total money expenditure, while incomes policies were used to maintain full employment. See, for example, James Meade, *Stagflation*, vol. 1: *Wage-fixing* (London: Allen & Unwin, 1982). In this case, of course, incomes policies could not be directed toward any specific distributional outcome. Nonetheless, the fact that government was directly intervening in the determination of incomes would obviously

mean that it could not regard the distribution of incomes as lying outside the area of its concern and responsibility – as Meade appears to recognize (see ibid., pp. 15–20).

36 See Bruce W. Heady, "Trade Unions and National Wage policies," *Journal of Politics* (1970).

37 The control of inflation, or price stability, may be regarded as a public good: Individuals and groups could benefit from it whether or not they had contributed to its achievement. Indeed, the maximum advantage would be gained by those who contributed nothing – for example, in the way of wage restraint – in the case where general control was achieved. The worst outcome would be experienced by those who did contribute in the case where, because sufficient others did not, control was not obtained. Accepting restraint always carries, therefore, a serious element of risk. See Frey, *Modern Political Economy*, chap. 3.

38 The contribution of major importance here is Alessandro Pizzorno, "Political Exchange and Collective Identity in Industrial Conflict," in Colin J. Crouch and Alessandro Pizzorno, eds., *The Resurgence of Class Conflict in Western Europe Since 1968* (London: Macmillan, 1978), vol. 2. See further Alessandro Pizzorno, *I soggetti del pluralismo; classi, partiti, sindicati* (Bologna: Il Mulino, 1980), chaps. 5–7; and "Interests and Parties in Pluralism," in Suzanne Berger, ed., *Organizing Interests in Western Europe* (Cambridge: Cambridge University Press, 1981).

39 See the discussion of the "ratchet effect" in political bargaining in Peter Lange, "Sindicati, partiti, stato e liberal-corporativismo," *Il Mulino* 28 (1979).

40 As an interesting indication of the growing recognition of the logic of this argument among economic analysts, see, for example, Peter Kenyon, "Pricing," and J. A. Kregel, "Income Distribution," both in Alfred S. Eichner, ed., *A Guide to Post-Keynesian Economics* (London: Macmillan, 1979), and compare the editor's own conventional Keynesian view, p. 175.

41 See Rudolf Meidner, *Employee Investment Funds: An Approach to Collective Capital Formation* (London: Allen & Unwin, 1978); and for valuable analysis of the context of the Meidner Plan, Korpi, *Working Class in Welfare Capitalism*, chap. 11; and Andrew Martin, "The Dynamics of Change in a Keynesian Political Economy: The Swedish Case and Its Implications," in Crouch, ed., *State and Economy in Contemporary Capitalism*. For more general reviews of the current positions of national trade-union movements on questions of their involvement in investment, see M. Donald Hancock, "Productivity, Welfare and Participation in Sweden and West Germany," *Comparative Politics* 11 (1978); and Andrew Martin and George Ross, "European Trade Unions and the Economic Crisis: Perceptions and Strategies," and Colin J. Crouch, "Varieties of Trade Union Weakness: Organized Labour and Capital Formation in Britain, Federal Germany and Sweden," both in *West European Politics* 3 (1980).

42 Although so far no national union movement has called quite explicitly for such an attack as the price of its cooperation in pay restraint, by the later 1970s union arguments to the effect that incomes policy and social policy should be "integrated" were widespread. See Gerhard Lehmbruch, "Problems for Future Research on Corporatist Intermediation and Policy-Making," in Schmitter and Lehmbruch, eds., *Trends Towards Corporatist Intermediation*.

43 Or, failing that, of course, to reject incomes policy altogether. This, for example, was the course followed by the French government under the Fifth Plan (for 1966–70), which was the first to propose the planning of prices and incomes. Union conditions for cooperation in incomes policy – including tax reform, guarantees of the expansion of employment, a voice in competition policy, and the transformation of collective bargaining – were turned down by the government. A former member of the Commissariat du Plan has observed: "Quite frankly, when the government grasped their

implications, they were taken aback." Jacques Delors, "The Decline of French Planning," in Stuart Holland, ed., *Beyond Capitalist Planning* (Oxford: Blackwell, 1978), p. 22. Delors's further comment is also of considerable interest: "The negative result of rejecting the chance to negotiate with the unions on prices and incomes was crucial not only in itself but also – which has been widely neglected by many commentators – for the institution of planning. It was a key factor in the decline of planning in postwar France."

44 Perry Anderson, "The Limits and Possibilities of Trade Union Action," in Clarke and Clements, eds., *Trade Unions Under Capitalism*, p. 334.

45 See, for example, Lord Kahn, "Thoughts on the Behavior of Wages and Monetarism," *Lloyds Bank Review* (January 1976).

46 See Heady, "Trade Unions and National Wage Policies" and Lehmbruch, "Liberal Corporatism and Party Government."

47 Heady, "Trade Unions," p. 169. See also Walter Korpi and Michael Shalev, "Strikes, Power and Politics in the Western Nations, 1900–1976," *Political Power and Social Theory* 1 (1980); and Walter Korpi, "Social Policy and Distributional Conflict in the Capitalist Democracies," *West European Politics* 3 (1980).

48 See Colin J. Crouch, "La politique dans les rélations industrielles: gouvernement et revendications syndicales dans les années 1970," *Sociologie du Travail* 4 (1979), and Pizzorno, "Interests and Parties in Pluralism."

49 Pizzorno, "Political Exchange and Collective Identity," p. 284.

50 See the excellent discussion of this issue in Norway in Don S. Schwerin, *Corporatism and Protest: Organizational Politics in the Norwegian Trade Unions* (Kent, Oh.: Kent Popular Press, 1981), esp. pp. 29–30.

51 Recognition of this point by the leaderships of national labor movements would seem to be not particularly well developed. The Swedish movement has probably given greatest importance to fostering a sense of class solidarity among union members. See further in this connection Marino Regini and Gösta Esping-Andersen, "Trade Union Strategies and Social Policy in Italy and Sweden," *West European Politics* 3 (1980). Also highly relevant here is the discussion by Wolfgang Streeck of the emerging contradiction in the West German trade unions between the "de-ideologization" encouraged by cooperation with their "social partners" and the need to preserve ideological traditions as a basis for the class solidarity that is required for such cooperation to be effective. See his "Qualitative Demands and the Neo-Corporatist Manageability of Industrial Relations," *British Journal of Industrial Relations* 14 (1981); and "Organisational Consequences of Neo-Corporatist Co-operation in West German Labour Unions," in Lehmbruch and Schmitter, eds., *Patterns of Corporatist Policy-Making*. Finally, on the Norwegian case, see the insightful paper by Ted Hanisch, "Markets and Politics in Wage Determination," (Paper delivered to the International Working Party on Labour Market Segmentation, Modena, September 1981).

52 See, for instance, on Sweden, James Fulcher, "Class Conflict: Joint Regulation and Its Decline," in Richard Scase, ed., *Readings in Swedish Class Structure* (Oxford: Pergamon, 1976); but compare Walter Korpi, "Unofficial Strikes in Sweden," *British Journal of Industrial Relations* 19 (1981). On Norway see Schwerin, *Corporatism and Protest*; "The Limits of Organisation as a Response to Wage-Price Problems," in Richard Rose, ed., *Challenge to Governance: Studies in Overloaded Polities* (Beverly Hills, Calif.: Sage, 1980); and "Incomes Policy in Norway: Second-Best Corporate Institutions," *Polity* 14 (1982).

It is apparently in Austria that liberal corporatist institutions have so far operated with fewest problems of the kind in question, though no altogether convincing analysis of why this should be so has been provided. See, however, Lehmbruch, "Liberal

Corporatism and Party Government"; Fritz Scharpf, "The Political Economy of Inflation and Unemployment in Western Europe: An Outline," Internationales Institut für Management and Verwaltung, Berlin, 1981; and Bernd Marin, "Organising Interests by Interest Organisations: Associational Prerequisites of Cooperation in Austria," *International Political Science Review* 4 (1983).

Various instances could be cited of unions being withdrawn by their leaderships from corporatist arrangements under some degree of rank-and-file pressure. See, for example, Tinie Akkermans and Peter Grootings, "From Corporatism to Polarisation: Elements of the Development of Dutch Industrial Relations," and Walther Müller-Jentsch and Hans Joachim Sperling, "Economic Development, Labour Conflicts and the Industrial Relations System in West Germany," both in Crouch and Pizzorno, eds., *The Resurgence of Class Conflict*, vol. 1.

53 Such a reaction would seem particularly likely where a combination of wage restraint and rising taxation leads to many workers' experiencing a fall in the real value of their take-home pay. See Richard Rose, "Ordinary People in Extraordinary Circumstances," in Rose, ed., *Challenge to Governance*.

54 In other words, just as it is not "moderation" in the usual sense that is required, neither is it "militancy," in the sense usually understood in Anglo-Saxon contexts, at least, of the aggressive but narrowly conceived pursuit of sectional interests. Rather, union strategy must turn, as was earlier implied, on the politicization of the essentially class issues of the control of investment and the goals of social policy.

Index

409